UNITED THEY STOOD

*The Story of the UK Firefighters'
Dispute 2002–4*

From Roger to the children: Sarah, Joseph, Rachel, Adam, Hannah, Judith, Miriam, and Ben

From Tom to Jennie, Jill, Kay and Liam

UNITED THEY STOOD

The Story of the UK Firefighters' Dispute 2002–4

Roger Seifert and Tom Sibley

Lawrence & Wishart
LONDON 2005

British Library Cataloguing in Publication Data.
A catalogue record for this book is available from the British Library

Printed in Great Britain by
Cambridge University Press

Contents

– kill the bill – history of the dispute – sunset clause –
settlement in the making
June – ghosts – recalled to settle – white paper
July to October – phasing – November – pursuing the
unreasonable
Long goodbye – January to August – stand-down – carry on
– actions – final curtain – employers renege – time to pay up
Conclusion

PART TWO: ANALYSIS AND AFTERMATH

LIST OF FIGURES AND TABLES

Abbreviations

ACAS:	Advisory, Conciliation and Arbitration Service
AEEU:	Amalgamated Engineering and Electrical Union
AEI:	Average Earnings Index
AFS:	Auxiliary Fire Service
AGS:	Assistant General Secretary
AMICUS:	Engineering Union formed from the Merger of MSF with AEEU
ASLEF:	Amalgamated Society of Locomotive Engineers and Firemen
BBC:	British Broadcasting Corporation
BVPI:	Best Value Performance Indicator
CACFO:	Chief and Assistant Chief Fire Officers' Association
CBI:	Confederation of British Industry
CCT:	Compulsory Competitive Tendering
CFBAC:	Central Fire Brigades Advisory Council
CFO:	Chief Fire Officer
CFS:	Community Fire Safety
CID:	Criminal Investigation Department
CMT:	Corporate Management Team
COSLA:	Convention of Scottish Local Authorities
CP:	Communist Party
CWU:	Communications Worker Union
DPM:	Deputy Prime Minister
EC:	Executive Committee
ECRO:	Emergency Control Room Operator
EO:	Employers' Organisation (part of LGA)
EU:	European Union
FBU:	Fire Brigades Union
GMB:	general union
HSBC:	Hong Kong and Shanghai Banking Corporation
HQ:	Head Quarters
HRM:	Human Resource Management
IDS:	Incomes Data Service
ILO:	International Labour Organisation
IPDS:	Integrated Personal Development System
IRMP:	Integrated Risk Management Planning
IRS:	Industrial Relations Services

IRU:	Incident Rescue Unit
JCACR:	Joint Committee on Audit Commission Report
JSCC:	Joint Standing Sub-Committee (of the NJC)
LCC:	London County Council
LGA:	Local Government Association
LRD:	Labour Research Department
LSE:	London School of Economics
LSI:	Long Service Increment
MI5:	Military Intelligence
MP:	Member of Parliament
MSP:	Member of the Scottish Parliament
MWA:	Member of the Welsh Assembly
NATFHE:	National Association of Teachers in Further and Higher Education
NBPI:	National Board for Prices and Incomes
NES:	New Earnings Survey
NHS:	National Health Service
NICE:	National Institute for Clinical Excellence
NIPSA:	Northern Ireland Public Service Alliance
NJC:	National Joint Council
NPM:	New Public Management
NUJ:	National Union of Journalists
NUM:	National Union of Mineworkers
ODPM:	Office of the Deputy Prime Minister
OFSTED:	Office for Standards in Education
PCS:	Public and Commercial Services Union
PCT:	Public Choice Theory
PFI:	Public Finance Initiative
PM:	Prime Minister
PPP:	Public Private Partnership
PSBR:	Public Sector Borrowing Requirement
PSPP:	Public Services Productivity Panel
RFU:	Retained Firefighters Union
RMT:	National Union of Rail, Maritime and Transport Workers
SNP:	Scottish National Party
SWP:	Socialist Workers Party
STUC:	Scottish Trades Union Congress
TGWU:	Transport and General Workers Union
TUC:	Trades Union Congress
UK:	United Kingdom
UNIFI:	bank workers' union now part of AMICUS
UNISON:	general union mainly for public sector workers
USA:	United States of America

Foreword

It is now some eight months since final agreement was reached in settlement of the FBU's Claim for Pay Justice that was lodged with the employers in May 2002.

Uniquely for a national dispute involving over fifty thousand workers, it took over two years to reach a settlement. During this protracted dispute we encountered many problems, some of which were impossible to predict. What started as a relatively straightforward pay claim, albeit with a few special features, developed into a complex political struggle impinging on both the criminal invasion of Iraq and on fundamental human rights and trade union freedoms, such as the right to collective bargaining and the right to strike.

Despite the nefarious efforts of some New Labour Ministers and a small group of New Labour councillors, the FBU has emerged bloodied but unbowed.

Pay is considerably improved. Equality both in pay conditions and procedures has been advanced for all minority groups, whether by occupation, grade, gender, race or sexual orientation. And not a single job has been lost as a direct result of the 2003 Pay & Conditions Pay Agreement. Furthermore, a new Pay Formula has been agreed, which, if implemented with goodwill, should ensure that the pay and conditions of a group of essential public servants is never again allowed to fall in relative terms or fail to reflect the skills, training, commitment and bravery of firefighters and Emergency Control Room Operators. These advances owe everything to the solidarity and unity of the FBU membership in their determination to secure pay justice within an even better Fire Service for the people they serve.

This book, produced so soon after the momentous events it describes and analyses, captures the story of our campaign. I do not agree with all of the authors' views expressed in this book. Neither will FBU activists. But I am convinced that the authors have produced a fair and accurate commentary on the events of 2002-2004; for this, generations of FBU members will be grateful. And it is to be hoped that the analysis provided will assist the labour movement and progressive people generally to learn the lessons of our recent history.

Andy Gilchrist
April 2005

Preface

This book was born in the seminar rooms of Keele University. At the start of the dispute both authors had close links with the Fire Service. Tom Sibley was working part time for the FBU, helping an already overstretched Research Department cope with the extra work involved in developing a major national campaign. Professor Roger Seifert was involved in developing education and training courses at the Fire Services College. Both authors have long records of trade union activity. Our perspectives on this dispute are shaped by our experiences and by our shared commitment to advancing trade union freedoms and workers' rights within a democratic society.

We would like to thank all those who gave of their time for extensive interviews and to all those too numerous to mention individually who helped with the preparation of the manuscript at its various stages. We particularly wish to thank our colleague Mike Ironside for his help with an earlier draft of the book. As usual his comments were very much to the point.

This project has been fully supported by the FBU following endorsement by its Executive Council. But the views expressed and the analysis developed are entirely our own. Of course we have been influenced by the views of FBU members since, like them, we supported the objectives of the union's pay campaign. We have also had the benefit of access to a wide variety of sources and many years of academic training and trade union experience. We hope this has enabled us to capture the essence of the dispute and to draw some useful lessons from it that will benefit labour movement activists now and in the future.

Most of the interviews were carried out by Roger Seifert.

PART 1: THE STORY OF THE DISPUTE

Chapter One

The UK Fire and Rescue Service

INTRODUCTION

This account of the 2002-4 industrial dispute in the UK Fire and Rescue Service was written in order to provide a time line of events as a record of the action; to provide some analysis of the dispute while memories were fresh and before hindsight distorted arguments; and to assess the causes and conduct of the strike itself within a broader setting of British public sector industrial relations after seven years of a Labour Government under the leadership of Tony Blair and Gordon Brown.

We set out to answer three questions: why did the Fire Brigade Union (FBU) make the claim that it did when it did? Why did the employers and the Government oppose the claim so strongly? How did the FBU deal with this very powerful opposition to their claim? At one level we would have expected this dispute to follow, more or less, the pattern of many other such actions by public sector workers and their unions. A claim is put forward by the union on the basis of falling relative pay along with concerns over aspects of the management of labour. And the employers respond with attempts to tie pay rises with conditions of service changes – called 'rationalisation' or 'productivity bargaining' or 'modernisation'; usually this involves additional managerial controls over all aspects of work under the umbrella heading of 'flexibility'. In the public sector the process also always involves Central Government directly or indirectly, in both the progress of the dispute and the final outcome. As Clegg noted, 'the last word lies with the Treasury, which they [the employers] must inevitably consult before agreeing to substantial increases in Government expenditure' (1972: 385).

When, as in this case, the process of collective bargaining involves strike action, further elements come into play. As Knowles said, 'strikes in the broad sense – collective stoppages of work undertaken in order to bring pressure to bear on those who depend on the sale or use of the products of that work – are about as old as work itself' (1952: 1). In particular strikes are seen as a rational response (Hyman 1989, Edwards 1992) to a combination of pressures and processes; those involved calculate the level of costs and benefits, and make an assessment of the risks of losing. But strikes by any group, whatever their special case, are highly visible social events. They attract media coverage, impact on other groups in similar situations, and become part of the political concerns of the day. They throw light into the shadowy corners of our political economy, and thereby threaten both the actual social order and the constructed social order projected as reality.

The book begins with a brief background chapter to provide information about the Fire Service for those uninitiated into its special ways. In particular we discuss why it is a public service, the organisation and management of the Service, the FBU, and the collective bargaining regime at the start of the dispute. We also discuss the background to the pay formula (the indexation of pay), the 'modernisation' reforms, and deal with the legacy of the 1977-8 strike.

Chapters two, three and four cover the claim and the dispute. They start in May 2002 with the FBU conference and discuss both the claim and the arguments underpinning it. The story then unfolds in the phoney war (later called 'fancy dancing' by John Prescott, the Deputy Prime Minister) of the summer of 2002, the intervention of Ministers, the employers' first offer and the setting up of the independent inquiry under Professor Sir George Bain (known as the 'Bain' inquiry/report). This was followed by the famously confused near deal of 21-22 November and the subsequent eight-day strike. From November 2002 to February 2003 there were more strike days, more intense media coverage, more direct intervention from Government leaders, more resistance from the FBU membership, and more pressure to settle. The subsequent invasion of Iraq in March 2003 allowed the Government to argue that support for the troops meant that they could not be used to cover for striking firefighters, and this helped bring about the June 2003 agreement. The final section of chapter four deals with the problems of implementing the June 2003 agreement, which had become more honoured in the breach than the application. The employers, now again left to their own devices by the media and Central Government, failed to pay the monies owing. In November 2003 this led to a brief outbreak of unofficial action followed by further negotiations. These dragged on until May 2004 when again the employers' failure to pay what was owed led to more unofficial action in a number of brigades. By late August 2004 the FBU was balloting its members for more strike action to enforce the deal that ended the dispute on 26 August 2004.

In part two of the book we discuss some of the issues raised by the dispute. In chapter five we discuss public sector employment and 'modernisation'; and we suggest that the underlying principles in this particular form of change come from an overarching acceptance of neo-liberal views of the benefits of global and local markets. This is translated through public choice theory to New Public Management (NPM): a set of actual practices – such as work intensification, flexible working, flexible pay and deskilling – which together indicate a shift in the balance of power away from the workforce to the managers acting as the agents of employers and the instruments of Central Government policy. We then discuss the role of the central state in the collective bargaining process; the question of pay determination, with special reference to pay comparability; and strikes by public sector workers to maintain their relative living standards. We argue that the practicalities of modernisation in labour intensive public services mainly involve changes in employment of staff. Finally we apply this to changes in the Fire Service itself.

In chapter six we attempt a brief overall assessment of the dispute and its aftermath. We conclude with a discussion of why the Government stepped in to prevent a negotiated settlement in late November 2002, thereby condemning all those involved in the Service to another twenty months of uncertainty and conflict. The book ends with a consideration of the impact of the dispute on those involved.

SEIZE THE TIME

Local Government in the UK has been subject to significant changes in recent years. These have mainly been concerned with corporate governance. The main thrust of policy from Central Government has been covered by the cluster concept of 'modernisation'. This includes, amongst other things, reducing the democratic account-ability of senior decision-makers; encouraging more private companies into the Service; weakening the employment position of most employees; and strengthening Central Government control of the entire functioning of the system. Such was the power of this reform movement that eventually it was bound to engulf all aspects of Local Government, including the Fire Service. In particular we look at the 1995 Audit Commission report, and we comment on the 1999 Local Government Act, with the introduction of Best Value (Vincent-Jones 1999), alongside the Single Status agreement for other Local Government workers (IRS 2000b). Later we discuss the impact of the election of a Labour Government in 1997, and the tragedy of 9/11 in New York, as part of the cocktail of events and issues that persuaded the FBU leadership and membership to act when and how they did. This accumulation of pressures and oppor-tunities created in the minds of the FBU leadership, activists and some members the view that the time had at last come for a push on pay and a new pay formula. The storm clouds were gathering: on the one side Government and Local Government modernisation of service structures, management and labour management were well on the way; on the other side the pay gap was widening, the job had changed, a Labour Government was half-way through a second term; and there had been a further shift in public policy and public opinion as to the value of the fire and other emergency services. Such is the calculus of political decision-making, and upon such thoughts actions are formulated.

When Oliver Twist was famously refused more food, Dickens leaves us in no doubt about what is happening. Two major reasons are apparent for the refusal: firstly, what was not given to the children could be kept by the rich trustees; and secondly, if they gave Oliver more, all the others would queue up for more. In addition to these two principal reasons we are presented with a host of minor ones, which include spite, selfishness, greed, meanness, doing what the powerful can do just because they are powerful, vindictiveness, and personal animosity. But what underpins all of these major and minor reasons is the prime motive: defence of the system in the interests of all those that own and run the system.

In the spring of 2002 the FBU decided to ask for more. Members and leaders alike felt that there were good reasons for optimism: they had a good case based on widespread and enthusiastic support among the members; they had strong public support enhanced by the 9/11 events; they had important support from sections of Labour MPs and the media; they worked in a relatively small and efficient sector and therefore the costs of the deal would be modest; the Government appeared secure with a huge second-term Parliamentary majority and sound public finances; the Government was under pressure over security, terrorism and the Iraq conflict; and the employers appeared to be weak, disorganised and divided. If there was ever to be a good time to ask for more, it was now. Seize the time seemed to be the correct slogan.

Our main argument is that this was a straightforward industrial dispute, with the union leaders asking for more, and the employers using a variety of tactics to try to control the outcome of the negotiations and the threat of strike action. A deal along traditional lines could and should have been made on 21-22 November 2002, with no further strikes and no further damaging and protracted bargaining. In our view, and we seek to show this in the book, the dispute did not end at that point because of direct interference from the highest levels of Government to prevent a settlement. We further argue that the main reason for this was to damage the FBU in order to push through further 'modernisation' programmes throughout the public services – including more privatisation, fewer national conditions of service, and greater central control over pay and pensions – and to secure an ideological victory over organised labour. The guiding mind behind this was that of the Prime Minister, Tony Blair.

Our intention is to provide FBU members and others in the labour and trade union movement with an account of the dispute that will assist the process of understanding what happened on a number of levels. For the firefighters it was not simply a sectional trade union struggle for better pay. It involved issues of public sector pay and management that are of general concern. It shone a light on Labour-Union relations in the era of New Labour modernisation. Above all it was a pay campaign conducted by a united FBU membership, in the face of Labour Government and media hostilities, and against the background of constant threats to restrict union rights at a time of impending war.

SOURCES

This work is based on extensive research of FBU sources; published Government and employer reports; and media accounts. It draws most from interviews with over forty FBU activists and officials in 2004; attendance at two seminars for FBU regional and local officials spread over five days in February 2004 and attended by some 150 strike leaders; and attendance at other FBU conferences, where we heard scores of other activists openly express their views.

It is inevitable that in the account of any strike the bulk of the evidence comes from the union side. It is after all the union leadership that tables the claim for an advance in wages, and it is the union conference of activists that decides whether to proceed with strike ballots and action. It is therefore through the eyes of union leaders, local and national, that the story is mainly told. Representatives of the employers and senior managers were also interviewed and relevant documents analysed. Neither Deputy Prime Minister John Prescott nor Nick Raynsford – who as Minister for Local and Regional Government within the ODPM had direct responsibility for the Fire Service – could be persuaded to help with the study; but the two leading negotiators (Charles Nolda and Phil White) for the Fire Authorities' Employer Organisation (EO) were very helpful when interviewed. George Bain and Frank Burchill also declined to be interviewed; nonetheless their public statements are on record and we have used these (Bain 2002, Burchill 2004). Others involved who agreed to be interviewed included Brendan Barber, then Deputy General Secretary, and now General Secretary, of the TUC – a key figure in the negotiations; Rodney Bickerstaffe, former General Secretary of UNISON – a go-between and someone consulted by the parties; Alan Simpson MP, a leading figure in the Parliamentary Labour Party and someone trusted by many unions to speak for their cause in the House of Commons, and Alan Doig, Chief Fire Officer (CFO) of Staffordshire and now President of the Chief and Assistant Chief Fire Officers' Association (CACFOA).

There are a few references to industrial relations in the Fire Service in general academic works (Clegg 1972, Bain 1983, Edwards 2003, Rose 2004). There are more in books on the nature of public sector pay claims (White 1999), public sector disputes (Morris 1986, Fryer 1989), and negotiations within a collective bargaining system (Beaumont 1992). There is relatively little written about the national Fire Service's industrial relations system itself, although there have been a few case studies of specific brigades (Swabe and Price 1983, Darlington 1997, Fitzgerald and Stirling 1999); a handful of research dissertations (Smith 1992, Jones 1993); some historical material (Segars 1989 and 1990, Bailey 1992a); and some studies commissioned by the FBU from academics on special issues (Linn, 1992).

A FAIR FIGHT?

Throughout the writing of this book we were struck by the depth of the union's democratic culture – of the way discussions and decisions in the FBU always involve a broad range of activists, and how at every stage of the dispute members were fully consulted before agreements with the employers were entered into. Members' involvement in the campaign and strike was very widespread and evident, and the constant contact between leaders at all levels of the union and activists and members was the hallmark of this closely-knit occupationally coherent organisation. The commitment from the leadership to consult was strong even at the most difficult times, and the fact that, after such a hard-fought dispute, the union has maintained membership levels and remains intact is in part testimony to that style of union government.

As we have noted, this account starts with the FBU conference decision to consider strike action over a pay claim in May 2002, and then takes the reader through key moments – the employers' rejection of the claim; strike ballot and results; the campaign prior to the stoppages; the stoppages and negotiations; the negotiated settlement that did not stand; and the final settlement. At each decision-making stage we attempt to capture the arguments of those involved – whether or not the original pay claim should have been entered; the employers' efforts to tie pay increases with conditions of service changes; the strike tactics themselves; and the nature of the agreement that ended the dispute. As part of this we consider the role of the media, the Government and the wider labour movement in changing the balance of decision making.

The central theme is the ways in which pay (the total remuneration package, including pensions) is determined for any group of workers in a market-dominated society, focusing on workers employed by sections of the state (in this case the local state – local authorities), for which there is no direct labour market. There is one purchaser of firefighter labour (a monopsonist), through a national agreement and national legal framework, even if there are many actual employers. In such circumstances the 'worth' of such workers is a highly contested matter. The workforce and their union tend to judge 'fair' pay with reference to other comparable groups as a starting point, and then to add special extras for the peculiar features of the job. Employers seek to ascertain the right quantity and quality of labour needed for the business, but at the least possible cost; and Central Government seeks control over pay, both as a factor affecting other macro-economic variables (inflation, borrowing, taxation), and as a means of maintaining influence over all other wage increases.

So we have two long-standing and traditional issues: what is a 'fair' wage for public sector workers, and how can such a contested wage be reached? The former is determined through complex social and economic factors, creating at times of low inflation some notional stability; and the latter is determined through collective bargaining within a broadly maintained Whitley-style mechanism. But when the level of wages is challenged and the machinery for peace comes under pressure, strikes may result.

We follow the model developed elsewhere (Ironside and Seifert 2003) regarding the actualisation of comparability claims and their place within public sector collective bargaining. These are, first, that felt-fair comparability claims are most likely to mobilise union members to take action when there is an additional sense of unfairness beyond the steady erosion of pay differentials; and in this case this was supplied both by the higher pay awarded to senior managers in the Fire Service, and by the special matter of the failure of the pay formula. Secondly, this is all the more apparent when members feel a strong sense of betrayal by their employers and/or Government Ministers: and in this case the employers had been unwilling to negotiate a pay rise, and later the Government intervened to support the employers. Thirdly, the action is more likely to start, and to be successful, if the demands have a unifying theme around a common claim developed from within the union's own decision-making processes; and certainly the claim and the tactics were agreed and discussed, and there has been unity within the FBU for most of the dispute. Fourthly, action is more likely to start and be sustained if the employers are divided (because of different problems in relation to labour market recruitment and retention); and in this case the employers were certainly divided – on party political grounds, between large urban and smaller rural areas, and, later and bitterly, between Central and Local Government. These points are usually the necessary conditions for strikes in the public sector, but clearly they are not sufficient to deliver higher wages.

THE UK FIRE SERVICE

We now present a brief overview of the UK Fire Service in terms of its origins, purpose, structures and institutions.

No citizen can isolate themselves on any island of self against the ravages of flames and suffocation of smoke. Hence, when fires start and spread citizens literally put all hands to the pumps. The social contagion of fire demands the social cohesion of those who put fires out, save property and rescue people. Once this general principle is established then, as with all other labour, the division of labour creates jobs and skills that allow some citizens to become employed as firefighters. The question arises as to who might employ such people, and whether full-time or part-time. The answer in most countries for most of the time is the state, local or national. This is because private ownership and control does not make any economic sense: profits would be hard to make if the Service put out fires in remote farmhouses, rather than in large supermarkets. Social solidarity and shared risk means that, as with the origin of many local services, local citizens collectively contribute to defending themselves from the shared risk. In addition equity and social justice require that some effort is made to ensure parity across groups of citizens. Social services need national standards of staff training and professionalism, national quality service standards, and national health and safety standards. These should be enforced and developed through national frameworks and finances enshrined in legislation.

Fire in society thus means firefighters, and eventually this leads to the creation of a Fire Service: funded, regulated, managed and directed through a combination of national and local politics, staff representation, community voice, and management control. The state run nature of the Service stems from the historical experience of citizens, and the continued support of a coalition of forces, including the workforce, the unions, the employers, the managers, politicians and the local community. Some of the time – and now is such a time – these coalition partners begin to disagree about the efficacy of keeping a particular service within the state sector. At such moments tensions emerge, debates are revisited, and powerful vested interests become involved.

The FBU, along with most other trade unions in the UK, the TUC, and until 1995 the Labour Party, is committed to and convinced by the need for a sizeable public sector, especially in the areas of public services and utilities. Many unions have statements in support of such a position as part of their constitutions, and their historic ties with the Labour Party for most of the twentieth century were based on the ideals and practices of public ownership. Public ownership, in whatever form, has been a hallmark of socialist and social democratic parties and Governments in Europe, especially since 1945. It has frequently been the single most important issue dividing such political groups from their liberal and conservative opponents. Support for public ownership is based on a combination of bitter experience when market alternatives failed, and on idealised notions of democracy and equity applied practically to basic rights such as the right to education, free access to health care, and shared community safety through the police and Fire Services. The role of the state in providing public goods and services is at the heart of modern political economy. It links the economic function of the state – as the protector of private business under conditions of monopoly capitalism – to its role in controlling the social and political consequences of private business activity. Hence the exercise of state power plays a central role in ensuring that private capital accumulation proceeds (and therefore also that the exploitation of labour proceeds), but within the political realities of representative democracy. So as the economy grows and international competition becomes fiercer, the state intervenes ever more robustly (Miliband 1973, Chomsky 1999) to secure such accumulation and exploitation, despite the rhetoric of a minimal state (Niskanen 1967 and 1971, Thatcher 1993). This creates an increasingly ruthless state elite, in order to protect the gains made from the uneven workings of markets and the interests of dominant large corporations.

Within the structures of representative democracy the workers themselves take political action, through trade unions, political parties, and pressure groups, to shift state action towards meeting the needs of working people and their families. The resulting tensions are expressed through struggle over the nature and the scope of public services. The business case focuses on state provision of services that are required by private businesses but cannot normally be provided by the private sector due to market failures, or incomplete markets, or the impossibility of markets (e.g. physical infrastructure, security forces, and a healthy educated workforce with the right attitudes). Alongside this there are citizens' demands for the state to ensure general welfare far beyond the narrow goal of reproducing the workforce. The debate about the nature of public service employment, the nature of public service work and the size of the public sector pay bill cannot be separated from analysis of the nature of state provision (Stiglitz 1986, Seifert 2002).

A central part of the argument for state ownership and control over the provision of goods and services is that market alternatives often fail to provide what is required to serve the public as citizens and user-consumers. We may also wish to have state provision for something that could be provided privately for reasons that have nothing to do with simple economics – for example for reasons of national security, social equity, or cost/risk factors. There are some 'pure public goods' that it is neither feasible or desirable to ration. To take the case of the armed forces as an example: if they were provided privately some people would not pay for them, but even though they did not pay they could still use them, since the armed forces cannot be used in such a way as to differentiate between those that do and those that do not pay. To avoid this 'free rider problem' the armed

forces are paid for out of general taxation. Two other frequently
quoted examples are the use of vaccinations and the Fire Service. In
the following quotation from Stiglitz (1986: 120-1), he refers to the
situation in the USA:

> In many communities, fire departments are supported voluntarily.
> Some individuals in the community refuse to contribute to the fire
> department. Yet, in an area where buildings are close together, the fire
> department will usually put out a fire in a noncontributors' building
> because of the threat it poses to adjacent contributors' structures. But
> there have been instances of fires at isolated noncontributors' build-
> ings where fire departments refused to put out the fire. The fire
> departments were severely criticized. This is an example in which
> exclusion is feasible; the fire department can withhold its services
> from those who do not contribute to its support. The fire departments
> claim that in the absence of sanctions, everyone would be a free rider.
> Why should they pay, if they can obtain the service for nothing?
> Because of the outrage that occurs whenever a fire department refuses
> to put out a fire, most communities prefer to provide the service to
> everyone; but to avoid the free rider problem, they require everyone
> to support it (through taxes).

Thus there is a fairly widespread consensus that the Fire Service should
be a public service. This does not, however, isolate the Service from the
contemporary pressures and conflicts over social provision.

ROLE AND STRUCTURE IN JANUARY 2002

The official website of the Fire Service (www.Fireservice.co.uk)
answers the question 'What is the Role of the Fire Service?' as
follows:

> As well as dealing with fires and other emergencies, we enforce fire
> safety laws, give advice about fire safety and carry out various emer-
> gency-planning activities, including helping the local boroughs and cities
> to plan for emergencies. These all form part of our services. We are
> governed by legislation and guidance and one law that is particularly
> important for us is the Fire Services Act 1947. It requires fire authorities
> to make provision for fire fighting purposes, which means not only
> putting out fires but also protecting life and property in case of fire.
>   You may be surprised to learn that we are not required to provide
> any non-fire rescue services, such as for road traffic accidents or help-
> ing people when their homes have been flooded. We decide whether to
> provide these services using the staff and equipment we use for fire
> fighting. We provide five main services: Community Fire Safety –
> Recognising that prevention is better than cure, Community Fire Safety

covers a range of initiatives that are aimed at reducing the number of fires and the number of deaths and injuries caused by fire. Legislative Fire Safety – A service that makes sure the people of the UK are not put at risk from fires in the workplace and similar buildings. We make sure buildings comply with fire safety legislation and issue fire certificates when designated buildings are assessed as being fully compliant.

Fire and Rescue Emergency Response – A service that responds to incidents and makes sure that the risk of injury, loss of life and damage to property is minimised. Special Services – A service that responds to other types of incident, for example, vehicle accidents, trapped people and animals, storms and floods. We charge for some of these services. Emergency Planning – Services that plan and prepare for large-scale emergencies, for example, large rail crashes, coastal pollution, severe floods.

Currently there are about 66,600 employees in the UK Fire Service. Some 59,000 are uniformed staff and their pay and conditions are contained within the so-called *Grey Book*. Of these nearly one third (18,000) are retained staff – these are part-timers but fully trained members of brigades, available on-call and typically employed in rural areas. The fifty-eight Fire Authorities employ these men and women. Fire Authorities are part of Local Government and are subject to general legislation and, of course, the possibility of political variation in the nature of their employers.

The employers were previously grouped into three employers' associations: the Association of County Councils (usually dominated by Tory councils), the Association of Metropolitan Authorities (usually dominated by Labour), and the Association of District Councils (usually Tory). This has now become the Local Government Association (LGA). The Fire Service comprises individual Local Government Fire Authorities. There are forty-seven such Authorities in England, three in Wales, eight in Scotland and one in Northern Ireland. In Scotland there are six Joint Boards (Central Scotland, Grampian, Highland and Islands, Lothian and Borders, Strathclyde and Tayside) and two Fire Authorities are a council department of a unitary authority. There is a single Fire Authority for Northern Ireland, operating under the aegis of its Health, Social Services and Public Safety Department.

Before the reform process of 2004 the structure was dominated by Fire Authorities responsible for employing staff in brigades and running fire stations. In turn such authorities were responsible to the Secretary of State, and interacted with Central Fire Brigades Advisory Council (CFBAC) and Boards, as well as with the Fire Service Inspectorate, the Fire Service College, and, in industrial relations, through the National Joint Council (NJC). Such a pluralistic and democratic structure is now seen as part of the problem for the implementation of change, and many Government statements have decried the lack of local management strength, parroting contentious

Figure 1: Existing fire authorities

From Our Fire and Rescue Service, ODPM 2003

Figure 2: Organisational structure of the fire service in England and Wales in 2002

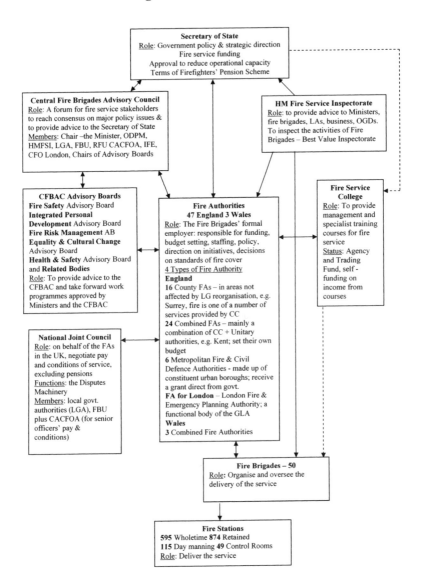

Source: Bain Report

management consultants' views that, 'chief fire officers' operational freedom is constrained by the inflexible national fire cover standards, crewing arrangements and shift patterns' (Bain 2002: 28).

The variety in local accountability structures is coupled with very wide variation in territory, composition and size of brigades. For example, the Isle of Wight has sixty-one full-time firefighters and 155 part-time retained firefighters, whereas London has 5,684 full-time firefighters and no retained staff. This variation means, as with all national public services locally delivered, an uneven level of provision and performance. The peculiar accountability structure has not, however, stopped development in management efficiency, or a culture of change by agreement. However, the 2003 White Paper, *Our Fire and Rescue Service* (ODPM), repeats Bain's demand for reform while offering little evidence that the problems of the Service have been mainly associated with structure.

FUNDING, PERFORMANCE AND PAY

As with most public services in the UK the bulk of funding for the Fire Service comes direct from Central Government. This always raises three issues. Firstly, spending comes from a mixture of taxes and borrowing, so that total public expenditure has an important impact on other macro-economic variables such as inflation and interest rates. Secondly, the allocation of resources as between types of Government spending is hotly contested within and between political groupings; and while there is no golden rule, successive Governments have tried to create basic formulae (with bits added on) to match the equity need of equal spending per person with variations in regional population. This system has often been seen as too rigid and centralised, but alternatives have failed; and there has been continuing debate about whether or not the solution to the problem is privatisation in some form. Thirdly, the freedom to spend the monies so allocated within any given sector raises questions of accountability – as between employers with legal duties, senior managers with operational obligations, staff with employment contracts, and the user/receiver of the service (citizens in a given community) with rights. As a result of this messy but democratic decision-making system, recent Governments have sought to tie specific funds to specific outcomes and/or targets. This, it is argued, gives senior managers more freedom to manage, but in fact it actually limits managerial discretion in important matters, through pre-digested views of best practice and best value.

With the exception of Northern Ireland, where 100% of the costs are met from central funds, Fire Services are financed to the extent of some 85% of their budgets by Central Government grant, delivered through the Standard Spending Assessment mechanism applied to Local Government generally (and the Fire Service element is not hypothecated); the remaining 15% comes from council tax. The total annual cost of the service in England and Wales is around £1.5billion, or some 2.5% of local authority expenditure (Burchill 2000: 7).

As funding becomes tied to outcomes, and as outcomes are measured by performance indicators, so the measuring of performance – individual, group and corporate – becomes more important as well as less reliable. The ODPM website (www.odpm.gov.uk) gives this account of the current ways and means of establishing performance and concludes that the Fire Service in 2001-2 (the year before the dispute) was very good:

> Best Value has been applied to local authority services since 1 April 2000. There are a number of different categories of fire authorities in England and Wales. Essentially these divide into 34 single-purpose authorities (London and the metropolitan fire authorities and combined fire authorities) and 16 county fire authorities where fire is provided by the county council as one of a range of services. Single-purpose fire authorities are Best Value authorities in their own right. For county fire authorities the duty of Best Value applies at county council level. The Fire Service BVPIs were included in the document 'Best Value Performance Indicators 2001/2002' which was published in December 2000. They were developed in consultation with Fire Service interests and replaced the indicators published by the Audit Commission up to and including 1999-2000. There are two broad categories of indicators, service delivery and corporate health. Service delivery indicators tend to show how effectively fire authorities are providing services, for example in relation to the incidence of fires and fire-related casualties. Corporate health indicators provide information on how well fire authorities are running themselves.
>
> The BVPI data for service delivery indicators give a direct brigade by brigade comparison under each heading … Where it is considered important to have comparisons in the performance of all fire authorities against particular corporate health indicators, such as sick leave rates, data have been collected from all authorities. The indicators serve to highlight variations in performance. Under the Best Value process, fire authorities will be required to compare their performance with that of the best and set targets for improvement.
>
> The essence of Best Value is seeking continuous improvement in service delivery and outcomes. It is therefore vital that authorities are able to establish a comprehensive baseline of performance against which they and the people they serve can judge the progress they are making.

This type of heroic account of potential improvement with no costs and no problems stems from a systemic approach to performance management borrowed over-enthusiastically from the Harvard Business School model of measuring performance through and by market achievements. According to the Government:

improving the performance of all our public services is a central objective of the Government. The fire and rescue service has a long tradition as a locally based service, responsible to the local communities whose areas it serves ... there is much that could be done to improve its performance ... we will introduce new systems to improve the overall performance of fire and rescue authorities (ODPM 2003: 45).

This sudden drive for improvement through innovation – born from Bain but gestated inside the employers for years – emerged from the chaos of the strike. It hardly reflects the considered public view of Government two years before:

> Fire Brigades and the Fire Service as a whole have attracted high ratings in both actual performance and public satisfaction surveys. That is recognised as flowing from effective management combined with a long history of nationally laid down standards of fire cover which predetermine the speed of response, and its weight in terms of number and type of fire appliances, according to density of population, terrain and the type of risk to life and property. These factors in turn prescribe the configuration of fire stations, the deployment of appliances and allied equipment and, crucially, the numbers of people to be employed. Thus individual Fire Authorities have rather less freedom than their counterparts in other sectors of Local Government to manage resources so as to reduce costs; indeed they may not close fire stations or take an appliance out of service without the approval of the Secretary of State, who will not give it unless he is assured by HM Inspectorate of Fire Services that the minimum standards of fire cover will still be maintained. Proposals of this nature are also commonly accompanied by a public outcry of considerable volume. Proposals by Fire Authorities for reorganisation within Brigades, resulting in a reduction of some 1,500 posts of all types and grades, were nevertheless approved and implemented over the period 1997-99 (Burchill 2000: 8).

Concern for service improvement within all Local Government services is long-standing. It is an obvious fact of life, but the argument tends to be hijacked for short-term political purposes, to claim that failure to reform is due to the traditionally minded and obscurantist behaviour of staff and their union activists. Endless efforts at improvement have generally reaped poor returns, often owing more to the ingestion of current management panaceas than to the development of evidence-based and staff-supported change. Thus in the 1980s the emphasis was on the benefits of management development in the Fire Service (Davies 1980); and more recently the Service has been dominated by management of change nostrums (Doyle 1996). What follows is a classic statement of New Public Management, which assumes that such matters can be determined by good management seen as a technical question, rather than an understanding that the delivery of the service depends on the workforce, and that their version of good performance may differ from that of the management (see chapter five):

> All local authority services are within the ambit of the provisions of the Local Government Act 1999 that require those responsible for, and employed in, these services to seek continuous improvement in the way they are delivered ... The 1999 Act, by giving statutory effect to the Government's proposals for best value for local authorities, not only creates an expectation of a need for change, but places a statutory obligation on Fire Authorities to make arrangements to secure continuous improvement in the way they exercise their functions having regard to a combination of economy, efficiency and effectiveness (Burchill 2000: 9).

It is useful to note for now that the Bain report thought that the pay system 'is not suitable for a modern, flexible service' and that 'the new, broader and more sophisticated Fire Service described in this report will need a new reward structure' (Bain 2002: 81). Until the recent dispute:

> firefighters' remuneration was also prescribed by a formula agreed in 1978 whereby they are paid in line with the upper quartile of male manual earnings, annual increases thus being automatic rather than the subject of detailed collective bargaining whether at national or local level. While this is recognised as being the bedrock on which relative industrial peace in the Service for over two decades is founded, and as having delivered no more than modest increases over time, it is a further – and unusual – example of the predetermined nature of the way in which the Service is run (Burchill 2000: 8).

Actual levels of pay at 7 November 2001 and their relative worth are shown in Table 1, while the machinery for determining the levels of pay is dealt with below. In its 2002-3 report on public sector pay Incomes Data Service (IDS) commented on the dispute:

> in 1979, shortly after the pay formula was introduced, the upper quartile of male manual workers' earnings was worth £107.8, or almost 92% of the upper quartile for all male employees (£117.5). Since then however, manual workers' earnings have fallen as a proportion of non-manual workers' earnings. Figures from the most recent New Earnings Survey (NES), for April 2002, show that the upper quartile of male manual workers' earnings stood at £432.5. This was worth 75% of the upper quartile for all male employees, which stood at £577.7 ... firefighters' average earnings have recently fallen as a proportion of average earnings for all occupations (IDS 2002a: 106).

Table 1: 2002 Fire Service Pay

WHOLETIME MEMBERS

	Annual £	Weekly £	Basic hourly rate £	Casual overtime rate £
Fightfigher (aged 18)				
During first 6 months	16941	324.74	7.73	11.60
After 6 months	17727	339.81	8.09	12.14
Firefighter (aged 19 or over)				
During first 6 months	17208	329.86	7.85	11.78
After 6 months and during				
2nd year	17982	344.70	8.21	12.32
During 3rd year	18843	361.20	8.60	12.90
During 4th year	19776	379.09	9.03	13.55
During 5th year	21531	412.73	9.83	14.75
(subject to being fully qualified)				
After 15 years' service (qualified)	22491	431.13	10.27	15.41
After 15 years' service (unqualified)	20694	396.68	9.44	14.16

	Annual (42-hour week) £	Weekly (42-hour week) £	Annual (40-hour week) £	Weekly (40-hour week) £
Fire Control Operator				
Aged under 17 years	14163	271.49	13170	252.45
Aged 17 years	14655	280.92	13623	261.14
Aged 18 years during first 6 months	15588	298.80	14514	278.22
Aged 18 years after 6 months	16311	312.66	15174	290.87
Fire Control Operator (aged 19 over)				
During first 6 months	15825	303.35	14736	282.47
After 6 months and during 2nd year	16539	317.03	15396	295.12
During 3rd year	17325	332.10	16131	309.21
During 4th year	18174	348.38	16920	324.34
During 5th year (subject to appraisal)	19827	380.06	18438	353.44
After 15 years' service	20682	396.45	19230	368.62

RETAINED AND VOLUNTEER MEMBERS

	ANNUAL RETAINING FEE	
	During first 3 years' service £	After 3 years' service £
Firefighter	1881	2055
Leading Firefighter	2055	2115
Sub-Officer	2115	2274
Sub-Officer i/c of station	2274	2475
Station Officer	2574	2913

The annual retaining fee may be reduced by up to 25% where cover is provided for a limited period only

	Turn-out fee £	Pre-arranged attendance fee* £
Firefighter	13.93	6.20
Leading Firefighter	16.27	7.20
Sub-Officer	18.47	7.95
Station Officer	20.79	9.52

* *Also extra payment for remaining on duty and payment for extra work*

FBU CIRCULAR

MEMBERS have been informed of the 3.9% increase to pay which arose from the Pay Formula this year. This increase produced a weekly rate of pay for the Qualified Firefighter of £412.73 with an annual salary of £21,531. The rates of pay for all members are attached to this circular.

Set out below is an explanation, as agreed by Annual Conference, as to how this year's Pay Formula was calculated:

PAY FORMULA
The formula was agreed in 1978 following the National Strike, and equates the earnings of qualified firefighters with the earnings of the upper quartile of adult mate manual workers. To achieve this the formula requires the following information:

1. The New Earnings Survey upper quartile figure.
2. The average earnings index.
3. The earnings of qualified firefighters.

UPPER QUARTILE FIGURE
The New Earnings Survey is published annually by the Office for National Statistics which provides information relevant to April each year. This year the

National Joint Council were informed that the upper quartile figure for adult mate manual workers was £430.00.

AVERAGE EARNINGS INDEX

As the Fire Service Pay Date is 7 November each year and the upper quartile figure is calculated on an April figure it is necessary to project the upper quartile to a November figure. This is done by using the movement in average earnings and the latest available figure to us was 4.5% which relates to August. This projection means that instead of using an upper quartile figure of £430.00 to calculate firefighter earnings we used £441.31.

EARNINGS OF QUALIFIED FIREFIGHTERS

The Union and the Employers jointly carry out a survey each year of the earnings of qualified firefighters. This survey showed that the qualified firefighter in August 2001 received earnings of £417.26 per week.

This earnings figure is made up of basic pay of £397.26, allowances of £14.25 and casual overtime of £5.75.

This total earnings figure is a 3.5% increase over last year which reflects increases in London Weighting Allowance, overtime and turnout fees.

These increases in the earnings of firefighters affect the calculation of basic pay and demonstrate very clearly what the impact of issues such as shift overtime would have on the pay formula.

The reality is with our formula that any increases in earnings of firefighters through allowances and overtime have a direct effect on the basic pay of all firefighters, the greater the increase in allowances and overtime the lower the pay increase!!

CALCULATION OF FORMULA

The following calculation therefore applied to the 2001 Pay Agreement:

Upper Quartile of Mate Manual Workers	£430.00
Projected Upper Quartile	£441.31
Firefighter Earnings	£417.26
Casual Overtime Worked	0.41 hours
New Basic Pay of Qualified Firefighter	£412.73

This resulted in an increase of 3.9% which was then applied to the pay rates for all members of the service and set out in the NJC Circular.

Mike Fordham
Assistant General Secretary

Source: Firefighter, Jan.-Feb. 2002

FBU – MEMBERS, HISTORY, POLICIES, STRUCTURE, GOVERNANCE AND POLITICS

The history of the FBU, like many similar craft or occupationally specific unions in the twentieth century, owes much to war and social upheaval. So while some firefighters did join more general unions, little was achieved until after World War One when a distinctive union was formed which quickly affiliated to both the Labour Party and the TUC. After 1945, along with other public sector unions, the FBU won the right to bargain nationally, and the Service was put on a statutory basis, with national standards of fire cover. For most of the 1950s and 1960s the union started the long march for better pay, pensions and conditions of service, especially working hours and training. By the 1970s inflation and various government policies had undermined morale and faith in the system, leading to a spate of government inquiries and local industrial action. This culminated in the 1977-8 strike and the pay formula. For most of the 1980s and 1990s the nature of the job changed, with the introduction of new technologies and the changing profile of local communities. Pay was only just protected by the formula, and employers became itchy to change working practices, especially the overtime ban and shift patterns. By the time of the election of the Labour Government in 1997, the pay formula no longer worked favourably, modernisation was in the air, and there was a changing of the guard in terms of the sentinels of collective bargaining.

Firefighters in big cities began to join unions, mainly local government manual unions, in around 1906. Following a dispute over union recognition in London in 1902, the London County Council (LCC) conceded the demand for a separate firefighters' union, which later become the Firemen's Trade Union. Firefighters in other brigades began to join the new union and by 1922 it had 2000 members. In the same year, members were balloted on a proposition to join the Labour Party and set up a political fund. This was agreed and the following year the Firemen's Trade Union affiliated to the TUC. The union was renamed the Fire Brigades Union in 1930. Like other workers in the early 1930s its members were faced with the prospect of five per cent wage cuts, but a skilful rearguard action eventually secured (in 1934) an industrial court order that allowed for equality with the Metropolitan Police (Bailey 1992b).

There then followed a major struggle on hours of work. With the election in 1934 of a majority Labour administration at the LCC, the FBU leadership saw an opportunity for a major breakthrough on working conditions. The LCC leader, Herbert Morrison, a future Home Secretary, fiercely opposed the union's claim for a reduction in the seventy-two hour week. Just like Bain today, Morrison argued that for much of the seventy-two duty hours firefighters were resting, and that 'weekly average of working was 29 out of the 72 duty hours' (Bailey 1992b: 35). The FBU leadership's response was sharp. Not only had Morrison greatly underestimated the hours of active work; he had totally failed to understand the social arguments for cuts in working time. Writing in *London News*, the FBU's General Secretary said this: 'firemen do not want to rest on trestles; they do not want to remain at work to "play games" [a response to Morrison's remark about firemen on day shift playing billiards], they want to go home like other workers when they have completed eight hours' (*ibid*). No progress was made on reducing working hours during the 1930s and when war broke out in 1945 the seventy-two hour week was replaced by continuous duty. Nevertheless, membership grew, if slowly, and stood at 2,800 in 1938 (1,700 of whom were in the London Fire Brigade).

In the early months of the war, John Horner was elected General Secretary of the FBU and he set the union on a path of membership growth and socialist politics. He pioneered a new approach to the Auxiliary Fire Service (AFS) that had been set up to tackle the exigencies of war. Rather than see this new force as a threat to the whole time firefighters' professionalism and status, Horner was determined to recruit and involve auxiliary firefighters in the union. FBU membership leapt to 66,500 (including 1000 women) by 1940. The bulk of these new recruits were from the AFS, but there was also significant recruitment into the union of whole time firefighters outside of London, partly due to a new positive approach to trades unionism by the public authorities. The war, with its aerial bombings, had convinced all those concerned of the need for a national service, and decisively tipped the balance towards central regulation of local authority control of the Service and the staff (Ewen 2003).

After the war, the Service was denationalised and handed back to local authority control on 1 April 1948. At the same time the FBU secured two important advances. Firstly, that wages and conditions were determined nationally, and secondly that the FBU was to be recognised as the 'one organisation competent to negotiate on behalf of all ranks' (Bailey 1992b: 82). Membership dropped dramatically with the disbandment of the AFS at the end of the war, but steadily rose thereafter from 15,293 in 1946 to 23,810 in 1960 as the FBU moved towards its objective of a 100% organisation.

For the FBU, pay and hours dominated the agenda in the 1950s and 1960s. Horner recognised that the first requirement was to establish the Fire Service as a modern operation employing skilled technicians who are often involved in personal danger while carrying out their jobs. In this period, firefighters spent hours a week on routine cleaning duties, while fire regulations were rudimentary and inspection regimes haphazard, even in high risk industries and premises. The Fire Service had to be rid of its 'mop and bucket' mentality, argued the FBU leadership (Horner, 1992: 355), if it was to be transformed into a modern Fire Service. So in this very basic but radical sense, with the development of the FBU's campaign *A Service for the Sixties*, the FBU were the pioneers in modernisation some forty odd years ago, along with other public service workers.

As far as wages and conditions were concerned, the FBU leadership was determined to re-establish the comparability principle, carrying forward the arguments and arrangements of the 1930s and 1940s, which linked, however tenuously, firefighters' pay and conditions with those of the police. To do this effectively required that the status of the job be upgraded, and Horner championed Fire Prevention activities as the way forward. The FBU leadership argued for fire prevention and inspection activities to be integrated into the job descriptions of fire-fighters. This overall approach was given official support with the publication of the Holroyd Committee on the Fire Service in 1970. Since then the FBU has fought for proper pay comparability – secured for some years under the 1978 pay formula – and for service improvements based on agreement with managers and their employers.

Today, the FBU organises only in the Fire Service and dwarfs all other workers' organisations. It has 52,000 members and represents over 80% of the Officer grade personnel below the level of Assistant Chief Fire Officer. Of the 18,000 retained firefighters over 9,000 are FBU members, and the vast majority of the 1,700 control staff are also FBU members. The other workers' organisations in the Fire Service are the Retained Firefighters Union (RFU), which has around 3000 members (including retired members) and a no-strike constitution, and two smaller organisations representing Officer grades – the Fire Officers Association and the Association of Principal Fire Officers. At present there is a single negotiating body, the National Joint Council (NJC) representing all grades below Assistant Chief Fire Officer. At the time of writing, in April 2005, talks were still going on, with ACAS help, on new bargaining arrangements brought in under the 2004 Fire and Rescue Services Act. The intention of Government was to complicate the bargaining structure and thereby weaken the FBU's dominant position, and to achieve this the employers had rejected ACAS recommendations for the best way forward.

Since the 1977 strike the FBU has been a remarkably successful union. Unlike almost every other union, the FBU's membership actually grew during the Thatcher years, illustrating how well the union had fought off cuts to the Service and protected its members' conditions. As we note later, the union has had a high success rate in local disputes involving proposals to reduce fire cover, or to attack the *Grey Book* defined working conditions. In recent years, under successive General Secretaries (including Ken Cameron, who retired in 2000), the union has been impressively active in driving through its *Fairness at Work* agenda, designed to tackle head on the militaristic, sexist and racist practices in the Service, which the employers, by and large, have failed to address. This work was recognised by the Home Office's *Thematic Review of Equal Opportunities*, and even Bain rather grudgingly conceded a leading role to the union in driving forward equal opportunities work.

The FBU has developed a highly representative democracy, given specific recognition to all minority groups by occupation, gender or sexual orientation. Each of these groups has its own publication, its own national committee and is represented on the Executive Council. Thus, for example, Michael Nicholas, was elected as the first black member of the Executive Council, and has been a regular speaker at TUC congresses for the last few years.

A number of commentators are interpreting the FBU's support for the existing watch and shift patterns and single entry promotional arrangements as being discriminatory against women and black workers who might otherwise be recruited. The FBU's riposte is that the current arrangements are important features of an efficient emergency service, and that the employers have spuriously used arguments in support of equal opportunity policies in order to undermine existing agreements (see the Merseyside dispute). At the same time the FBU argues that employers have done too little to improve conditions for women firefighters – for example in providing facilities such as properly designed uniforms for female firefighters, and female toilets in stations; or in increasing establishment levels to allow for special parental leave in the event of family sickness. Within a 24/7 emergency service, the existing shift systems actually make it easier for parents to organise child care than it would be in traditional 9-5 Monday to Friday working. The Inspectorate reluctantly recognised that the FBU has been at the forefront of campaigning to modernise the Service's approach to equal opportunities, recruitment policies and family friendly working practices. This was formally recognised when the CFBAC appointed the FBU General Secretary, Andy Gilchrist, as the first chair of its Equalities Committee.

This commitment to equality has been one of three pillars of recent FBU policy alongside improvements in health and safety, and pay. The importance given to these policies reflects both membership wishes and the broad left nature of the FBU leadership nationally as well as in most regions.

Rule 3 of the FBU states its objects thus:

(1) To organise all uniformed employees of fire brigades into one Union.

(2) To secure unity of action in order to improve the position and status of members and the service and secure that the numbers of uniformed employees of fire brigades, members of the Union and appropriate post holders within the Union, are as far as reasonably practicable, representative of gender and ethnic minorities and sexual orientation.

(3) To settle and negotiate differences and disputes between members of the Union in matters relating to their Fire Service employment, with employers, Trade Unions, or other persons.

Figure 3: FBU structure

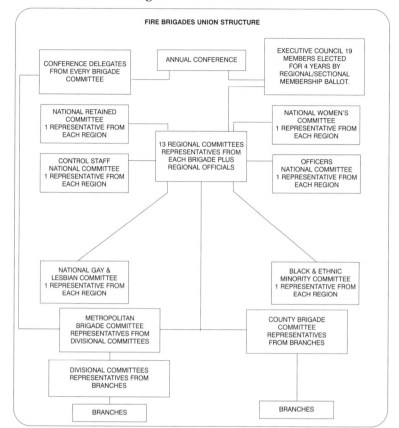

Source: FBU

(4) To promote legislation in the interests of the members of the Union and the service.

(5) To secure that only members of this Union are employed as uniformed members of fire brigades.

(6) To aid and join with other trade unions or societies having objects similar to any of the objects of this Union.

(7) To provide legal assistance to members when matters relating to their employment in the Fire Service or affecting their interests as employees in the Fire Service are involved.

(8) To further political objects to which Section 3 of the Trades Union Act 1913 applies.

(9) To administer from the general funds of the Union such benefit or welfare funds as may be instituted from time to time by the Executive Council in the interests of the members of the Union or of any section of the members of the Union.

(10) To administer any scheme or fund which the Executive Council may set up from time to time.

(11) Where possible it be the policy of the Fire Brigades Union not to conduct business with any organisations or in premises of said organisations where such organisations are unsympathetic to the Labour and Trade Union Movement.

The nature of decision-making in the union follows the usual pattern of UK unions, with the annual conference of delegates being the supreme body and an elected executive charged with carrying out policy on a regular basis. On most issues the senior elected officials manage the union within policy constraints and with regular contact with EC members. In turn EC members are in regular touch with local officers, activists and members. In a small and mainly homogeneous union such links are fairly easy to maintain, and are aided by organisational structures for minority groups and within regions.

The FBU corresponds to a closed craft union, as well as having some of the elements of industrial unionism, and is cited in the literature on unions as such (Coates and Topham 1982, Mathieson and Corby 1999). The essential profile offered is of a union recruiting within a limited craft and/or industrial sector (therefore 'closed'), and this tends to create certain features such as greater democracy, a leadership recruited from the occupation, and policies concerned with control over the supply of labour, protection of working practices, and strong resistance to management initiatives (Turner 1964). For most of the postwar period its national leadership has been roughly broad left in majority, encompassing activists from the Communist Party through to the centre of the Labour Party (Saville 1992). This loose coalition has also tended to dominate most regions, although London and Merseyside have a few activists from further on the left. Relations between the London region and the main body of the FBU have frequently been fraught, one example being when the London Fire Fighters' Federation 'broke away' from the FBU (Lumley 1973: 70).

THE ULTRA-LEFT AND THE FBU

Since the election of John Horner as General Secretary in 1939, the FBU has been a left-led union, with most elected officials and officers supporting what we know as broad left positions within the labour and trade union movement. In the early years after 1945, as in many other left-led unions, Communist Party members played the leading role in developing organisation and policy. But since the mid-1950s the Communist Party's influence has declined to be replaced by a more broadly based leadership that nonetheless pursued similar progressive policies. This continues to the present day.

Throughout this period there has been a small, organised Trotskyite presence, based in recent years mainly around the Socialist Workers

Party (SWP). Highly respected EC member Terry Segars from Essex played a leading role in developing a rank and file perspective, and the group produced *Red Watch*, an occasional broadsheet publication that was read by most activists. At most times and on most issues the leadership and the *Red Watch* faction worked together on industrial questions and FBU internal democratic and administrative issues.

The big divide, which became wider with the election of a New Labour Government and a re-alignment of the ultra-left with the formation of the Socialist Alliance and Respect, was the attitude to Labour Party affiliation. Here the leadership under both Ken Cameron and Andy Gilchrist fought hard to retain the link with Labour, arguing that the Party was based on the unions and that it could be reclaimed for progressive pro-working class policies from the Blairite clique. But the *Red Watch* faction argued that it was time to reshape the union's political work and to use its Political Fund in support of candidates and organisations supporting FBU policies. In recent times this has become a transparent effort to secure FBU financial support for both the Socialist Alliance and even more recently Respect.

Against this background it is ironic that the Labour leadership actively used its covert propaganda machine to paint Andy Gilchrist as an unreliable militant from the day he was elected as General Secretary of the FBU. For example Frank Burchill, for some years the independent chair of the NJC, was regularly briefed by Ministers and senior civil servants to the effect that Gilchrist was running with the Trotskyites and the Essex and Merseyside FBU industrial militants.

At the crunch time in the dispute Prime Minister Blair accused the FBU leadership of being 'Scargillite', and this was not intended as a compliment. In fact Andy Gilchrist came to the fore as part of the union's broad left leadership, in the same tradition as every other FBU General Secretary since 1945. His personal leadership style during the dispute was based entirely on collective decision making at EC level, informed by regular consultation with activists and members. At all stages the aim was to get a negotiated settlement endorsed by the membership. Not surprisingly, as the dispute dragged on some cracks began to appear in what was at the beginning of the strike a formidably united union. By November 2002 negotiations had produced the basis for a 16% two-year agreement, only for the Government to scupper the deal at the eleventh hour.

To reach this position the union leadership saw fit to cancel or postpone pre-arranged discontinuous strike periods in order to keep negotiations going and to show the union's total commitment to securing a negotiated settlement at the earliest possible date. Rumblings questioning the leaders' competence and democratic practice began from this time. At first they were small and isolated, remaining largely within the union's democratic structures, with the leadership's flexible strategy invariably receiving overwhelming endorsement whenever put to the vote at every level. But from the beginning of 2003 the '30k website' (see below) began to reflect a more concerted alternative voice, although the views expressed remained those of a very small minority. These minority views were encouraged and led, if not directly orchestrated, by the ultra-left and from this time on the website became a focus for the internal union opposition to the leadership. When the EC failed to carry the March 2003 Recall Conference, support for the views expressed on the 30k website began to increase within the union. But this opposition failed to obtain enough support to call a membership ballot of no confidence in the EC.

A number of vitally important democratic principles were tested to breaking point during the dispute. In particular, organised factions, who consistently opposed the decisions made by Recall Conferences and the elected Executive, used their own communications networks to undermine the elected leadership by calling into question the strategy and tactics employed during the strike, for example the Grassrooots organisation. This had the effect of chipping away at the membership's confidence in the leadership, and of advertising to the employers and the Government that there were differences to exploit. And perhaps most importantly, it gave the Government constant and reliable intelligence information about what the union was thinking and planning during what proved to be a protracted and difficult campaign.

Big and long strikes are rather like military campaigns. For those campaigning for justice, unity and support for the elected leadership are essential to success. As long as pre-strike decisions are made by an open and democratic process, within the rules of the union, and the leadership of the strike is determined by the same democratic processes, then it is essential to put some trust in the leadership if the best possible results are to be obtained.

For whatever reason, these basic principles of campaigning were turned on their head by those responsible for the 30k website. This non-elected, democratically unaccountable, and self-appointed alternative leadership had their own ideas and the means to spread them. For them anything went as long as it constituted an attack on the elected leadership. Of course alternative views were posted, partly because to do otherwise would have undermined the self-proclaimed image as a democratic forum. But the editors of 30k knew full well that the overwhelming majority of activists were both too busy and too loyal to their union to dissipate their efforts in fruitless debate in unofficial forums run by unelected and unrepresentative cliques.

During the dispute the 30k site managers made much of the virtues of democratic discourse. 'Let a thousand flowers bloom' was their attitude, and then the leadership would be better appraised of rank and file views. Yet to any honest outside commentator the official FBU structures are among the most democratic in the British trade union movement. At every key stage of the dispute members were directly consulted, after elected and representative conference delegates had thoroughly debated motions from both the brigades and the EC. So from every workplace upwards not a single FBU member was excluded from the democratic process that is governed by the rule-book. Those promoting the 30k site were seeking a second undemocratic bite at the cherry, and in doing so were playing into the hands of the union's enemies among the employers and Government Ministers.

Unfortunately the 30k site attack on democracy went further than an attack on the leadership, damaging though this was. It also used language and displayed attitudes that have no place in democratic discussion. For democracy to be a weapon for union advance, then differing views and the people who hold them must be treated with respect. Democracy also demands that the rules of debate are determined by the whole union and administered at every level by elected and accountable union officials and officers. The 30k site traduced both these democratic principles, and it did not stop there. Constant pressure was applied in a vain attempt to split the EC by demanding that each vote be recorded and that names be named on either side of a vote. This is to totally misunderstand the role of collective leadership during a strike – a majority vote must be binding on all, and to broadcast differences gives ammunition to the union's enemies, and encourages disquiet and possible disunity amongst members.

No doubt this attempt to name and shame had as much to do with personal ambitions in future EC elections as it did with spurious democratic principles. Not content with this attack on the integrity of the Executive, the 30k site leadership also questioned the rights of EC members elected by the FBU sections to vote on industrial questions. This attack on the rule book was probably motivated by expediency rather than principle – its authors hallucinated that they might get a majority for their views on the EC if that body simply represented the regions. But, whatever the motives, this challenge to minority group representation has sinister undemocratic undertones, and to raise such a potentially divisive issue during a dispute is the worst kind of opportunism.

Whilst the activities and arguments of a small group of political activists failed to convince the majority of FBU members, there is no doubt that confidence in the union's elected leadership is at a lower ebb than it was before the dispute. This has been reflected in recent elections for vacancies at EC and Regional Official levels, mainly in much lower turnouts than is customary in the FBU – a situation that has benefited candidates supported by the Trotskyite groups. This development, together with a recent conference decision to disaffiliate from the Labour Party, owes almost everything to the activities of the Blair Government during the dispute. Paradoxically perhaps, the supporters of a broad left social democratic and Parliamentary approach to progressive social change have been temporarily undermined by a Labour Government, to the benefit of members of small extra-Parliamentary political groups who seek to break the unity of the labour movement by destroying the Labour Party as a federal party of the working class. Such developments could have profound implications far beyond the ranks of the FBU, if the policies of the Labour Government and Labour Councils continue to attack public sector jobs and trade union rights.

NATURE OF THE JOB AND CONDITIONS OF SERVICE

The FBU leadership and activists have fought to win and to defend decent conditions of service for their members in stressful, dangerous, skilled and unusual circumstances. That is the nature of an emergency service. Once a pay formula existed after 1978 there was no reason why, in general at least, the union should renegotiate downwards hard won concessions: there was no need for the kind of something-for-something deal that was increasingly common elsewhere in the public sector in the UK in the 1990s. Employers and senior managers wanted changes to be made, but, while the union was always willing to negotiate some change, essentially the situation tended to favour what had been won. This cat and mouse game reached a crisis in the late 1990s when the employers sought to alter conditions outside the NJC, and this led to the setting up of the Burchill inquiry in 2000 to look at the workings of the NJC (see below). Subsequently, the dispute created the circumstances whereby working practices could be negotiated in exchange for more pay and a new formula. That is the heart of the 'modernisation' argument and fills the pages of the both the Bain report (2002) and the subsequent White Paper (ODPM 2003).

The conditions of service for uniformed fire staff are laid out in the *Scheme of Conditions of Service* issued by the NJC for Local Authorities' Fire Brigades (known as the *Grey Book*). This summary is based on the conditions at the time of the dispute, and chapter five discusses recent changes as a result of the strike action. The fifth edition agreed in 1998 states in point 4 of the Preface that:

> The Council wishes to refer to the joint nature of the decisions incorporated in this Scheme and to remind fire authorities of the value of affording opportunities to members of brigades, through their accredited representatives, for consultation ... the Council hopes that the Scheme will provide a sound basis for harmony throughout the Fire Services of the country.

So this represents a clear pluralist re-affirmation of the benefits of joint regulation for all those involved in collective bargaining for the sector. The document itself provides a clear delineation of operational and control staff ranks, with a brief statement of levels of concomitant responsibility. For example, 'a station officer' is to be 'responsible for the general operational and administrative efficiency of a station or a watch at a station' (section 1). Section 2 outlines the duty system and the hours of duty: for firefighters, leading firefighters and sub-officers, for example, 'the normal average weekly hours ... engaged in operational duty shall be 42'. This is now also undergoing change through initiatives such as 'Rank to Role' and the Integrated Personal Development System (IPDS).

There are three main duty systems: a shift system, day crewing, and day duties. The sub-section on pre-arranged overtime is discussed below in more detail as it formed a central part of the modernisation debate, as did of course shift systems, crewing and later even stand down time. For senior, leading and fire control operators the average hours was the same at forty-two, but they had only two types of duty system – shift and day. Other provisions in the Scheme include leave, such as annual leave (section III a), public holidays (IIIb), long service leave (IIIc) – another contentious issue – and special leave (IIId). Sick leave was dealt with under a separate section (IV).

Firefighters work on average a forty-two-hour week. The principal duty system operating in the Fire Service is the shift system. Shift-staffed pumps deal with some 75% of all incidents. Under the shift system, each twenty-four-hour period is divided into a nine-hour day shift and a fifteen-hour night shift. Firefighters work two consecutive day shifts then, after a twenty-four-hour break, two consecutive night shifts finishing at 9 am on the third day. They then have three clear days off. They thus work forty-eight hours in each eight-day period, which averages over eight weeks to a forty-two-hour week. Under this system, continuous cover can be provided by four separate 'watches' crewing each appliance

Pay is covered by section V of the *Grey Book*. Most of this section is not bothered with the determination of pay rates, but with issues such as qualifying periods and acting up allowances, while section VI deals with additional allowances such as accommodation, travel, meals, removal, and overtime (sub section 11).

Conditions of service of retained firefighters (section VII) include an obligation to attend: the station for training and maintenance duties (an average of two hours each week); the station promptly in response to a call at any time; and at any fire or other occurrence; or at any station for reserve or stand by duties. They receive: an annual retaining fee, drill attendance fees, attendance fees (when they respond to a call, but are not required to crew the appliance), turnout fees, extra payments for remaining on duty or other additional work, and a long service bounty.

Section VIII deals with suspension of members from duty under disciplinary regulations (currently being changed); and finally Section IX deals with miscellaneous matters including appointments and promotions; discipline; prohibition of outside employment and uniform. The document ends with Section X, namely the procedures for settling individual grievances and disputes between fire authorities and the representative bodies. This was subject to reform in 2000 (see next section). Section XI is the constitution of the NJC, and Section XII states the fairness at work principles – equal opportunities and equality.

THE JOB CHANGES

A report by the job evaluation expert Sue Hastings for the FBU into the 'changing role of the firefighter' over the last twenty-five years concluded, after detailed research, that 'this investigation has shown that changing technology and environmental changes, within and outside the Fire Service, have only increased the demands of the role of firefighters' (2002:12). While both the Bain report (2002) and the White Paper (2003) acknowledged such changes, yet the argument is around how to achieve changes in pay and actual working practices to meet the challenge of the new duties and requirement. The Government and employers insist on change by management, free of traditional collective bargaining responsibilities. Thus Bain makes the classic managerialist point that 'an important theme in this report is that managers must be free to manage'. In particular, to change core conditions of service such as shift patterns, crewing levels, and overtime (2002: 98-99). Included in this modernisation process is the desire to escape from the limitations, as they see them, of national agreements reached through the NJC. Indeed in *Our Fire and Rescue Service*, the arguments of CFOs are accepted without question, that they need 'greater freedoms and flexibilities' (ODPM 2003: 51).

While the benefits of change were being overstated, the costs were neglected. For example, a recurrent theme of reports into the Service over the last twenty years (starting really with the 1986 Audit Commission report) has been the inefficiencies that derive from sickness absence. Indeed better management of such absence is part of the modernisation programme (see chapter five). One aspect of this, as with other emergency service work, is the levels of stress experienced by staff. Both direct research (Moran 2001) and indirect research (Lusa *et al* 2002) has shown the extent of the problem and how it varies with periods of strike action and rapid change.

It has been widespread practice throughout the UK public services for conditions of service to be detailed in large national agreements subject to periodic renegotiation. In the traditional way of Whitleyism representatives of the two sides, in this case the FBU for the workforce and a group from the multi-employer side, would meet once a year to seek to negotiate changes. The outcome would be a national collective agreement named after the colour of its cover, and subject to implementation and interpretation locally. The difference between the Fire

Service and other services was that, after the 1978 strike settlement, pay was not (specifically) included in the negotiations and therefore the scope for negotiated change was much more limited from the point of view of the employers. For much of time from 1979 to 1998 this did not matter since the lead negotiators of the two sides (Charles Nolda for the employers and Ken Cameron for the FBU) both subscribed to a model that linked the good of the Service with the good of the staff in the Service. Only when this consensus cracked in the late 1990s, with the failure of the pay formula and the modernisation programme of the Labour Government, did the system fail, as the balance of power that had maintained it dramatically altered.

INDUSTRIAL RELATIONS AND COLLECTIVE BARGAINING IN THE FIRE SERVICE

Once those that control state power and resources resolve to include as part of their activities the ownership and management of certain services, the question of the determination of pay and conditions of the staff becomes centre stage. In most public services there is a high labour input with relatively high total labour costs. The control of these thus becomes very important, but while the state wishes to minimise its overall wage bill it must still recruit and retain the right quantity and quality of staff to run the Service to the required standard. After 1945, under the postwar settlement, good industrial relations and a fair system of employment appeared to be an essential part of the national-isation process. The preferred system, in one form or another, was that of Whitley: a national collective bargaining system based on the notion that its agreements would become effective national rates for millions of workers. This had been used for schoolteachers since 1919, and some parts of the civil service since 1918, but it was in the 1940s that it took off, with Whitley Committees in the newly founded NHS, the rest of Local Government, most of the newly nationalised services such as coal and railways, and, as part of this, the Fire Service (Whitley 1919, Clay 1929, Seifert 1992).

The Fire Service, along with the NHS and other sections of Local Government, came into being, as we would recognise it, in the late 1940s. The NJC itself was established in 1948 (and reconstituted in 1952 to include Scotland – see *Ministry of Labour Gazette* vol LX pages 89-90 for details of its constitution), based on the 1947 Fire Services Act, with a high level of national control and national pay and conditions. By the time of the 1959 Act central control was reduced, with more authority passing to the NJC itself, and the subsequent national agreement in 1963 was laid out in the *Grey Book*. 'The *Grey Book*'s provisions for addressing disputes were introduced in 1978 in the wake of the one national strike in the history of the Fire Service' (Burchill 2000: 5). The relevance of this reform of the NJC is made clear: 'thus the negotiations within the NJC on proposed changes to the *Grey Book* in 1998-9 took place against a background of the long tradition of central prescription within the Fire Service, and the drive to modernisation and change reflected in the Government's new legislation' (*ibid*: 9). This was crucial because all employers were under pressure from the centre to become more efficient, effective and economic (the three E's of NPM – see chapter five), through Best Value, and they had seen other Local Government workers make concessions through the *Green Book* on single status and local flexibility. There was, therefore, a strong movement amongst employers and CFOs to 'modernise' a Service seen as culturally backward, resistant to change, and lagging behind best practice elsewhere.

In March 2000 the Home Secretary, Jack Straw, ordered an inquiry into the machinery for determining firefighters' conditions of service under Professor Frank Burchill of Keele University (Cm 4699). It was presented to Parliament in May that year. It could be argued with hindsight that someone somewhere could smell smoke, and that this report was a harbinger of trouble to come. The specific causes of the inquiry are explained by Burchill in his letter submitting his report:

> On 14 October 1999 you instituted, at the request of the Local Government Association, an independent inquiry into the future arrangements for determining fire fighters' conditions of service. The Inquiry was in response to a breakdown in the arrangements then in place ... it was clear that the way forward was to retain voluntary arrangements ... nevertheless, there was, it seemed, substantial scope for clarifying, and amending the current procedures ... the most substantial changes in procedures are that in future a failure to agree will automatically go to conciliation, through ACAS; if either Side claims that an issue is not arbitrable in the future, that question will be put to an arbitrator ... it is a matter of some urgency ... to secure the appointment of an Independent Chairperson to the NJC (2000: i).

It is worth just briefly discussing the terms of reference of the inquiry and the main recommendations, since these are necessary to understand some of the formal aspects of the negotiations during the dispute. It started in 1999, when the employers sought to unilaterally change national conditions of service, which was immediately met by a threat of industrial action by the FBU (the so-called 'Smash and Grab' campaign). The details reflect the importance to the employers of change in working practices, 'modernisation'. In Appendix 1 of their submission to the Bain inquiry they supply five pages enlarging on the situation. In this view the employers had sought changes in the NJC method of working since 1992 in order to facilitate changes in conditions of service, and they had been blocked at every step by the FBU. Thus the employers created the crisis in 1999 in order to force an inquiry out of Government in the hope that reform of the NJC would open the door to more managerial discretion at brigade level. As the lead negotiator for the employers, Charles Nolda, later recalled:

> a concerted effort was made by the employers in 1999 to persuade the FBU to accept some changes to the national agreement, the *Grey Book*. This nearly came off at talks in Bournemouth, but the mood in the FBU hardened against any changes except in the context of both sides deriving benefit. Not unreasonable as a collective bargaining concept, many would feel, but the employers considered that the automatic pay indexation was the part of the bargain they had delivered for many years (2004: 385).

In the end the Burchill report, like the McCarthy one twenty-five years earlier, restated the centrality of collective bargaining as the main method to secure implementable agreements on every aspect of Fire Service work. The recommended improvements in the machinery were needed and welcome, but did not serve the employers' purpose. The key was the FBU's insistence on keeping everything national, and the FBU conference

> voted overwhelmingly to ballot for industrial action in the event of any attempt by employers to unilaterally impose local conditions. The employers decided to invoke the provision for unilateral arbitration ... the union refused to participate ... the employers then ... formally withdrew from the NJC. Local disputes were now taking place in a procedural vacuum. The employers sought external intervention via a Government Inquiry (Burchill 2004: 406).

The terms of reference for reform of the NJC included the notion that such changes were to secure 'best value, fairness at work, and effective procedures for the settling of disputes' (Burchill 2000: 1). Of course only the third of these was relevant, but reference to Best Value (see below on Local Government modernisation) and Fairness at Work (see below on New Labour) was made as pointed reminders as to the direction of Government policy.

The 1998-9 break down in the NJC machinery showed that the employers were ready to take tough action to secure changes in working practices, but that this was difficult within the context of a NJC in which there were no pay negotiations – pay being determined automatically through the pay formula. The employers wished to seek arbitration through ACAS, the FBU refused, and the employers then boycotted the NJC. It was the threat of FBU strike action in defence of the national agreement and the suspension of the NJC proceedings that prompted the employers to request the inquiry into the negotiating machinery. While the terms of reference of the inquiry excluded comment on substantive issues, nonetheless, as Burchill argued, there was a wider context. This included the reality that Fire Authorities 'have a duty to fulfil their obligations under the Local Government Act

1999 to seek continuous improvement in the delivery of their services to the public. Local Government services are under regular, detailed scrutiny by the Audit Commission' (2000: 2).

As Burchill suggests, the employers were somewhat divided as to the relationship preferred in decision-making terms: some wanted a continuation of a strong central system to prevent local competition wrecking efficiency gains; others wanted more flexibility at local level to reflect local need; and still another group favoured the *status quo* on the grounds that it allowed enough limited local variation to accommodate regional differences (*ibid*: 9). Burchill presents us with a range of criticisms of the existing bargaining arrangements and then some recommendations. These became more important as the dispute itself drew to a close and Burchill's own intervention as the chair of the NJC followed his prescription as to the value of a workable agreed procedure and the efficacy of negotiated settlements. The list of complaints contained the usual suspects: that the NJC had too many members (forty-five at the time); that the disputes procedures take too long; there was lack of clarity as to what was and what was not 'disputable'; that the *status quo* clause caused further delay; and that the atmosphere inside the NJC between the parties 'is adversial to the point of hostility' (*ibid*:10). The last point was understandable. After all, the employers had been under budgetary pressures for some time; successive Government-inspired reports had urged changes in labour management to save funds; the FBU had fought off determined efforts by senior managers in some brigades (sometimes through industrial action); and changes elsewhere in Local Government were now dominating the debate.

Burchill believed that in the end both sides were prepared to move forward to improve the negotiating machinery in order to allow a more orderly conduct to negotiated change (*ibid*: 12). He therefore recommended the 'reinforcement of the machinery' be done through the appointment of an Independent Chair of the NJC; that most business be done by a sub-committee with sixteen members also chaired by the newly appointed person; and that the chair, while being helpful, 'is not drawn into a mediation or arbitration role' (*ibid*: 15). Note that therefore conciliation is not ruled out in a rather pre-emptive sense. With regard to dispute resolution Burchill suggests that 'the reality is that anything within an employer/employee relationship is disputable' (*ibid*), and that no change should be made to the Disputes Committee functions since under the chair of Professor Brown there had been a marked improvement in speed, informal resolution and less wrangle on *status quo*. The final tranche of improvements came with the way the NJC dealt with disputes under section XI paragraph 12 of the *Grey Book*. This meant that there was unilateral reference to ACAS for what was in effect 'binding' arbitration. The nuance of change here is slight but important – the new paragraph will allow explicitly for a conciliation phase by ACAS. The intention was to prevent the parties from reaching final positions too soon and thereby restricting the terms of a settlement that might later be repudiated.

The NJC itself consists of an employers' side with twenty-three from the LGA, five from COSLA, and two from Northern Ireland. The union side has twenty-seven representatives from the FBU. After the Burchill report much business was done in a smaller Joint Standing Sub-Committee (JSCC) to speed things up and allow a more informal approach to bargaining, along with a newly appointed independent chair (Burchill himself). But events tended to bypass these reforms, and Bain felt that the situation remained too restrictive: 'under this machinery any aspect of firefighting which has an impact on terms and conditions, including policy issues, is subject to negotiation' (2002: 97). Bain goes on to claim that the machinery is too complex and is used to frustrate managers; therefore 'the system should be amended and simplified' (*ibid*: 98).

Figure 4: Disputes Machinery in the Fire Service

Stage of machinery	Action	Informative notes
First step	Referral of matter to the Join Secretaries of the NJC.	If a majority of both sides of the Joint Secretaries agrees, a decision is easily arrived at.
Referral upwards	If the membership can not reach agreement, the matter is referred to the NJC Disputes Committee.	
Second step	Both sides get the opportunity to put their case and the Committee tries to reach a decision under the watch of the Independent Chair	The NJC Disputes Committee is similar to the Joint Secretaries in that it is a small sub-committee – three members apiece from the employers and employees. An Independent Chair appointed by the NJC oversees proceedings; this post is currently held by Professor William Brown.
Referral upwards	Referral to the next meeting of the full NJC.	
Third step	If not resolved by the full NJC the only avenue left is ultimate referral to the Advisory Conciliation and Arbitration Service (ACAS)	The Grey Book (section 10.3) says 'in such circumstances it follows that both parties have voluntarily agreed to take part in the arbitration process when it is invoked and have agreed in advance to be bound by the arbitrators decisions.'

Source: Bain Report

PAY COMPARABILITY AND THE FIRE STRIKE OF 1977-8

Since our focus is on strikes by firefighters, we summarise the first national strike in 1977 before our detailed account of the 2002-4 action. The FBU (1997a) produced a twentieth anniversary account of the strike based on a compilation of newspaper and FBU accounts, but the only full account by an academic of the 1977-8 strike is by Bailey (1992d).

> The first official strike in the Fire Brigade Union's 59-year history began on 14 November 1977, and ended, after nine weeks, on 16 January 1978. If one image encapsulates the strike, it must surely be that of firemen on picket duty, huddled around braziers outside closed fire stations, acknowledging the signs of public support in the form of financial donations and tooting car horns (*ibid*: 229).

He continues, 'to go on strike had been a profoundly difficult step for people who saw themselves as uniformed servants of the community, providing an essential service that only they had been trained to provide'. The main cause was low pay. Their pay had fallen behind the average because successive incomes policies were enforced by Government Ministers on workers in the public services, but had been less firm when it came to private sector companies getting around the rules. The strike came after ten years of arguing the case for better pay: arguments based both on comparability and on the changing nature of their duties.

Ever since the formation of the national Fire Service in 1947 the comparative pay of firefighters has been a political issue. Until 1952 firefighters' pay was linked to that of police, but this link was broken following an Arbitration Board report which concluded: 'It appears to us that the proper way of deciding the remuneration of the Fire Service is not to relate it to police remuneration but to determine it on its own merits. Indeed to link it automatically to that of the police would be to render the existence of the NJC unnecessary' (the Ross award, see Bailey 1992c: 172-3). This followed the so-called 'Spit and Polish' agitation within the Service in 1951 (*ibid*).

Free collective bargaining did not serve FBU members that well in the 1960s and 1970s. Firstly, public sector pay as a whole fell further behind the private sector, where earnings tended to rise faster than basic pay and local bargaining became increasingly important. This process of widening wage differences tended to leave firefighters in a position where they were often chasing the pack in the wages league, but never leading it. For more years than not during this period firefighters' earnings fell in real terms. This was not the whole story. The 1960s and 1970s were the decades of incomes policies, particularly during periods of Labour Government. Such policies, which sought to restrict wage increases as part of an anti-inflation strategy, impacted most on workers in the public sector – for which the Government had either direct responsibility or considerable control on the purse strings; they also had more impact on workers whose earnings were overwhelmingly reliant on basic rates rather than additional elements such as productivity payments, overtime and shift pay. Firefighters fell into both camps and therefore fell down the wages league.

By 1966 firefighters were working a forty-eight hour week, and were 8.5% behind average male weekly earnings. Both sides within the NJC recognised that a special increase was required that year to assist retention and restore morale. The employers offered 7.5%, well in excess of the Government's 3.5% norm laid down in the White Paper on Prices and Incomes (Shepherd 1984). Matters got worse when a pay standstill was announced later in the summer. As a result the Government stepped in to block any increase and to refer the issue of firefighters' pay to the newly created National Board for Prices and Incomes (NBPI). With encouragement from the TUC General Council, the FBU EC decided to give evidence to the NBPI in the expectation that the strength of their case would be reflected in the justice of the NBPI's award. They were to be sadly disappointed. In May 1967 the NBPI report number 32 awarded a 7.5% increase from July 1968 over two years. In effect the increase was deferred for a year and then spread over a further two years. And there was to be a nasty sting in the tail. A pensionable bonus of around 10% of annual salary was offered to all firefighters prepared to work an extra shift a week. Within a year 90% of the Service was on a fifty-six hour duty system, thus undoing all the progress made since the war towards reducing working hours (Bailey 1992d: 233).

Yet the FBU's submission to the NBPI did mark an important turning point. It set out in detail firefighters' duties and activities, stressing increased skills and the greater diversity of tasks facing the Service in the 1960s. These included fire prevention and fire safety activities, and the growing incidence of special services such as rescues carried out at road accidents and other disasters. All of this required skills over and above those needed to fight fires, and the FBU's evidence showed that the firefighter of the 1960s was more akin to a skilled craft worker than the strong water squirters of the 1940s. The FBU's strategy was clear. It they were to break out of the low pay long hours culture, they needed to base future claims on the changing nature of the job and the skills needed to carry it out effectively. The FBU's case hit home in terms of the labour market arguments, as the NBPI report agreed, 'the failure of firemen's earnings to keep pace with other earnings has led to a significant increase in wastage. It has led also to an inability to recruit sufficient men to meet all the Service's requirements, both in numbers and in quality' (1967: 11).

The national strike came after neglect in some areas forced the hands

of the firefighters to take local action such as in London (1969) and
Essex (1970). As the pressure built up, the Labour Government of the
day commissioned a report by Sir Roland Holroyd of ICI (1970),
which more or less supported the FBU's own statement framed in its *A
Service for the Sixties* document. It recommended that, 'the earnings of
fully trained men with all round operational experience should be
comparable with the national average earnings of skilled craftsmen'
(Bailey 1992d: 234). So a notion of a pay formula reappeared out of the
crushing disappointment of the Government's decision to hold back
firefighters' pay. At this point a consensual mood appeared to favour
linking fire pay to that of skilled craftsmen. By 1971 another inquiry
under Sir Charles Cunningham examined the nature of the job and
linked it with the skills required by other skilled workers, and thus
started the formal idea of a pay formula. From 1970-4 pay policy under
Edward Heath's Conservative Government prevented any movement,
but a local unofficial strike in Glasgow in 1973 (Flockhart 1992) further
revealed the pressures on pay, and the use of overtime in some brigades
to supplement low basic earnings.

The Labour Governments of 1974-79 tried to hold to incomes policies, but, having raised expectations of greater fairness for public
sector workers, they suffered from a failure to deliver. The FBU called
for an overtime ban in 1974 and by 1975, having fallen foul of yet
another ill-considered pay policy, the union called for a three-month
'emergency calls only' ban in May 1975. Despite the FBU's narrow
and partial support for the TUC leadership's backing for further pay
freezes from Labour Ministers, sections of the membership and leadership felt they had come to the point of no return. If the FBU could
not secure pay improvements from a Labour Government in mid-
term, then when would they ever? In 1976 and 1977 there were
numerous short local actions, including one in Merseyside in May of
1977 (Roxburgh 1992), and an ACAS (1977) report into industrial
relations in London.

As Bailey notes, 'the brush caught fire in many places, extinguished
each time by executive intervention' (1992d: 240). These included
South Yorkshire, Northern Ireland, Merseyside, Essex and London. As
the crunch came, with Chancellor Denis Healey putting a 10% cap on
wages, the NJC set up a joint working party, with Lord (W.E.J.)
McCarthy as its independent chair, to translate the 1975 agreement on
job evaluation into a concrete pay formula. While the employers
accepted the working party report, they were bound by the
Government's 10% pay limit, and favoured both a reduction in the
working week (from forty-eight to forty-two hours) and a pay formula
based on 'McCarthy', as issues to be negotiated once the Government's
pay limits were lifted.

McCarthy had been a leading pro-Labour academic for some time
and had been ennobled by Harold Wilson. He was a main author of the

Donovan report (1968) and as such believed passionately in collective bargaining as a way of resolving conflict. As Bailey summarises,

> The McCarthy report recommended that the most appropriate comparison for the purpose of assessing a fireman's value was with 'the generality of jobs in the community'. The union's pay formula was based on this proposal to bring firemen's wages in line with adult male earnings (£78 a week) plus 10% to take account of the range of skills of qualified firemen and the physical dangers involved, or 30% in all. Negotiations on the NJC began in the autumn, with the two sides an ocean apart (1992d: 242).

The union launched its pay campaign and held rallies and demonstrations in Manchester, Birmingham, Strathclyde, Liverpool and Staffordshire. At the Eastbourne Recall Conference on the 7 November 1977, the Executive, and in particular the General Secretary, were defeated in their efforts to prevent a call for strike action. Government Ministers argued passionately against the strike and prepared the Green Goddesses for action. They suggested in alternative bursts of rhetoric that firemen were betraying the public, that the country could not afford to pay them more, that such a settlement would have a domino effect on other public sector workers, and that union militants had misrepresented the facts to members. The whole gamut of pious hypocrisy descended on the firefighters, then as now.

Pickets were mounted and 98% of FBU members went out on strike, including those in the control rooms and retained members – about 30,000 firemen according to the account in the *Department of Employment Gazette* (vol 86: 13). The level of support for the strike remained undiminished throughout its nine weeks. Ministers hoped that public opinion would turn against the firemen as tragedies were reported, and as other workers stuck in the low pay policy pit resented any group trying to break free. In reality the failure of the strike-breaking troops to deal with fires strengthened the case for better paid trained firefighters, and the solidarity of the dispute flummoxed Ministers, as well as political commentators accustomed to believing their own propaganda and myths. A key device for all parties was to agree that firefighters were a special case: that would allow a breach of pay policy without opening the flood gates of 'me-too' claims, or denting the shield of Government ministerial control over the economy. As the strike continued the union grew in solidarity and strength and cracks appeared in the resolve of the Government and employers.

At the Bridlington conference on 12 January 1978 the delegates voted to end the strike by a vote of 28,729 to 11,795, cast by representatives from sixty-nine fire brigades (from the *British Journal of Industrial Relations* Chronicle, vol XVI (2): 255). The decision was not universally popular with all members, but by now the employers were beginning to regroup and find a more aggressive and united voice; the Government Ministers with strong support from leading figures within the TUC had come to the end of their willingness to negotiate; and there were signs in parts of the country of the start of membership support ebbing away. As a result there were a few weeks of bitter and divisive argument within the EC and beyond amongst activists and members. The leadership were pulled and pushed and remained uncertain both of the mood of members and of the next step. The deal was 10% now (in line with pay policy), some changes in conditions of service, and a pay formula linking future increases in rates to earnings' improvements achieved by skilled craft workers. Bailey quotes one leader as saying 'none of the men is going back thinking he has won a victory' (1992d: 261).

Twenty-five years later whole sections of the FBU membership and activists refer to the clear and lasting victory of the 1977-8 strike, that delivered a pay formula, that allowed wages to remain comparable, that gave them a large increase in 1979-80, that allowed the FBU to fight off conditions of service changes at brigade level, and that did not put them through the heart-searching issue of taking strike action for a further quarter of a century. This 1977-8 strike has been referred to time and time again by the FBU leadership, the employers and Government Ministers. Its impact on the collective memory of those involved and still active is immense, and the lessons of history have been both learnt and misinterpreted by those involved in the recent action.

The great fear of many of the leaders of the Labour Government elected in 1997 was that public sector trade unionism in the form of industrial action over pay and to protect jobs could be the ruin of the new regime. Indeed most of them subscribed to the view that it had been the link with organised labour and the Winter of Discontent that had brought down the last Labour administration in 1979, and had made the Party unelectable for the next eighteen years. In fact the widespread action in 1978-9 arose from the then Labour Government's imposition of real wage cuts on low paid public sector workers

The Winter of Discontent refers to a number of strikes both in the public and private sectors at the fag end of the Callaghan Government in 1978-9. These disputes arose directly from the attempts of the Labour Government to restrict the growth in earnings to 5%, at a time when inflation was around 10%. This policy was a continuation of previous efforts by the same Government to hold back wages in a period of near full employment. Quite rightly, workers saw this as a policy of wage cuts and an attempt by a Labour Government to solve economic problems at their expense. At the General Election millions of working class voters deserted Labour and voted Tory under the leadership of Mrs Thatcher. It is part of New Labour's distorted version of history to present this episode as a trade union own goal rather than seeing it as yet another failure of Labour Government policy to address serious economic problems. If they believed that the 1977-8 firefighters' strike really was the harbinger of the Winter of Discontent, and that history was in danger of repeating itself, then Labour leaders had to make a difficult choice – between securing agreements with public sector unions on a range of issues including pensions, and one of imposing their programme of modernisation on hostile and reluctant groups. New Labour chose the latter, which left open the prospect of conflict with any group that felt strong enough and strongly aggrieved enough to challenge Government policy direction.

The lessons of the 1977-8 dispute, and of the usefulness of a pay formula, began to be re-assessed by the union in the early 1990s. This was because the nature of the Service and the job were being re-evaluated by Central Government and the Inspectorate; the pay formula, as noted, had began to wither away; and reforms of public services meant a changed atmosphere with regard to worker attitudes and employer expectations. By 1997 the in-coming Labour Government held out the promise of more resources, more bottom-up reform, and less privatisation and marketisation. Thus the changing of the guard at the FBU, with Andy Gilchrist replacing Ken Cameron, coincided with the changing hopes of the workforce and a reasonable view that some return to traditional industrial relations might emerge. Ken Cameron gave his considered thoughts on the 1977-8 strike and on the situation in 1997:

> it proved to be a tough nine weeks. We were taking action against a Labour Government and without the support of the TUC, though there were fellow trade unionists who did not let this deter them from giving the FBU both political and practical support. Despite these major obstacles the strike was solid – a key factor in our eventual victory ... not only were the public on our side, our members in Control rooms and our Retained members who, at that time, were not part of our pay claim, took the courageous decision to join us on the picket lines. Out of the dispute came our pay formula.

He continued:

> I constantly emphasise that FBU members, who are acutely conscious that they provide a vital emergency service, should not NEED to go on strike. We certainly never want to! Nevertheless, we defend our freedom to strike as a last resort ... all our recent disputes have been about defending front-line services, which, if diminished, put the public at risk ... we continue battling to convince politicians of the urgent need for adequate funding for the service. We hope that the fledgling Labour Government, unlike its four Tory predecessors, will listen to the voice of reason (Cameron 1997).

An important aspect of the 1977-8 strike was the use of troops by the Government to cover the operations of the striking firefighters (Whelan 1979, Peak 1984). Both Morris (1986: 131-5) and Hain (1986: 154-6) note that about 20,000 troops were deployed, using 800 Green Goddesses, in an unprecedented move at that time. Given the nature of the Service, other features were noted: that firefighters left the picket lines to help out in real emergencies, that nobody tried to use equipment held in stations for fear of crossing picket lines, and that the quasi-military disciplinary regulations of the Service were suspended through a form of Queensberry Rules approach brokered by ACAS (1977).

The pluralist model of industrial relations that dominated policy, especially after the 1968 Donovan Commission report, emphasised that good practice included that employers recognised unions for the purposes of collective bargaining; that such bargaining would tend to have a strong national element within the public sector, and cover both pay and most conditions of service; that strikes and arbitration could both be seen as part of this negotiating process; that the outcomes were more distributive than integrative; and that from time to time a complete failure of the system could be mended by recourse to pay inquiries. Inflation was part of the background that required annual pay rises and the machinery to deal with them, but the needs of service improvement (however defined) also meant that constant updating was part of the systematic adjustment based on changes in labour markets, technology, management, and user demands. By the 1990s the pay of firefighters had slipped, as the formula produced adverse results. In 1994 the FBU conference committed the Executive to undertake 'a review into potential improvements to the Fire Service pay formula, with a view to negotiating improvements with the employers'. This was done through the Labour Research Department (LRD), and they issued their findings in February 1996. This is discussed below in detail, but, alongside the 1995 Audit report into modernisation, the potential for future battle lines had been drawn.

MODERNISING THE SERVICE: ONE STEP FORWARD AND TWO STEPS BACK?

As elsewhere in the public services, there is an endless debate in the Fire Service about control over resources, objectives and managerial strategies, as between the centre, local employers, senior managers, and the staff, represented in this case mainly by the FBU. For obvious reasons the Fire Service has had less flexibility up until now for local variation because of the importance of the application of national standards within a national service. Thus both the specific legislation and the role of the Inspectorate prevent the type of developments seen elsewhere in Local Government and the NHS, such as changes in workload, skill mix, employees' rights, make-up of pay, and increasing sub-contracting policies. The Service remains unusually centralised, and this is reinforced by the role of the Fire Service College, with its dominant position in training. Nonetheless the wind of change was blowing ever more fiercely, especially after the 1995 Audit Report, itself building upon the arch free-market 1986 Audit report on 'value for money', with its recommendations that the NJC move towards renegotiating aspects of the *Grey Book* as part of the prototype for full modernisation.

The Fire Service has been short neither of introspection nor of Government-inspired reports. This is not surprising given the nature of the tasks undertaken and the logistical complexities involved in providing a cost effective round-the-clock fire and rescue service. Fire loss alone is estimated to cost over £7 billion per annum (at current prices), and when you add in the human costs involved in injury and trauma at road traffic accidents, rail tragedies, and flood damage, you are dealing with a major public service impacting highly on the quality of life in the UK. This service is provided for less than what is raised by one pence on the standard rate of income tax.

CACFOA produced its own report in support of job change, which included these points:

3.1.1 Since its inception, the Fire Service has been constantly expanding its activities in response to demands within the wider society. This expansion has led to the creation of a Service markedly different than that originally envisaged. The Service's response to fire-related emergencies is well known. Indeed, public satisfaction with the role of the Fire Service is consistently regarded as being exceptionally high. Throughout the mid 20th century, the resilience, reliability and adaptability of our firefighters caused society to place added demands upon their skills.

3.1.2 Through a process of evolution, the Service began to respond to other emergencies, including road traffic accidents, water rescues, people trapped in machinery and so on. The list of operational activity undertaken by today's Fire and Rescue Service is indeed comprehensive. Apart from this statutory responsibility for fire, the Service has limited authority or power to deal with these 'other' emergencies. It is, however, true that as the Service performs an increasing number of these 'other' emergencies, its ability to carry out such work in a cost-neutral sense was probably overtaken in the early 1960s.

3.1.3 Since that date, the Service has consistently struggled to reconcile this increased portfolio of activity within its existing constrained budget, allocated primarily for firefighting. If the Fire Service was to concentrate solely on fire and not respond to other emergency situations, the cost of providing these services to our society would be considerable. It is, therefore, our opinion that the expectations of the public and the recognition of those expectations by Government must provide the environment within which a clearly defined portfolio of operational activity is developed and agreed. Such a portfolio would determine what activities were carried out by the Fire Service in a given part of the country. Clearly, there would be geographical variations which would lead to a different portfolio, e.g. rope rescue, offshore firefighting and Co-Responder Schemes with the Ambulance Service. With a clearly defined portfolio of activity, the Fire Service should be allocated the appropriate level of financial resources to continue to provide this extensive range of civil protection services.

3.1.4 In determining the full extent of the functions of a Fire Service in our modern society, we must consider those elements of emergency response which our Service so capably delivers. We must also recognise the extensive role played by the Service in the planning for civil emergencies. This planning leads to a primary role for the Service in its response to all types of civil emergency. The Service often finds itself as the lead agency in response to all forms of civil emergency. This range of activity as a lead authority in times of crisis sits well within the flexible and responsive nature of our Service. However, this emergency response is not matched by our involvement in the pre-planning and organisation of such activities. Our Service often finds itself both marginalised and excluded from this crucial pre-planning role. The Service's unstinting performance in this role must be appropriately recognised, reflected and funded to properly align service delivery with public expectation of civil protection (CACFOA 2002: 6).

Perhaps the most influential report in recent years was that drawn up by the Audit Commission and published in January 1995. This was entitled *In the Line of Fire – Value for Money in the Fire Service*. In essence it argued that the Service had an excellent record in putting out fires and rescuing victims but, because of a restrictive national framework built mainly around intervention, it had not sufficiently developed its fire prevention role. The challenge was, in the Audit Commission's view, to introduce more flexible locally-determined provision with far greater emphasis on Fire Prevention work. Its approach is summed up in the following extract: 'Overall the Service is responding to 55% more incidents than 10 years ago … there is a financial cost (the marginal cost of responding to calls) and an opportunity cost (time spent fighting a fire is time not available for fire safety work)' (1995: 4).

The unwritten assumption here is that staffing levels should remain as they had been for the last ten years (with a 55% productivity improvement) and the workload redistributed such that increased attention to fire prevention would lead to less resources being needed to deal with fire intervention and rescue work. Perhaps a more logical position could have been to argue for immediate extra resources for fire safety work, and when it became clear that such activity had actually reduced fire incidence (perhaps five years down the line), to consider cutting back on resources allocated to fire cover work. When it comes to increased public expenditure on services, however, particularly during periods of Tory Government, calculations of long-term benefit are rarely taken into account. So the report fitted in with a shift noted by Darlington (1997) amongst others, that there was a tougher competition for funds, and that both the CFOs and the Fire Inspectorate had become more important and more politically active.

The report also recommended that, to secure greater flexibility of response, the existing national framework should be relaxed, and that local fire authorities should be required to draw up fire risk management plans. The Commission went on to say that, 'this approach should be introduced cautiously, but it would open up a range of possibilities for improving efficiency and effectiveness that cannot be achieved under the current framework'. As Fitzgerald and Stirling suggest, the so-called efficiency savings were focused on two main areas: 'to reducing sickness and leave allowances in order to maintain crewing levels with fewer staff', and through slimming down management by delayering (1999: 48). It is interesting to note that despite the independence of the Audit Commission's work it is clearly dominated by the conventional wisdom of the day in terms of what constitutes efficiency. This is discussed in more detail in chapter five, but efficiency is used by the Audit Commission in ways that parrot its use by Ministers and senior managers. Namely, it is taken to consist of a narrow short-term measure of resource mix and outcome monitoring, limited to any given unit of activity and closely linked with notions of market efficiency. This is in contrast to social efficiency, which is a measure more appropriate for public services, in which account is taken of activities over time and place, and of the wider social costs and benefits of the Service.

THE FIRE COVER REVIEW

Later in 1995 the Central Fire Brigades Advisory Councils (CFBAC) responded to the Audit Commission Report by setting up the Joint Committee on the Audit Commission Report (JCACR), which included direct representation of the FBU, who were happy to be involved in such an exercise at that time. Its governing principles were:

- public protection from fire must be maintained and, if possible, enhanced
- the safety of firefighters must not be compromised
- the primary focus of fire cover should more directly address the risk to life
- recommendations should be cost effective and consistent with the principles of best value for public money.

After extensive consultation, and evaluation of a number of brigade-level pilot schemes, the JCACR published its report *Out of the Line of Fire* in 1998. Its main achievement was to develop a risk assessment methodology incorporating the use of fire safety measures, which required brigades to adopt a response planning process based upon the concept of the Worst Case Planning Scenario. To develop this methodology further, to the point where brigades could implement it operationally, the CFBAC began what became known as the *Pathfinder Trials* in selected brigades, as the core element within a comprehensive Fire Cover Review. This Review was due for publication in the spring of 2002 but was delayed by several months, for reasons that have not been satisfactorily explained.

The Report was finally published during the dispute but before Bain, in October 2002. Among its main findings were:

- that increase of investment in the Fire Service could be self-financing by reducing property loss
- that an extra £1 billion investment a year could save an extra 40 lives, and £1.33 billion around 70 lives (the current annual budget for England and Wales is around £2 billion)
- that to achieve these results would require an increase of around 50% in the workforce, mainly in rural and suburban areas, with a significant increase in whole time station numbers
- that the implementation of risk based fire cover could be achieved without any changes to firefighters' national conditions of service
- that fire cover and fire safety were best regarded as complementary approaches to achieving public safety, not as alternative means of reducing overall risk to the public from fire and other hazards.

On fire safety the Report said: 'With the development of methods for quantitatively assessing the performance of various fire safety tactics, it will be possible in the future to develop fire safety strategies comprising a mix of fire prevention and fire intervention activities based on cost benefit' (B8 appendix).

The last point suggests that the methodology has not been developed as yet by which to assess the effectiveness of fire safety measures. In September 1998 the JCACR produced an interim report on the progress made by the Fire Cover Review team. It reported that at that stage no research had been commissioned into the relative merits of prevention and cure. The JCACR itself conducted a survey of practice in countries with comparable Fire Services to that of the UK. This survey 'found no examples of the prevention versus cure approach ... being either considered or have been implemented'.

The *Pathfinder Trials* produced important results and provide a good basis for the Integrated Risk Management Plans (IRMP) which local brigades are now required to push through at great haste. The methodology was found to be wanting, particularly when dealing with Worst Case Planning Scenarios in non-urban areas. All the brigades involved felt that this concept needed to be re-visited if it were to be useful in a world where budget constraints were real and there were other urgent calls on resources. While the FBU welcomed the approach it worried about resources and agreed implementation (FBU 2004). In the event the Government used Bain to bin *Pathfinder*. In a short paragraph Bain wrote off the six years of research that went in the Fire Cover Review (effectively from 1996-2002). Bain has this to say:

> the Pathfinder trails study has gained notoriety since early findings later shown to be unreliable seemed to indicate that a move to a risk based approach would require significantly larger numbers of firefighters ... chief fire officers who we have consulted tell us that Pathfinder work was directed only to fire cover (2002: 39).

As we have seen *Pathfinder* was flawed because it produced somewhat unrealistic results in terms of cost-benefit analysis, and the impact Worst Case Planning Scenarios would have on spending levels. From a fire safety angle it was not unreliable. In its final report *Pathfinder* showed that the methodology used provided 'a cornerstone of an integrated approach to fire risk management', and an 'evidence based method for assessing and responding to actual risk, taking into account the effect of fire safety measures'. The Bain report, therefore, was wrong on all counts pertaining to *Pathfinder*.

REFLEXIVE MANAGERIALISM

In May 2001 the HM Fire Service Inspectorate produced its own report, *Managing a Modernised Fire Service: Bridging the Gap* (Home Office). It adds to the argument that a modernising agenda for change was being fully developed and was to be applied to the Fire Service as soon as practicable. The control over the process therefore was important, and in 2001 it was mainly with the employers and senior managers. To gain any foothold in the process the FBU had to do more than resist, it had to become involved in a 'something for something' set of negotiations, and that was partly what led up to the May 2002 conference decision to ask for a pay rise outside the formula and a new formula. The Inspectorate's report makes it clear where the pressure comes from: 'the Government, which came to power in 1997, has been explicit in its expectations for the continuous improvement in the delivery of public services and the way in which Local Government in general and the Fire Service in particular is to achieve this' (2001: 1).

The document is written in a style of a typical management course – it is full of jargon and references to current fads; it is highly prescriptive (full of what ought to be); it is clearly managerial without reflection; and it heroically assumes it is both modern and relevant. As the overview continues:

> the modernisation agenda for Local Government has clear implications for the Fire Service. The requirement to meet the challenge of Best Value is enshrined in legislation and the principles of modernisation have equal value in the Fire Service as in the town hall. Value for money in terms of the quality and the cost of the delivered service must continue to be a driver for change and innovation (*ibid*).

The key emphasis of this 'scoping' review was leadership – an increasingly favourite notion within public sector management theory and practice, and one that conflates the psychology of motivation with the economic reality of employment, while conveniently ignoring power relationships. It seeks to explain the gap between leaders and the rest of the workforce in terms of a failure of understanding and communication, rather than as an expression of alienation and opposing sets of values. The report's main author, Graham Meldrum (the Chief Inspector), elaborates the need for cultural change to accompany management change within the limitations of the Government's White Paper, *Modernising Government* (1999). As the most recent Government report notes: 'in the last 23 years there have been seven major reviews of the Fire Service ... yet it is clear from the evidence received that none of these reviews have led to substantial change' (ODPM Report 2004: 7). It goes on to cite evidence from both the Government's own White Paper (*Our Fire and Rescue Service* 2003) and from CACFOA thus: 'on too many occasions in the past, we have had reports and reviews published on the future of the Service which have subsequently "gathered dust"' (*ibid*). Some in Government and most employers blame the workforce and the union for this, but others criticise poor management, incompetent employers, and largely indifferent Government Ministers.

A major part of the Meldrum document blames the workforce for the failure to modernise. Thus: 'the workforce does not appear to appreciate the scope of the work being carried out by the leadership of the Service under very difficult circumstances' (2001: 22); and 'the workforce seems not to appreciate or accept the validity of the wide range of tasks included in "Today's List"' (*ibid*: 24) – this is a reference to the Rank to Role reforms. Its emphasis on leadership mimics the USA-psychological models of management rooted in heroically simplistic views of how organisations 'behave' (Couch 2002). But despite much of the unitarist rhetoric of renewal, the report nonetheless maintains a clear understanding that change comes with and through the agreement of the staff, and that means the FBU as well. He argues that 'each Fire Authority should examine the practicality of establishing a local team, comprising members of the fire authority, trade unions and principal officers, to develop policy and strategy' (2001: 30); and later this becomes the first immediate recommendation (*ibid*: 57). So among the thirty-one recommendations for strengthening leadership, improving community accountability, and reducing the military tradition, is the assumption that all these vital changes can only take place with the co-operative compliance of the FBU and its membership. Both the Bain proposals and later the behaviour of the employers in the implementation of the June 2003 agreement, however, suggest that such co-operation has no place in the political battles fought out after the industrial action ended in February 2003. This particular service version of improvement and modernisation has been largely ditched for a more oppressively market-oriented position. As Fitzgerald and Stirling (1999: 51) show, previous attempts at changes based at brigade level involving new public management practices have foundered on the rock of the dominant industrial relations system. That rock had to be removed for real progress on the reform programme to take place.

THE INDUSTRIAL RELATIONS CLIMATE BEFORE THE 2002 DISPUTE

The employers' concern was that the union had blocked attempts to weaken the national agreement to enable local determination of flexible working, especially shift patterns. In a number of important local disputes concerning *Grey Book* conditions and cuts to equipment and personnel, the union had effectively used the strike weapon or the threat of it to force local employers to fully adhere to the national agreement. The importance of maintaining a national agreement for the FBU was paramount in its strategic approach to change. The dismantling of such national coverage elsewhere in the public sector had led to weaker union protection for members against worsening conditions of service and forms of privatisation. In a re-run of the 1977 strike, local disputes were setting the mood of the FBU membership and determining possible strike tactics if it came to a national strike. Two such disputes were reported in detail in the EC's *Annual Report* to the FBU's Conference (2002: 127-129). The first dispute led to a period of strike action in Merseyside, while the second in Berkshire was resolved following an 81.6% vote for strike action.

In Merseyside there had been a tradition of local disputes, such as the one in 1995 against budget cuts (Darlington 1997). The more recent Merseyside dispute mainly concerned a proposal by the Fire Authority to employ non-uniformed staff into Officer posts. This, argued the Officers' section of the FBU, was in direct contravention of the Appointment and Promotion Regulations and was subsequently referred to the NJC Disputes Committee for adjudication. The Disputes Panel, consisting of six members from both the employers and union side, unanimously decided in favour of the FBU. A day later the Corporate Management Team of Merseyside Fire Service met and decided to circumvent the NJC decision. This they did by resolving to employ non-uniformed staff in Officer position but to put the posts concerned outside of *Grey Book* Conditions of Service and therefore outside of NJC jurisdiction.

The decision of the CMT resulted in the registration by the union of a trade dispute on the basis that the NJC decision had been blatantly flouted. Merseyside FBU demanded that as a basis for settlement the employers 'immediately comply in full with the decision of the NJC Disputes Committee on the 3 May 2001 and forthwith discontinue the assessments and processing of the applications from non-uniformed personnel' (FBU *Annual Report* 2002).

The employers refused to meet the union's demands and the union went to a ballot of members for industrial action. On a large turn out, 83% voted for discontinuous strike action, but despite further attempts by the union to find a negotiated settlement the employers stood firm in their defiance of the national agreement. A series of eight-day strikes ensued and by the 24 July the union's national leadership was seriously considering calling a national strike in solidarity with Merseyside and to protect the national agreement. That same evening the Merseyside employers' representatives met with national and local officials of the FBU and agreed to comply totally with the NJC decision of 3 May. The ending of the dispute was fairly quickly followed by the early retirement on grounds of ill health of the Chief Fire Officer.

In Berkshire the issue was cuts to services. Late in 2000 the Fire Authority proposed to cut twenty-four jobs and reduce the number of special appliances. These moves were rigorously opposed by the union and some minor concessions were won at the December 2000 Fire Authority meeting. These concessions were not enough to meet the union's demands to protect jobs and services however, and after a two-month campaign 81.6% of the FBU members voted for strike action. Following protracted negotiations during April, the employers conceded all of the union's demands. Specifically, all cuts would be suspended and not reintroduced in any form without the agreement of the union, and the brigade would recruit back to the agreed establishment level.

The national employers were faced with new pressures too. The Labour Government's programme, particularly since its re-election in 2001, centred on the need to reform the public sector. In effect, through regimes like Best Value and a rather vague commitment to modernisation, the Government sought to raise productivity and to link this to a drive to improve service provision. In practice this meant new investment in public services would only be made where it could be shown that radical changes in management methods and changes in working practices were in place.

This approach struck a ready chord with many Fire Service employers and senior managers. Many had long felt frustrated by the ability of the FBU to block changes in working conditions which the union saw to be detrimental to its members. In recent years the employers' side had been defeated in its attempts to emasculate the national agreement on conditions of service (other than pay) in favour of local agreements (the 'Smash and Grab' dispute). Some of the more far sighted senior managers saw a possible trade-off between a step change improvement in salaries, which was overdue, and the strengthening of managerial prerogatives currently restricted by the prescriptive nature of national fire standards and the role accorded to the FBU in the *Grey Book* agreement. One LGA leader commented, 'managers too complained that service change became more difficult than it should, without the leverage of being able to negotiate pay and conditions in conventional fashion' (Nolda 2004: 385).

Of particular concern to the employers was their perceived right to use all resources flexibly, including the workforce, preferably without undue challenge from the union side. For many it appeared as a lifetime opportunity to put the FBU in its place – a union with the right to represent its members individually, but with few rights to consultation on Fire Service strategy and no rights to influence the way the job was organised on the ground. As Charles Nolda noted, 'as time went on local disputes, on occasions leading to strikes, increasingly arose. These disputes seemed essentially to be about who ran the Service – the FBU or management and the fire authority' (2004: 385). These approaches, which marginalise union influence and give far greater powers to local non-elected managers, accord very well with New Labour's overall approach to industrial relations in the public sector.

THE UNION AND NEW LABOUR

As we have seen the FBU weathered the Thatcher-Major years pretty well. The election of a Labour Government in May 1997 opened up new possibilities. Although expectations were not that high, the union leadership looked forward to a resolution of the longstanding problems resulting from the inadequacy of the funding formula for the Fire Service, together with new Fire Safety legislation which would make Community Fire Safety activities a statutory duty on Local Authorities, as well as widening the use of sprinkler systems and tightening the regulations on dwellings in multiple occupation and similar premises. At the same time the pressure from below to secure a sizeable increase in salaries was building.

Experience during the first Blair Government was tolerably good, although progress was not spectacular. The funding formula was tidied up to better reflect the range of services undertaken, but was not fundamentally reformed as recommended by the Audit Commission. Capital investment in equipment and stations was significantly increased, but radical reforms on the overall direction of the Service and on Fire

Safety were put on the back burner. Substantial progress was made on a Draft White Paper with the central objective of moving towards a risk assessed service based on locally drawn up plans and with much more emphasis than hitherto on Fire Prevention measures. These proposals fully backed by the FBU, but were never developed to the White Paper stage and were quietly dropped when the Minister, Mike O'Brien, was sacked. Alan Simpson MP thought this to be an important moment because the FBU had been led to believe the Government was supportive of their case, and therefore the union leadership felt badly let down when a new Minister in a new department in a new Government seemed to be much less helpful. This was in part the reason for the FBU leadership's distrust of Ministers and their reluctance to join in the inquiry under Bain.

With the election of the second term Labour Government in 2001 pressures for a pay campaign became even stronger. Significant numbers of firefighters were beginning to find it impossible to buy or rent affordable housing within reasonable travelling distance of their workplaces and house prices continued to rise much faster than their wages. This was particularly the case in urban centres and in the south of England. The second term Labour Government set its sights much higher regarding public sector reform. Not only did it press forward with PFI projects in the face of strong union opposition; it also asked to be judged by the success of its programme in delivering qualitatively better public services. The key to implementation, in New Labour's eyes, appeared to be the injection of private funds and private sector management techniques, opening up choice for users and enabling radical change, without the need to raise taxes or the public sector borrowing requirement. Much of this was presented as the search for efficiency in a 'what works' market, with increasing need to empower managers within stricter Central Government controls.

These policies evinced serious disquiet in unions representing public sector workers, as functions were outsourced and increasing numbers of workers taken out of public sector conditions of service, through a mixture of outright privatisation and PFI projects, leading to two-tier workforces. In New Labour parlance this represented modernisation; for public sector trade union activists it felt more like a return to an unprotected market system.

All this was part of a wider process of distancing New Labour from the trade union movement as the Government sought a new consensus of support around a strong market economy and public services delivered by anyone contracted by Government. To many union activists and members these policies became intolerable, and incumbent union leaders who remained prepared, for whatever reason, to give unstinting support to New Labour policies were becoming separated from their membership base. Sir Ken Jackson of the AEEU was voted out of office as General Secretary. This was just one example since 2000 of pro-Labour leaders being removed from office through union elections. Leaders more independent of New Labour were being voted in, such as Bob Crow of the RMT, Mick Rix of ASLEF, Tony Woodley of the TGWU, Mark Serwotka of the PCS, Andy Gilchrist of the FBU, Jeremy Dear of the NUJ, and Derek Simpson of AMICUS.

What defined them was neither their political positions nor that they represented a change of direction for their union. Some did, but others, like Andy Gilchrist and Jeremy Dear, came from the same broad left tradition as their immediate predecessors, Ken Cameron and John Foster. Their commonality was their independence from, and opposition to, the New Labour project; and their willingness to explore the political and institutional nature of their ties with the Labour Party.

THE EMPLOYERS TAKE THE OFFENSIVE

For many years now the employers in the Fire Service have bridled at the restrictions imposed on them by the *Grey Book* and the strength that this gives the FBU to block change. In particular these concerns relate to the need to negotiate local change on resource allocation, and the ability of the FBU to use the national disputes procedure to challenge any reduction or changes in establishment levels, crewing arrangements or appliance numbers. Despite the apparently burdensome need to agree change with their workforce, there is constant change in the Fire Service. Each year stations are closed, establishments changed (often reduced) and appliances withdrawn, often without union opposition. And the FBU's EC Report to Conference for 1999 records forty-nine instances covering the whole of the UK where the Home Office approved cuts in Fire Cover involving loss of jobs and appliances. For example in London, Barbican and Shooters Hill Fire Stations were closed with the loss of fifty-six jobs and two fire engines, while in Merseyside one fire engine was removed from Bromborough (the third pump) and one Aerial Appliance from Kirkdale, with the loss of thirty-six jobs. Even when such cuts are challenged by the union they are usually approved by the Home Office, albeit after rather protracted procedures.

In these circumstances it is difficult to see the FBU as an all-powerful barrier to change. The nature of the Service and the need to provide effective emergency cover round the clock all year round has led to a comprehensive national agreement covering in some details minimum standards for crewing arrangements and establishment levels; and these have been skilfully used by the FBU to protect their members' interests. In recent times neither the employers nor the Fire Service civil service has been happy with these arrangements. The main effects of the *In the Line of Fire* report of the Audit Commission in 1995 was for the employers to bring forward a comprehensive set of reforms, the chief of which was to introduce greater flexibility at local level. In a letter to the union dated 17 July 1998 the employers said this:

A significant majority of employing authorities support making amendments to the national scheme so that a framework of core national provisions can be applied at brigade level in a flexible way (FBU *EC Report to Conference* 1999: 11).

The Government had hoped that both the employers and the FBU would approach in a similarly constructive spirit the future negotiations that might arise from the decisions taken by the LGA Fire Executive at its meeting on 8 November 2000 that:

- the LGA supports the development through the NJC of a best value partnership agreement with the FBU, modelled on the agreement reached between the LGA and major Local Government unions in 1997
- the Employers' Side seek agreement within the NJC on a broad agenda for changes based on mutually agreed objectives for the Fire Service and a timetable for determining and agreeing modifications to terms and conditions of service that would be necessary to achieve this; and
- a pay formula and a 2.2.4 shift system be retained as part of an agreement on an overall package of modernisation and best value measures.

CONCLUSIONS

This chapter has provided an account of the Fire Service as it was in 2001 just before the dispute. The Service had undergone significant changes in the ways in which it was managed, the level of technology utilised, and in the job of the workforce. It had been subject to close scrutiny, and to regular reports from Government agencies, and two conclusions were commonplace: it was an efficient and effective Service in general, but it suffered from low pay and a managerial climate too traditional in its attitudes to women, non-whites, gays, non-uniformed staff, and to the management of all staff in terms of a hierarchical culture often secured by bullying and quasi-military disciplinary regulations. There was consensus that what was needed was a move away from its navy traditions to those of a more modern employer, while keeping the high performance achievements. It was also agreed that this could only be realistically achieved through the co-operation of the main parties: staff and union, managers and employers, inspectors, and Central Government. There was also consensus that the Service needed to move towards local risk assessment when allocating resources, and that fire prevention should be at the core of its activities.

Nonetheless this book is about an industrial dispute in the Fire Service. Despite the twenty-five year gap between this dispute and the one in 1977, there have been endless comparisons. The most important difference remains that the 1977 strike was part of a strike wave in the late 1970s, which Fryer suggests had several important features: the strikes were very bitter, with the use of troops in the fire strike an additional source of anger; in most cases, including that of firefighters, it was the first instance of official national action; the main impact of the strikes was on the public not on the employers; and most of the strikes were about pay comparability and the use of the NBPI to introduce new efficiency and/or productivity bargains. These strikes 'not only changed the internal character of several unions, [they] ... also sharply revised their public profile. Within less than ten years, public services unionism had moved to centre stage in British industrial relations and this was reflected both in the extensive (and often lurid and highly critical) attention paid to public service unionists and their leaders in the press and broadcasting media' (Fryer 1989: 51).

That account provides a summary of the strike wave associated with the Winter of Discontent and partly explains the hostility of Ministers to any public sector strikes given the history of the 1979 General Election. More important, however, is the role of the state in dealing with such disputes irrespective of time and place. Knowles explains:

> although the economic loss due to strikes ... has been small in most years, the shock effect of a well-planned strike may ... be very severe. A big strike tends to affect not only a single section of industry but industry as a whole; it may embarrass not a single employer but an Employers' Federation, and even the State itself. The State ... has sometimes behaved towards strikes like an Employers' Federation writ large (1952: 291).

Hyman, writing nearly fifty years later, repeats the special problems encountered by striking public sector workers when faced with Government imposed tight budgetary controls allied with avowed public policies on modernisation (1989: 225).

The Fire Service by 2002 exhibited many of the features most likely to create the conditions for a national dispute. There had been a sharp deterioration in relations between the FBU and the employers. It was also felt that Central Government had let matters drift and allowed low pay to seep into all areas of the Fire Service. At the forefront of much of this was the belief amongst Ministers that the FBU and its members opposed their notion of 'modernisation'. Indeed in his piece for the *New Statesman* in February 2002, Stefan Stern noted that 'the "M" word lies at the heart of the dispute with the firefighters' (Stern: 13). For these and other reasons most of those most involved believed something had to give: the pay formula, traditional attitudes, Central Government indifference, and local employers' inconsistencies.

Something did give.

Chapter Two

The Claim, the Campaign and John Prescott's 'Fancy Dancing'

INTRODUCTION

This chapter details the dispute from the May 2002 FBU Annual Conference with the agreed claim, through the campaigning months of May to October, into the start of industrial action in November 2002. It does so through a chronological account of events, with attendant arguments and analysis. It is largely based on newspaper accounts, FBU sources, documents and statements from employers and Government Ministers, debates in Parliament, and interviews.

The story of this, and indeed any strike, can be told in several ways from different points of view. As has been noted above, two elements dominated the debate: the comparable loss in pay was the main issue for the FBU and its members, and therefore a claim had to be made at some point outside the pay formula; and this was counter-posed with changes in the management of labour through renegotiated working practices, which was paramount for the employers, and part of the wider modernisation programme of the Government. What was left for the union activists to ponder then was the when and the how of the challenge. The time did seem portentous: there was already widespread support from FBU members, as illustrated in numerous motions to conference; there was strong support from the wider community for firefighters, especially after the events of 9/11 in the USA; and there was encouragement from sections of the labour movement, including friendly politicians, journalists and other leading union activists. There were even some friendly noises from sections of the employers and Ministers.

When the two sides met at the full NJC on 28 May to receive the FBU's claim, the union negotiators made it clear that they sought a negotiated settlement and that they recognised that the claim had a number of special features, not least the demand for a step-change increase in the qualified firefighter's rate. The initial response from the employers, in their letter of 7 June, neither surprised nor discouraged. The employers' side did not rule out any part of the claim, but it did insist that substantial improvements in pay had to be linked to 'modernisation'. After the formal tabling of the claim, the parties scheduled five meetings of the Joint Standing Sub-Committee (JSSC), for the sole purpose of reaching a negotiated settlement. Exchanges continued throughout the rest of the summer, with no apparent progress on two of the central issues – what value did the employers put on the work of firefighters, and how could negotiations be progressed so as to avoid a national dispute. On 2 September the employers came back to the full NJC with a first firm offer, of 4% with strings from 7 November; acceptance of the need to negotiate on a new pay formula for the future; agreement to parity for retained firefighters; and a commitment to a job evaluation exercise examining the relative pay position of emergency control room staff. Within a few days this offer was rejected by the FBU EC and, in an attempt to head off calls for national strike action, the Government announced the setting up of the Bain inquiry into every aspect of the management of the Fire Service, including pay and conditions.

TIMING

Support was high. The time also appeared right because the conventional wisdom was that the employers were divided and weak. Evidence for this had come from previous local disputes won by the FBU, and the partial national victory after the 1998-9 standoff. Messages from the employers were that they would trade more money for some changes in working practices. Behind them lay the might of Central Government. Ministers were no friends to local authorities and could not be relied upon to help them out. The Government itself appeared divided on several important domestic issues – such as top-up fees for university students, foundation hospitals, the entire Private Finance Initiative (PFI) project, and relations with the trade union movement in general. Added to this were the troubles over joining the Euro and the support of the Prime Minister for President's Bush belligerent statements against Iraq. The analysis was that, with all this on their plates, they might not bother with a skirmish in the Fire Service. After all the Service was small and therefore relatively cheap to finance, and it was considered to be one of the better performing and least awkward of the public services.

In addition, the Chancellor, Gordon Brown, had proclaimed many times with some justification that public finances were strong, and therefore Ministers could settle this dispute without any damage to the economy or their policies. The looming hostilities in Iraq and the more general terrorist threat had already provided the emergency services with a higher public standing than before, and so a settlement with firefighters would not do any political damage to the Government. And yet at a fairly early stage in the dispute powerful voices in Cabinet had chosen confrontation with the FBU as their favoured strategic choice, regardless of the merits of the case, the strength of feeling, the down-side risk to the Service itself, or indeed relations with the wider labour movement. Being tough with the unions played well both with focus groups and with New Labour's cultural elite.

PUBLIC SUPPORT

There has been a great deal of conventional wisdom that strikers need public support – because of the pressure put on political decision-makers; because it helps with membership morale; because it encourages the media to get behind the cause early on; and because in a public service, the public are the users. But what kind of public is this? In other disputes the loss of such support has been quoted as one cause of failure, as in the 1989 ambulance strike (Kerr and Sachdev 1991). The evidence for such arguments is rather thin, and it is difficult to see the mechanism between such support and the actual outcome of the strike. Of course public opinion is largely a false construct, since there are many publics, and some matter more than others. The one that matters most for the union members in dispute is that of community: family and friends, neighbours and local community, other trade unionists and workers. The extent of that tribal influence across cultures, towns and the country is less clear, but with high profile emergency staff such as firefighters it is likely to be greater than, for example, with the traditionally more isolated car worker, docker or coal miner. The fact of such support, however, was widely reported and widely treasured by FBU members.

The FBU strike bulletin was full of examples of support, including stories about donations: issue 2 told that 'Bristol firefighters collected £500 in just one hour'; and Tony Blair's famous father-in-law, actor Tony Booth, gave a donation to Glossop strikers in Derbyshire (issue 15).

There was a variety of support from overseas: 'the French firefight-ers' union, SNSPP, have pledged their support' (issue 2); five Chilean firefighters sent a photo of support (issue 15); and messages of support came from Ireland's Independent Workers Union (issue 25), Swedish firefighters (issue 3), Gibraltar firefighters, and those in the Falklands (issue 23).

Support also came from other unions: issue 10 reported that: 'Prospect, which represents more than 105,000 engineers, scientists, managers and specialists … has sent a message of support'. There were donations from local GMB branches to firefighters in Lambeth (issue 20), and the public services section of the GMB sent solidarity messages (issue 8). There was help with leaflet distribution from Kingston hospital UNISON branch (issue 3); the National Union of Students urged its members to support (issue 8) and waved supporting banners at their own national demonstration on 4 December 2002 (issue 18); Scottish UNISON gave a large donation (issue 18), and

Stockton UNISON also chipped in (issue 33), matched by NIPSA in Northern Ireland (issue 23); UNIFI members at HSBC sent support as did the NUJ (issue 38); NATFHE sent full support, indicating that their members in colleges had already suffered from so-called modernisation (issue 53); and the STUC Congress unanimously backed the FBU struggle (issue 61).

Many of the activists we interviewed stressed the importance of such support. Jim Quinn from Northern Ireland reported on the huge support for the Belfast march of 24 August, and John McDonald from the EC in Scotland noted the importance of links with the STUC and the generally high level of public support. Several commented on support from local trades councils, as Tony Maguire from Northern Ireland and Clive Protheroe from South Wales. In London several activists suggested that other unions did offer support, but that it was not really required.

If the time seemed right, the tactics needed to be sorted. They would be based on a strong claim backed by a campaign to win total support from members and the wider community; and a clearly stated desire to negotiate backed by the threat of action. When the threat had to be activated with a ballot, it was for discontinuous action – a few days here and another few days there. This tactic had worked in local disputes and was favoured by members and most activists. As we will see later, this on-off flexibility worked well at first, but it increasingly presented the leadership with harder and harder choices. As the dispute dragged on longer than expected and into the Iraq war, in retrospect some activists believed that these tactical decisions were mistakes that both damaged member morale and gave succour to the employers. At the time all evidence pointed the other way: there were no reports from any section of the union that a ballot for an indefinite strike would have won the huge majority (87%) that was achieved for discontinuous action. One reason for this is that such action limits financial loss to FBU members while still presenting the employers and Government with a high risk and high cost dispute.

Both Andy Gilchrist and Ruth Winters spoke of the claim in terms of the need to reverse the steady erosion of pay: the pay issue topped everyone's agenda, and member support was very high for a step-change pay rise. In all of this Andy Gilchrist stressed that the tragic events of 9/11 had not been a consideration:

> I had set out well before 2001 that the issue of pay was central to the future of the Fire Service. I would refute that 9/11 gave an impetus [to the campaign] ... and it certainly wasn't the origins of thinking about why pay was the number one issue ... what September 11 did do, which nobody in the Fire Service could ignore, for the first time, it crystallised in people's minds just what it means for somebody to go to work even with the outside possibility of not coming home.

Ruth Winters (the elected President of the FBU) agreed: 'No I don't think that was a great factor because ... we had identified the pay issue as a number one priority before 9/11'.

THE CLAIM

In May 2002 delegates to the FBU Annual Conference unanimously backed a new pay claim. It had been several years in the making, and was formally presented to the employers at a NJC meeting on 28 May. The pay formula had served the membership relatively well through the 1980s and into the 1990s. But by the mid-1990s the cracks were beginning to show. As manufacturing declined and occupational change accelerated, the relative level of craft workers' earnings (the upper quartile of male manual earnings on which the pay formula was based) began to fall (IDS 2002a). At the same time the nature of the FBU members' jobs was continuing to change, with more use of computers and other electronically controlled equipment, and a greater emphasis on fire prevention and special services. In addition, housing costs in many large towns, particularly in south England, were rising faster than earnings, making it impossible for a growing number of firefighters and control room staff to buy mortgaged accommodation within reasonable distance of their place of work.

The evidence for the relative failings of the pay formula comes from pay statistics, which indicated a relative fall of 21% since the start of the formula in 1977 (IDS 1991-1999); and in the same period, while average earnings rose by 380%, those of FBU members rose by 300% (LRD 1996, 2002).

These arguments surfaced with great force at the 2001 FBU Annual Conference. Delegate after delegate came to the rostrum to express dissatisfaction with the existing pay arrangements. Some stressed the failure of the pay formula (*Report of Proceedings*, FBU 2001 Annual Conference: 83-5). Most stressed the changing nature of the job and the increased range of skills required to carry out a seemingly endless increase in workload and responsibilities. Maurice Wilson, a delegate from Northern Ireland, put it like this:

> The Pay Formula has not for some years produced the level of earnings that reflects and rewards the ever-increasing levels of professionalism and range of skills required of our members. We have to be technically more skilled, procedurally more adept, well versed in legislation and increasingly more computer literate ... we are expected to be Community Fire Safety literate with teaching skills, communication skills, presentation skills (*ibid*: 83).

After a lengthy debate the Conference went on to adopt a detailed EC statement on the pay formula. This required the EC to investigate:

The change in the Firefighter and Control Staff roles, and the need to better reflect in a future pay formula these changes in respect of overall terms and conditions in relation to appropriate comparators. The resolution committed the EC to report back on these issues not later than Annual Conference 2002 (*ibid*: 167).

The FBU was not alone in recognising the shortcomings of the old pay formula. Writing in early 2002 the then CACFOA President Richard Bull said: 'It could be argued, however, that we have a long way to go to truly reflect that a firefighters' pay meets the requirements of the situation' (*Fire Magazine*, January 2002). In the same article he goes on to reveal that the average weekly take home pay of a qualified firefighter (after four years training and experience) was £263.23, and to say that this did not bear comparison with the earnings of a police constable (without overtime) or, indeed, other skilled workers. He concluded by arguing that the job of a firefighter is becoming 'more complex, more technical and more demanding', and that 'we have to ensure that the value of their position is fully appreciated and recognised'.

Even before the 2002 conference the FBU leadership had informed the employers at a meeting on 26 February that they would be asking for a substantial pay rise and that 'the formula is now outdated and needs to be reviewed'. The same press release (FBU 8.3.02) noted that the employers had agreed to make a joint approach to Alan Whitehead, the Minister, on this issue. At a meeting of regional pay campaign co-ordinators held at FBU headquarters on 1 March, Andy Gilchrist spelt out the issues facing them – that the case for an all embracing above average pay rise was clear, but that while the employers had expressed some support for their case in meetings on 6 and 26 February, the Minister had warned the FBU leadership that the Treasury would oppose any large pay rise. He went on to explain that the Government would fight them and that the employers would end up giving in to Government pressure. In such circumstances, he argued, it was essential to win over the members and through them to win public support. In a clear public statement of the case, Andy Gilchrist argued that a new pay formula was needed, 'to better reflect modern realities'; because 'basic rates for qualified firefighters are now far too low'; because of the need to 'recruit and retain staff, particularly in periods of relatively full employment'; and because 'the events of September 11 have reminded the public of the contribution firefighters make' (*FireFighter* January/February 2002: 2).

In an internal briefing document sent out on 25 April on behalf of Andy Gilchrist, activists were advised to stress that at the NJC meeting of 19 April the FBU had linked their pay demands with public safety, and wished to avoid confrontation. Alan Simpson MP was one of several people interviewed to note that much of the FBU's case was viewed sympathetically by senior figures in Government, and that

Mike O'Brien (the previous Minister) had suggested that an agreement on a new pay formula, moves to equality, and a step-change pay rise was within the realm of political acceptance – a view shared by senior figures at the LGA. Thus the first noises off stage from Ministers encouraged the FBU leadership to believe a negotiated improvement was possible.

In the run up to the 2002 Conference, the FBU EC had been busy putting the final touches to the text of the emergency motion. It had consulted widely within the union and commissioned two reports from outside bodies. The first report was on the pay formula itself and was carried out by the independent LRD (2002). The second was the work of an independent consultant on job evaluation, which looked into the rate for the job of a modern firefighter (Hastings 2002). Based on these reports and the views and expectations expressed during the membership consultation exercise, the EC drew up its four-point set of demands.

By the time the FBU delegates assembled on 14 May 2002 at Bridlington there was a widespread understanding within the Fire Service that it was time for a radical rethink about pay levels and that the pay formula was the obvious place to begin such a process. The 79th Annual Conference gave unanimous support to the EC resolution calling for a four-point pay campaign. Emergency Resolution 1 on pay read:

> The FBU Executive Council acknowledges the historical benefits of the Fire Service National Pay Formula in maintaining a reasonable level of wages for Fire Service personnel.
>
> However, since the 1980s the characteristics of the UK labour force have changed considerably. This has resulted in a significant decline in the manufacturing sector, which has made the Fire Service National Pay Formula less effective in delivering a reasonable living wage to those who render a vital emergency public service to our communities. Simultaneously, the jobs of Firefighters and Emergency Fire Control staff have become increasingly complex and skilled and this should be reflected in their wages.
>
> The Executive Council commissioned a report from the Labour Research Department on the Fire Service National Pay Formula, which was received in April 2002. The report comprehensively endorsed the above points.
>
> After widespread consultation, careful consideration and taking full account of the LRD report the Executive Council are recommending to this Annual Conference that we mount a vigorous campaign in pursuit of a fair wage for Firefighters and Emergency Fire Control staff. This should include:
>
> i   An improvement in the basic pay for Firefighters to £30,000 by November 2002. Existing differentials across rank structures

should continue to apply pending the outcome of the Rank Structure Review.

ii As a Trade Union committed to equality and fair treatment for all members and in recognition of their pivotal role Emergency Fire Control Staff to receive the same wages as Firefighters of their equivalent rank.

iii Firefighters working the Retained and Volunteer Duty Systems can be expected to do the same job as their Whole time counterparts. They should be trained to the same standard and receive the same pay and conditions.

iv A modern Fire Service demands a highly skilled and motivated workforce. FBU members are already committed to these important principles. This should be reflected in a more appropriate and relevant Fire Service National Pay Formula.

The Executive Council believe that the above points reflect the FBU's commitment to modernising the Service. It is our wish to pursue and resolve these issues in negotiations with our Employers. It is our express wish to avoid confrontation. If however this is not possible then the Executive Council will recall Conference and recommend that members take strike action in pursuit of a fair wage for Firefighters and Emergency Fire Control staff (FBU *Annual Report* 2002: 97-8).

This motion was carried unanimously following an enthusiastic debate. The launch of the campaign started with a speech in support of the resolution from FBU General Secretary Andy Gilchrist. In a wide-ranging address he made many of the points that subsequently formed the basis for the arguments up and down the country, from Westminster to Wick and from the FBU HQ in Kingston, Surrey to Belfast. The basic case is that: 'the pay of firefighters and emergency control staff has not kept pace with workers who have similar skills' (*ibid*: 98). This is supported by explicit reference to comparators, and the changing nature of the work and workload: 'despite being consistently understaffed according to the Government's own figures, and years in which the workload not only rose dramatically, it became more hazardous, more complex, new skills have been required, years in which your training was restricted because of a lack of funds' (*ibid*: 99). He was clear that FBU members were not the only ones to suffer from such concerns. While embracing the need to modernise he rejected that this might mean more private finance, best value, and the introduction of local pay. In contrast, the FBU modernisation proposals would include a commitment to equal pay for all in the Service, an abandonment of the second job culture which 'has always been opposed by the FBU' (*ibid*: 100), greater controls over the excessive pay rises of CFOs, and a recognition that a better trained and equipped and supported fire force is self-financing in the long term as incidents and their consequences are reduced.

Every subsequent speaker from all brigades supported such arguments and sentiments, and argued the need for a united front. All expressed agreement with the justice of the cause, reported massive support amongst members, called for unity, and claimed they were ready to take strike action if necessary. Many referred to Ministerial support for the high performance of the Service; others expressed anger at pay rises for CFOs, and key activists underlined their backing for the equality agenda in the claim.

It has been argued elsewhere (Ironside and Seifert 2003, 2004) that for public sector strikes to take place with a chance of success there has to be a strong sense of a loss of worth – a collapse in the felt-fair comparison with other jobs. This impulse is frequently made stronger when there is an additional sense of unfairness, often triggered by large pay rises to senior managers within the Service. Hence the reference to the pay of CFOs throughout the dispute. The tenth issue of the FBU strike bulletin reported that: 'Strathclyde CFO Jeff Ord, who once again has spoken up for the muddled Bain proposals, should remember that he's got no need for fair pay as he has already accepted his £25,000 pay increase for this year taking his salary to over £120,000'. A year after the strikes started the *Mirror* reported that: 'controversial fire chief Jeff Ord will pocket £300,000 after secretly being named boss of all Scotland's fire brigades' (4.12.03:19). The Glasgow *Daily Record* reported that the new CFO for Tayside, Stephen Hunter, had been given an eight per cent pay rise worth £6,500 at a time when employers would not even discuss the firefighters' own pay claim (28.8.02: 21); and when the CFO for Central Scotland was reported as having asked for a 29.3% pay rise, or £22,000, the local FBU representative responded furiously (*Falkirk Herald* 27.11.03).

£30K

The four pillars of the claim warrant further discussion here, as do the underlying assumptions. Firstly, the much-debated £30,000 pay target. We are concerned at how this figure emerged and the basis for the argument. The assumptions were clearly that, firstly, current pay comparability was falling behind; and, secondly, the nature of the job had changed sufficiently to be worthy of a redefinition within the ranks of the nation's job hierarchies. A central question was where the figure of £30k (a 40% rise) had come from. Andy Gilchrist explained its genesis in interview:

> If you are going to ask people for more money, you have to tell them what you want, which sounds obvious but sometimes people just go in and say we deserve more money. We thought it was responsible, and indeed I'll use the word 'professional', to say this is what we do for you as the employer and this is what we're prepared to do in the future. And

this is what we think we are worth. And that phrase gathered a momentum of its own, and it's a phrase coined in this very office, this is what we think we are worth. It wasn't something people dreamt up … We actually engaged people to do some work for us, professional academic work, because it's very difficult to say what you are worth. To the person where you lift their two children out of a bedroom, you're probably worth a million dollars a day. So we did that and that produced this association with professional workers, because Sue Hastings actually looked at particularly the type of job we did, the elements that make it up, and then of course when we gave that to people at the Labour Research Department they said if that's what's being said about the job, then this is where you should be in the pay league.

The actual figure of £30k came from taking the evidence from the four main sources together. The LRD report (2002) did not put a figure on it but referred to substantial slippage since 1977, and that average male earnings were approaching £30k; the job evaluation report by Sue Hastings (2002) gave a 16% rise based only on the terms of the scheme; the IDS (2002b: 6) figures suggested a 21% rise just to restore the relative position of 1979; and finally Government data based on call-outs per employee revealed a 50% increase in productivity since 1992. Andy Gilchrist clarified this:

We also said at the start that we were always setting out to negotiate not to go on strike. This was never a sort of covert way of getting our members on strike or starting the summer of discontent that you've described or indeed bringing down the Labour Government. This was about saying what our members are worth. Mick Harper, in his last year as FBU president, was constantly stressing this. We expected our employers to say, well, we agreed with a lot of what you say but we don't think you're worth that. We think you are worth this. You end up with something in the middle. That was what the purpose of the process was and in the very early stages that's what I believe the local authority employers were intent on doing.

National Officer John McGhee provided further evidence of this:

In terms of coming up with the figure of £30,000, I've got to say that Andy approached us with that figure on the basis of some of the research that had been done. We felt that if we presented it properly, it was justifiable. We knew it was going to be a tough argument … it was a just pay claim and I think it was well worked out in terms of what we could achieve and what we'd been asking. The pay claim was about the realignment of pay.

Assistant General Secretary Mike Fordham explained more fully about the arguments behind the claim and its tactical dangers:

It emerged over about fifteen years because there was a lot of feeling amongst activists that the pay formula wasn't delivering. The executive then, for reasons that all seemed right at the time, but with hindsight weren't, consequently took a view that basically they maintained the status quo. We had a pay formula and didn't want to risk any change that might open things up.

He then pointed out that there was a catch-up element to the claim:

We knew that was the case but it was a matter of where does the trade union actually start doing anything. I believe it's right trying to take things forward ... So that in itself gave us a problem of size, how could it have been delayed so long and if there is an ongoing problem within the relationship it's automatically a build up of size.

So I think it was a natural thing after having a leadership for so long and a change in leadership you are going to get a change in position. So part of the size thing [£30k] was catching-up after many years of slow decline, part of the size thing was expectation amongst our own membership, part of it was actually saying well if we are going to make this change – certainly some of us knew that other change was going to come with it despite what some of the rhetoric might have said – you might as well go for it in a big way. This is a once in a generation chance, take it. The research that we did showed a gap. It didn't actually say of course what that gap in financial terms exactly was. Therefore it was a political judgement to put a £30,000 figure on it.

Initially it was the leadership. We'd looked at the research, so to reach a position: we then made a recommendation to the executive, and that became the decision. This was the full-time officials, together with the President, Mick Harper, with Andy saying this is the level to aim for and we then made that as a recommendation to the executive, and the executive ... unanimously supported that position as a target.

PAY DATA

There was evidence for this assumption from the LRD report, which itself was based on the New Earnings Survey (NES) material supported by IDS. The pay formula linked firefighters' pay to the upper quartile of male manual earnings (in 1979 this was around 6% higher than average male earnings). Significant changes to the labour market and occupational structure became evident in the second half of the 1980s and accelerated throughout the 1990s. The pay formula's comparator group, the skilled time-served craftsmen, which was a pay setter for decades, is now a dying breed. At the same time the firefighters' job has changed.

In the aftermath of the 1977-8 strike a pay formula was agreed, partially based on the McCarthy recommendations and partly a compromise related to both the Clegg Commission and the prevailing conventional wisdom about public sector pay. It was kept in place because the three main parties were powerful enough to secure it, and because it represented the least worst way of arranging pay increases for this group. The FBU and its members saw the formula as a way of maintaining comparable pay in a period of hostile Conservative Governments, and having watched with dismay the 1984-5 miners' strike they were relieved not to have to mimic that method of securing jobs and pay. The Local Government employers were equally happy to maintain the formula: they had much bigger fish to fry, with contracting out regimes, strikes by manual and white-collar staff, and the burden of financial reforms (Ironside and Seifert 2000). For its part the Government saw no mileage in dealing with firefighters: a small and relatively cheap group on the margins of Local Government activity, with a formula that did not outrage pay norms, although it did cut across some of the free market rhetoric of leading Conservatives such as Keith Joseph (Halcrow 1989) and Michael Heseltine (1987).

In 1996 the LRD published its report for the FBU on the operations of the pay formula from 1979-1995. It was based on a motion carried by the union's 1994 Annual Conference, that the EC undertake a review into potential improvements to the Fire Service pay formula, with a view to negotiating improvements with the employers. This corresponded with the 1995 Audit Commission report into the Fire Service, as part of continuous efforts by the employers and senior managers to develop management techniques increasingly used in other parts of the public services. What considered view there was from the relevant Ministers and civil servants in the Home Office lamented, rather vaguely and lamely, the lack of progress as they saw it in the Fire Service (Linn 1992) on such matters. Taken together, the emerging concerns of Local Government decision-makers (both senior managers and all party politicians) about the Fire Service in the mid-1990s began to stack up the case for radical change.

The more important point is that the pay of the main comparator – skilled male manual workers – was itself falling relative to others in the labour market. Non-manual workers and those on higher earnings received much larger pay increases as national collective bargaining declined in industries with large numbers of skilled manual workers, and as the changing structure and technological advancement of UK industry rapidly altered in the 1990s (Cully *et al* 1999; Millward *et al* 2000). The obvious solution was to renegotiate the formula at some point. There had to be a shift away from the upper quartile of male manuals, and there had to be some technical changes relating to a period of low inflation and therefore relatively low percentage pay rises.

Doing nothing no longer seemed an option. Some of those interviewed and some conference speakers argued with hindsight that the pressure for change was not as compelling as it appeared to be at the time, but there is no evidence that they voiced their concerns at that moment. By now, therefore, there was widespread consensus within the FBU that change was needed. The main issue was when to ask for the change, given the attendant risks. The overwhelming feeling we received from interviews was that the claim was 'good and just' (Jim McMullen from Manchester); that the £30k was a genuine call from conference (Dave Whatton from West Midlands); that there was 'strong support for the £30k' (Tony Maguire from Northern Ireland); that it was a 'just cause' (Jenny Griffiths from South Wales); that they were convinced by the 'rate for the job argument' (Sandy McNiven and John Cairns from Strathclyde); and that because the old pay formula had not been working well for some years there was need for 'catch-up' element in claim (Gordon Fielden from London). Without exception, all of those interviewed and all of those we heard speak at the four conferences we attended in 2004 said that they and their members had understood that the £30k claim would come at a cost in terms of changes in working practices.

From the early 1990s the operation of the pay formula failed to deliver acceptable pay increases for firefighters and others in the Service. This situation was made worse by Government policies with regard to public sector pay and finances more generally. For example, in 1991 IDS reported that firefighters were to receive a 9.5% pay rise from November 1990 under the terms of their formula. In case this is mistaken for a generous deal, at the time inflation was at 10.9% and rising, and average pay rises for white-collar Local Government staff were 9.4%. IDS go on to report that:

> the joint Home Office/National Joint Council working party, set up to examine pay and conditions in response to the 1986 Audit Commission paper on value for money in the Fire Service, produced its report on 31 July 1990. This concluded that the current arrangements should continue but that 'there should be greater flexibility in working arrangements' (IDS 1991: 45).

This would appear to be important, since even at this time the employers and external Government agencies made it clear that changes in conditions of service, especially concerning staffing levels and overtime, were open to local negotiations. This was pertinent since in the aftermath of the 1989 ambulance dispute there had been a move towards local productivity bargaining, as a forerunner of a more general approach by Government Ministers that public sector pay rises above inflation had to pay for themselves. In other words pay rises could come from savings, normally a euphemism for job losses.

For the next six years, 1992 to 1997, pay rises would be limited to whatever came from savings during a period of continuous public sector paybill freeze. This picture did not change with a Labour

Government. In 1997-8 the basic pay increase was 4.8% in the Fire Service, contrasted with inflation at about the same level and others averaging between 3-5%. As IDS conclude about Labour: 'in 1998, the Government's public sector pay policy is set to be as tough as in any of the previous four years' (IDS 1998:1). In 1998-9 the 41,000 whole time and 18,000 retained firefighters received 5.6% from the pay formula, along with control room staff. The new Ministers were firm that only 'affordable' claims could be met, and those that did not undermine the target of 2.5% inflation set by Gordon Brown.

As we shall see later, Central Government was determined to push on, in a period of low inflation, with long-term pay agreements. A significant increase in two to four-year deals was reported by IDS in its survey, including a three-year agreement for teachers in Scotland and two years for staff in Customs and Excise. The arguments in favour of such deals are explained in the Treasury's guidance to departments and include: benefits from longer term financial planning; to allow for modernisation of services to be carried out in a partnership of management and unions; and that they provide 'a clear and stable basis for implementing modernisation and reform' (IDS 2002a: 15; 2002b: 4).

ROLE CHANGE

The evidence for role change (Hastings 2002) is very strong and was based on another report using job evaluation, and a series of wider reports from Fire Service managers and relevant Government departments (HM Inspectorate 2001). While both these provided a clear-cut and largely uncontested case, in themselves they do not provide a simple equation for the £30,000 figure.

In interviews with us, Sandy McNiven and John Cairns from the Strathclyde region of the FBU accepted the argument about slippage and were convinced that £30k was the right rate for the job. Mick Flanagan, an officers' representative from South Wales, and Jenny Griffiths, the fire control representative also from South Wales, agreed that they compared badly with other similar jobs and that now was the time to catch up. Many others expressed their total conviction that they were worth the full £30,000, as in the case of Kerry Baigent, the National Secretary of the women's committee; others saw it as a decent negotiating position, such as Jim Quinn from Northern Ireland, and Gordon Fielden and Katy Lane, both from London region.

The arguments for the target became a major part of the initial campaign to win FBU membership support and wider union approval. They were paramount during the prolonged negotiations and at the centre of the propaganda and industrial war during the strike action itself. In addition they became part of the post-June 2003 settlement debate inside the FBU, and coloured the analysis of events, as well as re-emerging in the long drawn-out end of the dispute in the late summer of 2004.

THE DRIVE FOR EQUALITY

The second and third pillars of the claim were further evidence of the FBU's desire for, and commitment to, equality throughout the Service, as would be expected from a progressive union. In contrast, most senior managers and employers had done very little to change the culture of prejudice in the Service, and the Government's pious words were never matched by action.

Figure 5: FBU leaflet on control staff and the pay claim

Dear Brother/Sister,

The Fire Brigades Union is just that, a Union. It is a Union of people of the same or similar occupations, in this case Firefighters and Emergency Fire Control Operators, joined together to advance the pay and condi-tions of its members for mutual benefit.

As a Trade Union we either move forward together or we do not move forward at all. As part of the Fire Brigades Union, Emergency Fire Control staff have played a major part in the development of the Union, an Emergency Fire Control Operator is now the President of the Fire Brigades Union.

In relation to the pay claim it is worth remembering that:

- Emergency Fire Control Operators are employed under the same Grey Book conditions of service as Firefighters.
- Emergency Fire Control Operators work the same shifts and shift patterns as Firefighters, including nights and weekends.
- The rank structure and pay differentials are the same as, or broadly similar to a Fire Station.
- Fire Control rooms have seen a massive increase in workload since 1977 and at the same time seen huge cuts in Control Room personnel.
- The same period has seen a huge increase in new and ever more sophis-ticated technology within the Control room without this being reflected in pay levels.
- The job of an Emergency Fire Control Operator can be both stressful and demanding. Stress levels are actually higher amongst Control staff than firefighters.
- Until recently Control staff have had to endure a recruitment freeze leading to chronic understaffing which meant on numerous occasions watches working below the minimum staffing level required for the Control room to function properly.
- The Control staff on duty at any given time has had to deal with what-ever level of workload that comes in, however great that may be. There is no facility to call for assistance.
- Should the need arise Control staff can be called on to work for the

whole of their shift without a break. There is no such thing as 'relief duties' in the Control room.

- Control staff have to maintain a constant watch. Stand down periods are therefore much shorter in Control than on a Fire Station.
- In recent years the rest facilities available for Emergency Fire Control Operators has been far less than on Fire Stations.

In every Industrial Dispute in Merseyside, Essex and Derbyshire Fire Services, official or otherwise, FBU members in the Control room have actively and wholeheartedly supported the stance taken by the Fire Brigades Union and voted overwhelmingly in favour of industrial action to defend jobs and conditions of service, even when not directly affected by the proposals.

Unity is strength; all sections of this union have to move forward because in the end nobody wins unless everybody wins.

Y.... because we are *all* worth it.

The second pillar was exclusively about the 1700 control staff, nearly all of who are women. In this part of the claim the EC was eager to bring the reality of equality into the Service, rather than to endure more years of empty rhetoric from the employers. It was important for securing significant levels of unity within the union during the action; for providing a FBU version of modernity as opposed to a dominant employers, and Government account of what a modern service would include; and for trying to tie control staff closer into the Fire Service and thus to afford protection from ideas of merger with ambulance and/or police. The claim itself sought to raise the basic rate of pay for all grades to 100% of that of a firefighter, from the existing level of 92%. Ruth Winters spoke of the reaction to the claim and eventual settlement:

> We still represent something like 80% of the control staff and they were as solid as any firefighter during the dispute, and I actually think they felt totally part of it for the first time in a long time … actually they're happy with the 95% in the sense that it is an improvement on the 92%. Obviously a 100% would have been better but I think by that time they had realised that they were never going to gain everything anyway. They were also happy to be part of a national pay formula, and the fact that they also got a 16% pay rise backdated.

Other control staff representatives agreed with this. Jenny Griffiths noted the problems of police and ambulance control rooms and argued convincingly for separate control for fire. Val Salmon, the EC member for control staff, felt her members had become a full and accepted part of the union during the dispute.

The third pillar of the claim sought to include as equals within the

Service all retained staff. This would help dispel the myth of the FBU as uninterested in and unrepresentative of retained staff; and it would thereby help counter the media – and at some points Government and employers' flirtation – with a tiny retained staff union; and it served to provide a totally united front to employers. This involved 18,000 staff, of whom about half were members of the FBU and involved in the dispute. One retained FBU representative interviewed, Wayne Howells from South Wales, explained the importance of this element of the claim for his members as part of becoming fully integrated into the FBU, and to combat what he saw as a 'scab' union (the minority Retained Firefighters' Union).

The fourth and final pillar was a statement for a new pay formula, needed to deliver a modern high quality, high performing service with highly skilled and motivated staff.

NEGOTIATE FIRST, STRIKE LATER

Having laid out the claim and the main arguments, the final section of the resolution explains the tactics – negotiate in good faith and if neces- sary as a last resort strike. So the second day of the conference, 15 May 2002, saw the claim agreed, the arguments endorsed, and the tactics supported. The press generally reacted cautiously, with those papers sympathetic to the FBU putting down markers for their future cover- age. The *Mirror* quoted Dean Mills, a FBU regional official, with reference to the 9/11 tragedy in New York: 'if a similar tragedy occurred here we would respond with the same dedication as US colleagues. The only difference is the funding and higher pay they receive' (14.5.02: 2). Kevin Maguire writing in *The Guardian*, noted that the relevant Cabinet Minister was Stephen Byers, already on his way out, as the department of Transport, Local Government and the Regions was about to be re-organised; he pointed out that this would hardly help other Ministers, such as Alan Whitehead (then the Minister responsible for Fire Service), in dealing with the demands coming from the FBU conference (16.5.02: 8). Meanwhile the *Morning Star,* the FBU's strongest supporter during the dispute, quoted Andy Gilchrist asking a question on the lips of many traditional Labour supporters, namely: 'why are public sector workers considered fair game when company directors, financiers – those who move capital around the globe to maximise their profits and who care nothing for the havoc they bring to the lives of workers – are praised by the Government?' (16.5.02: 4).

THE CAN OF WORMS?

The way in which the claim was formulated, and the threat of strike action to secure it, has been described by some, including the former FBU General Secretary, Ken Cameron, and Charles Nolda of the LGA (who were the lead negotiators for their organisations for many years and used the term independently in separate interviews), as a 'can of worms'. The argument matters: with a formula, pay rises were automatic and therefore there was no basis for standard practice collective bargaining, and no chance for the employers nationally to trade conditions for pay improvements. Such changes in the 1990s had filtered through to other Local Government and state sector workers, with pay rises increasingly tied to worsening conditions of service, greater managerial controls, more insecure jobs, and moves to local pay bargaining. When local Fire Authorities with assistance from CFOs had tried to change the *status quo* the FBU had mounted successful campaigns, as in Essex and Merseyside. This time, however, it appeared that the 'can of worms' was going to be opened anyway: if not by the FBU in a controlled set of negotiations, then by the employers under severe Government pressure.

Ken Cameron explained how it appeared in the early 1990s:

> I found it fairly easy to make the argument that we shouldn't throw the baby out with the bathwater, and we should look at another formula to take us forward. But there was also the argument about conditions of service, what people did, and that was never highlighted to the extent that it is now.

We asked about how he had withstood the pressures from below to abandon the formula from the mid-1990s onwards. He argued that:

> people would have had one or two reservations that this pay formula is a load of rubbish, and we ought to get rid of it. But it was inevitable that the formula had to change.

The first eighteen years of the pay formula were administered by Conservative Governments deeply opposed to improving public sector workers' wages and conditions of service. Only with the election of a Labour Government in 1997 did it become possible to campaign for a step-change improvement with some possibility of success. This possibility became a probability when Labour was re-elected for a second term with a large majority. In order to achieve both a larger than usual settlement and a new formula, the FBU had to stand outside the existing formula, and that move meant that the employers had a chance to trade more pay against conditions of service. That was clear. So once negotiations started, both sides had good cause to take a strong line. But this can contained more worms than most – the Government soon became a player, at first hesitantly and half-heartedly but then with increasing confidence and clarity. Once opened, to mix our metaphors, how could the genie be put back into the bottle?

NEGOTIATIONS START

The conference resolution became the substance of the FBU's 2002 pay claim tabled at the NJC meeting of 28 May. On that day all members of the EC, along with regional officials and campaign co-ordinators, received a summary of the pay research (circular 2002HOC0446), and the next day they received another summary, this time on the research on the 'value' of a firefighter by Sue Hastings (circular 2002HOC0449AG). At this very early stage both sides – in the person of Phil White for the employers and Andy Gilchrist for the FBU – argued for the need for 'sensible and sound negotiations' as well as for a possible joint approach to Government for extra funding (FBU press release 28.5.02).

In line with standard procedure the FBU claim was referred to the Joint Standing Sub-Committee (JSSC), which met on 6 June to consider the claim. At this meeting the employers' side made it clear that it saw pay improvements and changes in working practices ('modernisation') as being intrinsically linked, and that this view was shared by Government Ministers. As one participant recalled of the delaying tactics of the employers, 'a statement was made by the employers to which the employees' side agreed to respond at the next meeting. This took place on 18 June 2002. The meeting was simply a variant of the 6 June meeting' (Burchill 2004: 409). In fact there were five meetings of the JSSC between 28 May and 23 July. By the third meeting, 'the employers proposed that the NJC should ask the Government to set up an independent inquiry into pay and modernisation issues' (Employers' Organisation 2002a: paragraph 3.3). By the fifth meeting the FBU made it clear that it was the NJC that should decide the issue and not an inquiry.

On the following day (7 June) the employers' side sent the FBU a five page letter detailing what it called the 'Employers' Modernisation Agenda', and concluding that 'at an appropriate time during the forthcoming negotiations we will be replying to your pay claim in the context of this modernising agenda'. The letter also included an offer to discuss special payments for special duties, something never apparently picked up on during the dispute. As the employers themselves pointed out about their ideas:

> some are within the NJC's remit and others are not. Some involve action by the NJC, some involve action by Government, some involve policy changes by the FBU (such as lifting their ban on voluntary pre-arranged overtime), some involve FBU acceptance that it is legitimate for fire authorities to do certain things (in relation to co-responding) (Employers' Organisation 2002a: paragraph 4.6).

The letter is signed by Phil White, Assistant Secretary to the employers, and pointedly does not respond to the union's pay claim.

His boss at the LGA, Charles Nolda, thought:

> the £30k policy that the conference endorsed in 2002 set the FBU on a
> collision course with the Government, with the fire authorities as an initial
> obstacle. Even with some evidence that the upper quartile pay formula had
> put the FBU's eggs in the wrong basket (manual workers' pay now moves
> more slowly than whole economy pay as a consequence of de-industriali-
> sation); even with a large reservoir of public goodwill towards the Service;
> even with the events in New York of 11 September 2001 fresh in minds, it
> was decidedly foolhardy to demand a 39 per cent pay rise for a service
> where on average 80 people were applying for each vacancy, despite nearly
> full employment in the wider economy (Nolda 2004: 386).

This labour market point was also emphasised by the *Economist*: 'firefighters do come quite low down in the public-sector pay league. Yet,
interestingly, this does not seem to deter applicants' (7.9.02: 38).

In a circular to all members dated 21 June the FBU General
Secretary dismissed the employers' letter thus:

> their agenda is far from 'modern'. It is simply a repeat of the same wish
> list which began with the publication of the Audit Commission report
> 'In the Line of Fire' in 1995 and culminated in our 'Smash and Grab'
> campaign. It is quite clear that the Employers are intent in ignoring our
> current pay claim and want to start 'Smash and Grab 2'! (Circular
> 2002HOC0513AG).

The EC made it clear to the employers that it considered that the
latter's agenda was neither modern nor a framework for progress.
Indeed much of it was a rehash of the Audit Commission (1995) *In the
Line of Fire*, which sought to destroy the *Grey Book* Agreement on
conditions of service, and which the union had vigorously opposed at
the time. But it was not only on wage levels and the pay formula that
change was afoot in the Fire Service. Throughout the 1990s there had
been an active debate about the development of the Service, which had,
by the turn of the century, produced a consensus about the need to
move from a service based on prescribed national standards to one
based on local risk assessment, with much greater emphasis on fire
prevention (FBU 2004). If, it was argued, greater resources could be
put into Community Fire Safety, with better building designs and
locally framed risk assessment plans with more flexible use of
resources, lives could be saved and property loss reduced. On cost-
benefit grounds a win-win situation was possible – more initial
investment, particularly in fire prevention, could bring much larger
savings for society as a whole. This consensus was to be broken as it
became clear that the Labour Government favoured cost savings rather
than extra investment.

In this part of the late spring the employers were already trying to persuade Government Ministers that the FBU had opened the way for a new inquiry linking pay with changes in working practices, and that such an inquiry should now take place with all the parties involved, and with a clear remit to put 'modernisation' at the head of the reforms. At this time the Government seemed unimpressed by the employers' request, since the FBU had signalled its lack of interest in such an inquiry well before negotiations had started. We will see later that Ministers subsequently changed their minds and set up the Bain inquiry.

Phil White explained:

> Well, we knew some months in advance that the resolution of conference was going to be for a pay increase and a change to the pay formula. We saw that as an opportunity because twenty-five years of the old pay formula meant that the balance in negotiations was tilted towards the FBU who never came to us for anything. We tried to, on separate occasions, make changes to conditions of service, famously in Bournemouth in 1999, where the union just sat tight and said 'no we don't want anything, we're not going to give it up and status quo shall continue'. So because the formula meant we had got nothing to bargain with, the pay claim gave us an opportunity. We had already started work … on our modernisation agenda and as soon as we got the formal claim, we responded with we were prepared to talk about pay if you are prepared to talk about these other things.

When I asked 'did you expect a £30k claim?', he replied: 'we weren't expecting £30k … I think their conference the previous year had sent the executive away to look at the pay formula because the view, quite rightly from their point of view, was that they had fallen behind … I think our initial anticipation was for a claim to reform the pay formula. The figure of £30k was a surprise'. The central issue for the employers was that the claim, according to Phil White, 'unlocked the key to the door, which meant that everything was up for grabs. Our response was that we were prepared to bargain, we were prepared to talk about pay levels and pay formula in the context of what we were calling modernisation'. The employers had already decided not to make a counter offer to the claim, but continued to argue that any negotiations would have to be about modernisation. This was the chance for which they had been waiting for twenty-five years – a real bargaining exchange.

THE CAMPAIGN

JUNE 2002 – THE LONG WAIT

The FBU was waiting for the employers to formulate their response and counter the union claim with their own offer, in time-honoured collective-bargaining fashion. This failure of the employers to respond early and clearly fuelled the resentment amongst the workforce, adding to their sense of betrayal by employers. The employers saw it as a chance to wait and see how the FBU would set up their own case before pushing the change agenda. The reaction of the union was to grasp the importance of the massive and enthusiastic membership support for their case in order to make the threat of action to the employer real. This few weeks enabled the union to rally their membership through a series of public events. It also brought the case to local communities, boosted morale, and gave the union leadership a chance to sort out organisational arrangements if a strike was to come. Throughout June the membership rallied behind their claim. On 11 June 12,000 members and supporters marched in London to demand pay justice on the largest ever FBU organised UK-wide demonstration (FBU press release 11.6.02). The *Coventry Evening Telegraph* reported that:

> fifty Coventry firefighters were today taking part in a massive demonstration in London to fight for better pay. City firefighters were part of an eight coach convoy from the West Midlands ... Mark Bridges, Foleshill fire station's branch representative at the rally, said 'the gist of the rally is to get firefighters' pay up to a reasonable level because we have fallen back over the years' (11.6.02: 2).

The Times covered the event in a dismissive fifty-five words (12.6.02:11), while the Cardiff edition of the *Western Mail* reported that fourteen coaches had taken 450 Welsh firefighters to the London rally and quoted the FBU Wales official Dick Pearson: 'we hope not to be forced into taking strike action' (12.6.02: 3). A sentiment echoed in reports up and down the country, as with Brian Harvey of the FBU speaking in Torquay (quoted in *Herald Express* 13.6.02: 2).

Brendan Barber from the TUC addressed the rally: 'I know that the FBU has not entered into this campaign lightly. But the mood of the union's recent conference and the message from the fire stations up and down the country is clear. The time for change is now. I hope that the employers and the Government have been listening – I urge them now to respond' (*FireFighter*, pay campaign special no 2, July 2002: 4). This hint of action was reported elsewhere: 'the union is mobilising around the campaign and warns that while it wants to avoid confrontation, it will recall its conference and recommend strike action if necessary' (*Labour Research*, June 2002: 5).

Between 17 and 21 June a series of well attended mass meetings was held in every region of the union while the war of words continued. A crucial part of any claim and subsequent negotiations is support from the membership. Such support persuades the employer that the lead union negotiators have a realistic chance of calling for action if necessary, and prevents the employers appealing over the heads of the union leadership direct to the members. It also allows the union leaders to call for ballot on their terms and at their timing, thus allowing for maximum pressure on the employers, and in this case the Government too. The FBU campaign over the summer months was an outstanding success by any standards. John McGhee played an important co-ordinating role as he explained in interview. On being asked what was the crucial thing they had done to persuade their people, he replied: 'I think in the early stages when we took the campaign to our members ... we agreed to set up a series of campaign co-ordinators, appointed by regional committees:

> Every brigade was asked to appoint someone and eventually the communication tree we wanted actually came from campaign co-ordinators. We'd had a batch of regional co-ordinators, regional officials through the 'smash and grab' campaign. We just kept them going and gave them a new role ... we identified with them early on that we needed to have this communication tree that would get information to members. For example, Andy would phone me and say this is what's happened, here's the message and I could put it out to campaign co-ordinators who could put it out to the brigade co-ordinators who would then put it out to the branch co-ordinators for the members ... it was done by text, it was done by phones, it was done by e-mail, but mainly by mobiles.

I asked Ruth Winters about the campaign organisation. She replied:

> I do think the organising was very good. I do think we actually involved as many people as we could. We did, contrary to popular belief now, we spent a year asking people and building up whether this was going to be our goal or not, and I think that was why it was important.

When asked about members' reaction to critical press stories about the claim, she said:

> I think our members reacted by saying well no it's not, it's not outrageous. I think when we were talking about £30k against £21,500 our people were quite happy to argue that and felt good. I don't think our members ever felt they were worth any less than the thirty grand to be honest.

Meanwhile the employers were considering the substantive issues of a 'something for something' deal. They were also pondering their tactics – the threat of a FBU strike was politically significant, but the desire of the FBU to win a large pay increase made the employers believe that it was possible to win real concessions from the union negotiators. In addition there were some who wanted to call the union's bluff and test whether or not they had the backing for a strike.

A critical part of the cost-risk-benefit analysis undertaken by both sides at this time was the question of the funding for the deal. The employers had to work within restrictive Government pay guidelines rooted in the annual cash settlement between Local and Central Government. Such amounts have been at the heart of much of the traditional tensions between Whitehall and the shires and cities, but since the mid-1980s the centralising tendencies within the British state had secured greater controls for the centre thus undermining both local democracy and community cohesion. These were being replaced by a combination of the political expediency of Westminster and the economic requirements of business, both local and national. The bottom line for the employers was that they could not fund any above average pay rises, even for relatively small groups, without increased financial support from Central Government.

Two crucial arguments now emerged. Firstly, the FBU, with some independent research support, argued that the pay rise would create a better trained and higher performing workgroup. This in turn would improve productivity and save lives, reduce damage to property and increase safety; all of which provided financial benefits as well as welfare ones. The problem – or issue – is that such benefits accrue to individuals, companies, the community and insurance companies rather than directly to Local Government employers. In any traditional welfare model (see chapter 5 on social efficiency) that would be enough to convince politicians, locally and nationally. But in some important corners of political life this is no longer enough.

Compartmentalised economics, free market calculations and the erroneous separation of economic from social and political worlds has created a false accounting, in which artificially created units of accountability are pitted against some incongruous definitions of (market) efficiency and cost effectiveness, thereby allowing rational people of good intentions to make poor decisions. Andy Gilchrist constantly argued this wider case, as in a letter to *The Guardian*: 'the first essential is to ensure the public services can recruit, retain and train staff. Only then will the public see a marked and consistent improvement in the services it needs and demands' (21.6.02: 21).

The immediate outcome was that the employers could not fund the pay claim and could not be persuaded or persuade others that such a claim might be self-financing. Therefore only Central Government could meet the funding gap – real or assumed.

The second argument emerged more forcefully and with the voice of Gordon Brown, Chancellor of the Exchequer. It was clearly in the minds of the negotiators, Government Ministers, and other trade union leaders, including at the TUC in the summer. This was that a larger than normal pay rise, however presented, might encourage other public sector workers to follow and thereby unleash a summer of industrial unrest. The Government feared a spate of 'me-too' claims, creating a

domino effect on public sector wages. This view was repudiated by the
TUC leaders and other general secretaries of large public sector unions.

While the economic case was still being calculated inside the Treasury,
with its later statements about knock-on effects, the likelihood of such a
rush of claims seemed remote. The industrial relations mechanisms for
how a pay rise for fire staff could trigger similar claims remained unclear;
for example, it was unlikely to affect staff covered by Pay Review Body
arrangements. Nonetheless being a pay setter was as attractive to the
FBU leadership as it was worrying to employers. John Monks made it
clear at a seminar, even if half in jest, that he did not want to be TUC
General Secretary when industrial action brought down yet another
Labour Government! This was a sentiment echoed in the Cabinet room
by a generation of Labour leaders brought up with a distorted view of
the events of 1978-9 during the 'Winter of Discontent'.

JULY 2002 – GOVERNMENT PUTS ITS BIG TOE INTO THE WATER

The month started with a historic moment for the FBU as Ruth Winters,
a fire control room operator from Lothian and Borders, became the first
elected woman President of the union, a position she took up at the
September recall conference. On 3 July, along with many colleagues, she
was demonstrating outside the LGA conference. It was later alleged in
Parliament and elsewhere, that John Prescott held secret talks with leaders of Fire Authorities at the conference, and made it clear that the
Government wanted a large part in the forthcoming negotiations
(*FireFighter* vol 30 (4), August 2002: 4-5).

By early July it had become clear that, despite their earlier promise to
bring forward proposals on pay, the employers were still not prepared to
answer the central question which the union side had raised during NJC
Sub-Committee meetings since the beginning of June. This was simply to
tell the union the value they placed on firefighters and emergency control
room staff, and to express this in a pay offer which could then be the starting point for meaningful negotiations. It later transpired, through a leak
to the media, that the employers had indeed prepared a paper on pay but
that Ministers had intervened to prevent this from becoming the basis for
a realistic offer. According to both *The Guardian* and the BBC this would
have taken a qualified firefighter to £25,000 by November 2003, subject
to progress on the employers' modernisation agenda.

'FANCY DANCING' OR THE OFFER THAT WAS NEVER MADE

An independent consultancy firm reported that 'one of the key points
in the dispute was the Government's vetoing of an offer worth 16 per
cent over two years, linked to an extensive programme of modernisation including a new pay formula, changes to the pay/grading
structure, and provisions for more flexible working' (IDS 2002a: 106).

On 9 July there was still no pay offer at the NJC meeting. While all of this was rightly seen as early manoeuvrings, Mike Fordham remains convinced that 9 July was the date that set the logic of strike action. As he said:

> With hindsight there is an issue then of how much the setting of that ambitious target provoked the reaction from the other side particularly Government. I also believed that events showed that until July 9 our tactics were working well in that we were negotiating with the employers, they promised to make an offer on July 9 and that offer in many of our minds at the time and still to this day would sometime later have been a satisfactory conclusion to the dispute and the strikes would not have taken place.

At this time there was evidence of a split among the employers, with some publicly pushing for a joint union-employer approach to Central Government for more service funding to resource both pay and modernisation developments. 'The employers therefore told the FBU at a negotiating meeting on 9 July that they had concluded that only an independent inquiry into pay and modernisation could secure the new money needed to improve their pay' (Employers Organisation 2002a: paragraph 2.6).

Charles Nolda noted:

> we spent much of May and June sort of saying … we'll talk about everything but not coming to the point on the pay side of things, then, I think it was some time in July we produced a paper which had £25k in it … over two years.

The politics behind this delay and the subsequent low offer were made clear:

> at first the only nudge from on high was don't rock the boat by unsettling the FBU, but after John Prescott became involved in early July he made all the noises you would expect to be made by a Minister … he made it clear that any offer made by our side had to be within the current Government pay policy and that there would be no extra funds from Central Government and at the same time we had promised we would give a response to the claim in July, and we produced this paper for the employers which was £25k over two years with lots and lots of strings … it was sent to civil servants and the civil servants didn't react adversely to a 16% pay increase … the conclusion that our side reached was that we should be arguing for a pay inquiry, which was the point that the LGA put privately to Prescott at their conference.

Later he admitted that John Prescott told them in early August to make the 4% offer in early September. As Phil White agreed, the offer was designed for the FBU to refuse. This would enable Prescott to choose to announce an inquiry 'which we had been privately urging on civil servants since before the FBU submitted their original claim'.

The carrot offered by the employers to the FBU to join in a joint request for an inquiry included an agreement in principle to change the pay formula, to instigate job evaluation for control staff, and to consider a higher than average pay rise in exchange for modernisation. On 17 July the FBU rejected these advances.

Togetherness was not to the taste of the parties, and mixed messages appeared from the rank and file. On the one hand even in Merseyside, a traditional hotspot for FBU action, there was apparently some co-operation:

> Both sides have indicated they want to work together to lobby the Government for more money to fund a substantial pay increase for fire-fighters … Les Skarratts, FBU Merseyside convenor, said: 'we welcome that they agree with us that we should earn more … if local employers can recognise our pay demands, then there is no reason why this shouldn't be extended to the national employer body' (*Daily Post* 11.7.02:13).

Elsewhere sympathetic CFOs such as Ronnie King from Mid and West Wales added their voices to a joint approach to fund a deserving case for higher pay and a new formula; and support came from some councillors such as Councillor Dunn, chair of the Derbyshire Fire Authority.

On the other hand, and in a different part of the country 200 fire-fighters held a meeting at Grimsby Town Hall. It was reported that: 'Mick Headon, FBU regional treasurer, addressed the meeting and said that there was "growing anger" among union members that could lead to strike action … as an organisation, we do not want to take the British Fire Service on strike' (*Grimsby Evening Telegraph* 16.7.02:3); and on 15 July Mid and West Wales FBU members lobbied their employers in Carmarthen (FBU Welsh Region press release).

On 22 July there was a large rally in Glasgow. 'Defiant union members from across Britain marched on Glasgow's George Square to highlight their "scandalous" pay' (*Daily Record* 23.7.02:15). This time the event was properly covered by *The Times* with an obviously more worried tone (23.7.02: 9). It was estimated that over 5000 marched that day to force the employers to make an offer (FBU press release 22.7.02). But such rallies, while geeing up FBU members and winning some wider support, had little impact on the employers' negotiating strategy. This was at first based on the setting up of an independent review with joint support, leading to Government being able to release some additional funds if and only if pay was tied with modernisation.

On 23 July the employers effectively confirmed that Ministers had placed them in a negotiating straitjacket. They asked the union to support them in a joint approach to Government to request an independent inquiry into pay and modernisation in the Fire Service. It was at that JSSC meeting that the employers made it clear that they were handing effective control of the dispute to the Government. The FBU EC's response was to argue that these matters were for the NJC to determine and that if there were to be a joint approach to Government, it should be to seek extra funding both to finance pay justice and to invest in the Fire Service that had suffered decades of underfunding.

Frank Burchill later wrote his account of these meetings with a comment on costings, an issue that emerged later in the dispute as a vital debating point between the parties. He reported that the employers 'produced a response of some substance', namely that 'nothing is agreed until everything is agreed'; and that firefighters should have a new pay formula within a national grading system, but that the Government would not fund any additional payments. As he continued, 'it was at this meeting that the employers' side raised the issue of an inquiry ... on the basis that this represented the only way of securing additional funding' (Burchill 2004: 409). Two more July meetings did nothing to further the discussion, but Burchill tells us that part of the employers' proposals contained a letter of 21 June sent to the 'Technical Working Group', made up of

> ... nine employer representatives from the NJC; a team of people referred to as 'multi-disciplinary support' – a representative of the IPDS; a representative of the ... LGA Labour Group; the ... CFO of the London Fire and Emergency Planning Authority ...; a personnel representative from LEFPA; somebody from communications from LEFPA and an employers' organisation consultant on communications; a finance representative and members of the employers' organisation and LGA secretariats (*ibid*: 410).

The letter included two papers: one of them was 'a draft document designed to be put before the FBU at the 9 July meeting', and proposed a 16.1% pay rise, taking pay to £25,000 over a phased period. This would add 9% to the paybill over and above the normal settlement. The other paper spelled out the costs of the options of such a 9%, about £85 million (*ibid*).

Burchill then reports that the paper did agree that there was 'a shortfall in current firefighters' earnings against those of more meaningful current comparators' (*ibid*). The view is that this was about £1500, added to the new year on year pay increase from a new formula the total rise could be 18%, or 7% increase in real terms, to be funded by Government (*ibid*).

EMPLOYERS PASS THE BUCK

In the event the employers, influenced by the Government, wrote to the Deputy Prime Minister immediately after the NJC meeting of 23 July. In their letter the employers asked the Government to set up an Independent Inquiry to make recommendations on both pay and modernisation. The employers justified their requests as follows: 'It has become increasingly clear to the employers that even if we were to make significant achievements in relation to our modernisation agenda, there would not be sufficient money available to fund any settlement through negotiation'. The employers' press release of the same day was even more blunt: 'The Government had made it clear that it will not bail us out financially if we negotiate a deal we cannot presently afford'. Ministers were sending a clear message that they were not prepared to consider the reasoning behind the firefighters' claim for a step-change increase, nor was the Government prepared to put right in the short term acknowledged shortcomings in the prevailing funding arrangements for the Fire Service. The employers had simply passed the baton to Government through a so-called independent inquiry, in the hope that the union's power to resist management-imposed change would be ended. Thus for political reasons the way was paved for the Bain report and the trap had been set for the FBU leadership.

The union's response to these events was set out in a circular sent to every member on 25 July. It stated that, despite being given every opportunity to do so, the employers had refused to table an offer on firefighters' pay, 'despite on one occasion a commitment to do so'. The letter went on to explain that 'the employers indicated they had indeed been prepared to make an offer on pay at the NJC meeting of 9 July, however Government had told them in no uncertain manner that there would be no new money to fund any offer. As a result they had clearly decided not to make any offer'. The letter showed the extent to which the FBU leadership was both informing and consulting with its members at every stage. The tactics remained clear: 'for the union's part the route in terms of seeking to resolve our pay claim is through dialogue, discussion and negotiation with the genuine aim of avoiding unnecessary confrontation'; and if no 'good faith' offer was made at the scheduled NJC for 2 September, then the FBU leadership would recommend industrial action to the planned recall conference on 12 September (Circular 2002HOC0588AG).

We know from accounts by Andy Gilchrist and later by John Prescott in the House of Commons that they met to discuss the negotiations. This private but not secret meeting on 8 August was an indicator of the depth of the Government's concerns about a possible strike (*Labour Research*, September 2002: 5). John Prescott wanted to know what the FBU wanted, and the union's General Secretary told him they needed an offer to get the negotiations underway. As a result Prescott contacted the employers' side and apparently instructed them to make an offer but to keep it so low that the FBU would have to reject it out of hand. In addition the offer should be in line with other public sector settlements in order to sow doubt in the minds of potential FBU supporters in other unions. Some may be surprised that a set of independently-elected employers from across the political spectrum took their lead from Central Government. The myths of decentralisation, of local democracy, of free negotiations, of each group of workers making a case based on the market and skills, and the Labour Government's concern for public sector workers, were all dispelled in that one moment of *realpolitik* – do as we say or take the consequences, financially and politically. From that moment the Prime Minister, through the ODPM, seemed to take over the dispute: the employers knew it, as did the FBU leadership. As a consequence the union had to recalculate the odds; the employers had to involve themselves in elaborate shows of strength, and the Ministers had to win, as they saw it, this aspect of the battle with their own workers and supporters.

The union leaders were worried but not surprised by the early intervention by Government Ministers, although, given limited industrial action by other Local Government workers, it still seemed an improbable fight for Government to start. In interview Andy Gilchrist stated that:

It would be inappropriate and wrong for us to go directly to Government because we are not employed by Government. What we always knew of course was that if you are employed by the public sector the Government will have a view, particularly if you are looking for a significant rise.

On the role of Government at this time, he stated:

The first time that I ever met John Prescott actually was what I call a very informal one to one ... when the sub-committee meetings had broken down because of the infamous intervention by Government, and we had said, well, in the absence of negotiation we are not going away and we are only left with the one industrial weapon, what do we do? I think then the Government took an interest and I got an invitation to meet John Prescott, who was the nominal head of the Fire Service, being the Deputy Prime Minister ... and that was the first time I had met him. Ruth, Mike and myself together subsequently met with Prescott a number of times to clarify points.

Mike Fordham was more explicit about the intervention of Government and in particular some senior civil servants:

Well ... I'm a 'conspiracist' by nature. I think the role of the civil service within Government acting in this dispute has been particularly powerful and particularly destructive. I think we have a civil service that is not used to the Fire Service, because we changed Government departments about three times in twelve months. We've changed Ministers, we've been all over the place. We had been with the Home Office for most of the time and the Home Office dealt with us in a certain way and we were used to that.

When asked if there was a political guiding mind, he responded:

I think there was. We were dealing with a civil service that we hadn't got any experience of. I've been a national officer for twenty-five years, and hadn't dealt with that type of civil servant before. The Home Office civil servants, honestly, are seriously different people with different backgrounds. They are not what people refer to as career civil servants in the context of the others, and I think therefore we underestimated the politicisation of the new breed of civil servant. There was also a very very close relationship between the civil servants (Clive Norris in particular) and the responsible Minister who was Nick Raynsford.

We also had the problem, which was greater than we had expected, namely the internal politics within New Labour of 10 Downing Street, 11 Downing Street, and Prescott's office. The games that were played at the time behind Minister's backs did not help. I had a particularly close relationship with Ian McCartney and I learnt things about what was going on.

So going back to the claim, the claim was justified. I know that I remain convinced it's justified, but maybe the consequences of the claim weren't thought of. Certainly, and I've had this discussion, I think there was maybe a lack of examination by the executive of the consequences of the claim, certainly by conference. At that stage I don't actually attach any blame to them because we were involved in a campaign. If we say our members are worth £30,000 they are going to say 'yes we are, aren't we?' There was an expectation with the delivery, a massive expectation with the delivery and we built an expectation, we told people we could deliver it, we told them they were worth it, we asked them if they were worth it, they said 'yes, we're worth it!'

AUGUST 2002 – FROM BAD TO WORSE

For most of August the negotiations went nowhere, although there were some contacts at office level. As the clock ticked nobody seemed able or willing to avert a further call for strike action and therefore a ballot. In early August the employers in particular upped the *ante* with increasingly strident calls for the FBU to back off their claim, agree to changes in working practices, and to participate in a joint review of the Service. John Ransford, the LGA's director of education and social policy, was quoted as saying that: 'at a time when other key public service personnel are negotiating far smaller increases, it seems unbelievable that the FBU are holding a gun to the heads of their employers over a wage demand that simply cannot, and would not be met' (*Daily Post* 2.8.02: 5). He was clearly worried by the threat of a fire strike, and he wanted to isolate the FBU and especially its leadership from ordinary public sector workers and their union activists. Elsewhere the employers were reported as putting more and more pressure on Tony Blair to fund a deal in which, on the back of an independent review, modernisation would be traded against pay. The employers knew that this was a very good chance for them to claw back some conditions of service issues from the FBU in exchange for better pay, and were genuinely anxious to get Central Government to join them in seizing the time. More reports suggested the FBU was prepared for strike action (*Guardian* 2.8.02: 7), but all the while there was some correspondence between the two sides as they tested out their relative positions.

The FBU had already set the deadline of 12 September for their Recall Conference and now local FBU groups were gearing up to get in a large strike vote. Matt Lee, chair of the Derbyshire FBU, said: 'the committee decided unanimously that it should recommend its members to support the ballot for national strike action' (*Derby Evening Telegraph* 5.8.02: 5). As the month of August drew to a close there was still no offer from the employers. There was another rally, this time in Belfast, attended by over 3000 determined and good-humoured firefighters – the crowd turned out waving banners and blowing whistles (*Sunday Herald* 25.8.02: 5). Jim Barbour of the FBU restated the union's position:

> we have said all along that we want to avoid confrontation. This remains the case. However, we are absolutely determined that our firefighters should receive the proper salary for the professional job they do. We are not asking for special treatment, but fair treatment (*Belfast News Letter* 22.8.02: 2).

In the last week of August the pressure mounted. The Government ordered Green Goddesses to be prepared and for troops to start training for the eventuality of a strike. As the *Independent* noted, such actions are designed to 'worsen' relations between Government and firefighters (25.8.02: 2); and the *Mirror* reported that: 'Ministers have established Doomsday plans to pulverise the FBU's industrial action planned for October' (26.8.02: 6). Needless to say references were now being made to both the Winter of Discontent in 1978-9 and to the NUM strike of 1984-5.

THE 4 PER CENT POISON CHALICE

The employers sent an interim offer letter to the FBU dated 27 August. They suggested that it had three new elements: a 4% offer, an undertaking to increase that if the inquiry so recommended, and yet another offer to jointly approach Government for the funding (Employers Organisation 2002a: paragraph 3.5). The offer appeared to have been inspired by John Prescott in order to force the FBU leadership to reject it and call for a strike ballot. In the mind of Government, this would create the conditions for an independent review requested by the employers, with the effect of splitting the FBU away from other public sector workers and their unions, and making sure that Central Government now controlled events. The *Morning Star* reacted by reminding its readers that the employers' demand for an inquiry based on modernisation was 'a shorthand for privatisation and job cuts' (29.8.02: 6). For those in any doubt, in June 2002 the Scottish Executive had asked the management consultants Deloitte & Touche to consider a scheme to privatise through Public-Private Partnership (PPP) the Highlands and Islands Fire brigade. The pattern seemed strangely familiar: an under-resourced public service with no new public money and a pay dispute, leading to a call for private money and ownership as the only solution (*Sunday Herald* 23.6.02: 4).

The ploy of a low offer worked. In Scotland, John McDonald of the FBU EC, said: 'when it comes to the employers' proposals, it's disgusting it's taken them three to four months to come back with any kind of response. We're insulted they are offering us a mere four per cent and we don't need an inquiry to know we are not paid enough' (*Daily Record* 29.8.02: 4). In South Wales the FBU executive member, Mike Smith, told the press: 'there is so much frustration at the employers' intransigence and lack of willingness to settle the claim … there have been five meetings so far with the employers but they have been a waste of time' (*South Wales Echo* 30.8.02: 28). Tam McFarlane, regional pay co-ordinator for the south west FBU, said: 'our executive council will consider the proposals of the four per cent offer, as is their duty. But to be honest the offer is little short of derisory' (*Western Morning News* 30.8.02:1). Brian Moss, Staffordshire FBU secretary, added his voice: 'the sense of feeling we have in Staffordshire is that the offer made by the employers so far is unacceptable' (*Sentinel* 30.8.02: 3). And the *Gloucester Citizen* reported that: 'dozens of fire-fighters from Gloucestershire and beyond packed into Hucclecote Rugby Club to hear the latest on pay negotiations … several raised concerns about the prospect of industrial action but following the private meeting the FBU officials said they had been guaranteed 100% support from full-time firefighters, retained firefighters and control crews' (30.8.02: 3).

These reports and many others point to an important element of the dispute and strike to come. Most firefighters were unhappy about taking strike action and were keen to avoid it, but they were completely loyal to the union. The FBU leadership could be confident that they would achieve both a high vote for strike action in the ballot and subsequently total backing for strike action once it started. The hope was that such strong feelings and support would further put pressure on the employers and Ministers to settle. As September came and the stakes were raised this was a realistic way forward, and there was no dissent inside the FBU to any of this.

All of this informed speculation became formal bargaining reality when, at the next scheduled meeting of the NJC on 2 September, the FBU leadership announced that if acceptable offer was not made at that meeting then a Recall National Conference would be held on 12 September to authorise preparations for a national strike.

As Andy Gilchrist recalled:

> What John Prescott found ... actually he found it funny but it made him rather frustrated at the same time was that they [the employers] never made us an offer. Now my point was, tell us what we're worth. I remember him sitting there saying, 'what have they offered you?' I said not a thing. Now he found that, with his trade union background, astonishing. Even if it's going to be insulting and derisory you are duty bound to make some sort of offer. That's why I believe he did actually say to the employers you've got to give the bloke an offer to take to his members when you get to 2 September national joint council.
>
> Then they offered us 4%. We said that's derisory and insulting. I think at some point the employers had been told by Ministers to negotiate us out of a problem. When they were going to offer us £25 grand plus strings, I think somebody in Government said don't you dare do that. Then the employers rightly said, and this is all speculation on my part by the way, well hang on a minute, if we are not going to be allowed to do what you've asked us to do then we are going to do nothing. So we ended up with a daft situation where I couldn't tell our members what was being offered. So I remember John Prescott saying repeatedly, well it's crackers. They've got to make him an offer, and they did on 2 September. They came back with a formal offer from the national council and I think after that the course was set for at least a ballot if not industrial action.

Mike Fordham added about Government activity over the summer:

> Well, we were no longer dealing with an employer who had any say ...they were not the power. It was the classic problem of the monkey and the organ grinder. We were in a position where Government made it clear to us that they had no respect for the employers, no respect whatsoever. Now I'm pretty sure when they met Prescott he probably slagged us off as well, he certainly slagged the employers off big time right up front with us. He showed no respect, and that's for both the

professional employers, as I call them the bureaucrats, the employer's organisation, and the elected employers. Whatever he thought about us he told us anyway to our face that he did have respect for our professional abilities, but he thought the claim was outrageous.

In answer to the direct question: 'So then they came out with the 4% offer which allegedly was prompted by Prescott', he was equally direct with his response: 'yes, he told them to do it'.

SEPTEMBER 2002 – CALL FOR ACTION

As we have seen the employers' response at the 2 September NJC was to make the first concrete offer of 4%. As the employers later stated: 'the positions of the two sides did not change on 2 September, even after an adjournment during the meeting to allow each side to confer privately. The meeting closed with the FBU's general secretary saying that it was quite clear that both sides had a different approach, and that they [the FBU] would now pursue theirs separately' (Employers organisation 2002a: paragraph 3.7). Andy Gilchrist, writing in the *FireFighter,* said of the offer: 'this was for a miserly 4%, thus ignoring the years of inadequate settlements and strongly felt and expressed views of their workforce' (Pay special, September: 3). In face of this provocatively disappointing offer the FBU EC decided to press ahead with the Recall National Conference on 12 September at which it would seek delegates' support for a strike ballot.

Charles Nolda later confirmed this: 'the Government was at first reluctant to commission such an inquiry ... eventually the Government agreed that an inquiry would be set up if talks broke down in the NJC. This meant that the employers would need to make a specific offer in reply to the FBU's claim' (Nolda 2004: 387).

On 3 September Nick Raynsford issued a statement that effectively set up the Bain Commission with its terms of reference. The ODPM's *News Release* (2002.0308) for that day quoted him as saying to the CACFOA organised Fire Conference in London Docklands that: 'one option which has been proposed is for an independent review to consider both fire service pay and modernisation of the Service ... clearly it would be best if all parties participate in the review'. He went on: 'I want to make it crystal clear that there is no reason why a programme of investment plus reform cannot go hand in hand with a fair deal for firefighters'. As the employers recall, 'the following day the negotiating phase was drawn to a close by the Minister's announcement at the Fire Conference that he was minded to set up a Review. When consulted by ODPM on what should be in the Review's terms of reference the employers' chair indicated that they should cover pay and modernisation issues' (Employers Organisation 2002a: paragraph 3.8). Two days later, on 5 September, the formal announcement setting up the Review under George Bain was made. The Minister stated that 'this review provides an alternative to what would be unnecessary and deeply damaging industrial action'. He then outlined the terms of reference in full (ODPM *News Release* 2002.0310). As discussed below, the selection of the chairman and stated terms of reference were made by Government Ministers with no consultation with the FBU, and therefore, as others have said, it could never have been an 'independent' inquiry.

The morale of the FBU membership remained high despite the failure to reach a negotiated settlement. Over a thousand FBU members demonstrated outside the NJC talks on 2 September and it seemed a foregone conclusion to most observers that any Recall National Conference would be unanimous in recommending industrial action in the absence of a realistic offer on which to negotiate. At the following week's TUC conference, delegates voted unanimously for the following statement moved by General Secretary John Monks on 10 September:

> After receiving a report from the General Secretary of the Union the TUC General Council today expressed their full support for the FBU in their campaign for a new fair pay deal in the Fire Service. Britain's firefighters deliver a crucial service that is enormously valued by the British people. They know that if a disaster strikes their firefighters will be there to help, whatever the dangers, prepared to put their lives on the line. As the Local Government have accepted, the formula by which Fire Services pay has been set for the last quarter of a century is now out of date. The FBU have made clear throughout, their wish to avoid industrial action. The employers should come to the negotiating table without delay to reach a fair and just settlement so that a deeply damaging industrial dispute can be avoided. The TUC will be briefing all its affiliates on the issues involved in the FBU's pay campaign. The General Secretary has been asked to keep in close touch with the FBU in the days and weeks ahead and the TUC will be doing its utmost to promote a fair settlement for all Fire Service workers (TUC 2002: 35).

It was the Congress chaired by Sir Tony Young, who the following week was appointed to the Bain Review team, a review that effectively blocked the search for a negotiated settlement for three months, and provoked rather than prevented strikes.

Tony Blair addressed public sector reform and his notion of what constitutes modern trade unionism in his speech to the TUC. After explaining to sceptical delegates that Saddam's weapons of mass destruction posed an immediate threat to world peace, he went on to offer a rather one-sided notion of building a partnership in order to reform the public services.

He started by saying 'we are modernising the whole welfare state' (*ibid*: 113); he then said: 'We will listen to you on genuine concerns about the workforce conditions. I ask you in return to listen to us on the need for reform'. Here the Prime Minister can be seen to be limiting the trade union role to that of protecting conditions of service. There was no inkling of genuine social partnership in which the workforce delivering services could, through their union, influence the content and implementation of reform. Then he turned his attention to the so-called awkward squad. He said:

> I simply say it would be ironic if just at the moment that trade unions were achieving such a partnership some of you turned your back on it ... It happened in 1948, in 1969 and in 1979. The result then was the folding of the Labour Government and the return of a Tory Government. Not this time. It will just be less influence with a Labour Government (*ibid*: 114).

So here were the two central messages from the Prime Minister: we intend to press ahead with public sector reform in the way we determine and you will have no say on central strategic questions; and we will simply ignore alternative views, partly because we know that there is no credible Parliamentary or electoral opposition. What Mr Blair neglected to tell his audience is that in 1948, in 1969 and in 1979 it was precisely at the stage when the Labour Government stopped listening to the views of the unions that its electoral prospects plummeted. These were all incomes policy years – years in which a Labour Government responded to failures of its own economic policies by asking organised workers to take cuts in the purchasing power of their wages and salaries. In every case workers protested, the TUC eventually got round to opposing such policies, and mass disillusionment was translated into Labour abstentions or Tory votes at the following elections. Labour did not 'fold' as Blair claims – they were defeated at the ballot box.

Blair's speech was made two days before the first FBU Recall Conference, which voted unanimously to proceed to a ballot of the membership recommending strike action should the existing 4% offer not be substantially increased. In the previous week the Government had moved extremely quickly and without proper consultation to appoint the Bain Commission following the FBU EC's rejection of the employers' first concrete offer. Throughout August the Government had maintained that the FBU pay claim was a matter to be resolved within the NJC, with the totally unrealistic proviso that any settlement had to meet existing budgets and plans for public expenditure for the rest of the Spending Review period. Such restrictions prevented the employers from making an offer which could even form the basis for negotiations, and since they were not prepared to join with the FBU to put a united Fire Service case to the Government, they felt compelled to hand the responsibility over to Central Government via a so-called Independent Review.

During the summer the Civil Contingencies Committee (a Cabinet committee set up in 2001 in the wake of fuel protests, flooding and the foot and mouth outbreak) was actively planning its fire cover assuming that a strike was likely. The Civil Contingencies Secretariat ... is a co-ordinating body and centre of expertise for improving the resilience of Central Government and the UK in the face of disruptive challenges that can lead to crisis. It also supports the Civil Contingencies Committee, chaired by the Home Secretary' (www.continuitycentral.com).

The Civil Contingencies Committee has a response co-ordination facility codenamed Cobra, and it was Cobra's role to activate and oversee the implementation of the Government's contingency plan to provide alternative fire cover in the event of a strike. This plan became known as 'Operation Fresco'. During the strikes some 18,600 members of the armed forces were deployed in firefighting duties, using a rather ancient fleet of Green and Red Goddesses (yellow in Northern Ireland), fire appliances, and working a two twelve-hour shift system. All these personnel received at least one week's basic training in firefighting, topped up before the dispute (Pyper 2003: 493-4, Burchill 2004: 414).

These contingency plans worked fairly well during the strike periods with 9,300 personnel deployed on each twelve-hour shift (against the normal deployment of around 9,000 whole time firefighters on each shift; but with an attendance record of around 40% of that carried out by FBU members, productivity was well down. The Government made some attempt to use Cobra's experience as a justification for introducing joint control rooms and for cutting night cover, but this proved rather short-lived in face of FBU counter claims and professional scepticism.

Two days after the TUC Congress debate, delegates representing FBU members from all brigades met in Manchester to take stock of the situation. The outcome was never in doubt, as speaker after speaker reported that the membership was ready and able to go into the second national strike in the union's history. Delegates voted unanimously in support of an EC resolution calling for a ballot authorising national strike action in support of the four-point pay claim submitted at the end of May.

DISCONTINUOUS ACTION – A TACTIC FOR OUR TIMES

An important decision to be made was what type of action was to be asked for on the ballot paper. A large majority of activists reported back to the EC that an indefinite strike was not in favour with the membership, and that the overwhelming preference was for discontinuous action. This meant a few days here and a few days there. A tiny minority in the union did feel that an indefinite strike was a better tactical option, but at this time it was a view with little support. The benefits of discontinuous action appeared to be that it kept the employers on the hop, it allowed for flexible interchange of action and negotiations, and it meant members' loss of pay was less hard to bear. When I asked him about the on-off discontinuous action, John McGhee replied:

> Most of the members I met during the dispute understood at the time why we cancelled particular strikes, and that was fine if we were talking with the employers, the members didn't want to go on strike. They were happy if we were talking that is what they wanted to hear. There was a group of people who never liked the decision ... people like that exist in every dispute. You take a ballot and are going on strike and that's it. There were those who thought our strike was going to lead to a revolution in the public sector. Why would we do that? But the majority of members were pleased that we never took them out on strike when we were negotiating.

Ruth Winters also made clear the position when I asked her the reasons for that tactic:

> Well one reason was quite clear. We were being told that our members weren't up for an all-out strike. Another was that discontinuous action – which you can use as and when – allows you to be more flexible. When you suspend an all-out strike that's a different inference ... we'd used it in local strikes and the executive had discussed for months what kind of discontinuous action to take. In the Essex strikes they were using on-off hours. In the Merseyside strike they were using days here and there, and then changed over to shifts, and then they upped it to an 'eight-dayer'. But when you talk about a local authority it's totally, totally different from a national strike, and that's why we discarded it in terms of that particular way of doing.

In contrast, Mike Fordham, however, noted the difficulties of discontinuous action in a national dispute:

> we've had discontinuous strike action in brigade disputes that have been successful in Essex, Merseyside, Derbyshire and elsewhere. One of the things we only learnt while running a national dispute, is that it is very different from running an industrial dispute with a regional employer. Apart from anything else the Government's role in it is different; and the whole issue of communication is different. The strategy of discontinuous action does allow negotiations between days out ... but it also allows the employers to say we're not talking to you while there is a threat of strike over us. Now, they didn't do that to us in the local disputes in Essex and Merseyside, but they did do it in the national dispute. We then came under pressure to call off strikes because there were talks taking place. So

it was a tactic that worked well for us at first, but the employer learned how to turn it to their advantage. The biggest problem with discontinuous action is the lack of togetherness and the difficulty of communicating. When we were on the picket lines for nine weeks in 1977 we were together, it was a very close atmosphere. To be honest it was great atmosphere, a good dispute to be in, a good dispute. When you are there for on off, on off, different people on off, and all the rest of, it's not that same spirit.

Andy Gilchrist was reconciled to the outcome:

> when the EC decided to run a ballot for discontinuous action that was not my favoured option. All out continuous action was my option. It was clear, from the Executive, that we might have got a majority for that but not a big enough one to sustain an indefinite national strike. I think people too easily forget that. What we knew we could get was a big majority for discontinuous action. Now this was not a mistake, this was people looking at things compared to what we had done before. Discontinuous action had been immensely successful in Essex in particular and Merseyside ... against a local authority that didn't want to face strike action.
>
> So although I was saying 'hard and fast' early on, I was already thinking we need to get a negotiated settlement. That's why we put the message into my sound bites – give us an offer and we'll look at it.

The EC was in no doubt that a big majority 'yes' vote was almost a certainty. The case had been made, the activists were up for it, and the feeling of injustice among the rank and file members was palpable. Not many expected the full £30,000 but most felt that as long as firefighters and control room staff made their feelings clear and stayed united then the justice of their case would sooner or later persuade the Government to think again. Accordingly the EC began to put in place a strike strategy in anticipation of a big 'yes' vote, so that the momentum gained by a democratic mandate could be seized. Previous experience in local disputes as well as the national strike of 1977 had shown industrial action short of striking to be ineffective. Work to rules, which effectively meant dealing with emergency calls only, had failed to move employers in the past, since their only statutory duty was to protect the public against death or injury from fire. For all the lip service given to Community Fire Safety and Fire Prevention in its broadest sense, neither the employers nor the Government saw the withdrawal of these services as of serious concern.

By now it was front page news even in *The Times*, which reported that strikes were almost certain to start in October: 'the Government is preparing to buy off Britain's firefighters with an interim pay deal to avoid a national strike that could divert thousands of troops now preparing for war against Iraq' (13.9.02:1). Kevin Maguire, writing in *The Guardian* on the same day, considered the dispute to be 'the most serious industrial threat to Tony Blair since 1997', and quoted both Sir Jeremy Beecham (head of the LGA) and Nick Raynsford, condemning the union's claim and urging it to join in the review (13.9.02: 2).

PREPARING TO STRIKE

Once the 12 September Recall Conference had supported the EC's recommendation to ballot for strike action, a number of organisational decisions were activated. The media reported a 51,849 to 0 majority in favour of the recommendation to strike, and that none of the twenty speakers from the 242 delegates had spoken against the decision or the strategy. Under the banner headline 'firefighters roar for strike action', the *Morning Star* reported both the unanimous support for a strike vote and that: 'Ministers have already worked out a strike breaking strategy and are planning a union bashing propaganda campaign' (13.9.02: 1). Elsewhere reports indicated that the vote was intended to force the employers back to the negotiating table to achieve a realistic settlement (*Independent* 13.9.02: 1).

Andy Gilchrist was quoted as saying that the Bain inquiry was 'a dangerous distraction' (*Morning Star* 13.9.02:1), and Mike Fordham added: 'pay and conditions of service is solely the property of the NJC for Local Authority Fire Brigades and has nothing whatsoever to do with the Government' (*Labour Research* September 2002: 5). In anticipation of the FBU's opposition to Bain, Nick Raynsford urged them to 'submit their case to the review and avoid a damaging and dangerous strike' (ODPM *News Release* 2002.0316). His version of the Government case was that, while it was up to the parties to settle their dispute, yet once it was clear (when this occurred he does not say) that a settlement was unlikely, then the Government had a duty (to whom is unclear) to intervene.

The FBU decided to produce a National Strike Bulletin to go out to stations several times a week and to set up a National Pay Campaign Co-ordinating Committee with representatives from every Region and Section. Each region was expected to replicate this form of organisation. A number of unions, notably UNISON, RMT and ASLEF, provided assistance with specialist help, and printing and mailing operations whenever required. Particular attention was given to relations with the media.

POLITICAL LOBBYING

A number of initiatives were taken to promote the campaign with MPs, Members of the Scottish Parliament (MSPs), Members of the Welsh Assembly (MWAs), and members of the Northern Ireland Assembly. The results were mixed. Jim Quinn, the chair of the Northern Ireland FBU, told me that the Northern Ireland Assembly, following extensive lobbying by the union, gave the campaign unanimous support. Unfortunately it was stood down early on in the dispute and replaced by a direct rule administration. In Scotland friendly MSPs blocked attempts to repeal Section 19 of the 1947 Fire Act. This was reported in issue 25 of the strike bulletin, which had noted that a coalition of SNP, Liberal Democrats, Scottish Socialists and rebel Labour members had combined to narrowly defeat the Scottish Executive. John McDonald (EC member for Scotland) told me that political support was patchy – although the outrageous attack on the FBU by Dr Richard Simpson, the deputy justice Minister, did lead to his resignation. At a business dinner he had called striking fire-fighters 'fascist bastards'. Unfortunately for him this was widely reported (*Express* 27.11.02:14).

In Wales the devolved Assembly was kept fully abreast of events, and individual Assembly members interceded with the ODPM to urge that he use his good offices to promote a negotiated settlement. The *FireFighter* strike bulletin issue 15 announced the launch of a FBU support group amongst Labour MPs, which would be convening local community meetings, launching petitions and opposing reforms that mean job cuts. This group were particularly effective during the main debates in Parliament on the dispute and Fire Bill. Alan Simpson confirmed this in interview with me, as did Paul Routledge:

> the firefighters' dispute is the cause of much coming and going at Westminster. The day after both sides went to ACAS, leaders of the FBU came in for secret discussions with the Parliamentary Labour Party trade union group. The group's chairman, Tony Lloyd ... refused to say anything, but we may assume it was a much-needed fence-mending exercise. Ian McCartney, the Minister assigned by No 10 to act as a go-between, was busily ingratiating himself with the union, having previously accused its leader, Andy Gilchrist, of 'losing the plot'. And friendly noises, too, from John Prescott. When Ken Cameron, the former FBU leader, came into Strangers' bar for a quick snort, the DPM (as he loves to be known) was soon on the terrace with him, exchanging Anglo-Saxon pleasantries (*New Statesman*, 12.9.02: 14).

Andy Gilchrist pointed out the efforts made to brief politicians and to win their support:

> it was very important. There were two groups in particular we met with: the Campaign Group of Labour MPs and the trade union group. We gave them stand-up presentations about where we were ... the Campaign Group were the people who asked the difficult questions of Ministers, but we got surprising support across the Parliamentary Labour Party from all manner of people who understood the morality of our case. Some still had a problem with how we were doing it, by being

on strike. We did meet the Liberal Democrats and in all fairness we didn't do very much in Westminster with the Conservatives because we felt that was probably a pointless exercise. Now the Liberal guy turned out to be completely ignorant in terms of the Fire Service and so he proved no worth at all. What we did manage to generate was a sizeable reaction among the backbenchers of the Labour Party, which was of considerable embarrassment to Ministers at the time. And we did a lot of what I call the famous informal briefing: we sent loads of papers, there was a lot of meeting up with key people and saying this is how it really is, this is what's going on tomorrow, this is happening next week.

Every member of the British House of Commons received direct mail from the union at crucial times during the campaign, and the General Secretary addressed full meetings of the Trade Union Group of Labour MPs on two occasions. The Socialist Campaign Group of MPs gave regular support to the union and the FBU was able to place Parliamentary Questions, as well as giving a number of MPs extensive briefings before important debates on the Fire Service.

In the House of Lords, Baroness Turner and Lords McCarthy, Wedderburn and Lea were extremely helpful in pushing union-friendly amendments to the draconian Fire Services Bill that threatened the right to strike. Although these amendments were unsuccessful they put down important markers for the future by obtaining assurances from Ministers that the Act was not intended to be used to block strikes which are otherwise lawful.

BOYCOTT BAIN

Following the rejection of the employers' 4% offer in early September 2002 the Government in the person of Nick Raynsford moved swiftly in support of the LGA's request to set up an inquiry into the future of the Fire Service. Prescott announced that he was setting up an inquiry, as requested by the employers, into pay and modernisation in the Fire Service, and invited the union to give evidence and present its views on the inquiry's terms of reference. The EC quickly decided that such an inquiry was a distraction from the need to find a negotiated settlement. It therefore determined not to have anything to do with it. This decision of the FBU leadership to not only boycott the inquiry but to actively attack its existence, its terms of reference and its membership was in line with its stated policy.

The FBU issued a ten-point statement entitled 'Why not trust the Government inquiry?' They argued that the inquiry was too broad and covered 'modernisation' as well as pay; it could add nothing to existing knowledge, given that they had already buried the findings of previous inquiries such as the one on Emergency Cover; and there was no promise to fund any pay increase. There were other more tactical reasons for rejection – the fact that the idea came from the employers;

that the timing of the announcement by Government indicated that it was there to delay action and take the momentum away from the union; that its terms favoured the employers because they emphasised the trade off of modernisation against pay increases, and that the FBU felt it could not trust a Government pretending to allow the employers to negotiate while pulling their strings. Indeed some specific 'old chestnuts' from the employers were included within the terms of reference, such as cutting night-time crewing levels. The composition of the committee and the speed of its deliberations – it was to take weeks rather than the months required – also suggested that the civil servants would dominate its findings and write its conclusions in line with Government policy. This position was repeated in the media resource information circular sent out by John McGhee on 24 September to all Brigade Secretaries and Chairs (2002HOC0803JMcG).

It was difficult to see how 'independent' the report would be. Finally, of course, the FBU leadership could not be seen to join with an initiative that they had attacked since its first flotation. Rodney Bickerstaffe, who had been approached to sit as the trade union representative on the inquiry, told me that he felt the FBU had no option but to reject the basis of the inquiry at the time. This view was repeated much later by Lord McCarthy, who felt that as neither the terms of reference nor the chair of the inquiry had been agreed it could not be seen as independent of Government. On the other hand both the lead LGA negotiators, Phil White and Charles Nolda, and the then Deputy General Secretary of the TUC, Brendan Barber, told me in interview that had the FBU joined in it was possible that more pay would have been forthcoming, without posing problems for Government in terms of other 'me-too' claims. All the activists we interviewed shared the views of EC member John McDonald that there 'was no need for Bain', and the leadership's rejection of Bain was fully supported, according to Matt Wrack, by the London regional committee of the union.

Charles Nolda told me that he wanted the FBU to join Bain, but 'Bain without the FBU was better than no Bain for us'; and Phil White added, 'it would have been best to have them on board but not having them on board was not a show-stopper'. Later they admitted that:

> the reason we had asked for an inquiry was because we had hoped to be boxed in, we hoped to avoid having to answer the very difficult question 'what is a firefighter worth?'. Which is the question that the FBU were asking us. It's a very difficult question to answer and we really didn't want to answer that question in the public gaze ... and we were hoping that in time-honoured fashion a committee with the FBU's involvement would come up with a judgement.

The Times, now fully on board with regard to attacking both the FBU and the Government's handling of the dispute, reported that:

> John Prescott decided yesterday to press ahead with an independent review of the firefighters' pay despite fierce opposition from union leaders ... The Deputy Prime Minister had hoped to avoid a 'deeply damaging' strike by securing firefighters' support for the review, which will look at pay and modernisation of working practices. Nick Raynsford, his deputy, said that the Government would impose the review with or without co-operation from the union (6.9.02: 9).

On the same day, but with less fanfare and coverage, the FBU's East Sussex Brigade Secretary, Jim Parrott, sent an open letter to the editor of the local paper in which he argued that the FBU had rejected the Government's offer of an independent review of Fire Service pay and conditions because the reviews had already taken place. He claimed that since 1999 there had been eight reviews of the Fire Service. So another review would add nothing new and therefore was seen to be just a device to wrong-foot the union.

By the 20 September the inquiry team was in place. It consisted of Professor Sir George Bain (the chairman), Sir Michael Lyons and Sir Anthony (known as Tony) Young. Sir Michael Lyons was formerly Chief Executive of Birmingham City Council and is now Professor of Public Policy at Birmingham University. Tony Young was the Senior Deputy General Secretary of the Communication Workers Union, which subsequently criticised his involvement in the Inquiry. The three have much in common: none had any experience in the Fire Service and all three had received knighthoods under the New Labour Government. Ken Cameron was amongst many trade union leaders unimpressed by this threesome, and limited attempts to get Rodney Bickerstaffe involved came to nothing when he refused to be considered if the FBU themselves were unwilling to participate in the inquiry.

But more important than the inquiry's make-up were its terms of reference and the timescale given to complete it. The terms of reference were as follows:

> Having regard to the changing and developing role of the Fire Service in the United Kingdom, to inquire into and make recommendations on the future organisation and management of the Fire Service to:
>
> Enable it to undertake the full range of responsibilities that are appropriate to it;
>
> Enable it to respond effectively to all the operational demands that may be placed upon it;
>
> Enable the responsibilities of the Fire Service to be delivered with optimum efficiency and effectiveness.

In the context of the above, such recommendations should include considerations as to,

> The pay levels and conditions of service that are appropriate taking full account of the wider context of pay arrangements, levels and their affordability across the economy;

> The most appropriate arrangements for determining future pay and conditions of service of whole time firefighters, retained firefighters, voluntary firefighters and fire control room staff.

If the inquiry was to serve any purpose at all in resolving the dispute then the review group would need to report within a few months. The terms of reference made it extremely difficult for the FBU leadership to play an active part in the review process, because they made it clear that appropriate pay levels should take into account the 'wider context' and 'their affordability across the economy'.

The FBU knew full well that these conditions effectively ruled out recommendations in line with the union's main argument – that FBU members' pay failed to reflect, or even come close to, the rate for the job they did for society. The terms of reference also made pay improvements conditional on changes to working practices, which had been flagged up by the employers over the last decade and a half. 'Optimum efficiency' and 'effectiveness' were seen as management-speak for cuts, overtime, increased casualisation of hours, and more day-shift only stations. The FBU had long signed up for a risk-based Fire Service with more local control and greater flexibility in the use of resources, but this was in the context of the *Pathfinder* approach of an expanding service with substantial increases in investment and many more whole-time stations.

Not surprisingly, the FBU leadership saw the Bain inquiry as an attempt to get both the employers and the Government off the hook. Time and again FBU negotiators had asked employers and Ministers to tell them what they thought a firefighter was worth and then to negotiate a settlement. Now the EC felt they were being faced with a Government-appointed inquiry which, by its terms and reference, could award no more than 4% without strings, and might well go on to fundamentally challenge many of the conditions of service and FBU policies (such as the overtime ban) which members greatly valued. The union was also acutely aware of the absurdity within the terms of reference. The last Government-sponsored inquiry into the overall management of the Fire Service (the Holroyd Committee 1970) had taken three and a half years to complete its report, and it had not been faced with the complications of an industrial dispute. Now Bain was being given less than three and a half months, with somewhat broader terms of reference than Holroyd, to complete a similar exercise. The result was easy to predict. Bain could do no more than reheat the many existing reports (mainly produced in the Thatcher years) under the guidance of a Civil Service secretariat wedded to the approach of the Audit Commission Report of 1995 (*In the Line of Fire*), whose main thrust was to end constant crewing in the interests of greater flexibility. Indeed, in his letter to the Deputy Prime Minister of 16 December accompanying the final report, Bain said this: 'The purpose of the Review was not to conduct a root and branch examination of the Fire Service; there was not time for this. Nor was there a need. The major issues facing the service have been well documented in a series of reports over many years'.

In effect Bain was used by the Government to hold the line on public sector pay and to promote a particular version of modernisation, with increased overtime and casual on-call working at its core. Bain did not hold off industrial action. So whatever the merits or demerits of the arguments and conclusions in the Bain report, our view is that the act of commissioning itself was aimed at dislodging the FBU from the high ground of their case; it therefore was part of the employers' and Government's negotiating tactics against the union. It was to be expected that the FBU would reject it, and it seems odd that the employers were surprised by such a rejection. Even if Government Ministers had wrongly believed that the FBU would sign up to Bain, they were happy to take the opportunity of the union's opposition to paint the leadership as unreasonable.

Indeed the Government seemed determined to string out the negotiations until Bain reported. So the three and a half months between the employer's offer of 2 September and the publication of Bain on 16 December were wasted as far as the search for a negotiated settlement was concerned. The overwhelming majority of stoppages occurred during this hiatus, at some considerable cost to the public purse and with increased risk to public safety. Predictably enough, Bain also produced a straitjacket, restricting the possibilities for negotiators, particularly on the employers' side. Indeed, at one stage the employers made any offer conditional on the union accepting Bain in full.

The inquiry was expected to report before Christmas 2002. All this confirmed the EC's views that such an inquiry could neither be independent nor assist in resolving the dispute. The terms of reference were too broad as far as the future management of the Fire Service was concerned, but they were very narrow on pay: Bain's recommendation would need to fall within current Government pay policy for the public sector, and be directly linked to the perceived savings available from a 'modernisation' programme of job cuts. In essence, any increase in pay above the going public sector rate would have to be self-financing through cuts to establishment levels and services. This is the straitjacket the Government put Bain into, and the timescale involved meant that the inquiry could not possibly carry out its remit to review the management of the UK's Fire Service. So it was almost a foregone conclusion that Bain would produce a report that replicated all the cost cutting notions of the Thatcher/Major years, in particular those from *In the Line of Fire*, while making any above cost of living pay rises conditional on acceptance of the cuts agenda.

Meanwhile the union concentrated on finding a negotiated settlement, but Bain was now a roadblock to this, as the employers and Government played for time, waiting on the convenience of the three knights. However the results of the strike ballot served to concentrate minds on all sides. On 27 September ballot papers were sent to all FBU members; a few days before John McGee had circulated local FBU Brigade officers with a media information pack, containing a clear case on the substantive changes in the nature of the job, a clear message from the majority of the public in support of the pay claim, the strongest possible case for parity for control room staff and retained firefighters, and a rebuttal of the argument that the costs of funding the claim would escalate throughout the economy leading to pay chaos and inflation. It was particularly strong on the reasons not to trust the Bain inquiry: 'how can we trust an inquiry with no finish date and no commitment to fund any pay increase for firefighters? How can we trust the "independence" of an inquiry when the Government has already made clear that there is no new money? ... Why should we trust this inquiry when the Government used the same tactic to trick the Prison Officers?' (Circular 2002HOC0803JMcG).

The FBU had already on 12 September officially informed the Clerks to all Fire Authorities of a notice to ballot under section 226A of the 1992 Trade Union and Labour Relations (Consolidation) Act. In a four-page letter attached, Andy Gilchrist argued the case once more:

> it has been made clear on your behalf that nothing can be agreed until everything is agreed. The position is summarised in a letter sent by Ted George, the Chair of the Fire Service National Employers to the deputy Prime Minister on 23 July 2002. In that letter Mr George makes it clear that: 'the national employers ... are prepared to discuss the possibility of increases in fire service pay but ... this would be subject to wider negotiations that delivered the Employers' ... modernisation agenda'.

He went on to say that since there was no more money there could not be a negotiated settlement, and therefore only an independent inquiry backed by Government could deliver the extra funding and so avoid a strike. The FBU, by rejecting the employers' national position, also endorsed by Charles Nolda in a letter to Andy Gilchrist on 27 August, could now lawfully have a trade dispute with each Fire Authority, since each one had agreed to stick by the national position of their representatives on the NJC.

On 27 September the ballot papers went out with the question: 'Are you prepared to take part in industrial action consisting of a strike?'

OCTOBER 2002 – VOTE 'YES' AND TALK MORE

'Firefighters' union gets massive vote for action' (*Labour Research* November 2002: 5). The ballot result was announced on Friday 18 October. On a huge 83.5% turn out, 87.6% voted for strike action. In Northern Ireland, where papers were counted separately, an astonishing 96.6% voted to strike. This was unprecedented support, in a ballot where every paper went to members' homes and was returned directly to the independent Electoral Reform Society for validation and counting.

The EC moved quickly and announced on that same Friday what it called the first series of strike dates. These amounted to six periods of strike action between the end of October and Christmas Eve. They started with two forty-eight hour strikes, planned for 29 October and 2 November, and finished with four eight-day strikes starting on 6 November, followed by another three eight-day strikes with four days non-striking in-between. They deliberately excluded 5 November and the Christmas period, traditionally days when public safety is at the greatest risk from fire damage. The first response from Government was not encouraging. Later, some FBU activists when interviewed wondered why the EC had announced the dates so far in advance since, they argued, that gave time for the employers and Government to prepare for cover and feed the media with anti-FBU stories. At the time of the announcements such objectors were silent, and in any case legal aspects of strike taking meant dates had to be set. In addition it was part of the bargaining tactics of the union that by setting dates the FBU appeared as responsible as it could, and it gave a further chance of movement on the offer because the threat of action was now so real.

On the day the strikes were announced, John Prescott stormed out of a Press Conference when questioned about the dispute, and on the same evening Nick Raynsford labelled firefighters as criminals, a statement he later withdrew. Ted George, the chair of the national employers' group, reacted quickly by denouncing the pay claim as 'unrealistic, unaffordable, unreasonable and unjustified' (*Evening Standard* 17.10.02:15). In contrast, FBU regions were issuing advice to strike committees: 'All branches should have established strike committees ... a branch strike committee should include representatives of each watch ... [they] will need to consider picket rotas, press liaison, fund raising, branch finances, hardship cases, and contact with local unions' (*FBU Organiser – official strike bulletin of the London region* 18.10.02).

Meanwhile the Bain inquiry was taking evidence, as pressure grew to produce an interim report (later called a 'position' paper) with recommendations on pay. The one-sided nature of the evidence was further emphasised when 'the independent chair of the NJC was invited to give evidence to the review body but declined to do so. It was felt that given the position of the FBU submission of evidence would jeopardise the independence of the Chair in any subsequent negotiations' (Burchill 2004: 411). Indeed Frank Burchill went further in informal conversations with us, indicating his distaste for the inquiry and its threat to both the negotiations and the future of national bargaining through the NJC.

As a result of the overwhelming strike ballot for industrial action, employers and the Government were forced to reconsider their positions, and talks resumed between the union and both these parties. To assist this process the FBU Executive called off strikes planned to begin on 29 October (forty-eight hours), 2 November (forty-eight hours) and 6 November (eight days), in line with their avowed negotiating strategy and the original Conference motion (IDS *Report* November 2002: 4). The extent of Government intervention was clear: 'contacts initiated by the Deputy Prime Minister resulted in the FBU cancelling the first two blocks of their planned industrial action, in return for the employers agreeing to meet them in the NJC on 30 and 31 October' (Nolda 2004: 387).

The last week of October proved to be one of intense activity, behind as well as in front of the scenes. The FBU leadership, armed with an unequivocal vote in favour of strikes, had reasonable grounds to believe that large sections of the trade union movement supported them, because of the official position of the TUC and the active backing of a number of individual unions. They were supported by all the main rail unions, the safety of whose members might be affected during a firefighters' strike. Indeed the press were full of potential horror stories: 'the country will be plunged into chaos ... rail services will be cancelled ... high rise buildings may have to be evacuated and hospitals and other public services will have to put into practice emergency procedures ... motorists in particular will be at risk ... London Underground has said 19 stations will close' (*Daily Mail* 19.10.02: 6). There were also threats to sporting events, especially football matches. In the event none of this materialised, save for the closure of some central London tube stations.

In addition, trades councils up and down the country backed their local FBU, as did an important section of Labour politicians and activists. This went hand in hand with public support and local sympathetic press coverage. The employers had punted all on the Bain inquiry and stood behind that, urging the FBU to wait for its findings and then join with them in asking Government to fund the recommendations. The Government itself played more complicated games, with a good-guy/bad-guy act from the Prime Minister and his Deputy leading to endless speculation as to the extent to which it was an act. Certainly it was Tony Blair at first, later backed by his Chancellor, who appeared to take the hardest line.

It was the statement made by John Prescott to the House of Commons on 22 October that concentrated the public and media attention onto the dispute for the next two months. From that point the firefighters dominated the national and local news, brought into focus the political predilections of senior Government decision-makers, tested the resolve and unity of both the FBU and the wider trade union movement, and demonstrated where the balance of power lay in Britain in 2002. The statement and subsequent debate raised many relevant points concerning how the dispute had got this far, and what was now happening. One major issue was the extent to which, if at all, the Government had intervened, and the reasons for such intervention. This is important, because a critical part of policy with regard to the public services is the extent to which such services are 'free' to manage their own affairs independently of Central Government. Indeed, a central plank of New Labour – and a view that was problematic for old Labour as well as the Thatcher Tories, is a denial of the centralising tendency of the state. It controls but does not manage, and it manages but does not own. Prescott therefore started with this point:

> fire service pay is the responsibility of their employers, the local fire authorities, and the Fire Brigades Union. The negotiating process started earlier this year and the FBU lodged its claim on 28 May. It demanded a 40 per cent, no-strings-attached pay increase for firefighters, a 50 per cent increase for control room staff and a review of the 1978 formula that governed their wages (col 125).

He went on:

> the employers responded to the FBU's claim by indicating that any significant pay increase had to be matched by modernisation. But little progress was made over the summer because the FBU refused to consider the employers' modernisation proposals.

In reality no progress was made because the employers refused to make an offer before 2 September:

> I want to be particularly clear on one point about the negotiations over the summer: at no point did the Government intervene in the negotiating process. Sir Jeremy Beecham, the leader of the Local Government Association, has made that clear on numerous occasions. I made it absolutely clear that we had played no part in the negotiations when I met Andy Gilchrist on 8 August. He accepted the Government's position, but made it clear he wanted a 40 per cent increase and no inquiry (col 125).

Now comes the case for intervention. Prescott continued:

On 2 September the employers offered the FBU a 4 per cent increase, plus an agreement to establish a new formula that would link increases in firefighters' pay to increases in the economy in general. The employers also invited the FBU to join them in asking for an independent review to be established. They also gave an undertaking that any increase in pay agreed by the review would be backdated to the 7 November pay settlement date. By any standards that was a reasonable offer. Nonetheless, the FBU rejected it (col 125).

The Deputy PM then reached the punch line:

> it became clear that there was no prospect of a solution being found through the normal negotiating process. The employers made it clear that the negotiations had broken down, and requested a Government review. In those circumstances, the House will recognise that the Government could not stand aside. Fire disputes are different from most disputes. People's lives are put at risk and the Government have a responsibility to secure people's safety. So we acted quickly and decisively (col 125/6).

So at this time his claim is that the Government intervened in two ways: through the setting up of the Bain inquiry and by preparing the Army to cover striking firefighters. He also claims the reason for the interventions was a failure of the negotiating process for which he blamed the FBU entirely. MP's questions centred on certain important aspects of the case. First was the question of when the Government intervened. David Davis for the Tories claimed that he had been told that the Deputy PM had been involved in informal talks with Local Government leaders on 3 July during the LGA conference, and 'as a result of that intervention, the employers failed to meet their commitment to make an offer by 9 July' (col 129). Prescott's rebuttal was clear: 'I did not interfere in any way with the firefighters' negotiations' (col 129). This is not a view shared by the FBU leadership.

Other points that emerged included a discussion about the independence of the Bain inquiry, and in particular the speed with which it would finish its deliberations. Two aspects were discussed with regard to the inquiry itself. First, the delay in setting it up in the first place. The employers had been asking for an enquiry since the early summer but Government only agreed in early September. Prescott explained:

> when the General Secretary saw me in mid-August he was complaining that the employers had not made any offer and that there was to be a meeting in September. It seemed ridiculous that the employers had not made any offer. We made it clear that they should make an offer to find out whether the firemen would accept it (col 130).

In answer to a question from the Labour MP Elfyn Llwyd on this issue he replied that it was 'silly' that no offer had been made and that therefore there had been no chance for the FBU to reply. He added that after the 8 August meeting with Andy Gilchrist he spoke to the local authority negotiators and subsequently an offer was made. (That offer was pitched so low as to make FBU rejection certain and thus the Government could claim that negotiations had broken down and announce the inquiry.)

Secondly, some MPs sympathetic to the FBU, such as Alan Simpson, urged that the Bain report be accelerated to help negotiations. Others, such as Andrew Miller, referred to the 1972 Wilberforce inquiry into miners' pay which had taken only eight days to complete its work (Hughes and Moore 1972, Ashworth 1986: 309-311). There was also some concern about the conduct of the strike if it got underway. MPs raised questions about safety arrangements with Green Goddesses, about adherence to the TUC code of conduct that governed disputes with the potential to endanger public safety, and about the role of the RFU and those wishing to work.

A further issue of interest that was touched upon, which became a major feature later, was the costs of the strike, the settlement and of modernisation. John Prescott put the argument against funding the claim like this: 'if £450 million were to come out of the local authority budget, the money would basically be coming from other people's wages and conditions' (col 135). He later poured scorn on the FBU argument that a better paid and trained workforce would save about £600 million in fire damage: 'unless the insurance companies have discovered a way of transferring dividends to the Government in order to meet a wage requirement, however, that does not seem a sensible way of dealing with the problem' (col 140). He also made much of the wider Local Government pay settlement of 7.9% over two years, as the going rate; it was what Government stood firm on. An interesting point for a Government concerned with free labour markets and loose ties with public services!

The next few days saw increased speculation in political circles as to how the PM would deal with the issue, and whether the trade union movement when it came to the crunch would allow the FBU to become isolated. A number of strands emerged. Other unions made loud noises that a firefighters' strike raised safety issues for the railways and tube (RMT and ASLEF), and unions as far apart industrially as NATFHE and the GMB asked members about their safety concerns.

Secondly, the PM decided to lead the charge against the FBU. The London *Evening Standard* reported that:

> Tony Blair has made his most confrontational attack yet on the firefighters, comparing them to Arthur Scargill's militant miners … the comparison makes clear that Mr Blair is determined to face down strik-

ers without concessions ... Mr Blair has told colleagues he cannot and will not give way to the firefighters' 40 per cent pay demand because it would put the economy at risk ... he revealed to aides that he was privately told by senior moderate union leaders that they would not be able to control their own members' wage demands if the firemen were given an inflation-busting settlement (23.10.02: 2).

So the genie was out of the bottle: pay deals were not based on labour markets, were not based on skills, were not based on negotiations between employers and unions, but were subject to Government pay policy rooted in the limits of public expenditure and borrowing. So once again it was clear that it was okay to borrow for war but not for welfare!

Thirdly, on 24 October *The Times* drew attention to a possible settlement through a meeting between John Prescott and Andy Gilchrist. Some of the hope rested with the PM himself pressing for an interim version of the Bain report, which might then allow some movement on pay in exchange for modernisation. This in turn could give the Government a way of increasing the available funds from Central Government. The report continued in a peacemaker fashion by declaring that: 'Mr Gilchrist is not a throwback to the ranting self-destruction of Mr Scargill and the last miners' strike. He is a modest, articulate but ultimately ordinary father of two children, still surprised to find himself in his union's top job'. In a telling end comment the reporters note: 'the FBU has choreographed strike plans so that there is a delay before the escalation into eight-day actions. Mr Gilchrist believes the first walk-outs will force the Government to make a deal. Downing Street appears to be ready to let the FBU strike go ahead, believing public opinion will swiftly turn against the firefighters' (24.10.02: 15). In fact public opinion remained solidly behind the firefighters' claim throughout the dispute.

As the dispute inched towards a strike, the pressure became intense as threat was turning to the real thing. On 27 October the *Independent on Sunday* could state that:

the threat of strikes by the fire brigade lifted last night when union leaders emerged from a day-long meeting to say they wanted to resume talks. The decision by the executive of the FBU means that two 48-hour strikes scheduled for this week and next week are definitely off. But the FBU warned that an eight-day strike from 6 November could go ahead if talks with employers break down. Nonetheless, the announcement came as a huge relief to Government Ministers who were facing the prospect of the worst public sector industrial dispute since Labour came to power. John Prescott, the Deputy Prime Minister, who spent five hours in talks with union leaders last week, said: 'I am delighted that the FBU has agreed to sit down with the employers for talks on pay and modernisation. I hope that this can now lead to a final settlement of the dispute' (27.10.02: 4).

EVEN FANCIER DANCING

'The next few weeks were known informally (following an expression of John Prescott's) as "fancy dancing", a period in which the employers were trying to keep the FBU at the negotiating table without pre-empting Bain's report. This may have been an impossible task' (Nolda 2004: 387). This was clearly a critical moment, and one that has been chewed over many times by FBU members and activists since the strike. At the time it appeared a tactical triumph for the leadership's position. After all the FBU had managed a successful campaign so far with public support, had worried senior Government Ministers, and had pushed their own employers back. The on-off style of strike threat appeared to be winning an acceptable negotiated settlement, but there was unease within the FBU itself. Some felt that the moment had passed; that members could not be turned on and off so easily; and that the Government, in playing for time, had seized the tactical advantage – with a war looming, preparations for strike breaking ever more ready, and the propaganda of reasonableness being pushed back into the faces of the FBU negotiators.

On 27 October the EC called off the first three strikes and prepared for new talks, with some hint from Government circles that the pressure was so intense that the employers might move their position. This decision was greeted mainly with relief and support amongst the membership, but some were less than happy: 'FBU officials in London have been contacted by hundreds of FBU members in recent days. Many, many members have expressed a growing feeling of frustration and anger at the slow pace of the pay talks, the lack of information coming from those talks – and at the cancellation of strike action when nothing appears to be on the table' (*FBU Organiser* 7 November). These tactics were not without problems. In particular two questions emerged: first was the question of whether the threat of strike action was more potent than strike action itself. Phil White told me that: 'we would be quite happy to admit we were all very worried … and fear of industrial action played a huge part in the whole process leading up to November'. This was supported by activist pro-strike feelings and their own reports that the membership was 'up for a fight'. Officials such as Joe MacVeigh from London told me he visited all the fire stations in his patch and the message was the same. The second issue was whether the members would support longer strikes and longer strike activity. At this time nobody really knew, but after the eight-day strike in November things changed and a new consensus emerged from within the membership that a deal needed to be done sooner rather than later.

At this point even the very hostile *Financial Times* reported that 'for the first time in two months the employers and FBU are to sit down and talk, as opposed to conducting megaphone diplomacy'. It continued:

where the news is less reassuring is in hints that the employers may be prepared to be a little more flexible over 'modernisation' – New Labour speak for getting a set of working arrangements that bear some relationship to the 21st century. As the talks begin, the employers must remember that if there is to be any more money on the table above the 4 per cent offered, it must be money for real improvements, not token ones. The package the employers seek is already pretty modest. It does not involve redundancies. It does not touch the cost of the firefighters' costly pension scheme. It does not take away the popular two-shift working system that allows them generous time off and, in many cases, the pleasures of a second job (29.10.02: 20).

At the 30 October meeting of the NJC there were further pay talks. Some progress was reported on the issue of equality for retained firefighters, and on an agreement on a new pay formula based on the associate professional and technical category. But nothing was happening on equality for control staff, and even less on the pay claim itself. This lack of progress on pay was, as Frank Burchill noted, because 'the employers were inevitably "waiting for Bain"' (Burchill 2004: 412).

Here then is the voice of the City of London financiers, of the business case, of powerful lobbyists, of the majority of the press, and of senior civil servants: one of contempt for workers such as firefighters and of visceral hatred for trade unions – the voice of the guardians of an economic policy designed to keep their supporters rich at the expense of the rest. Which voice was heard loudest in Whitehall and Westminster, and which voice expressed the policy preference of the Government?

EMPLOYERS RALLY BEHIND MANAGEMENT RIGHTS

The increasingly sidelined employers had their own problems, as their thinking remained rooted in the immediate past. In the run up to the dispute the employers were feeling rather jaundiced about their relationship with the FBU. This is clearly reflected in their evidence to Bain. Both the LGA and the Employers' Organisation (EO) submitted detailed views, and any objective reader cannot but be struck by the employers' antipathy towards the FBU. For the LGA, above all else – including years of substantial underfunding – it is the position of the FBU that is the biggest block to improving services to the public.

The Employers' Organisation complained about an adverse balance of forces, in which the good guys (the EO) were saddled with a statutory duty to protect the public while the baddies (the FBU) were both over-powerful and irresponsible in constantly using the threat of strike action to block change. To those outside of the Fire Service it is difficult to reconcile this view of the world with the fact that firefighters are so low in the wages league table and that there have been only two national strikes in the whole eighty year history of the FBU.

What united the employers was their fairly recent opposition to the prescriptive nature of the *Grey Book*, which sets out in some detail a framework covering a wide range of working conditions and staffing requirements.

While generally embracing the principles inherent in Best Value, departure from the strictures of the *Grey Book* was seen by some as risking an unwelcome return to significant local variations in conditions of service, and as likely to create a competitive regime through local processes of negotiation, which would not be an advance on the efficiency of the present centralised system. Others saw the *Grey Book* as inhibiting (for example in the duty systems, of which three main types are permitted) the best allocation of resources against demand, and limiting progress in redressing the under-representation of minority groups and women in the Service. A third viewpoint was that, since it had proved possible in practice to negotiate sensible local arrangements which were different from those laid down in the national Scheme (which is not a statutory one), a good measure of flexibility was already available, and this might be compromised if that were a formal provision of the Scheme itself. The more explicit the proposals for flexibility, the more likely they were to be resisted.

It is now clear that the second perspective, that of seeing the *Grey Book* as a barrier to change, had emerged as the dominant one among the employers. Thus the EO's evidence to Bain says: 'fire authorities are being inhibited by Conditions of Service from taking management decisions that allow resources to be used in the way they judge best. It should be the responsibility of management to determine crewing levels and there can be no justification for this provision remaining'. Not much sign here of social partnership or negotiated change, let alone industrial democracy. Later in their evidence the LGA underscores the point: 'the overall effect is to give the FBU a powerful influence that seriously undermines the ability of fire authorities to manage their service' (Employers Organisation 2002a: 19). And like a headmaster giving advice to a new teacher on ways of dealing with an unruly Fifth Form, the LGA says: 'In our view the most effective way of dealing with this problem would be to place the FBU in a firm but fair environment in which it was made clear that such methods would no longer be tolerated or accepted' (*ibid*). This apparently represents the zenith of employer thinking on the nature of modern participative management in the public services.

NOVEMBER 2002 – FAILED TALKS AND THEN STRIKES

November was the month of dashed hopes, bitter action, and repositioning the union to face the full might of state power. It started with the release of an interim report from Bain and a two-day strike. Both seemed to have paved the way for a settlement on the 21–22 November, and indeed many of those involved that day and night believed that enough had been achieved for a fully negotiated deal. But, at what appeared to be the eleventh hour, someone high up in Government dramatically changed tack. It was decided to ride out the forthcoming eight-day strike and then hit the FBU hard.

On 4 November the EC replaced the previously announced strike date, of 6 November, with a new forty-eight-hour strike due to begin on 13 November, thus giving the employers a further nine days to come up with a realistic offer. The figure of 16% had been widely discussed as one with which the employers had originally been willing to start the negotiations, and the FBU negotiating team, Andy Gilchrist, Ruth Winters and Mike Fordham, believed that that was now a possible point of return.

The NJC met again on 5 and 6 November before the EC met the employers on 7 November. All these talks pushed back strike dates, as each side hoped to conclude a deal before any action. The NJC agreed to meet again on 12 November. But the interim report (the position paper) from Bain was released on 12 November. It had been widely leaked by the Government over the previous weekend. Bain recommended 11.3% on the total paybill over two years, conditional on the biggest reform of working practices and management/industrial relations' structures ever seen in the Fire Service. These reforms were clearly intended to cut jobs and to enable Fire Authorities to pay any increase in salaries within their current budgets. Fewer firefighters, more overtime and rest day working, extra responsibilities including paramedic duties, for an increase of £10 a week in take home pay. This was the gist of Bain's recipe for Fire Service pay. By 11 November the *Evening Standard* in London could report that a FBU spokesman had 'denounced the 11 per cent offer as "an insult wrapped up in razor wire" ... this is the work of Government hawks who want to provoke a strike' (11.11.02: 2). The deal on offer through the agency of the interim Bain report was a little above average pay rises, in exchange for large scale changes in working practices – a not-very-much for something position.

Far from providing a basis for settlement, Bain was flagging up what many had suspected since the announcement of the Inquiry: that the Government had no intention of recognising the validity of the union's claim despite the overwhelming vote from members, and the overall strength of the arguments for step-change improvements in 2002. The employers were at this stage tied to Bain, and the talks on 12 November consequently made no progress. Once again the employers, now closely gripped by Central Government minders, offered 4% now and 7% in one year's time, and all tied to modernisation. This was not what the FBU had bargained for.

So the strike started.

Chapter 3

The Strikes

INTRODUCTION

This chapter deals with the failed negotiations of the 21-22 November 2002 in which a settlement was prevented by the direct intervention of Government leaders. This meant that tough talking was replaced by hard action. The FBU took its members out on strike for eight days, and during that time the Government attacked the FBU leadership, its motives and actions, and the whole basis of independent trade unionism and collective bargaining. The strike ended and negotiations started up again after immense pressure from all sides. Some of these talks were at ACAS, others inside the NJC's sub-committees, and others still as part of a complex shuttle of informal contacts.

THE MARTINI SOLUTION!

The first national fire strike for a generation began at 18.00 hours on 12 November. It was of forty-eight hours duration and was totally solid. Widespread public support was evidenced by visits to picket lines and donations to hardship funds. The news across Britain exploded with strike stories and reactions to the action. The BBC news carried a quote from Andy Gilchrist the day before the strike: 'the intervention of the Bain report yesterday, which set out some of the most dangerous and damaging proposals that anybody in the fire service in living memory can remember, I think scuppered the talks today'. In reply John Ransford of the LGA claimed that: 'we should be able to use firefighters where and when they're most needed to protect our communities. We are unable to do so because the FBU prevents change. All other workers are allowed to work overtime, but firefighters are prevented from doing so due to restrictive union policy'. He continued to lay down the line that the employers supported by Ministers wanted change to modernise the service in the interests of the community, and painted the union leadership and activists as obstructive barriers putting their members' vested interests before public safety. A familiar argument – that not only do managers know best but workers will only change when forced by a heavy stick and a juicy carrot!

This became known as the 'Martini solution' to staffing the Fire Service – anytime, anywhere, anyplace – and was bitterly resented by firefighters.

Paul Routledge, writing in the *Mirror*, backed the FBU thus:

> firefighters will be fully justified in going on strike today after the breakdown of negotiations ... they called off three strikes for which they had voted in a secret ballot, in order to give peace a proper chance. But their moderation was in vain. Instead of grasping the olive branch, the employers shoved it down their throat. And the 'independent' inquiry chaired by Professor Sir George Bain proved an illusion ... Labour MPs must now rally to the firefighters' cause, and shame their Government, our Government, into paying the firefighters what they are worth (13.11.02: 16).

There were plenty of reports of public support for the pickets, as when 'a black cab shot along Harrow Road, its driver waving and blasting the horn in support of the firefighters on picket duty outside Paddington fire station' (*Evening Standard* 14.11.02: 4). The reaction to this first two-day stoppage was cautious in terms of the more conservative media. Many agreed with the *Independent's* assessment that for Tony Blair it was the 'biggest industrial crisis since he became Prime Minister' (13.11.02: 1); and others were keen to quote his deputy's call 'don't walk, talk' (*Financial Times* 14.11.02). The *Economist* thought this was 'Tony Blair's Waterloo'. In a typically reactionary analysis, the article first suggests that any deal along the lines mooted: 'would spell the end, almost before it has begun, of the Government's attempts to show that by a combination of generous funding and modernisation it can provide efficient and highly valued public services'. It then attacks John Prescott for both sleepwalking in the early stages of the dispute and for claiming that a special case might be made for the Fire Service. Finally the labour market argument prevails: 'the queues of people wanting to join the fire service suggest two things: the firemen are not currently underpaid; and if the incumbents don't wish to provide a decent service, there are many people who would be happy to' (23.11.02:11-12).

As the two days ended it appeared that the FBU had come out of this first skirmish in a stronger position. The strike action was solid, public opinion remained largely in support, and other unions helped out without a fuss. Ministers, taking their cue from the Prime Minister, heaped abuse and vitriol upon the firefighters. John Reid and Nick Raynsford, in particular, accused the FBU of playing into the hands of terrorists, and Paul Routledge firmly believed at this stage that 'victory over the FBU camp has got the upper hand in Number 10' (*Mirror* 15.11.02: 8).

PICKETS, STRIKERS AND COMMUNICATIONS – FINKS, SPIES AND PROPAGANDA

When strikes start, the union involved has to ensure that everyone comes out in a show of solidarity; that any picketing remains effective but within the law; that actions, statements and behaviour of members remain within union policy and lawful; and that there is co-ordination and communication between strikers, local officials and national officers. In this era it also requires clear advice on dealing with the media – what to say, how to say it and when to say it. There were also public relations issues, and a need to make sure other unions supported the action, either individually or through local trades councils working with the TUC centre. There was much preparation involved. There was also the realisation that many sensitive issues were being discussed over various airways.

It was assumed that MI5, some local CID, a handful of FBU members in the pay of the media and/or employers, and elements within the media, would spy upon FBU leading activists, bug HQ phone calls and e-mails, send out disinformation, hound to the point of persecution FBU leaders, and seek to vilify the strikers themselves. Those in charge of the FBU campaigns understood this and were to some extent ready for it. John McGhee explained: 'prior to that we had done some work with some media people behind the scenes. We had done work with the *Press Association*, the *Guardian*, and the *Mirror*'. In answer to the question, 'was someone from the EC feeding the employers information?', McGhee answered as follows:

> Well, we also know that every single thing that we did on the Executive the employers knew about … actually there were times when whole conversations had been quoted … we knew that [there was a leak] before we went into the dispute. We had a conversation about it and we told people that … you have to presume that everything you write on your computer that is connected to the network will be read, everything you say on a telephone will be listened to … we went into telephone shops and bought six mobile phones with completely untraceable numbers and gave them to key people, and then told them that the minute you break that circle, you've got to tell everybody. If you accidentally break that circle and you phone anybody then we have to … dump them, we'll start again.

Geoff Ellis confirmed this: 'I think all the phones were bugged obviously'. He was the official in charge of communications at FBU HQ. In his interview he explained the conduct of the campaign. First he discussed regular contact with members and the wider world:

> What we did earlier in the campaign, we stopped publishing the *FireFighter*, because it was too slow to get articles in and then to get

information out to the members. We did a pre-strike bulletin initially, which we tried to do on a minimum of three-a-week if we could, in order to get information out in the build up to the ballot result. When we took the strike action we changed it to an official strike bulletin that again we tried to do three times a week, but it depended on what was happening. We needed to get information out as quickly as we could to the membership ... we did it online and put hard copies in the post to every branch

One of the things we did do early on for which the feedback we got was very good ... we were putting anything like press releases or bulletins on the website, and sending an e-mail to all our users to tell them it was on there. We set up one press co-ordinator in each region, and what we would do is, whenever we'd send out a press release, we'd send it to them, so we'd drop a hymn sheet, if you like, of key messages. We had problems when they went out, because the media were picking them up before the officials, who weren't happy about that. I set up a group text on my phone, and the text said check your e-mail because there's a press release gone out or whatever. I then extended that to all EC members and then we ... got a programme ordered through the internet, a web-based programme, to set up a database of all our officials, although they were in different groups. So any time we put anything out on the e-mail we could text, group-text, officials to say this has gone out on e-mail, and it was a very very quick way of getting information to officials. And they were, we discovered afterwards, they were then setting up their own groups to members and to branches so information was going very very quickly to branches.

When the strike started we were trying to get news from around the country – 'tell us what's happening' – which was hit and miss. Some worked, some didn't. I think the truth is, as soon as anything went outside the executive council it had to be put up for consumption. Because of the technology available to people nowadays we had to accept that, as soon as anything was outside of that executive council, it was leaked.

I asked about the £30k website, which later became a major source of internal dissent, helping those opposed to the conduct of the strike to exploit differences inside the union as well as to attack the leadership afterwards. He replied:

I think when the £30k website was first started up we actually encouraged it, we used it. I say used it, it was a benefit to the campaign, to the campaign pre-strike, to the ballot result ... It was the same person [running the website] who is doing it now and I actually gave him some funding initially to help set it up. I was very keen to get information out very quickly. I didn't think that our website could be used as a bulletin board type website, because we didn't have the resources to control it, and we couldn't have our own website being abused by people within or without the union. So I was really keen not to do that when they set it up. Initially the bulletin board side of it was only a small part and that was just information, but our information. The trouble was it got taken over by rumour and scaremongering, and the fact side of it disappeared, and it got to a point you couldn't tell what was factual and what wasn't. There were so many people reading it, media, Government, employers whatever, getting information from that site and taking it as fact, and a lot of it wasn't, a lot of it was misinformation.

In terms of dealing with the media and handling the campaign he continued:

We had three or four good journalists who we could trust who we could brief on a regular basis and put stuff out through, and of course could get stuff back through them as well which was quite useful. We had another wider group of probably up to a dozen journalists who we could trust.

This was for both [TV and press]. People that we knew would put our side without distorting it too much. Of course then we had a gang of other people who we knew that whatever you told them they were going to distort it. And we had the decision to make – do we speak to them knowing that they were distorting what you were saying, or do we ignore them and let them write what they like anyway and discredit them? We had some fair old discussions about it.

That was my main brief, it was the media stuff. We had a fair bit of support in that area from other unions as well. I mean UNISON set up an office, their office, and helped us staff it on strike days ... we made use of RMT's press officer Derek Kotz and ASLEF's press officer at the time Andrew Murray did a lot for us as well. So we had other unions helping out, which was quite good.

Certainly, initially, we seemed to get core messages across. Our members were standing up in forecourts of fire stations giving the same message. When it started we were nervous about where we sent the press releases, where we could go to speak to someone, we were nervous, although we've got officials that we know are going to be reliable. But towards the end we didn't care, we just said 'look, just go to a fire station, just go where you like' – because our members were good at giving our message across on camera, live. We were just so gob-smacked, and I think, you know, from the media themselves, they said they could-n't believe it, they thought we'd trained all these people up – a lot of them were just, like, angry firefighters, I've got a point of view, brilliant.

But the difficulty was, once the Government machine stepped in we didn't have the resources, we weren't big enough, we weren't, I don't know, we weren't big enough to take on the state like that.

The minutiae of strike action is worth reporting since it provides an account of the inventiveness of local activists up and down the country with regard to presenting the national case within a local culture of receptiveness. It is also a reminder to those who indulge in conspiracy and betrayal theories, to those who believe politics is the stuff of TV chat shows with experts and leaders, and to those who subscribe to the view that people do not care any more – to all the Cassandras and Jeremiahs – that in terms of social action, workers still exercise potent power, and their actions still worry those in authority anywhere in the land. It challenges the desiccated conventional wisdom that collectivism is dead, and it does so through a myriad of methods, including humour. For example, Gateshead fire station displayed a poster comparing the Minister Nick Raynsford with cartoon hard-heart Mr Burns – the nuclear power station owner from the *Simpsons*.

Many regions produced their own bulletins and information pamphlets. In Wales the FBU strike bulletin, *Branchline*, carried regular stories, providing local and national reports, countering media and employers' efforts to undermine the strike, and supporting the union in all its forms. This was supplemented by leaflets to give out to the public with clear statements of the case, and of the role of the employers and Government, and asking for support to improve public safety. The Welsh region also produced important information pamphlets – 'organising for strike action', 'organising your finances for strike action', 'fair pay for the fire service', 'why £30k?' and, in issue 4, 'negotiations and enquiries'.

Such materials were widespread and helped inform members and local people; they kept the activists busy with the propaganda war, maintained the link of local FBU branches with other branches and with HQ, and enabled a rapid response to changing events and media distortions. There was a flurry of such materials in the middle of November as negotiations reached their climax and the eight-day strike started. For example, in an angry newsletter from the Northern Ireland FBU dated 19 November 2002, Jim Barbour of the EC launched into an attack on Sir George Bain, arguing that his report had 'sabotaged those talks': 'perhaps it is not surprising that the Bain report is so full of half-truths and misleading comments. Sir George is a busy man': as a well-paid University Vice Chancellor (a full-time job), his work on the report could be seen as 'moonlighting'! In Manchester the strikers held a public meeting on 25 November and issued their leaflet for local rallies on 29 November at Town Halls in the region. In London the official strike bulletin, the *FBU Organiser*, was coming out three times a week in November. In calls for action the bulletin's authors condemned Bain and the employers in issue 4 (12 November); proclaimed total support for action and solidarity in issue 5 (14 November); and provided stories from the picket lines in issue 6 (15 November). Other stories from the first strike action told of firefighters leaving their picket lines when lives were at risk, as in Worksop in Nottingham. Other local bulletins, such as *FBU Matters* in Berkshire, reported support of picket lines for each other in terms of the distribution of hot food and cakes given by the public! (issue 12, December 2002).

Needless to say there were huge numbers of support messages to HQ; these included one from the North Staffs Miners' Wives Action Group; another from the relatives of an elderly women who had tragically died in a house fire at the start of the strike, and notes from activists in support of the leadership. Everyone we spoke to and heard speak at various conferences confirmed this story of high morale, with largely supportive local media coverage (Sandy McNiven and John Cairns), very active and participative local strike committees (Jim Quinn, Dean Mills, Kerry Baigent, Gordon Fielden).

TO PICKET OR NOT TO PICKET?

A key aspect in keeping public support and putting more pressure on the local employers was the willingness of FBU members to leave their picket lines to attend life-threatening incidents. This was clearly a very difficult issue for the union and its members. Attending such moments of danger meant good press, that firefighters could keep the high moral ground – and that members could be easier in their minds. But in so doing the strike's impact may have been lessened; Ministers may have felt that this was a strike for which FBU members did not have the stomach and heart; and, as injuries were reduced, Ministers could claim that their contingency measures were working. It was a hard call to make.

In the FBU's second strike bulletin there were reports of three cases of strikers leaving picket lines, in Nottinghamshire, Shropshire and Surrey. In all cases the reports indicated the heroism involved and the over-riding concern for public safety. This sentiment was echoed by Jim Quinn, who told of the decision to leave picket lines to put out a fire in a Belfast hospital. Similar examples were given by John McDonald from Scotland and Mick Flanagan, an officers' representative from South Wales. Activists from the London region told me of the very real dilemma this issue posed for them and their members. The problem was recognised by the FBU and they sent out a press release on 15 November: 'the tragic deaths of the seven fire victims lost during the two nights of the national fire strike have exposed the penny-pinching hypocrisy of Government and fire chiefs' plans to cut the number of Professional Firefighters on duty and ready to save lives every night of the year, every year'.

At this stage the FBU leadership felt that they might have done enough to push the employers into good faith negotiations. Andy Gilchrist agreed:

> I feel the debate about did you get it right or wrong, was it a victory or
> defeat, was the wrong discussion. I actually do hold the view that just

about every official did our very best in the circumstances we found ourselves in … the other thing is the industrial action was to do one thing – to get the employers to the negotiating table to make what I would call a substantial offer … It wasn't to bring the Government down, it wasn't to wreck the Party, it was to get the employers back to where I believe they should be: answering that fundamental question, what do you think your workers in the fire service are worth? We cancelled the first forty-eight hours of strike because they [the employers] said they were going to talk to us. Now I know with hindsight some people would say that was a mistake. I don't think so, because, equally, if we hadn't had talks, and we'd have said to our people, they definitely would have still gone on strike, but they would have said to me privately on the picket line – because in-between the talks I'd have got to a picket line – they'd have said we needn't be out here … I'm talking about ordinary members, people who actually just wanted me to get in to talk on their behalf and get them a reasonable settlement.

So when I look back at why we cancelled strikes, I'm conscious that we always had a good reason, and we never did it unilaterally. It was always with reference to the Executive Council, and we had to win the argument, myself the AGS and the President. 'Why do you want us to cancel this Andy? Well, are we going back to talks? Alright!' Because the vast bulk of people don't want to be on strike … if you're on a low wage anyway the last thing you want to do is lose half of your wages.

John McGhee expressed the excitement and solidarity of the start of the strike action:

there was an incredible feeling on the picket line. I mean on the first day I visited picket lines in Newcastle … I travelled down from North East England to Cambridge and I finished up in Bedfordshire. The mood was that people weren't happy about being on picket lines and about being on strike, but there was absolute resolve, absolute steely resolve. It would be wrong to say it was all gung-ho, it wasn't, but here was a resolve that we've started something and we'll see it to the end.

This sentiment, the immense strength of feeling and determination, was repeated in every interview and speech we heard. There were no dissenting voices from within the FBU at that time.

THE TWELVE DAYS THAT SHOOK THE SERVICE
We now come to the twelve days that shook the Fire Service, the Government and the union movement. There was intense debate, informal soundings and media spinning in the run up to the resumed negotiations on 19 November. Then came the famous deal in which a negotiated settlement was snatched out of the hands of the parties and recycled through Downing Street, to be left in lingering tatters until the

summer of 2004; then the eight-day strike; then the long hard road to a settlement in June 2003; and finally the anguished frustration of non-compliance by the employers until August 2004.

On 19 November the FBU Executive put forward its own view of Fire Service modernisation. This was very much based on the Government's draft White Paper published in 2001 but subsequently abandoned, for reasons never explained by Ministers. The EC's approach was to show, as confirmed by the *Pathfinder* trials and research carried out on the union's behalf by Cap Gemini (2002), that extra investment now could save many lives and over £3 billion a year to society as a whole in reduced NHS and insurance costs. In a letter to John Prescott, enclosing the FBU modernisation document, the General Secretary said:

> As I have stated many times we would have no difficulty discussing a significant increase in pay in conjunction with an open and progressive discussion on modernisation ... it is our sincere wish to avoid future strike action and we believe a genuine commitment to deal with pay linked to modernisation as set out in the attached document could be the basis for achieving this.

Under pressure from Government Ministers, the employers agreed to resume negotiations on 19 November. At these talks the FBU negotiators indicated that the union's opposition was not to modernisation but to cuts in the service. In the run up to these talks the Government threatened to allow troops to cross picket lines in order to utilise the red fire engines. This particular bit of nonsense was mischievously encouraged by the Tories and elements of the press, but dismissed elsewhere as impractical and dangerous. These suggestions tended to backfire, since some local employers and CFOs openly opposed such moves, and this allowed the case for trained firefighters to do the job to be strengthened (*The Times* 16.11.02: 14). In the same edition and page of that paper, it was reported that plans to gain more central control over the Fire Service were uppermost in Ministers' minds:

> a confidential Whitehall document shows that legislative proposals for 'greater central Government direction and control' over the Fire Service had been earmarked for inclusion in a Bill last year. The legislation was shelved while Ministerial responsibility for the service was shunted around between the Home Office, the Department for Transport and, most recently, the Office of the Deputy Prime Minister. This week's strike has convinced some senior Ministers that any long-term pay settlement for the firefighters must now be overseen by Whitehall. They blame local authority employers for allowing terms and conditions to ossify over 25 years.

Such reports of course made a deeper hole for the employers to keep digging in, and fuelled the long-standing grievances between local authorities and Central Government.

Elsewhere right-wing papers continued their attacks both on the firefighters for having two jobs, and on the Government for deploying useless Green Goddesses (*Mail on Sunday* 17.11.02: 17). Later in the same edition Joe Haines, formerly press secretary to Harold Wilson, demanded that: 'Blair must crush the firefighters for all our sakes'. His argument is familiar if somewhat hysterical:

> this country is now facing the rebirth of the Militant Tendency-inspired strikes which wrecked a Labour Government, ruined the economy and destroyed the savings of millions of ordinary working people. A motley group of hard-line Left-wingers among trade union leaders – Marxists, Trotskyists, Socialist Workers and Scargillites – is determined to humble the Government (*ibid*: 26).

This kind of argument matters for two reasons: firstly, this line is shared by many in and around the Cabinet, namely that it was militant trade unionists that brought down the Callaghan Government in 1978-9 through the Winter of Discontent'; and, secondly, it is a myth bought into and favoured by sections of the wider public. Of course it remains an oddity of this analysis that such apparently weak groups – compared with the media, large corporations and the Government itself – can have such a major impact on the country.

On the eve of what became the most important set of negotiations, more mixed messages were sent out from Central Government. John Prescott was meeting both employers and the FBU at separate times; then the Prime Minister himself hinted at some element of a self-financing deal; but then, in contrast, Gordon Brown robustly rejected the idea of more money. Brown argued that such a settlement, tiny in itself, could not be reconciled with his 'no risks with inflation, no short-term quick fixes, no unacceptable spending beyond our settlement of last July, no inflationary pay awards' mantra (*Evening Standard* 18.11.02:15). On the same day *Guardian* reporters Kevin Maguire and Patrick Wintour had got hold of a leaked document which claimed that the employers had been willing to offer a 16.1% pay rise in July, but that Ministers had refused to fund the deal: 'The leaked 24-page paper, which conceded that firefighters had slipped in the pay stakes, proposed phasing in the award over two years – 6.8% this month, 4.35% in April and 4.2% next November. It demanded the modernisation of working practices which both the Government and the Bain interim report have called for'. Indeed on 18 November the FBU issued a press release with clear evidence of the 9 July offer that was never made. The accusations from Andy Gilchrist were serious: 'the Government stepped in and stopped this offer [16%] being made on 9 July. It is clear to us that senior members of the LGA, including Sir Jeremy Beecham and John Ransford, have been lying ... Government Ministers have also been lying'. So, with reports of John Prescott seeking a last minute negotiated settlement but being opposed by Blair and Brown, together with a well-timed leak aimed at splitting the local employers from the Government and giving to the wider public a view that the FBU was willing to settle, all seemed to be in place for a final deal.

On the day the talks opened the *Mirror* ran a four-page special which made much of the 16% offer made four months before and Prescott's failure to act at that time. The banner headline on the front page ran: '16%? Most people wouldn't do this for two jags, four homes and £124,000 a year. Would they Mr Prescott'. This attack was coupled with one by Charlie Whelan: 'it's time for Tony Blair to get his tanks off the firefighters' forecourts. The PM may think that smashing trade unions will boost his macho image but forgets at his peril that firefighters are heroes and most of us think they're worth £30k a year for daily risking their lives' (19.11.02: 4). On the back of that there were other reports indicating growing public support for the strike, and even *The Times* acknowledged: 'firefighters ready to call off strike: Government's three-year pay offer would break deadlock' (19.11.02: 1). But others reported a different story: 'why the Government will not surrender to the firefighters', wrote Donald Macintyre in the *Independent* (19.11.02: 16). He argued that, 'while holding out the encouraging prospect of serious negotiations in the fire dispute, Gordon Brown was at his most magisterially unequivocal yesterday, warning that the union was pursuing the wrong claim at the wrong time and with the wrong methods'.

The importance of all this press reporting is that everyone was positioning themselves indirectly, through leaks and off the record remarks, to friendly journalists. The battle in the public sector especially is partly fought on the terrain of public opinion, and in particular on the opinion of key activists in the unions, the Labour Party and the wider circle of the politically interested. Hopes for a settlement were examined like the entrails of an unlucky chicken, and post-talks blame was already being shared out between the FBU leaders, the employers, and various factions in Cabinet. Papers swayed from the anti-Blair *Guardian* – 'Blair has been burned already: however it is resolved, he is the loser in the firefighters' dispute' (20.11.02) – to the ardently pro-FBU *Mirror* – 'Paul Routledge on why the dedicated and disciplined firefighters union won the argument' (20.11.02: 7). The pro-Brown *Financial Times* wanted to blame Prescott and the employers, arguing that no settlement was possible without more money (20.11.02), while the extremely anti-FBU *Sun* claimed that the union had been exposed 'as bullies, extremists and opportunists' (21.11.02: 8). By now further leaks from the talks indicated things were not going well, with the

Evening Standard believing that 'eight-day fire strike looks set as Blair gets tough' (20.11.02: 1).

21-22 NOVEMBER: GOVERNMENT INTERVENES TO PREVENT NEGOTIATED SETTLEMENT

By 21 November the talks had developed into full negotiations aimed at reaching a final settlement. Significant progress was achieved and a position paper drawn up. This would have been the basis for delivering 16% by November 2003, and would have allowed the eight-day strike planned to begin the next morning to be suspended so that final negotiations could begin the following week. Around dawn on 22 November the Office of the Deputy Prime Minister intervened by refusing to give the employers the freedom to pursue this line of negotiation. The employers were nearly as furious as the union about the Government's intervention. In a circular to his members the employers' side Secretary Charles Nolda said:

> The draft agreement prepared overnight by the joint secretaries ... was endorsed by the FBU, but not by the employers following a last minute request from Government sources that the Employers should not endorse the draft until Ministers had considered it. This is a new procedure of which we had been given no prior notice.

The TUC also reacted angrily to the Government's blocking tactics. In a letter to all Trade Union General Secretaries, TUC General Secretary John Monks indicated that: 'The TUC is defending the draft agreement as robust, fair and workable – and is doing all it can to help the FBU in this new, difficult phase of the dispute'. Those involved believed Ministers had agreed to these proposals – which included 16% phased in from November 2002 to November 2003 in exchange for modernisation – prior to the negotiations; indeed such an understanding formed the basis for the employers' behaviour.

In the early evening of 21 November John Prescott told the House of Commons once again that: 'the employers have released some details of their pay offer. It amounts to a pay increase of 16% over two years linked to modernisation'. So he knew full well what was on offer. So what did he have to say about funding it? 'I have repeatedly made it clear to the House that any pay in addition to the original 4% offer has to be linked to modernisation'; and he ended by saying, 'we have to be fair to all – to nurses, teachers, ambulance workers and the police. We cannot and will not accept rises for firefighters that are unfair to others' (*Hansard* 21.11.02 col 885/6). Again the argument is that an above average pay rise would endanger economic stability and fall foul of the Government's unofficial incomes policy for the public sector. He also noted that 16% could be funded through Bain's forthcoming proposals. He therefore knew both what was about to be offered and what it would cost, more or less, before he went to bed that night. The subsequent collapse of the talks, the turning point in the dispute, was therefore neither about costs nor comparability, but about defeating the FBU and humiliating the employers. The stamp of ruthless central state control is the hallmark of New Labour's technique of governance.

Reports from the talks suggest that the parties were very close to a form of words that would have settled the dispute. Indeed the FBU reported that:

> after many hours of difficult negotiation and discussion a form of words was accepted by the EC as a forward to suspending strike action and having further talks next week ... the Employers in their discussions to agree this form of words ... felt they would eventually be able to sign up. Astonishingly, during the hours of dawn, intervention by the Government in the form of the ODPM effectively blocked this opportunity to make progress (Circular 2002HOC0931AG).

This was supported by the independent chair, Frank Burchill, 'there was an understanding by all present ... that an agreement had been reached. At 6.10am news came through that Prescott had refused to authorise the deal without seeing its details' (Burchill 2004: 414). It was also suggested that the union side as well as independent onlookers believed a deal had been struck; but employers' representatives were less forthcoming in their account of how near to a done deal they were. What appears to have happened was that, after many long hours of negotiations, the employers were still nervous and tested the proposals through a senior civil servant, Clive Norris, whom they believed to be in contact with the Deputy PM. The union side thought that, given previous assurances from Prescott, he would approve the deal. But at some moment it was put on hold, whether by Prescott himself, or by Gordon Brown, or by senior civil servants. Thus the eight-day strike had to go ahead. The moment had gone: a hair's breath away from the dispute being resolved.

I spoke to all the main negotiators and some other witnesses to these events. Unfortunately, Frank Burchill, the independent chair of the NJC, declined to be interviewed, although both he and Charles Nolda produced brief published accounts of events (Burchill 2004, Nolda 2004). The FBU side were clear as to what had happened. Mike Fordham explained:

> Certainly we were working on the basis, and I'd been told by politicians I was talking to that they shared a priority, to avoid industrial action if they could. There was still a belief that people did want a negotiated settlement and the idea of a national strike was ... well, all stops were pulled out to avoid it ... And again in good faith certainly on the official side of what we knew in that long day and long night was that there was

a willingness to reach agreement. Now I believe if we'd have had Tory controlled employers that night we'd have reached agreement, that's the view I hold. What became the problem again was that we had Labour politicians working with a Labour Government and therefore kowtowing to the Government ... And again there was the interesting link between Raynsford and Shawcross and Norris.

It should also be noted that the best man at Nick Raynsford's wedding was Ken Knight, later to become the CFO in London and special advisor to the Government on the Fire Service. There was a hint of a London-based New Labour political freemasonry being involved through close social and personal links, with people determined to block the FBU's case.

Now certainly I do know that throughout that night Ministers were approving the wording of the agreement we were working on. I know that because I was in the room with people like Barber and Monks, and Raynsford had been the relevant Minister and he was agreeing to it. So certainly at that stage when we went back to our executive and the employers went back to their side, which was about one o'clock in the morning, we genuinely – and I say Monks and Barber were involved as much as anybody else in that – thought that Prescott had approved the terms of the agreement. And whatever people want to say now, what I remember about that is we ended up changing some words from 'within forty-eight hours' to 'as soon as possible', and that was looking good as we headed for the weekend ... but we needed to get Prescott's approval to change it from 'forty-eight hours' to 'as soon as possible'. We had to get him out of bed. Now I do not believe you get a Deputy Prime Minister's approval for that sort of change if you haven't already got his approval for paying 16%.

So we were told at the time that Ministers had approved it. Then of course we started to wait for the employers' answers in text between me and Phil White, and there was delay after delay after delay. My first reaction was something was going wrong again. I also know that the message came from Norris to the employers' secretary, that Ministers will not consider the deal till nine o'clock in the morning. Now the person that told me Brown was stomping round Whitehall was a journalist. It wasn't one of the employers. I do know first hand that it was the employers who told them that the Government could not approve, would not finance such a deal until they considered it. They could not consider it until nine o'clock in the morning. In making that decision they must have known we had no alternative but to call that strike. They must have known that, they're not daft, so it's a conscious decision in my mind that Government determined that strike was going to go ahead.

Of course what happened then was the bulldozer hit. We were told that Blair had put us top of the list above Iraq. They rode straight over us in every sense of the word and it was like getting run over by a bull-dozer. We got hammered during that period of time. Now, in my mind, that was a very very successful tactic by the Government and employers' side. The employers were, they were passive, but they went for it and then the Government denigrated us, they denigrated the employers, they denigrated anything they could touch.

We probably shouldn't have ridiculed Prescott for not getting out of bed! No, he didn't like it, and he was out of bed, that's the more important thing, and although he's apparently thick-skinned, he's not, he's thin-skinned as hell.

I indicated that I had been told a different story by Charles Nolda and Phil White from the employers' perspective. Mike Fordham thought, however, that his version was the one most likely to be accepted once the dispute had ended. Andy Gilchrist also spoke of that day and night:

At the meeting, John Monks and Brendan Barber were the serious players and obviously myself, the President and the AGS. We got to the stage where we had a document spread out in front of us and it had to have what they called political cover. John Monks certainly was on the telephone to the politicians. I can't think who it was he spoke to; it might have been Ian [McCartney]. I don't know, but after those phone calls out in the hallway the word came back to go back to your side and if you can sell this it's done in the morning. And we went back to the executive. We told them what the outcomes could be and they said we would be prepared to recommend this to our members. In other words this dispute could be over on that basis. It is interesting now, the deal we've got now, which some people complain about, is actually better than that one. Perhaps that tells its own lesson.

Anyway, we waited around for this phone call you see, we phoned up the secretary on their side and said after, I don't know, an hour and a half, we were going for it. There was a few minutes chat about how are you getting on, and they said that we'll get back to you, it's getting a bit difficult. Then we got a phone call at five, gone five o'clock, that things had gone seriously wrong. We thought, blimey, you know, this is a bit serious, and then we got a phone call, whatever time it was, quarter to seven, seven o' clock, saying no it cannot be agreed because the Deputy Prime Minister, that's how it was put to me, has got to look over it. And I said, well, are you not going to look over it now, and then the famous 'no' came out, he's not in the office till nine o' clock. I think everyone in the room on our executive found that deeply insulting since they had spent the best part of twenty-four hours on their feet trying to reach an agreement. It might have been disingenuous to suggest that he had not been involved until then. The fact that Prescott appeared to be saying this can wait till nine o'clock did not go down well, didn't go down well at all. I've got to say our EC said, well, if that's the approach, then Government people therefore are not serious about wanting to stop this, then we're not. I was given a clear message by the EC to take that piece of paper and do what you want with it, we've got a strike to organise.

As that morning unfolded I went home, and that was that. I think it was significant that at that meeting Ian Swithinbank, who was a senior member of the employers' side, said they were in touch with all sorts of people including, I understand, the Treasury. I don't know who but I'm sure he might have got a phone call, and on our side John Monks and Brendan Barber both spent a lot of hours through the night trying to get it sorted.

Brendan Barber later told me in interview that he and John Monks were completely sure that a deal in principle had been struck, and that Ministers had a rough idea of the costs of the settlement before the negotiations had started. It is inconceivable that such an array of leading figures from the industrial relations world would have been there and been involved unless the message from the Government was to settle within pre-arranged parameters. Barber went on to explain how he and John Monks had gone for breakfast in the belief that a deal had been done, and could not believe it when the news filtered through at about nine in the morning of a breakdown in talks. They immediately went over to see John Prescott and explained again to him that a strike would be very damaging and that the deal on the table was not only reasonable but presentable as well. Apparently by now the Deputy Prime Minister's mood had changed. He had gone from being conciliatory to being hardline and uninterested. He was now deaf to the arguments from the TUC leaders, and was clearly preparing for weeks if not months of FBU and union bashing.

The version of this crucial moment from the two lead negotiators from the employers' side, Phil White and Charles Nolda, again differs in some respects from these other accounts. They explained to me in interview what happened. Charles Nolda started:

We knew that evening that we were very very close indeed and that there was one big issue between the two sides, which was not the money or when the money would be paid, but it was how we would express the strings, and in particular how the second and third stages of the money would be dependent on progress in negotiations upon parts of the package. And we knew that it was very important to leading people on our side, and indeed to Ministers, that somehow the Audit Commission should be involved in this. The position that we are now in is that the Audit Commission are arguably saying whether or not pay should be released, because they've got to say whether or not modernisation was on track locally. We knew that was not acceptable to the Ministers that night. And what we got to in the negotiations was a form of words – my guess is before midnight – that had the Audit Commission as a player but not as a potential showstopper ... a player that would be a sort of arbitrator along with others if parties couldn't agree on how the strings would apply. And Phil and I knew that that form of words was not quite right from the Government's point of view. So we arranged, or it was arranged, that there would be a political discussion between somebody representing the majority political position on our side and the Deputy Prime Minister.

They then explained the sequence of events and telephone calls. John Monks spoke to Prescott at about 1.30 am on the phone, and this was followed by another call between Prescott and one of the political leaders from the employers' side. The outcome of this second conversation seems to have been a block by Government on what had been agreed. So, according to White and Nolda, the employers got back to work to find a form of words acceptable to Ministers. This new formulation was then faxed over to the FBU leadership in their hotel at about 4.30am. Nolda continued:

> At 4.45 my mobile went off. Still talking, we were in an employers' meeting, and I was talking, Phil answered the mobile, and it was Clive Norris, who was the senior civil servant in charge, and, my guess is, my personal guess is what happened was that John Prescott didn't like the sound of what he'd heard in the political conversation that I've referred to earlier, and got Clive Norris out of bed and told Clive. I think Clive was obeying orders. Clive was told to make sure that any offer the employers made, that the employers should not make any offer, any new offer, until it had been cleared by the Government. Now, that was the message that Clive delivered to Phil White.

The NJC, under which some of these negotiations were supposed to be taking place, has no role for Government. There is no formal constitutional position that allows Ministers to intervene, but as Nolda elaborated:

> the Government had no role constitutionally in these negotiations. But obviously our employers are all political animals, the majority of them are Labour, and they weren't going to – it was very clear very very quickly – they weren't going to say to the Government, well, we don't care, we've got a constitutional position and this is where we've got to, and we are going to make an agreement. It has to be said that before this call came through the employers were having some difficulty with this position ... and I think it was, it was getting, it was starting to split on party lines, and one of the ironies of this is that before Clive Norris came through it was Labour that was in favour of doing the deal and the minority Tories and Lib Dems who were for not doing the deal.

When asked 'When you say Norris was obeying orders, whose orders do you think they were?' the reply was, 'Prescott's, or probably Prescott's, my guess is it would be Prescott's private secretary'. They then suggested that the role of go-between played by Clive Norris was mainly on behalf of his own Ministers, with Prescott as the main influence and Gordon Brown making it clear that he wanted nothing to do with any deal. The question was why had Ministers allowed these talks to start at all, given their apprehension about looking weak if the likely deal was struck. Nolda continued that:

> Ministers knew from earlier on in the week what the proposition (which is basically the proposition in the July paper) that the employers' organisation had produced on the night contained, which hadn't surfaced until it was leaked by, we think, one of the members of the employer's side. So Ministers had known about this and had given a sort of ok to it earlier in the week. But I think that that may have been an ODPM take, and what we got subsequently was a more corporate Treasury take on the proposals. Added to that was the fact that in the course of the night the strings had been weakened, or apparently weakened – you can argue that the version that emerged in the night would still have enabled the employers to negotiate the changes in working practices they thought necessary within the level of earnings required by Ministers.

I suggested that, nonetheless, as freestanding employers it was still possible to reach an agreement without Government approval. Nolda put me right:

> My first thought was 'well, the constitutional angle is that we would make an agreement if we wanted to', but it was a stillborn thought. I didn't voice it, because it was perfectly clear that people within the employers' side who had been supporting this proposition were from the same political party as the Government. It was perfectly clear instinctively, and from everything that was being said, in body language and in words, that those people would not want to pick a fight with Ministers.

Phil White expressed the views of the employers' negotiators when it all went wrong:

> Well, I think we all felt gutted because we had had, we thought an hour earlier, we had a deal. And we thought we had done a deal and we thought we had done very well. But this became one of a number of – I mean we're still not out of the wood yet – I don't know how many times we had been to the wire on this, but it must have been at least half a dozen, and that was the first one.

Nolda continued:

> I think my perception is that the Government – whoever Government is in this context – somewhere in a very short space of time the objective changed. We were in no doubt that up to a very very late stage, the Government's objective was to avoid a strike. And suddenly, I think with the benefit of hindsight, the potential impact of this deal on public sector pay policy became more important than avoiding a strike. Now when that happened, and whose influence occurred to alter the position, I don't know, but that was the major change. Avoiding a strike, I think, seemed to me very much the important thing for Government, but then suddenly it was the pay deal implications. Now maybe that doesn't point towards the Treasury but that's the shift.

In a later written account Nolda argued that:

> The employers made an offer early in the afternoon that was in line with Government's requirements. This referred explicitly and in detail to the Bain modernisation agenda; involved the Audit Commission in advising whether all the required modernisation agreements had been satisfactorily completed *and* implemented at local level; and stated that the package (16 per cent over two years) would impose significant extra local costs over and above any efficiency savings which might be generated by modernisation ... a revised version of the earlier offer was drafted in the small hours of 22 November – *the same overall pay increase* and exactly the same references to funding as before, but with different wording on the linkage between those pay increases and the delivery of modernisation ...The employers' representatives in the small group meeting under Frank Burchill's chairmanship were fully aware of the political sensitivities surrounding the changes in wording between the two documents. Contrary to popular belief, John Prescott was contacted from the employers' side in the small hours of 22 November.
>
> This may have been why, later in the night, at about 4am, when the employers were about to decide on the second draft, a mobile phone rang. A senior civil servant was calling to say that the second offer (the text of which he had not seen) should not be made until the Government had seen it and considered it. Up to that point the Government's official position had been that they were not directly involved in negotiations.
>
> The Government has no direct constitutional role in the fire service negotiations. The employers could have made the offer (which the FBU had already decided to accept) and agreement would have been reached. Although no final decision had been reached when the call came, the indications were that the employers were about to decide on a very narrow majority vote to make the second offer. For the first time, and the only time in this long dispute, they were about to split on party lines.

But the civil servant's call changed everything. Notwithstanding the constitutional position, the employers decided unanimously not to make the second offer … [as a result] the eight-day strike went ahead. Attitudes hardened politically. The opportunity for a freely negotiated settlement disappeared for several months (Nolda 2004: 388-9).

John McGhee told me:

It was a strange day because when we got together, I think everybody hoped we would reach a position and that the strike would be cancelled, but the longer the day went on there was a kind of strange feeling that they [the employers] seemed to be more stuck in. There was a real mixture of we'd think we were getting somewhere and then we'd be pulled back. Progress was slow and it began to look as if we were going to settle this. We were getting somewhere and then in the middle of the night, Monks and Barber were there, we reached a position at quarter to five in the morning … we voted to cancel the strike.

When asked: 'when you look at the two agreements – the first one they offered and then the second one you almost got – there does seem to be a feeling of great achievement and how do you explain the employers conceding so much ground?' McGhee replied:

We had felt for some time that the employers were not allowed to freely negotiate, but that somebody had said settle this. They had been allowed to go back to the July position … I don't know about the politics from their side, but when you've got John Monks and Brendan Barber there saying that's fine get off to bed that's it, sorted, and then suddenly in the morning somebody on the television is saying this is unaffordable – where did they get him from?

This was a reference to Professor David Metcalf from the London School of Economics, a pro-government academic. Frank Burchill tersely commented on this:

the author [Burchill] left at 3.30am believing an agreement had been reached and that the dispute was over. Waking up at 7am and watching the early morning television news it was with some surprise that he saw a Professor of Economics condemning the union and the employers … for attempting a costly and irresponsible settlement. It was difficult to establish what was most surprising – the collapse of the deal or comments on its content by an apparently independent non-participant while part of the process was still unfolding (Burchill 2004: 421).

McGhee carried on:

The press would never get out of bed for all that crap, but they managed to get somebody from the London School of Economics who managed to re-cost the offer and say it was unaffordable. It wasn't costed ... no of course he didn't read the proposal ... There was clearly an agenda somewhere else ... we can only deduce from that that Gordon Brown was involved.

I think everybody was a bit shocked, by then I don't know if angry would describe it. We just wanted to get on with it and went into almost the mode of, right, this is what we're doing with it [the strike]. We've now got to go and make sure it's solid. This is it, we've no choice ... There was such a short debate once they came back saying this one was off, the popular strike's back on, everybody's agreed. There was no big view to keep it cancelled and hope ... we also knew that because of the warped trade union legislation we couldn't say, well, we'll cancel the first date and take the members out later. We had to go out at nine o'clock the next morning or not, we couldn't say, well, let's wait until nine o'clock the next day – we had to give seven days notice for a new strike.

At this point Tom Sibley commented that this was an interesting point – the inflexibility was built into the legislation. McGhee carried on:

We called a strike and we were faced with no choice but to take that strike action. I mean people just had to. There was a big feeling of anxiety amongst the executive members because they wanted then to get back to their regions and their own staff in London two hours before the strikes were due to start. So they were all going to be travelling. So a crowd of us went round to Euston fire station. Then of course we'd been up all night so we needed to sleep. Andy was going to be up in a couple of hours ... and I was talking to the press, and then of course Geoff sent off stuff to members trying to explain to them what had happened.

So extraordinary Government tactics made the eight-day strike unavoidable.

Once the strike started on 22 November the press was again full of blame and speculation, but the real change came from Ministers. They now went on a blistering offensive against the FBU in Parliament and across the media, signalling for the first time a clear intent to defeat the strike and defeat the union. First, though, came the accounts and analysis of the night of the long faces. *The Times* provided one of many accounts of that evening:

negotiations continued through the night with the firemen's leader walking back and forth through the streets of London for meetings with his union colleagues and the employers. Hopes for a deal rose at 2.15am, when a cheerful-looking Andy Gilchrist emerged from the Euston Plaza Hotel to report that talks were at 'an extremely delicate' stage and that he was returning to the FBU's base to await documents from the employers ... the shuttle diplomacy had started well after midnight at the end of a roller coaster day that began with hopes high that the strike would be called off as the employers promised the firefighters a 16 per cent pay rise ... as the talks resumed after midnight – with Mr Gilchrist leaving the Hotel Russell in Bloomsbury on foot at the same moment that the employers' negotiators left their headquarters at the New Connaught Rooms in Covent Garden for a supposedly discreet meeting at the Euston Plaza Hotel – troops were standing by to crew Green Goddesses again.

The heart of the debacle was that Ministers refused at the fence of using central funds to help support the extra pay for modernisation offer. In the end the Government's position on funding tied the employers' negotiating hands, and the FBU found the changes in working practices a change too far to agree. As the report continues:

> recriminations flew, with the Government rejecting what it saw as an attempt by the union and some local authority employers to bounce it into a deal. One senior Government official said of the union: 'they have walked away from modernisation and opted to protect their Spanish practices'. Gordon Brown also effectively vetoed any above-inflation deal that did not include modernisation (22.11.02: 1).

The press stories accumulated, with the FBU blaming the Government for pulling the plug on a basis for a negotiated settlement because of Treasury fears of a domino effect on wages and eventually on inflation. The Government blamed the FBU for refusing to modernise but also criticised the employers and especially their negotiating team. The employers blamed the FBU for lack of flexibility and Government for lack of clarity. Most headlines, though, concentrated on the hapless Deputy Prime Minister and his alleged failure to get out of bed: a fabrication that allowed all sides to blame the most easy of targets and deflect attention away from the real hows and whys of the breakdown. For example, the headline in the *FBU Organiser* on Friday 22 November was: 'Wakey! Wakey! Prescott stays in bed – we strike!'.

By 23 November most eyes were on the strike, to see what impact it would have on actual public safety, and also the impact on the political barometer. The dogma of the Treasury had combined with the political instincts of Number Ten to overthrow the craven employers' position, and let the firefighters, and by default the labour movement, go hang. The risks of defeat for Government and employers was relatively small – some additional cash (not theirs) and some immediate loss of political face, but nothing as damaging as a run on the pound or floodgates of pay demands; but the risks to the FBU and its members were far more significant. They included union survival and the ability of the workforce to resist managerial changes and maintain living standards. In such an uneven game of poker those with the most to lose have the weaker hand.

THE EIGHT-DAYER

The mixed emotions of bitter betrayal and defiant determination came clearly from all those FBU members interviewed at the start of the strike. One FBU bulletin reflected, 'when the Government talk about modernisation what they really mean is more ways to save money. When firefighters talk about modernisation we talk about more ways to save lives'. These feelings were made stronger when in the early part of the eight-day strike Government flirted with several unpleasant but pointless adventures, such as use of legislation to outlaw the dispute, the use of the army and civilian HGV drivers to scab, and a lock-out of the strikers thus making life harder for the pickets.

Andy Gilchrist felt:

> People were extraordinarily angry as they embarked on the eight-day strike, and when they kicked off there was absolutely not a problem. Eight days, eight days was a tough event, and of course the attitude of Government seemed to be, well, we'll get by and people die in fires anyway.
>
> Our problem seemed to be that our people were saying do we have to do this much strike, in these chunks, in this sort of way. Lots of members were finding that hard, and didn't warm to the prospect of spending a lot of time doing lots and lots of strike action. So then that began to focus your mind on what are we doing here. So at the end of the eight days there was again the promise of talks, so it was no hardship to cancel the next eight days and get involved in negotiations. This wasn't talking to officials, this was talking to people who actually were stood out at ten o'clock at night. No, you can't fail to react to that. If you don't I think you are acting almost irresponsibly. It wasn't, as I say, one or two people, this was the vanguard of our membership saying 'we'll do it Andy but it's not very nice mate'.

This point was made to us by most of the activists to whom we spoke. That there was real anger at the collapse of the talks, confidence in the leadership and solidarity in the membership, but there was also some anxiety as to where all of it was heading. Mike Fordham added his views:

> There was internal pressure as well as external. The external pressure was immense, no doubt about it, and it hurt. It hurt because I think it then impacted upon the second bit, indeed our membership, they'd never experienced that. They'd never experienced denigration, they were the most popular public servants in the world, they did a brilliant job, every-

body loved them. And it switched, and the Government literally turned them into a bunch of lazy people demanding exorbitant pay rises, holding the country to ransom, putting the troops at risk. The whole thing that started to develop had a massive hit on the confidence of the membership.

Some blame was attached to the Bain inquiry. MPs and journalists had already asked why it was taking so long, others questioned its independence, and many more thought it part of the problem and not part of the solution. Sir George Bain was clearly irritated by these comments and protested in a letter to the *Independent* that: 'this review has not been set up to avert the strike, but to present a long term solution to the issues behind the strike – pay and modernisation in the fire service', and later he added: 'I want to produce a credible and independent report' (24.10.02: 21).

The *Mirror* maintained its support for the firefighters while attacking the Government:

> so just who is in charge of the Government's attempt to sort out the firefighters' dispute? Is it John Prescott, the Deputy Prime Minister, who has now woken up enough to realise that a rise of 16 per cent is the basis for a settlement? Or is it the Chancellor, Gordon Brown, who insists there can be no more money for the firefighters? No wonder there is confusion – among the employers, the union and the public. The whole thing is a shambles. Of course there is only one person who should be in charge – Tony Blair (25.11.02: 6).

The paper's line of argument reflected widespread concern that Brown had intervened against the deal brokered by Prescott, and that, as John Edmonds, General Secretary of the GMB, said in the same edition: 'throughout this dispute the FBU and even the employers have shown a willingness to compromise. The only people who have not are Ministers' (*ibid*: 4). The warfare metaphor – being practised for the forthcoming invasion of Iraq, and dusted down from the coverage of other periods of industrial unrest – now came very much to the fore. Class warfare was clearly in the minds of key commentators and decision-makers. Thus, for example, Martin Wolf of the *Financial Times* stridently urged the PM on: 'On Friday morning, all seemed lost. But, at the very last moment, the Government extricated itself from a disaster, albeit ineptly. It refused to finance the irresponsible 16 per cent pay deal reached between the employers and the FBU. That would have been a calamitous defeat. Now, as the first eight-day strike proceeds, the Government has a chance of victory' (25.11.02). To add to the loud voices against the strikers came the heavyweights of the CBI attacking the 'me, me' attitude of the firefighters. *The Times* joined in with its version of son of the Winter of Discontent, with long lists of strikes and potential strikes. As always the right-wing press has to balance its act: condemning strikers and Government alike, but not wishing to give credence to the possible re-emergence of union strength. Thus: 'Gordon Brown insisted yesterday that £500 million would be needed to fund the 16 per cent pay deal for firefighters as he rubbished the package and gave a warning about the impact on public sector pay' (25.11.02: 4). And the *Sun*, mimicking the right-wing slogan about the IRA, declared 'no surrender on strike' as the position of Tony Blair: 'the PM will echo Maggie Thatcher's famous war cry, saying he is "not for turning"' (25.11.02:1). It also stated: 'battling Tony Blair wheeled out his big guns yesterday – as he prepared to take personal command of the war against militant fire union bosses. The PM will refuse to cave in to the FBU pay demands that threaten to wreck Britain's economy' (*ibid*: 8).

BLAIR'S OFFENSIVE
This then became the first major propaganda weapon, explained by the *Independent* thus: 'Tony Blair will make a direct appeal to voters today for support in the Government's battle with the firefighters by warning that caving in to their demands would jeopardise jobs, inflation and mortgage rates' (25.11.02:1). But at the same time, just as union leaders such as Bill Morris of the TGWU, Derek Simpson of AMICUS and John Edmonds of the GMB were attacking the Government for a mismanaged botch, Government messengers were seeking a more conciliatory posturing from Ministers in order to allow peace a chance. Only the *Morning Star* reported the actual progress of the strike from the picket lines, with stories of rallies in Glasgow, public donations to the FBU fighting fund, firefighters leaving pickets to help if lives were in danger as in Halifax and Cornwall, and quoting support from TV actor Ricky Tomlinson (25.11.02: 4). But just as the papers on 25 November were full of the strike, that afternoon Tony Blair stood up in the House of Commons to make his statement on the dispute – to be available for all the news on 26 November.

He made five substantive points. He explained in summary form what he took to be the essence of Bain's report on modernisation, namely that:

> full-time firefighters should lift the ban on working alongside part-time ones; that overtime, where it is needed to be worked, could be worked; that management could change, where necessary, the rigid shift system of two days on, two nights on, then four days off to provide better services; that firefighters could be allowed to do basic training as paramedics and carry resuscitation equipment such as defibrillators; that the fire service could share control rooms with other emergency services to provide efficiency of response; and that action be taken to improve the management of sickness in the service to reduce the extremely high numbers who retire early through sickness and ill health (col 23).

Secondly, he stated on several occasions during the debate the conditions for an agreement: 'the potential deal that may have been reached last Friday morning between the union and the Local Government employers was unacceptable for the simple reason that it was not funded through modernisation. In addition, the agreement to modernise was only to talk about it, not a firm commitment to do it'. Thirdly, he commented on the conduct of the negotiations and dispute, with particular reference for the need for a negotiated settlement, and that pickets had left their posts to attend emergencies under the 'gold command situation' (col 31). Fourthly, in this area he also spoke at length about the use of troops to cover for the striking firefighters.

Finally he spoke of the wider economic case for refusing the deal:

> the Government cannot be asked to find additional money outside agreed Government spending limits; to do so would risk fundamental and lasting damage to the economy. If the Government were to yield to this claim for pay increases way above inflation and not linked to productivity, the consequences across the whole public sector would be huge. Nurses and soldiers – after all, many of them are manning the appliances at the moment on pay far below that of the firefighters – as well as teachers and police officers would also seek similar claims, and all that we have done to produce the lowest inflation, the lowest unemployment and the lowest mortgage rates in Britain for decades would be put in jeopardy. This is a course we cannot take (col 24).

Both this argument on the economic consequences of the claim and the earlier one about the nature and meaning of modernisation are contested versions of reality, and alternatives are discussed in later chapters. The FBU sent a open letter in reply which refuted most of the points made. Robert Taylor, in a typically shrewd piece for the *New Statesman*, argued that Blair was playing a dangerous game with public sector unions and their members' pay, and floated the notion that Bain, having done the Government's bidding with the firefighters, might be used to chair a wider reform of public sector pay – conjuring up the ghost of Hugh Clegg and incomes policies by any other name (18.11.02: 15). In contrast, The *Economist* gave Blair robust advice about how to deal with 'the Neanderthal world of the fire service', in which 'the shift pattern is archaic and cushy' and they enjoy 'batty working practices' (23.11.02: 34). The answer was to seek guidance from elsewhere – from the apparently flexible French firefighters, the near-privatised Danes, and the Austrians and Germans, who made greater use of volunteers. But the unsigned article suggests that all this would be too much for both Government Ministers in need of some union support and fire service managers, themselves afraid of change (30.11.02: 27-8).

On the same day at a press conference the Prime Minister signalled an all out Government propaganda campaign to undermine the union. He said: 'the FBU leadership claims that the Government somehow wanted this dispute ... this idea is palpably absurd.' And then he went on to describe how and why the Government had intervened to block a negotiated settlement, the basis for which had been agreed by both the employers and union sides.

He proceeded to pluck a few figures out of the air to show how the proposed settlement threatened the stability of the whole economy. He said it would add £500 million to the costs of the Fire Service – while the employers' estimate was £70 million per annum above the 'going rate'. He then claimed that if it was applied across the whole of the public sector it would cost an extra £16 billion or 30% on the tax bill for the basic rate taxpayer. This was clearly desperate stuff, and was later repeated by the Governor of the Bank of England and the Chancellor of the Exchequer. (The actual cost of the full FBU claim (the four points) was 40p per week per household on council tax, and the cost of 16% over two years about 10p per week on council tax.) The Prime Minister went on to call on Sir Jeremy Beecham, the head of the LGA, to put together a new and more focused negotiating team which would consult Bain about the financial parameters for any settlement. 'A slimmed-down team of Local Government negotiators, led by Sir Jeremy Beecham, chairman of the LGA, will meet civil servants today to discuss the proposals' (*Daily Telegraph* 27.11.02: 1).

On the next day, 26 November, the Deputy Prime Minister was involved in a further exchange in the Commons. This time there was more detail on the negotiations, as well as a repeat of the five points made by the PM the day before. He said:

> Following the breakdown of negotiations on Friday morning, I held a discussion with Jeremy Beecham on the way forward. Sir Jeremy is the chairman of the Local Government Association, but he is not a member of the negotiating team. He agreed with me, and has made it public, that the document negotiated between the employers and the employees on Thursday night and Friday morning abandoned the essential link between pay and modernisation that has been the touchstone of the Government's approach to the dispute. I met Sir Jeremy again last night. He was working to put together a new group on the employers' side, which will oversee the process of modernisation of the fire service, drawing on the work of the Bain review ... officials from my Department met the employers yesterday and they are meeting officials again today to work on the costs and benefits of modernisation proposals.

Here comes the heavy hand of Central Government: 'We will continue to work with the employers to help them to come to a clear view about the process of modernisation and the costs of any pay deal for the firefighters' (col 165). So the blame is passed squarely to the employers and in particular their negotiators.

He then repeated the line that the Bain report was the basis for a negotiated settlement, trading pay for changes in working practices, under the jingle of modernisation. He went on:

> Bain also set out a route map for achieving that vision. He proposed a four-strand approach to negotiations, under which discussions would begin on the whole package of reforms at the same time but would be completed according to different time scales. The first strand would be completed in four to eight weeks, the second in about six months and the third in about a year. That model involved a direct connection between staged payments and the implementation of modernisation. Sir George recommended that, in exchange, the firefighters should receive 4 per cent pay rise immediately and a 7 per cent rise next November. Each rise would be linked to the implementation of modernisation. The fourth strand would depend on action to be taken in partnership with local authorities and central Government, and would take longer to complete (cols 167/8).

Thus the Deputy Prime Minister explicitly linked job cuts to the money required to reach a pay settlement. He told Parliament that 20% of the UK Fire Service personnel would be retiring over the next few years, which could pave the way for natural wastage and cuts in establishment levels. To the ex-shop steward and seafarer's rank and file leader this appeared to be totally unproblematic. Throughout the dispute Prescott was focused on cost cutting to pay for above-inflation pay increases, rather than investment in modernisation to improve the service.

Much of the debate reflected wider concerns about the consequences of the strike, and many FBU-friendly Labour MPs tried to win more concessions on the argument from Prescott. David Borrow, for example, pushed about what a firefighter was worth if not £30k, and the deputy PM fudged the answer (col 176). Later Michael Weir asked him to repudiate alleged statements by the deputy justice Minister in Scotland, Richard Simpson, that firefighters were 'fascists' and 'bastards'. Another duck and dodge. Some raised the issue that the FBU did not appear to be negotiating with anyone who could directly deliver the deal, and this once more pushed the Government into an unconvincing litany of the relationship between the employers and Ministers in this area.

As the strike continued, the Government's line hardened, and they united behind the Blair position of defeating the union leadership and the claim. *The Sun* was the champion cheerleader in this. Thus, for example, Trevor Kavanagh reported: 'Tony Blair couldn't have been firmer. This strike will not succeed. There will be no extra cash without reform' (26.11.02: 6). He went on luridly: 'union hardmen last night ominously joined forces to turn the fire strike into a new class war – and bring down Tony Blair's New Labour'. This followed the headline on page 4: 'You're like Scargill and like Scargill you'll lose', aimed at Andy Gilchrist. This point was taken up by the *Daily Mail*, 'echoes of Maggie and the miners as PM tells union: you cannot win' (26.11.02: 4). The more educated but no more politically sophisticated right-wing press saw a group around the PM as taking on the union – composed of Gordon Brown, Alastair Campbell and Philip Bassett (*Financial Times* 26.11.02); but this group were also spinning against the employers. The commentators in the *Independent* felt that two clear points had emerged: firstly that Tony Blair was now in charge and would force the issue to a conclusion the Government could paint as a victory; and secondly that the dispute had thrown light on the disarray in public policy on public pay. Before that Donald Macintyre had characterised the dispute thus:

> a weekend of wildly contradictory statements by Cabinet Ministers, a heavy-handed, and largely unforeseeable, last-minute intervention to stop a provisional deal to get the current eight-day firefighters' stoppage called off on Friday morning – giving their union a new pretext for militancy in the process, a search, not always fully justified, for some scapegoats, and some rather cavalier treatment by some Government spokesmen of the facts of the case had all contributed – whether justifiably or not – to a mounting sense that there was a good deal of confusion and even near-panic at and near the centre of Government (*Independent* 26.11.02: 20).

Of course one key development was that Central Government, in the person of Nick Raynsford, was to deal directly with the employers to hammer out an agreed clear line that could form the basis of a negotiated agreement. The real losers at this point were the employers. As the eight-day strike went on, for the first time real costings of various outcomes were being discussed. Although the figures were challenged, at least they now openly existed, with £450 million being estimated as the cost of the 16% possible settlement over 2002-4 period. This was linked to a possible £160 million of short-term savings, with more to come after three years. These costings then brought with them a wave of speculation about where savings would come from – with the possible answer of jobs. The *Mirror* was in no doubt: 'John Prescott finally admitted yesterday that up to 10,000 firefighters could lose their jobs in modernisation of the service. This came as a Government-backed report – leaked to the *Mirror* – recommended not cuts, but huge new investment and extra staff' (27.11.02: 5). This Fire Cover Review document, a genuinely joint report, appeared to undermine the case for the one true version of modernisation put forward by Ministers. So the balance of opinion now swung back to the FBU. Nobody out in the communities wanted job cuts and no local employer could endorse them.

As the rhetoric was ratcheted up, compromise appeared closer; but the illusion was ever greater than the chances – 'The deputy prime minister adopted a tough line in public to dampen already faint hopes of a breakthrough in the increasingly bitter dispute' (*Guardian* 29.11.02, 11). But at the same time, while the FBU was heading for a second eight-day stoppage, informal activity was becoming frenzied, with involvement from the TUC and ACAS behind the scenes, along with whispered asides between the leading political figures and former General Secretaries, Ken Cameron and Rodney Bickerstaffe. Cameron told us that:

> One of the first things Presto did when we went on strike was to ring me and spend three-quarters of an hour on the phone at home with me. I told him what I felt, and we had quite a friendly conversation, and I said to him I hope you realise I'm going to ring Andy now and tell him what you said. I don't work behind people's backs. But, I don't think Prescott was ever in charge. I believe that Blair and Brown were in charge. I can't excuse Brown, because he's holding the purse strings, he's the person whose dictating what they can and can't do in terms of finance. And although it's not a great amount of money they thought that if we allow this to happen what's going to happen in other unions?

THE FALL OUT FROM THE EIGHT-DAYER

Like the previous forty-eight hour strike, the eight-day strike was totally solid. But when the FBU EC reassembled over the first week-end of December, many of its members reported disquiet among the rank and file, giving the first indication that long strikes were unsustainable and risked splitting the union. In the overwhelming majority of regions members were saying 'no more eight day strikes'. Against this background the EC agreed to call off the next eight-day strike, due to begin on 4 December, and to accept the TUC's advice and ACAS invitation to explore the possibility of finding a negotiated settlement involving the assistance of ACAS mediators. To keep pressure on the employers and the Government, the FBU leadership was at pains to stress that the next scheduled strike, due to begin on 16 December, remained live.

Most of the press presented this as a climb down by the union. Apart from the *Guardian*, which reported it straight under the headline, 'Fire strike off for new peace talks' (3.12.02), and the *Morning Star* and the *Mirror*, the rest of the printed media was determined to describe these events as a union defeat, brought about mainly by blunders made by the leadership. In particular the press singled out Andy Gilchrist's speech to the Socialist Campaign Group's conference on 1 December in which he called for a campaign to change New Labour into real labour. This the establishment press presented as an own goal that changed the balance of forces irrevocably in favour of the Government. The argument was that the speech had lost support for Gilchrist within the union, and had lost support for the union within the wider world.

Thus the *Independent* reported:

> Andy Gilchrist has really blown it now. As if his handling of the strike had not been inept enough to date, the leader of the FBU has now linked the dispute with his desire to replace the Blair Government with a 'Real Labour' one ... Mr Gilchrist was foolish to address the hard-left Socialist Campaign Group ... the initiative is now with Ministers. And they are pressing it home with some brutality (2.12.02:14).

And *The Times* of 3 December proclaimed in big headlines 'Fire strike is suspended as union hard-line crumbles'; and it went on to quote 'informed sources' (probably Phil Bassett – a former journalist with *The Times* and *Financial Times* before becoming a key figure in Tony Blair's press department) as suggesting that, 'the union's decision to back down was due to an internal fall out after Mr Gilchrist's speech on Saturday in which he suggested that his aim was to overthrow new Labour with real Labour'. Similar assessments were made by other broadsheets including most of the Scottish press. But it was all based on unattributed sources and was almost certainly spun from Whitehall, with Phil Bassett's No 10 fingerprints on it. In the light of subsequent events it appears unlikely that Gilchrist's remarks about New Labour would have been the cause for any divisions within the FBU: eighteen months after that meeting the union delegates to conference voted overwhelmingly to abandon New Labour altogether by disaffiliating from the Party.

But when the dust had settled it was clear to all that the Blair writ ruled. By refusing to encourage the search for a negotiated settlement, which appeared to have received considerable impetus during the 21-22 talks, the Government was sending a message that no settlement was possible outside of Bain. In addition, any agreement had to be within the current resources available to Fire Authorities. Initially the Government got a bad press for its brutal blocking of the negotiating process. John Prescott, who is still distrusted by sections of the establishment press, took the brunt of the criticism, but the Government as a whole was damaged by its clumsy intervention.

For example, in the *Sun* for 26 November the self-regarding Trevor Kavanagh, the paper's political editor, who always seems to have access to Government thinking, had this to say: 'the FBU has wrong footed the Government and made monkeys of both their employers and John Prescott. Outrageously, they have won the support of TUC chief John Monks who was thrown the trade union movement behind them'. Whilst it is surprising that such half-baked saloon bar wind bagging can be passed off as political analysis, there is little doubt that it accurately reflected the thinking and prejudices of the Prime Minister's press officers. Mr Kavanagh may not know much about democratic culture and collective bargaining practices, but he is well practised in the art of reflecting the interests of the rich and powerful.

The Government's first response was to attack the employers for making what was said to be an uncosted offer covered by a blank cheque to be signed at a later date by the taxpayer. But this was disingenuous: the employers knew full well that a negotiated settlement could not be reached within the current resources available to Fire Authorities, and had been saying so since the previous June. So the position reached on 22 November, before the Government's intervention, was not that of a concrete offer but the basis for further negotiations linking pay improvements to agreed changes in working practices, including talks with the Government about funding implications. In a real sense this had been a triumph for the FBU's position first outlined in the June talks, when the union had urged a joint Fire Service approach to Government to fund a better service including a step-change improvement in salaries for all employees and a new pay formula to protect the real and relative value of earnings. Ignoring all this, the Government moved quickly to undermine the employers' position. Their competence was questioned in public statements by Ministers, and the Prime Minister intervened to announce a new streamlined and focused negotiating team on the employers' side, to be led by Sir Jeremy Beecham. He also announced very clear guidelines about what could be offered, and that negotiations would be closely monitored by both Government departments and the Audit Commission.

The message to the union was loud and clear. Not only was their strike strategy under pressure, because the membership had strongly indicated its reluctance to take on long strikes; in addition, the Government had taken over the reins and was now centrally directing the negotiations. So when on 30 November the TUC brokered ACAS talks as a way forward, the union leadership saw this as an opportunity to take stock in the run up to the Christmas and New Year. In this period Bain was also due to report and it was now clear to all sides that the Government's strategy was to delay a settlement until the main elements of Government policy had been endorsed by Bain.

The strike ended on 28 November, with Ministers on the offensive, having gained complete control over the employers, sown seeds of doubt amongst some public sector union leaders, and provided an armload of anti-FBU propaganda to the media and wider public. The employers were for the moment sidelined, and the FBU leadership now faced a very difficult situation. While the strike remained solid there was clear concern amongst members, whose loyalty to the union was never in doubt, that more strikes might not achieve better results.

Later this created some soul searching among activists. Helen Hill thought that they had lost some public support during the strike, although all agreed that there had been no strike breaking. Some welcomed the strike as bringing the members together more (Mark Watt and John Robinson from South Wales), while others noted that the mood in the FBU was swinging away from any more eight-day strikes but still in favour of shorter and sharper ones. Levels of activity did drop after the strike with no night time picketing, but some activists from the London region assured me that their members wanted the longer strikes and were at a loss to explain the EC's position of calling off strike days.

By this time many commentators assumed that the union now had little option but to negotiate what it could at ACAS, but that any pay rise would have to be financed by job losses. But, as the New Year was to show, the struggle was far from over. There were to be more strikes before a settlement was reached, and, when it was, it looked more like the position agreed at the NJC in November than the Bain recommendations published in December.

WHAT WAS TO BE DONE? THE POLITICAL BALANCE OF FORCES

Following the breakdown of talks, the political climate began to change. The FBU leadership judged there to be three distinct approaches at the top level of Government at this time. The first approach, associated with John Prescott, was to find a negotiated settlement approximating to Bain, who was due to report in a few weeks. The second, the Treasury position, was to look for a negotiated settlement strictly in line with existing public sector pay policy, namely that no extra Government finance was available to 'oil the wheels' for a settlement. Thirdly, there was Tony Blair, who saw the political importance to New Labour of defeating a perceived militant union and put this political requirement before the need to find a negotiated settlement. This position was probably shared by the majority of senior civil servants outside of the inner circle of Fire Service professionals. For example, Professor Frank Burchill, addressing a FBU National Education School in December 2003, told his audience that he had been informed by senior civil servants that there was a strong view in Government that the dispute provided an opportunity to 'crush the union' (*Firefighter*, 31(4) December 2003).

Andy Gilchrist's speech to the Socialist Campaign Group of MPs was seen as a useful tool in this battle. As *The Guardian* noted, Ministers were now convinced that the FBU was heading for defeat, aided by the Government's ability to link the dispute with the politics of the union leadership (2.12.02). But elsewhere the speech was well received and widely reported, as it took up a theme previously developed by a number of trade union General Secretaries, including John

Edmonds and Bill Morris, leaders of Britain's two largest general unions. This served to point out the growing distance between New Labour and the mainstream of the British trade union movement, a distance that often appeared to be welcome to New Labour. Arguing for a trade union-led campaign to recapture the Party for Socialist values, Gilchrist had called for New Labour to be replaced by Real Labour. This was shorthand for a change in Labour's policies, to refocus Labour's whole approach to become worker friendly rather than being designed to please the CBI and the pro-Tory press. It was not a call for changes in leadership personnel but an argument for a radical change of Government policy, and its broad concerns were shared by many in the labour movement.

New Labour spinners and much of the press had presented the speech as being proof positive that the firefighters' dispute was in fact a political one, designed to undermine Government policy, with rank and file trade unionists being used to serve political ends. Thus on 2 December the *Independent* argued: 'Above all it was foolish of Mr Gilchrist to get into a position which is where the Prime Minister wants him, of depicting the strike as an attempt to undermine the authority of an elected Government'. It continued: 'If the legacy of the firefighters' strike is … a further weakening of the role of unions in Labour's constitution, it will be all to the good'.

In an article which appeared in the *Guardian* (4.12.02: 21) Andy Gilchrist answered the criticisms:

> My call on Saturday was simply to work within the constitution of Labour to reclaim the Party for Socialist values and pro-working class policies … If we fail in these objectives the Labour Party will be lost to its New Labour colonisers and the organic unity between party and unions will be destroyed.

And on the issue of addressing political issues in the middle of industrial disputes he had this to say:

> of course it suits John Prescott to offer avuncular advice about keeping out of politics. But individual members and affiliated unions still have the right to criticise the Government … It's called democracy.

In reality Gilchrist's speech was of minor importance. Contrary to press reports and speculation it produced no dismay or discussion within the ranks of the FBU at any level. The overwhelming majority of FBU political activists fully supported the sentiments of Gilchrist's speech and recognised that, with few exceptions, the FBU's parliamentary support came from the Socialist Campaign Group membership. Thus, while meetings did take place between FBU leaders and the officers of the Trade Union Group of Labour MPs, there is no evidence that the latter used their influence to enhance the firefighters' campaign. Indeed, during the debates on the Fire Services Bill, leading officers of the Trade Union Group supported the Government's taking powers to impose a settlement and determine terms and conditions of employment in the future. In the run up to the big TUC/FBU demonstration in support of the pay campaign, held on Saturday 8 December, the Trade Union Group declined an invitation to be represented on the platform of speakers, for 'fear of politicising the dispute'.

As many trade union leaders recognised, it was the Government's actions which made an already politicised dispute even more so. The *Financial Times* of 26 November said: 'Alastair Campbell is thought to be keen to take on the union to dispel any perception that the Government will give into union demands as the last Labour administration under Jim Callaghan did'. Here we have the voice of No 10 and the views of Tony Blair. And we also have the reappearance of the ghost of the Winter of Discontent, looming up to frighten the horses – and used both ahistorically and inaccurately: the Callaghan Government conceded no public sector union demands outside of its incomes policy limits. But trade union leaders had a different take. The *Guardian* of 25 November quotes a number of union leaders condemning the Government's handling of the November talks. Bill Morris, TGWU General Secretary is quoted thus: 'peace deal scuppered by a mysterious hand in Government'. In the *Guardian* of 22 November TUC General Secretary John Monks described the Government's approach as a 'clumsy shoot from the hip'.

DECEMBER 2002 – AN ICY WIND

In early December ACAS intervened to try to find a way to a negotiated settlement (Roberts 2002); as Nolda noted, 'ACAS conciliation became the cover for resumptions of negotiations' (2004: 389). Kevin Maguire explained what had happened:

> under the cover of a very public war of political threats and industrial reprisals, the two sides in the fire dispute spent a long weekend privately talking peace. Both sides last night insisted that secrecy had been crucial as neither wanted to be seen to blink first in the highly charged atmosphere ... union leaders and local authority employers, in a rare display of unity, agreed that the involvement of the conciliation service ACAS offered the best – and perhaps only – prospect of a negotiated settlement before Christmas (*Guardian* 3.12.02: 4).

But any talks now became further confused by a leak of the final Bain report to *The Times* on 5 December:

> As *The Times* can reveal today, Sir George has followed up his first report ... with an even more radical package ... The Bain proposals on

'modernisation' are substantial. He insists that firefighters adopt new shift patterns, work jointly with other emergency services whenever that is practical, agree to voluntary overtime work (an option that the FBU has banned), allow full-time and part-time firefighters to serve together in what are termed 'mixed crews', and adopt realistic disciplinary regulations (5.12.02: 23).

On Saturday 7 December the FBU and TUC organised a joint demonstration in support of Fair Pay in the Fire Service. On a bitterly cold day over 20,000 demonstrators marched through Central London in a colourful and noisy display of unity and solidarity. The *FBU Organiser* reported that the 'mood on the demonstration was defiant and determined' (strike bulletin issue 11, 19 December); and the *Morning Star* reported on its front page that, 'the biggest, noisiest and most colourful trade union demonstration for a generation left no-one in any doubt about the massive support that exists for the firefighters' (10.12.02). John Curran, the Grampian regional FBU representative, told the Aberdeen edition of the *Press and Journal* that, 'the mood among marchers was "resolute and determined" ...the march has reinforced the tremendous support among workers for the leadership. All that those negative reports have served to do is make members more determined' (9.12.02). At the same time the FBU was telling all its members that it had accepted an offer of help from ACAS, and that: 'our dealings with ACAS have so far proved to be helpful and constructive ... because we are in a strong position and in order to maintain this momentum the EC have decided to cancel the strike action due to begin on Monday 16 December for eight days'. It went on to say that another meeting with ACAS on 19 December, three days after the final Bain report, should prove useful, and that negotiations would then take place with the possibility of an offer in mid-January. In the meantime new strike dates were issued in line with legislation, for 27 January 2003 (circular 2002HOC0973AG).

On 16 December the full and final Bain report was issued amidst statements in the House of Commons, and renewed media speculation about the future of a dispute which had seen the union pushed back day-by-day from its original objectives. The Bain report endorsed and embraced the full gamut of requests from fire chiefs, Fire Authorities and management consultants to alter the working practices of the staff, and, at the same time, to re-organise the service itself along the lines already favoured elsewhere in the public sector. This involved changes in financial structures, lines of accountability, the involvement of the private sector, and, crucially, changes in the relationship of the service with Central Government. This required legislative changes as well as managerial ones. We comment elsewhere in this account on the extent to which these recommendations simply repeat dogmas and mistakes rooted in a neo-liberal approach to public services. But for now all parties were buried in the detail of Bain, and its part in resolving the dispute.

Again it was *The Times* that led the way in revealing Government intentions with regard to a new Fire Bill and FBU opposition to much of Bain; it also showed that there still remained enough fudge around specific changes, and the phasing and nature of extra payments, and the type of self-financing deal, to allow a settlement (16.11.02: 2). On the same day John Prescott made a statement to the Commons: 'the report describes a service where legislation is out of date, management practice is out of date, and the rules and regulations that govern the overall framework and the day-to-day work of the fire service are old-fashioned and restrictive' (col 552). He failed to note the contradiction that such an 'old-fashioned' service had the best performance record in the public sector on targets achieved and had been recently assessed by the Audit Commission as a 'high performing service'. He noted that, 'the report's first and most fundamental recommendation is to move to a system of targeted fire cover that is based on a careful, professional assessment of the real risk of incidents in each local area' (col 552). He went on to list other important areas for change: more collaboration between brigades; changed working practices; and repeal of section 19 of the Fire Services Act 1947. He went on to accept this last recommendation, and linked this with a White Paper to be produced in the spring of 2003.

On pay he said:

> The Bain report commissioned two studies to compare pay for fire service roles with pay for jobs of similar weight elsewhere in the economy. The report concludes in paragraph 8.19 that there is no case for significant increases in pay based on the existing pay system. However, it calls for a new reward structure ... the final report proposes an 11.3 per cent pay increase over two years, subject to the implementation of the common-sense reforms that it sets out. The report does not rule out further pay increases in future, but as with the 11.3 per cent increase, any increases would be subject to the implementation of the modernisation programme (col 554).

As we show (chapter 5), the pay research for Bain was badly flawed.

Despite Prescott's wishes for the dispute to reach a negotiated compromise through ACAS, he was giving the employers a clear sign that Government would not be helpful in giving them fresh room to manoeuvre, and he further upset the employers by his total disregard for any say they might have in the outcome. Despite protesting that, 'it is not my intention to take over the negotiations', he argued that 'we are doing exactly what every other Government have done: they have pointed out what their public pay policy is' (col 558).

Despite the rhetoric of self-funding and hands-off dealing, however, he admitted in answer to a question from Edward Davey that, 'therefore, a judgement would have to be made as to the transitional funds' (col 561). Later Dennis Skinner asked: 'is my right hon. friend aware that the most interesting and important part of his statement was the new provision that referred to transitional funding, up-front, to resolve the modernisation question?' This provoked a further comment on the famous collapsed deal:

> people accused me of sabotaging the agreement at 5 o'clock in the morning, even though I had made it clear at 3 o'clock to both the general secretary of the TUC and the employers' negotiators that I could not sign a blank cheque. However, one of the difficulties was that they did not know what savings could be made ... transitional payments will need to be agreed for a three-year period (col 566).

So neither employers nor civil servants had bothered to do the figures, but once done (however managed), the agreement would cease to have to be self-financing in the immediate period, as long as it was in the future. But this was the exact point made to Prescott by Andy Gilchrist and derided by Labour's Deputy Prime Minister at the time.

The talks at ACAS went on until the week before Christmas, and at that time the employers announced that they could be in a position to make an offer during the week commencing the 6 January 2003, although Phil White described this period as 'just play-acting' on behalf of the employers. In the light of these developments, the EC decided to suspend the eight-day strike due to start on 16 December. Then on 19 December Prescott announced amendments to the Local Government Bill to repeal Section 19 of the 1947 Fire Services Act, creating the possibility of imposing a settlement.

The complete take over of the talks by Government Ministers allowed them to seek to impose their overarching policy on public sector reform onto the Fire Service, and thereby turn a pay-for-conditions dispute into something larger. The three features of Government intention here, as elsewhere, include cutting costs per unit of activity, involving private sector finance and management, and helping local employers and managers to dominate the decision-making process within the industry. The so-called cuts agenda became a major issue, since Ministers had to present their case carefully: after all, this is an emergency service and to cut it at this time appeared to be at odds with overwhelming public sentiment, and with policy on terrorism and civil protection. Reporting on this issue was uneven. Left-wing papers such as the *Morning Star* were happy to provide stories of the absurd consequences and choices such budget control meant – as with the case in North Wales, where there was a trade-off between a new £600,000 ladder and the use of specialist appliances (3.1.03: 10). But for most of the press it was the same pattern of attacks on the FBU leadership – for being variously incompetent, stupid, corrupt, out of touch, stubborn, too left-wing, and flying in the face of twenty-first century mores. The right-wing stories were torn between hatred of the union and contempt for the Government, while the pro-Labour writers in the *Mirror* and *Guardian* pleaded their case for a quick negotiated settlement based on a pay-for-conditions agreement.

As the year ended a combination of events was making life very difficult for the firefighters and the FBU leadership. The Bain report, although hotly contested and later largely ignored, was a stick that was used to beat the FBU in the propaganda war; the eight-day strike while solid and successful, had not shifted the balance in the FBU's favour as expected; the Iraq war plans, with the fear of associated terrorist attacks, cast a long and dark shadow over events; and Government Ministers were briefing the press on a daily basis to be as hostile to the FBU case and leadership as possible, while not attacking firefighters as such. Mike Fordham expressed some of this:

> Andy, Ruth and myself went on a tour of Britain in a minibus. We were in difficulties, no doubt about that. And then John Prescott saved us. Not deliberately, I'm sure he didn't, but he did, and he went and made his statement on the imposition. We were actually in the minibus when phone calls came through that he was going to do it, and we listened to it on the radio and our reaction was 'thanks John'. He gave us another impetus to have a go at imposition and Government bullying. The TUC had to get involved. They could not avoid getting involved on the imposition argument. We were called out of meetings, we'd gone up to Yorkshire on the first day, and we'd been called back for the TUC steering committee, and they went 'oh shit it's going to get bigger this'. To be honest John's decision to announce possible imposition in Parliament gave us a mechanism for keeping the dispute alive and giving us something to work around.
>
> The members' mood was still incredibly solid, but an interesting change is that when we arrived at the fire stations there were lots of people there at each one. It was a pre-planned thing, they knew we were coming, and Andy would do the speech and I'd stand at the back with Ruth talking to members. They were saying one thing at the front of the group and a different thing at the back of the group, and then when we broke up and had tea with them privately they were saying to us how are we going to get out of this? I don't want to do this again.

John McGhee noted that:

> There was then a further debate on our Executive … we are now arguing to get 16% back on the table. So in effect that was the reality, and I think most people on the Executive understood that. There were of course officials who said that they thought we should go further. But

there was the membership who was saying not eight days again, we are not doing eight days, we can't afford to do eight days, and people were starting to say eight days is not hurting the Government, it is only hurting us.

Ruth Winters added with reference to her members' mood:

No, no I don't think anybody particularly liked it. There were some areas of the country where I would honestly say forget the strategy … they would have gone on strike for as long as it took if it was going to be productive; there were some who never really wanted to go at all in the first place … again I would say the huge bulk of members didn't particularly want to go out, but actually felt they needed to get something. If it's what they had to do, it's what they had to do, and that was probably the main bulk of the members I would say.

So while the union re-assessed its own strategy and the Government pushed on with its reform programme, the employers watched as their decision-making powers were taken away. Charles Nolda explained:

the Monday after the debacle on the Friday morning, Blair held a press conference in which the line hardened up. Until that point the agreed proposition had been the 16% over two years subject to strings, but on the Monday following the theme was much harsher, that the strings must give us savings to allow us to pay 16% over two years. So it becomes a self-financing proposition and to underline it the Government and the LGA, which is the main political player on our side, accepted that the employers will not make any offers without clearing them first with the nominated civil servant which is to be Clive Norris! How did we feel about that? Well, we realised that it's going to take a lot longer to resolve the issue than appeared a week previously, a lot lot longer because our hands are tied … and the forthcoming legislation has meant a much stronger position for the employers and a much weaker position for the union.

So the eight-day strike had left the Government in charge of the dispute, the FBU concerned to get their negotiating objectives back on track, and the employers believing the time for payback was nigh. As Charles Nolda noted, 'there was a general understanding that, having been on the back foot in negotiations with the FBU for years and years and years, suddenly the employers were on the front foot'. Phil White added:

you don't know what the implications of a strike are and you are worried. We were worried, the Government was worried about the implications of a strike. So for years, from the FBU's point of view, ever since the last national strike in the late 1970s, it is a very strong card and they threatened to play it. But once they played it and the country didn't fall apart, didn't burn to the ground, there's a tilt in the balance of power and I think the employers and the Government knew that. And again there's a bit of hindsight involved in this. I don't think we felt compelled to rush into reaching an agreement. I think we felt time was on our side. We didn't have to, there weren't deadlines. The FBU continued to set deadlines, but we didn't feel as if we were slaves to their deadlines. That's the change.

2002 came to an end and, despite threats of more strikes from the FBU, everyone knew by now that the time had passed for threats of action and action. The New Year would see more hard bargaining at first, with a few short stoppages, then the tragedy of the Iraqi War, and some vicious personal attacks on Andy Gilchrist; then there was a vital intervention from the chair of the NJC, Frank Burchill, to resolve the dispute, and finally, after further antics from Ministers, a settlement in June 2003. This was to be phased in and linked with reform, but by the end of 2003 this deal also had been botched by the employers; it took another nine months of wrangling, unofficial action, local unease and disgruntlement before a final agreement was made in August 2004.

So the pendulum swung.

A NEW YEAR – NEW NEGOTIATIONS, NEW LABOUR INTERVENTIONS, AND NEW STRIKES

The first week in January saw a more optimistic note from some sources as talks were to be held with ACAS, and there were calls for a more balanced debate, as when *The Scotsman* requested the publication of the *Pathfinder* report, which called for more investment rather than just reliance on the Bain report (4.1.03: 8). But such early optimism was soon to be doused by leaks of the new offer in hand: 'to begin with no progress was made. The employers bound themselves tightly to the Bain agenda' (Nolda 2004: 389). As David Turner of the *Financial Times* reported:

> Local Government employers are to propose 11.3 per cent in return for sweeping changes in fire service practices, with 4 per cent immediately and the rest to come later in the year if there is clear evidence that change is taking place. That is considerably less than the 16 per cent offered by employers late last year, which was also linked much less closely to a transformation in the way that fire service staff work (8.1.03: 6).

His analysis was that Ministers were strengthened in their dealings with the union by their view that the eight-day strike had not been the actual and propaganda disaster for them once feared.

On Thursday 9 January representatives of the employers' side of the NJC outlined a framework offer which stuck to the Bain recommendations (4% in 2002 plus an average of 7% in 2003), subject to unreserved acceptance of all the proposals on reform. For the first time this was linked to a specific proposal to cut jobs – 2% year on year for the next four years, or over 4000 whole-time posts. This was clearly a long way short of what had been proposed in November. Consequently the EC agreed to recommend a further strike for Tuesday 21 January for twenty-four hours. As the *Financial Times* explained:

> the threat of more fire strikes loomed last night after the firefighters' union leader warned there was 'little point' in more peace talks if employers refused to raise their planned offer ... [this] highlights the severe constraints that Ministers' hardline stance on fire service pay and practices has placed on the negotiators who represent fire service employers (10.1.03: 2).

The *Evening Standard* reported that the employers were sticking rigidly to Bain, and this had made things worse: 'Linda Smith, treasurer of the FBU's London region, said: "our members are extremely angry and fed up with being reasonable. If we don't get an increased offer soon I think the correct response would be more strikes"' (10.1.03: 2).

The next day, 11 January, the papers again reported the new strike wave to come as the union refused to seek the help of ACAS after the Bain-inspired employers' offer. As the Iraq war loomed the union felt that Ministers might be more willing to settle. Ministers felt, however, that the public would turn decisively against the union in the event of war, and that this might cause splits inside the FBU. Ministers were also keen to demonstrate their control over Local Government employers, and force them down the road of modernisation that Central Government, especially senior civil servants, felt that lazy and limited local councillors had failed to secure. The *Daily Mail* quoted Andy Gilchrist as saying that it was no longer a dispute over pay but over the future of the service, with the proposed loss of 4,500 jobs, associated with 150 station closures, and that: 'the straitjacket conditions attached to this offer threaten the future and safety of our fire service. We could not agree to this without compromising our obligations to the community we serve' (11.1.03: 2). This widely quoted sentiment had two clear purposes: an immediate attempt to counter Government propaganda by appealing directly to the public; and an important re-statement of the fundamental issue of what role do workers in public services have in running their services. This central contested issue pits the workforce and their union against a management definition of best practice and modernised procedures. In so doing it raises major concerns of the balance of power in our society, and the drift to less democratic control, less worker voice, and less user say in public services.

In a letter to employers' side Secretary Charles Nolda, dated 11

January 2003, Andy Gilchrist sought clarification that the understandings reached at the NJC in November still stood. These related to a
new pay formula, retained firefighters' parity in pay rates, and pay
parity for Emergency Control Room Operators. He emphasised that
negotiations could not continue on the basis of one side (the union)
being required to 'unreservedly commit' to the other side's agenda
(employers based on Bain). At ACAS the following day the employers
agreed to reconsider their position and to let the union know within
the next forty-eight hours. In the event the employers refused to budge
and it appeared to the EC that another impasse had been reached.
Accordingly strike dates were set for forty-eight-hour strikes beginning Tuesday 21 January, Tuesday 28 January and Saturday 1 March.

The FBU's position was marginally strengthened when leaked documents supported its allegations about the service cuts:

> Plans to cut staffing levels at some city fire stations by up to 10%
> provoked the new wave of fire strikes due to start on 21 January, it has
> emerged. Leaked papers from a meeting of the fire service employers
> early last week shows that they want to force through the cuts in return
> for better pay over the next four years. They also want a 2% cut across
> the board in the service every year (*Sunday Times* 12.1.03: 2).

The shift in the FBU case was now clear:

> Roddy Robertson, chairman of the FBU Scotland, said his members
> regarded Government proposals for modernising the fire service as
> 'dangerous' as it could put lives at risk … [he] said 'this dispute is now
> all about job cuts, reducing the number of firefighters and reducing the
> level of cover we can offer the Scottish public' (*Scotsman* 12.1.03: 5).

By the start of the next week *The Times* could report that:

> firefighters are likely to be offered a 16 per cent pay rise over three years
> as their employers try to avert another series of strikes. The Local
> Government employers are due to meet this morning to discuss their
> offer … sources close to John Prescott … conceded that a 16 per cent
> offer would be acceptable, provided it was funded through modernisa-
> tion (13.1.03: 4).

As part of the changing backdrop to the strike the FBU was reported
to be considering changing tactics, with a move to very short strikes
lasting only two hours (*Financial Times* 13.1.03:1). This tactic was
mooted alongside more pressure on Government from the firefighters'
parliamentary support group – made up of MPs such as John Cryer
and John McDonnell – which argued for a more flexible approach to
negotiations; while Geoff Ellis, senior national officer of the FBU, was

reported as saying on the BBC's *Today Programme* that, 'we have still got employers refusing to make us a serious pay offer' (*Evening Standard* 13.1.03: 4).

On 14 January: 'fire union leaders and employers were returning to the negotiating table today for talks at conciliation service ACAS' (*Coventry Evening Telegraph* 14.1.03: 3). As the talks faltered so the rhetoric again blossomed. The *Morning Star* led the charge for the union: 'the Government is taking issue with not just the firefighters but with all working people and with trade unionism itself ... every responsible and conciliatory stance by the union has been perceived by Government Ministers as a sign of weakness and treated accordingly' (15.1.03: 2). As the brinkmanship rushed headlong to the brink: 'Charles Nolda, their [employers] chief negotiator, said the sides were to meet at ACAS on Monday on the eve of what would be the third strike in three months' (*Guardian* 15.1.03: 7). Nolda, ever seeking a negotiated settlement, realised throughout that this was a chance for the employers to win concessions on working practices that had eluded them for years. He was quoted as saying that the talks had been 'friendly enough' and that some 'delicate points' had been covered (*Daily Telegraph* 15.1.03: 2). Local FBU activists reflected their anger, frustration and hope. As the Plymouth *Western Morning News* reported:

> Dave Chappell, chairman of the FBU in Devon, said the proposed reforms of the controversial Bain report would 'wreck the UK fire and rescue service'. He added: 'this is no longer just about pay, but for us to protect the public service offered by fire brigades across the UK' ... station officer Brian Harvey, another FBU member and head of Blue Watch in Exeter, added: '... our firefighters do not want to go on strike – after all, the consequences of them not being at work could affect not only the public but their own friends and family – but we have been backed down and have no other option'. Terry Nottle, a firefighter at St Austell, said: 'when we are out and about in St Austell, the majority of people say they support our action'. Mike Tremellen, secretary for the FBU in Cornwall, said the resolve of the firefighters remained in place (15.1.03: 4).

As the next strike day approached there was no evidence of attempts to prevent it or resolve the stalemate in negotiations. Instead a trickle of stories aimed at undermining the union appeared. The first full-time fireman to cross a picket line was in Plymstock. Andy Gilchrist immediately visited the station where he spoke to FBU members and apparently stiffened their resolve (Plymouth *Evening Herald* 16.1.03: 13). Meanwhile, in Aston, Steve Godward was having his case for dismissal heard at an industrial tribunal. He was dismissed in December by West Midlands Fire Service chief Ken Knight 'for gross misconduct for allegedly trying to prevent the Army using fire brigade equipment' (*Birmingham Post* 17.1.03: 7). In Northern Ireland there was a spat between Jim Barbour of the FBU and Rosemary Craig from the Northern Ireland Fire Authority, after she walked out from a NJC committee meeting, and he called for her to be sacked. This fissure amongst the employers was calmly reported as, 'there appears to be difficulties in arriving at a common negotiating position for employers across the UK' (*Belfast Telegraph* 16.1.03). These reports were capped by the anti-union *Daily Mail* in a typical piece of malicious spin: 'firemen yesterday pulled back from calling a new wave of strikes, in a move that will be taken as a sign the union fears it is losing the dispute ... but experts believe [not named] the climb down shows the union has realised it cannot win' (18.1.03: 6).

On 21 January there was a twenty-four hour strike, which was again completely solid. The day before saw an unpleasant, but not unsurprising, twist as Andy Gilchrist himself came under increasing personal pressure. Barrie Clement in the *Independent* noted that the ultra-left in the FBU wanted an all-out indefinite strike and had upped its public attacks on the leadership, while at the same time it was reported that there had been threats of violence against the family of the General Secretary (20.1.03: 11). Later that day the Deputy Prime Minister made a new statement in the Commons. He restated the Government position: 'I must repeat to the FBU and its members that further strike action will achieve nothing. It will only make it more difficult to settle this dispute' (col 21). He was tough on the Government response to public safety issues and especially over the gold command (col 23). He was less than clear in responding to a question from Alan Simpson pointing out that it was hard for ACAS to help when Ministers had laid down such rigid preconditions (col 29), and even more fuzzy in his answer on job losses when asked by Dennis Skinner and John Cryer (col 30).

Despite a meeting between Andy Gilchrist and John Prescott on the morning of 20 January, there was no backing off on the Bain preconditions. *The Times* was happy to report that: 'John Prescott warned firefighters yesterday that they would gain nothing by going back on strike' (21.1.03: 2). Again the strike was solid:

> Nuneaton and Bedworth firefighters joined their colleagues across the country today on the picket lines ... FBU representative Pete Muir said that the action was now about much more than just a pay dispute (*Coventry Evening Telegraph* 21.1.03:1).

And:

> more than 200 full-time members of the Lincolnshire FBU stopped work this morning ... they were joined by around 200 men and women

from the fire services' 500 retained firefighters ... a march from Lincoln High Street to the county council employers' headquarters was to be followed by a rally ... Lincolnshire FBU membership secretary Mick Burrows was manning a picket line at the city's South Park fire station this morning. He said: 'none of us want to be here, but now it is about more than pay. Cuts cost lives' (*Lincolnshire Echo* 21.1.03:1).

The Tories, scenting a wounded beast in the FBU, now started to bludgeon their way into the dispute. First Bernard Jenkin, the shadow defence secretary, said 'his message to pickets was: "you are a bunch of idiots, frankly, and you are a disgrace to your country"'. Then Nick Raynsford and his colleagues alleged that the army was providing a better service than professional firefighters. More insults came from the *Daily Telegraph*, with a headline 'firemen led by donkeys' – mimicking the famous 'lions led by donkeys' comment about British generals in the Great War at Gallipoli. The clear tactic was to attack the union leadership while being seen not to attack popular firefighters. After attacking the employers for lack of clarity and resolution, and then Government Ministers for being unprepared and then ducking any legal action against the FBU, the paper turned on the FBU leadership:

> Most firemen now know that they are likely to end up with not much more than 11 per cent over two years, and that even this will depend on their accepting substantial modernisation – and perhaps significant job losses. The union's main concern yesterday seemed to be to find a way of saving as much face as possible, before returning to the negotiating table. The sooner it does so the better. For the rank and file, all this will be hard to swallow, but at least they should be spared any more point-less (and payless) days on the picket line. When this dispute is finally resolved, the firemen should find themselves some better leaders (22.1.03: 25).

This view was at odds with most of our interviewees' beliefs. Indeed Dick Pearson, the FBU secretary for Wales, told us that he felt the fire-fighters were worth £30k and might still get it. Meanwhile the employers agreed to further talks on 23 January at ACAS without pre-conditions, that is without the union being required to give an unreserved commitment to Bain. Within days it was clear that the employers' agenda remained unchanged, and at the EC meeting on 27 January it was agreed to proceed with strikes set for the 28 January and the 1 February.

The Government, with its eyes now on the forthcoming Iraq inva-sion, pushed ahead with its attacks on the FBU and announced major changes; for example: 'town centre fire stations will be sold and new ones built near motorways and on council estates, under a massive shake-up of the service being planned by John Prescott' (*The Times* 24.1.03:1). The next day reports claimed that John Prescott had backed an initiative from the Scottish employers to remove the Bain condition from negotiations:

> Scottish local authority leaders have persuaded their English counter-parts to drop a crucial condition to further talks … the national negotiating body has now agreed to drop the commitment that the FBU commit itself 'unreservedly' to total Bain (*Scotsman* 25.1.03: 3).

In the spirit of tit-for-tat the FBU asked their lawyers, Thompsons, to challenge the Government's haste in repealing section 19 of the 1947 Act (*Independent* 27.1.03: 2).

This did nothing to prevent the two-day strike starting on 28 January. Once again the strike led to angry accusations, with John McGhee blaming 'the employers and the Government for the fresh round of strikes, rounding on the town hall chiefs for refusing to continue negotiations with ACAS scheduled for today and Thursday' (*Scotsman* 28.1.03: 5). By now the costs were being added up, with one estimate that the dispute had so far cost the Government £70 million (*Guardian* 28.1.03:1).

The Government turned the screw. On 28 January 2003 John Prescott announced to Parliament that he would be taking powers to impose a settlement, and heavy hints were dropped that it would be 'Bain' and no more, which was less than the employers' offer. It was around this time that press stories began to appear about the Attorney General's powers to injunct strikes if they were seen by the courts to be a threat to public safety. In the background was the threat of war – the real possibility that substantial numbers of British troops would be deployed in an early invasion of Iraq. All interested parties, not least the FBU leadership, knew that it would be difficult for the union to sustain its strike strategy in the event of war, and the Government was busy putting in place legal measures necessary to frustrate any further industrial action.

So the FBU membership was faced with a three-pronged pincer movement. There was the threat by Central Government to impose a settlement on inferior terms to that offered by the Local Government employers. There was the likelihood of British troops being part of a large invasion force and therefore at serious risk which arguably could be compounded if British military forces were overstretched by additional firefighting duties – with all that would mean in terms of lost public support for the FBU. And finally there were the powers available to the Attorney General to injunct strikes – powers more likely to be used in the event of war. What was now needed was a way to settle the dispute within the national conditions of service of the NJC.

Chapter 4

A Negotiated Settlement and its Implementation

INTRODUCTION

Into an already delicate situation was thrown a bombshell in the shape of a Fire Bill that contained the threat of Central Government imposition, thus effectively ending free collective bargaining in the Fire Service. At the same time, early in 2003, the Government prepared the nation for its invasion of Iraq. These acts together made further strike action very difficult, and the rest of the story was about the beginning of the endgame: bringing the employers back into play, achieving an agreed peace, side stepping around the Bain report, and finally winning an agreement in June 2003 that eventually – after another year – was implemented in August 2004.

A FIRE BILL FOR THE NEW CENTURY?

On 28 January 2003 the Deputy Prime Minister announced that the Government would be bringing forward legislation to give the Secretary of State powers to set terms and conditions of employment and to redeploy equipment in the Fire Service. This measure was to become the Fire Services Bill, and was widely condemned by the TUC, other unions, and many employment law specialists, as totally contrary to the UK's treaty obligations under international law.

Essentially the Bill proposed to give the Government powers to impose a settlement, undermining the rights of workers to secure through voluntary collective bargaining improvements in their terms and conditions of employment. The Bill clearly offended a cornerstone of fundamental International Labour Organisation (ILO) principles, specific ILO Conventions covering the rights of Public Sector Workers, and Chapter 6 of the European Social Charter. Much of this was conceded in the legal opinion, prepared by Government lawyers, commenting on the Human Rights implication of the proposal legislation. These issues were strongly pursued by both the FBU and the TUC, but despite meetings with John Prescott and the protestations of a number of Labour MPs, the Government held firm, conceding only to demands from the Tories that this be a time-limited measure (a sunset clause for two years eventually).

During the Bill's Second Reading in the House of Lords the Government met unexpectedly strong opposition. In particular two doyens of the labour industrial relations law community, Lords Wedderburn and McCarthy, fought the good fight for well-established democratic principles concerning the right to strike. It was not simply that the Bill offended ILO Conventions, which in their opinion it clearly did. It also highlighted the dangers to the right to strike presented by a breach of statutory duty. The Secretary of State was taking new powers to direct the work of the Fire Service, as well as to impose terms and conditions of employment, and these could be argued in the courts to be new statutory duties. Thus, argued Wedderburn in particular, it would be open to any citizen in the land to injunct the union should it consider taking industrial action against any actions taken by the Secretary of State using the powers given under the Bill.

With the invasion of Iraq only a few weeks away the FBU decided to postpone further industrial action. The impending invasion also meant that the Government was under great pressure to construct an end to the hostilities at home. Ministers chose the tougher option in the hope it would be faster and more decisive – to change the law and threaten to impose a settlement. This decision provided a get out of jail card for the union, and meant it could maintain unity, gather greater wider union support, enable friends in Parliament and the media to challenge the Government, and allow the sidelined employers back into the fray.

At 12.31pm on 28 January the Deputy Prime Minister made this statement to Parliament:

> The House will be aware that all sides welcomed the resumption of talks after last Tuesday's 24-hour strike. The chair of ACAS agreed terms of reference for those talks with both the FBU and the employers. The terms of reference are very wide and say that both sides should 'bring their respective agenda to the table and neither side would seek to rule any issue in or out'. Despite that, the FBU executive decided yesterday to go ahead with further strikes, and at 9 o'clock this morning the FBU walked out for the fourth time. It will be on strike for 48 hours and at present it is scheduled to walk out again for a further 48 hours on Saturday morning (col 719).

What Prescott did not tell the House was that at this stage the employers were insisting that modernisation as proposed by Bain was non-negotiable. After a lengthy attack on the FBU's conduct of the dispute, he announced:

as a matter of priority, I will introduce legislation in the public interest to take new powers of direction over the Fire Service. Those powers will, I hope, bring a new and much-needed sense of reality into future negotiations ... I will draw on provisions in the Fire Services Act 1947 that were repealed in 1959. Those provisions allowed a Secretary of State to specify the pay, terms and conditions of the Fire Service (col 720).

Patrick Hennessy, writing in the London *Evening Standard*, reported that: 'Tony Blair today announced sledgehammer new legal powers in a bid to end the firefighters' strike. A Bill to be rushed through Parliament within weeks will give the Government powers to impose a pay settlement on the FBU and to set the conditions under which firefighters work' (28.1.03: 1.2). He went on: 'the new powers should end the current spectacle of Ministers sitting on the sidelines during fire disputes, making tough statements without any effect while council chiefs carry on tortuous negotiations'. Meanwhile the next day's morning papers picked up on the threat of imposition. As *The Times* noted: 'Prescott uses emergency powers in historic breach with Labour allies. Draconian powers to force unions to bow to the Government's will on pay were announced'. But it also was happy to note the potential for internecine strife, with comments from other union leaders, such as Bill Morris of the TGWU and Paul Kenny of the GMB, worried about the unprecedented steps (29.1.03:1). *The Guardian* was quick to put all blame onto John Prescott's shoulders:

[his] decision to seek new legal powers in an attempt to halt the most damaging industrial dispute to hit new Labour is a high-stakes gamble by the only real union heavyweight in the cabinet. The Deputy Prime Minister's announcement that he personally plans to take control of pay negotiations from around Easter, threatening to sideline the FBU, sparked predictable public anger from TUC leaders and more surprising private condemnation from some fire authority employers (29.1.03: 6).

Was this just a bluff to force a settlement? Well Prescott hinted it might be when he answered a question from Jim Cunningham MP, who argued that: 'he may well bring in legislation to compel arbitration, but he cannot compel agreement'. Prescott replied, in a variety of phrases, that he wanted a negotiated deal now (col 730). The next day (29 January), in reply to John Lyons MP, Prescott said: 'the question posed to me is whether the actions that I proposed yesterday will have the effect of imposing conditions on firefighters. All that I seek to impose is negotiations' (col 866); and later: 'if negotiations fail and deadlock continues, I would come to the House and ask for powers for compulsory arbitration' (col 867) – a classic misunderstanding of the nature of arbitration. He meant, of course, imposition. On the same day and at the same time, Lord Bassam of Brighton was making the same statement to the House of Lords. There Lord McNally mocked the Government's handling of the dispute:

> the Statement has all the hallmarks of a panic measure rather than a considered strategy. This is not surprising because, during the course of the dispute, I can think of at least seven Ministers who have been wheeled out at various times to try to explain Government policy ... Can we be told whether there is a coherent policy towards the public sector ... is this emergency legislation part of the review of the Employment Relations Act 1999? (*Lords Hansard* 28.1.03: cols 1018/9).

Meanwhile, 'military crews battled to control a major fire in the centre of Glasgow last night after striking firefighters refused to cross picket lines to help out' (*Scotsman* 30.1.03: 2). But the strikers still remained solid: 'Tam McFarlane, FBU spokesman for the South West, said there was a "grim determination" to see the dispute through' (*Bristol Evening Post* 28.1.03: 2).

FEBRUARY 2003 – STRIKES, THREATS AND IMPENDING WAR
A further two-day strike with continuing solidity on 1 and 2 February persuaded the Government to promote another round of ACAS talks. The role of ACAS was intermittent – according to senior officials we interviewed they were around and knew what was happening, but their involvement varied from actual intervention to 'running alongside' (i.e. pushed away from the formal negotiations while presenting to the public a feeling of doing something). Despite some mischievous press reports of a FBU leadership split (*Scotsman* 1.2.03: 2), FBU members remained loyal: 'Branch secretary of Tyne and Wear FBU branch, Steve Hedley, said: "the Government is saying that the unions should nego-tiate, but to that I say, two months ago we were negotiating. The FBU and the employers reached a settlement, but it was scuppered by John Prescott's intervention"' (Newcastle *Evening Chronicle* 1.2.03: 9).

On 3 February Mr Prescott met with the union and employers to clarify a number of issues. He confirmed that the employers would be allowed to enter into constructive negotiations without preconditions, excepting that Ministerial approval would be needed for any settlement which required additional Central Government funding. On this basis the EC agreed the next day not to set further strike dates and to resume talks at ACAS the following week (*Independent* 3.2.03: 4). 'Tom Neal, FBU secretary for Leicestershire, said ... "we've got to be optimistic, but we've been optimistic before. We are hoping there's going to be an agreement – there's got to be eventually"' (*Leicester Mercury* 3.2.03: 2). Meanwhile, the poor atmosphere in the West Midlands between the CFO, Ken Knight, and the local FBU became worse, with accusations and counter-accusations of intimidation at Oldbury fire station (*Birmingham Post* 3.2.03: 1).

Pressures had developed on all sides to start a negotiating process that would this time have an agreed outcome. As the *Independent* reported: 'a top-level emergency meeting was convened last night in an attempt to avert weeks of fire strikes. For the first time since the conflict began last year, all sides, including the Deputy Prime Minister, John Prescott, met face-to-face to try to break the deadlock' (4.2.03: 2). David Turner, writing in the *Financial Times*, reported that: 'FBU leaders and Local Government employers have taken heart at Mr Prescott's words, which suggest a freedom to debate the "modernisation" proposals that have become the biggest obstacle to the dispute's resolution' (5.2.03: 2). While most commentators noted this subtle but important shift in the Government's position – one that gave enough scope to the parties to negotiate – papers such as the *Daily Mail* saw it as the FBU backing off in light of what it claimed was falling public support, as war fever began to hit the country (5.2.03: 41). The next day the *Daily Telegraph* reported a telling development – the recommendations of review bodies for teachers and others in line with inflation. The view was that this would put pressure on the firefighters to reach a more modest settlement (6.2.03: 8).

On 10 February John Prescott met FBU leaders again, to clarify certain issues ahead of renewed talks between the parties at ACAS (*Coventry Evening Telegraph* 11.2.03: 17). Elsewhere Mr Justice Moses dismissed a legal challenge by the FBU against the Government's proposed changes to the Fire Act (*Financial Times* 13.2.03: 4). On 15 February the FBU agreed to allow a four-week cooling off period for negotiations to continue. The Government was clearly relieved not to have to fight this battle with the crisis in the Middle East near to boiling point. In addition the costs of the dispute were now gauged to be about £200 million in total, with £20 million in Scotland (*Scotsman* 18.2.03: 1).

With talks now firmly underway most of the media turned to other matters, the Cabinet became uninterested, and the negotiators got down to negotiating with each other while keeping their respective constituents on board. Throughout these weeks of intensive negotiations, the FBU members were kept informed of developments. This was directly, through circulars, but more usefully through regular meetings of representatives from all brigades with the EC and national negotiators. On 21 February such a meeting took place, in which Andy Gilchrist was able to lay out a structure for the talks on all aspects of the claim, based largely within the framework of the NJC. It was at this time – and not before to any extent – that opposition emerged from within the FBU to the position of the national leadership. It came in the form of criticism of the cancellation of strike days and was mainly heard from leading activists from the London region. This was familiar territory at one level. The London region committee had a tradition of attacking the broad left national leadership, partly based on the objective labour market realities in London, which gave firefighters a very strong position, and partly based on ultra-leftist opposition fuelled by the leadership ambitions of senior members of this group.

MARCH 2003 – WAR AND A POSTPONEMENT OF LOCAL HOSTILITIES

March was a month of on-off seesaw bargaining sessions. Strikes were called and cancelled, threatened and rescinded; offers were made and rejected, new offers were accepted by the FBU EC but rejected by activists, splits opened and closed again; old offers in new dresses were proposed; Ministers at first gave a helping hand to the negotiations, but as war moved from possible to probable the hand became an iron fist of imposition and emergency legislation. As the month ended a crucial intervention by Professor Burchill, the independent chair of the NJC, opened a new avenue for both parties to walk down together.

In the run up to the expected new offer from the employers, the union leadership sent out clear messages to their members, the wider public and the politicians: 'FBU sources said that the union was prepared to accept sweeping changes to working practices in return for a significant pay deal', but no deal was possible 'which involves big cuts in jobs and closures of fire stations' (*Wales on Sunday* 2.3.03:18). On the same day the *Mail on Sunday* ran the first of an oft-repeated tale of Andy Gilchrist's curry dinner (2.3.03: 3). The story typified the dumbed-down coverage of the dispute aimed at undermining the FBU leadership with cheap jibes: it was much harder to attack the substance of the union's case, the reasonableness of the leadership's behaviour, and the solid support of members for their union.

The Guardian now returned to some serious effort at reporting the dispute with the widely held view that the employers would offer 16% in three phases. This would be linked with modernisation of working practices, and was dependent on £30 million transitional funding from Government (6.3.03: 9). Such an offer was indeed made early in March. This was described as a final offer. It outlined a three-stage pay agreement giving 16% over thirty-one months, by 1 July 2004 producing a £25,000 per annum basic salary for qualified firefighters. It also offered a guarantee of a new pay formula for at least two years. But much of the language on the proposed new conditions of service was of 'management rights to manage' rather than the need to seek consensus and agreement.

Not surprisingly, therefore, the EC at its meeting of 6 March decided to recommend that members reject the offer at branch meetings organised in the run up to the Recall Conference on 19 March.

Over the next few days the parties sought to marginally re-position themselves in anticipation of further Government nudges and a new offer from the employers. The *Financial Times*, for example, urged the FBU: 'to beat a strategic retreat by accepting the offer tabled yesterday by the employers'. The article was trying to appeal over the heads of the FBU negotiators directly to members. It is unclear why the paper felt they would read and/or take any notice of its views, yet it went on: 'members will find it hard to stomach, since the union did a good job of convincing them they deserved £30,000 a year. But they should take the opportunity to accept a deal that many others in the public services can only dream of' (7.3.03:18). On the same day the *Evening Standard* could report that: 'activists are now meeting at the TUC in London to discuss the decision by their executive that a 16 per cent pay offer over three years is unacceptable' (7.3.03: 2). Once that decision had been taken the new war of words started: 'firefighters' representatives from all over Britain expressed "outrage" yesterday at the latest pay offer and called for fresh industrial action' (*Independent* 8.3.03:6). Anger was in the air, and there was a push from some activists for an indefinite strike. By Sunday the *Observer* thought that: 'firefighters' leaders are ready to offer significant concessions when they meet the Government for talks tomorrow in a bid to resolve the deadlock over the long-running fire dispute' (9.3.03: 9). Andy Gilchrist was preparing the ground for his meeting with John Prescott and some reports indicated, this might include lifting the thirty-year overtime ban. The Gulf war was now the key issue for the Government and this put immense pressure on the union negotiators.

All was now ready for a new offer and further shadow boxing was involved through the media over the extent to which the overtime ban was to be removed and under what circumstances. On 12 March as the parties met again the FBU arranged a lobby of Parliament: 'A delegation of Devon firefighters was expected in London today to lobby MPs over pay and reforms' (*Express and Echo*, Exeter 12.3.03: 4). The London *Evening Standard* could report later that day that 'hundreds of firefighters from all over the country were lobbying MPs at Westminster today' (12.3.03: 2). The immediate issue was the Government's proposals to remove the right of appeal to the Secretary of State on public safety grounds on station closures and cuts in services.

Two days before there had been further words in the House on the proposed changes to the Fire legislation. While the debate centred on repeal of section 19(4) of the 1947 Fire Services Act, Nick Raynsford sought to put a moderate gloss on the employers' proposals thus:

> it is simply not the case that the reforms of working practices would involve unacceptable changes to firefighters' terms and conditions. The proposed changes allow a more flexible approach that will enable Fire Authorities to respond more effectively to today's risks and challenges. That will not mean tearing up all the terms and conditions enjoyed by most firefighters. Firefighters would continue to work, as they do now, an average 42-hour week. The majority could continue on the same shift

system that applies now. Some would have the option of changing working patterns: for example, to work days only, as some wish to do. Some
would be able to work overtime if they wanted. Nor will local fire chiefs
be free to impose draconian changes on firefighters without regard to
national considerations, as some who are hostile to a settlement suggest
(10.3.03 col 107).

But Raynsford did not tell MPs that the main purpose of the reform
was to give CFOs greater powers to change working practices unhin-
dered by the requirements of national fire cover standards. The *Mirror*
made clear what happened on 12 March: 'firefighters will stage a 24-
hour strike next Thursday, union leaders announced yesterday. The
move came after the FBU executive rejected the employers' revised 16
per cent pay offer' (13.3.03:10). The new offer still had too many
strings attached to be countenanced by the union negotiators; the decision to call more action was aimed at rallying membership support, and
was the final chance to take action before war fever engulfed the country's decision-makers and cheer-leaders. Immediately, doubt was
thrown over the exact nature of the new offer: 'John Prescott blamed
firefighters' employers yesterday for drawing up a pay offer that was
open to misinterpretation and then rejected' (*The Times* 14.3.03: 2). In
contrast to this conciliatory tone, the *Daily Telegraph* repeated the
threat to take legal action to ban the strike under the 1992 Trade Union
and Labour Relations Act if the nation was at war (17.3.03: 8).

THE BRIDGE TO BAIN
Into this deadlock stepped the independent chair of the NJC, Professor
Frank Burchill. As he said, 'the negotiations took place at ACAS
Headquarters, with the Independent Chair acting as mediator'
(Burchill 2004: 415). In informal discussions with us at the time of the
dispute he carefully considered his position as chair of the NJC, and
felt it was within the spirit of his role that a form of mediation by him
was possible. He referred to this in several conversations with us at the
time as 'the bridge to Bain'. With the help of the TUC leadership he
brought the two sides together on 17 March, and by 18 March the
employers had submitted a new offer (which they described as final),
which went some way to meeting union concerns on the way the new
working conditions were to be formulated and agreed.
    The new offer, brokered with the assistance of Brendan Barber, was
seen as the only possible way out for the union at this stage. Kevin
Maguire, writing in *The Guardian*, said that: 'the end of the most serious industrial confrontation to hit the Labour Government – whenever
it comes – is going to be messy'. And later, quoting Andy Gilchrist:
'"to reject the offer would be foolhardy ... I'm worried we would be
the first casualty of war ... this is not the time to tear this union apart"'
(20.3.03: 12). The EC felt able to recommend this offer to a Recall

National Delegate Conference held in Brighton on 19 March. The *Independent* claimed: 'an end to the seven-month-old fire dispute was closer last night after firefighters' leaders accepted a revised offer on pay and working conditions' (19.3.03: 2).

But delegates at the conference were not convinced and after a rather angry debate they voted overwhelmingly to reject the EC's advice. Making the best of what was a clear defeat for the national leadership, Andy Gilchrist said:

> today showed that ours is a truly democratic and representative trade union. Today our representatives made it clear that in their view the offer was not acceptable and they will be advising members during the consultation period to reject it. The logic is that, if it is agreed that it is unacceptable, then no doubt they will be asking for new strike dates. (*Morning Star* 20.3.03: 4).

Delegates also backed a brigade motion to call off strikes in the event of war. On 20 March the EC decided to circulate the amended final offer to all members' home addresses, indicating that it had been rejected by the Recall Conference. The circular asked members 'to consider this offer ahead of a new Recall Conference to be held in 2 to 3 weeks time'. In the event the Recall Conference was arranged for Tuesday 15 April. The document received by the members indicated the progress made in the recent negotiations. The biggest advance from the union's perspective was a new acceptance that changes to duty systems would be subject to local joint agreement and not be subject to management imposition.

The Government moved quickly following the Recall Conference's decision to reject the offer. On 20 March, John Prescott told the Commons that he was seriously considering using his powers to impose a settlement. Heavy hints were put about that any imposed settlement need not be as 'favourable' as the employers' final offer and that he could be returning to Bain's 11%, directly linked to job losses. This was not a surprise to the EC. In a letter to members dated 20 March the General Secretary explained that the threat of imposition was among the reasons why the EC had recommended acceptance. Later that day the FBU President and General Secretary met Prescott, who explained that he was under some pressure to ban strikes in the Fire Service and hinted that imposition was the lesser of the two evils. In all of the negotiations since the turn of the year the spectre of war and the threat of intervention by the Attorney General to injunct strikes as being a threat to public safety were never far away. Now the union was faced with the strong possibility of imposition by a Government, and which included some senior Ministers with a clear agenda to crush the FBU as an effective force in the Fire Service.

As the Government sensed further division and discord at every level within the FBU, it knew this was the moment to be even harder. On 20 March 2003 John Prescott rose to make a statement to the House of Commons on the fire dispute:

> As the House has just heard, military action is now under way and we are in a grave and serious situation. Our armed forces are now actively engaged in the Gulf. The continuing fire dispute means that 19,000 members of the armed forces are engaged in providing emergency fire cover at home. Therefore, although the FBU has called off its latest strike, which was due to start at 6 o'clock this evening, the threat of a further strike means that we must still hold those troops in reserve rather than release them for other military duties ... I regret to say that, last night, the FBU recalled conference rejected the latest offer from the employers. I will be calling in the local authority employers and the FBU to meet me this afternoon. I am sure that many Members will be astonished that the conference has rejected an offer of 16 per cent by July 2004 linked to common-sense changes in working practices. It would mean that every qualified firefighter would earn at least £25,000 a year compared with the present level of £21,500. That is a far more generous deal than most other workers in both the public and private sectors have settled for. It is double what their old formula would have given them, more than double what other Local Government employees have settled for, and compares with public sector pay settlements running at about 3 per cent a year (col 1101).

While John Prescott was right on the comparative benefits of the pay package, it is difficult to see how the return of overtime working and rest day working can be construed as common-sense modernising reforms. Having made his point on the fairness of comparable pay awards, he then tackled a series of by now familiar points: yes there was transitional funding but no more would be forthcoming; there will be legislation 'to impose terms and conditions within the Fire Service and direct the use of Fire Service assets and facilities' (col 1102); the FBU should hold a secret ballot of all members on the new offer rather than use the internal union consultative machinery; and – in reply to a question from Vernon Coaker – local CFOs would not have new powers to impose changes in working practices without agreement. The statement was used to put new frighteners on the FBU leadership and to remind the local authority representatives that Central Government still ruled their roost. In reality the statement helped to give the FBU's campaign new energy, by allowing the leadership to rally members and those from other unions including the TUC, around opposition to imposition. It also infuriated the employers with its threat to move towards a national Fire Service with centralised national controls.

As we have seen, the initiative for the 18 March talks had come from Frank Burchill. Fearing that the talks had reached an impasse and worried by the employers' apparent insistence that any improvement in pay must be accompanied by changes in working practices determined and imposed solely by the employers, conditions he knew were impossible for the union to accept and entirely alien to the principles on which the NJC was based – he felt impelled to use his position to bring the two sides back for further talks. He knew that the main problem was a predilection by some on the employers' side to sit tight and wait for the divisions within the FBU to widen. Some of the employers were in no hurry to settle. Burchill knew that a war of attrition would also be a protracted one, which would do considerable damage to morale in the Service and set back prospects for modernisation. He also felt that with some fine-tuning and a bit more time, the document agreed on 18 March could and should be the basis for a settlement.

His problem was to find a way forward consistent with the principles and past practice of the NJC. Two overriding concerns suggested themselves. The first was to preserve the role of the NJC in promoting change by agreement; and the second was to promote the localisation of duty systems in line with the Bain Report. To achieve these objectives Burchill needed to suggest amendments to the 18 March document that strengthened the commitment to negotiated change. He knew that the stumbling block to an agreement was no longer pay but the way in which new duty systems were to be introduced.

Over the next eight days there was a surge of activity designed to settle the dispute. First Burchill intervened with new mediated proposals. These were acceptable to the FBU but were received with hostility by Government Ministers and the lay leadership of the employers. The Government was preparing to go to war and deal with striking firefighters in the appropriate manner, through tough legislation and the language of bans, impositions and further threats.

The press was full of stories of what had been said and done for a few more days, before the story faded to be replaced by images of war. As the *Mirror* reported, John Prescott's statement 'inflamed union leaders and some backbenchers' (21.3.03: 23). Elsewhere there were reports of a mood swing amongst FBU members with the onset of war. With John Prescott back-pedalling on his imposition threat, there was a view that this was the time to settle (*Guardian* 22.3.03: 12). Brendan Barber of the TUC was widely quoted as being angered by the proposals and his views were themselves supported by a cross section of union leaders.

Against this background the EC met on 26 and 27 March. It decided to recommend to the next Recall Conference that, in line with the decision of the 19 March Conference, it should set new strike dates, but that these were not to be activated while UK troops were involved in the Iraq War. The union negotiating team then began yet again to informally explore possible ways of re-opening negotiations.

APRIL 2002 – BURCHILL'S PROPOSALS AND THEIR REJECTION

On 2 April Frank Burchill sent a letter to both the employers' side and the union outlining a possible way forward. These became known as the Burchill proposals. Their essence was to strengthen the agreement by including the requirement that change in working conditions be agreed with the union within the context of the requirements of the Integrated Risk Management Plans (IRMP), and that any failure to agree on these issues should be subject to arbitration.

The reaction to the Burchill proposals was immediate. The FBU EC saw them as a way to secure an agreement acceptable to the membership and safeguarding the union's position at local and national level. Radical change, some of it distasteful to many FBU members, was down the line, but with an agreement based on Burchill the union could remain a major representative force, with an important role in seeing that the modernising process benefited both the membership and the public. The employers and the Government were angry that Burchill had intervened at all. The hawks in their midst felt that they had the FBU on the run and that the union leadership should be left to swing in the wind. They wanted a settlement but they could afford to wait until pressures within the FBU either forced the membership to accept what their delegate conference had rejected, or led to a catastrophic reduction in the union's standing with the workforce. This, some felt, was their chance to destroy the FBU as an effective national force.

While hard and important negotiations were taking place inside and outside of the NJC against the backdrop of war, small groups of FBU members turned inward with some premature attacks on their own leaders. Such increasingly open and noisy splits were quickly picked up by the media and expanded into a sustained attack on Andy Gilchrist, in an attempt to discredit his role and thereby weaken the union in its dealings with employers and Government Ministers. One report captures the mood: 'firefighters in Greater Manchester are bidding to oust their national leader. Crews at Philips Park, one of Manchester's busiest stations, have passed a resolution of no confidence in the FBU national secretary Andy Gilchrist' (*Manchester Evening News* 3.4.03: 11). Such moves could have escalated via stations to the brigade committee and then to the conference scheduled for 15 April, but in the event these criticisms were few and far between.

Before then Barrie Clement, writing in the *Independent*, gave a clear view of developments:

> private proposals tabled by the independent chairman of the national negotiating forum late last week looked set to be rejected today by a meeting of fire authority representatives ... however, it was still hoped the blueprint might form the basis of an eventual settlement. The proposed deal, drawn up by Frank Burchill, professor of industrial rela-

tions at Keele University, who presides at pay talks, found favour with officials with close links to the union. One said: 'This has potential to settle it because it will not cost the Government a penny extra.' The Burchill document offers firefighters a greater degree of protection for existing shift systems and declared that changes should be introduced only after a process that seeks to reach 'agreement' with the FBU rather than 'consensus'. The word 'agreement' is seen to be more precise. In a leaked letter to Andy Gilchrist ... Professor Burchill says: 'differences between the parties are far less than perhaps they would recognise'. He argued for changes 'of a minor nature' in the wording of the proposals, which he says are 'always open to interpretation'. He said: 'It would be tragic at this stage not to reach a signed agreement, given the almost total proximity of the parties'. He adds: 'An enforced outcome rather than a signed and agreed one is unthinkable' (7.4.03:10).

The Times reported that 'both the Government and the employers said that the proposals were unacceptable ... the proposals give union representatives greater powers to obstruct changes in working practices' (9.4.03: 15). Yet, as it turned out, the employers' response was rather more measured than the Government's. In a letter to Burchill dated 9 April they made it clear that their main concern was that by insisting on change by agreement the Burchill proposals 'would make it too difficult to secure the changes necessary to modernise'. And later in the same letter the employers indicated that the proposal concerning duty systems 'appears to restate the existing requirement that there must be the same number of firefighters on duty around the clock'. As Burchill himself later recalled, 'a proposal would simply offer an option that did not exist – a plausible way back to the negotiating table for both parties. It had become obvious that the FBU preferred this. The employers, whoever they were, could simply ignore the option if they wished and ridicule the proposer' (Burchill 2004: 415).

The Government took a different line. According to Minister Raynsford, the Burchill proposals would cost £100 million a year. The issue of costs became contested, but remained as a major justification by Gordon Brown for not giving in to the FBU demands. This was based on the stale argument that to grant such pay increase would have a domino effect through comparability to other public sector workers, and that this in turn could cause havoc with macro-economic variables such as inflation, interest rates and unemployment. The more sustainable view is that Government leaders did not believe that at all, and in reality acted from other motives – to politically isolate unions, and to reassure voters, MPs, and media that this time a Labour Government was able to deal with union militancy.

The employers' main objection was that, by insisting on change being negotiated and agreed, Burchill was handing the FBU an opportunity to challenge any modernisation proposals which did not meet the union's approval at national level or have the members' support locally. The FBU's London region shared that view, arguing in their 17 April *Pay Claim Update*, that the Burchill proposals would 'retain constant crewing ... retain the right to veto any decision at local level ... retain the right to unilateral disputes procedure'.

This is a clear indication that trust had broken down entirely and that the employers were increasingly responsive to and nervous of Government pressure. As we have seen, at the November 2002 negotiations the parties were in agreement on the basis for a settlement, which included acceptance by the FBU that pay improvements were linked to reforms in working practices, and that where agreement could not be found on specific changes then they could be submitted for independent and binding adjudication. But by March 2003 the employers' position had changed completely. For example, they argued the extreme proposition that disputes procedures could only be invoked in circumstances when both parties agreed that this was appropriate. By March 2003 the employers felt they had the upper hand and needed to stand firm for an agenda for change not shared by the union and its members.

It is clear, then, that the employers' response to Burchill was hasty and ill considered. As Burchill said in his letter accompanying the proposals, the precise words in any agreement are always open to interpretation. For example, the employers in their reply to Burchill said that his new paragraph on crewing 'appears to restore the existing requirement that there must be the same number of firefighters on duty around the clock'. In other words, one of Burchill's main proposals was open to misinterpretation, but this could have been cleared up in further talks. For example it would have been very difficult for the FBU to insist on constant crewing everywhere in the context of local risk assessment plans, and it could be argued that Burchill was simply preparing the ground for variable crewing, provided that it could be justified on risk assessment grounds rather than imposed for cost cutting reasons. Similar arguments could be made about the employers' objections to Burchill's proposals on working hours (para 3.1(ii)), which in any reasonable interpretation opened up the possibility of local Fire Authorities organising, by agreement, a variety of shift patterns according to risk-assessed needs.

Burchill's own account stresses that his intentions were to achieve a negotiated settlement within the NJC, and that he realised that his 'unprecedented' intervention would anger both the employers and the Government (Burchill 2004: 416). And so it did. On 10 April Nick Raynsford wrote to Burchill and four days later he received another letter from Sir Jeremy Beecham (*ibid*). Both were critical, and particularly questioned the costs involved in the Burchill solution. Raynsford said at the start of his letter, 'I was surprised to learn that you had produced unilaterally a new package of pay and modernisation proposals, which goes beyond the employers' final offer to the FBU'. With this second intervention from the NJC Chairman both parties probably recognised that this was the last possible chance for a settlement within a national bargaining framework, and that both parties had no real interest in waiting for the enactment of the Fire Bill, or indeed for the outcome of the Iraq conflict.

The FBU EC met on 7 April to discuss the Burchill proposals. It decided to endorse them and to recommend that the upcoming Recall Conference adopt them as the basis for future negotiations with the employers. The EC also decided to challenge Raynsford's assertion that Burchill's support for democratic procedures in determining new working practices would add a further £70 million to costs. The union tested this by asking Fire Authorities to cost 'Burchill', and not one reply was received supporting Minister Raynsford's costings, reflecting the total unreality of the employers'/Government position. The £70m that Raynsford asserted would be added to the costs by the Burchill proposals had, he claimed, been based on information from Fire Authorities. Mike Fordham subsequently requested FBU (letter 2 May 2003) brigade secretaries to write to local Fire Authorities asking for the responses on this claim: in one answer Dave Green reported that no details of costings had been supplied to the ODPM from Lincolnshire, Derbyshire, and Leicestershire. In a letter from Councillor Duggan, chairman of the combined fire authority in Bedfordshire and Luton, to FBU brigade secretary Mick Syme, he says, 'neither the brigade nor the Authority has been requested to provide the information to which you refer' (letter dated 27 May 2003). We have read through another twenty-two such letters from Fire Authorities throughout the UK and the answers were the same: no request for any information had come from the ODPM. So for Ministers to accuse the FBU, or Frank Burchill, of not basing their proposals on costings seems very rich, given they also had no basis for their figures.

The Recall Conference met in Brighton on 15 April. It overwhelmingly rejected the employers' offer of the 18 March, and decided by a two to one majority to consult members on the Burchill proposals. By a big majority it recognised 'that the FBU membership will not take strike action during the current hostilities in Iraq'. In a circular to all 'home addresses' the next day, the General Secretary asked branches to meet urgently so that the EC meeting due to be held during the week beginning 12 May could be 'fully appraised of members' views'.

As Kevin Maguire reported in *The Guardian*:

firefighters' leaders yesterday threatened to call fresh strikes when the war in Iraq is over after rejecting a three-year, 16% pay offer tied to radical changes in the way they work. A meeting in Brighton of 250 delegates from all brigades voted overwhelmingly to turn down a package that the union's executive had originally recommended in March. The recalled conference of the FBU instead supported a proposal tabled last month by Frank Burchill (16.4.03: 9).

With a majority of two to one the recall conference delegates supported the EC's line to recommend these proposals to the membership. Opponents, however, felt that Burchill only represented vague heads of agreements, and had in any case been rejected by the employers (*FBU Organiser*, strike bulletin issue 20, 1 May 2003). In contrast, John Drake from Gloucestershire, representing a majority position, said: "'I think it was a very positive conference with a good outcome in that we are sticking with rejecting the employers' pay offer ... the Burchill document could form the basis for an agreement between the FBU and the employers and it is very much hoped that things would go that way'" (*Gloucester Citizen* 16.4.03: 6).

Informal talks with the Government and employers' side continued during late April and early May. The failure of the national employers' side to respond positively to the 'Burchill' proposals led to increased pressure from local Fire Authorities, MPs from all parts of the UK and local councillors to re-open negotiations and to reach a reasonable settlement quickly. In response to such pressure employers' leaders started to threaten to go back on their March offer. Sir Jeremy Beecham, chair of the LGA, was reported as saying that:

> unless firefighters come to a swift decision they would be jeopardising the existing pay offer. As time goes by, it's getting increasingly difficult to see how we will achieve those savings by November. That may change the order and size of the instalments ... of course there has to be consultation with the workforce, but it's not appropriate for any workforce to prevent the management, particularly in a publicly funded service, from carrying out the processes that are deemed appropriate (*The Journal*, Newcastle, 26.4.03:29).

The FBU negotiators met with the leaders of the LGA and COSLA on 6 May to hammer out the basis for an agreement around some elements of Frank Burchill's proposals, themselves based on the essence of what had gone before. Thus the logjam of bargaining positions had been broken sufficiently to allow a trickle of progress to be made.

KILL THE BILL

On 8 May there was a major debate in the House of Commons on the second reading of the Fire Bill. It was presaged by a number of press reports of the threat of further cuts in the Service directly from Central Government. 'The FBU said draft guidelines sent privately to local councils across the UK could mean 10,000 jobs axed nationwide. Yorkshire and Humberside regional chairman Malcolm Peel said the plans could leave already stretched services facing further cuts' (*Yorkshire Evening Post* 8.5.03). The next few days saw further reports of the rebellion by twenty-seven Labour MPs against the legislation to impose pay and conditions. 'The controversial bill has placed firefighters on a fresh collision course with the Government, fuelling fears that the FBU may plan a fresh wave of industrial action' (*Scotsman* 9.5.03: 6). The *Morning Star* added its voice: 'left Labour MPs pledged yesterday to continue the fight against the Government's draconian plans to impose a settlement on the firefighters and to cut the Fire Service' (10.5.03: 6). The Commons debate on the second reading of the Fire Bill was long and eventful. Labour MPs quizzed Ministers at length as to their real intentions, and on the principle of imposing conditions of service on a group of workers represented by a trade union in dispute with their employers. Much of the debate centred on the Burchill proposals: FBU supporters amongst MPs had been briefed by the union that it would accept a settlement based on those heads of agreements and form of words; but the employers and Ministers were keen to attack the proposals as giving far too much scope to the FBU to negotiate on behalf of members in the future.

Arguing that 'the FBU sets great store by the Burchill proposals', Tony Lloyd asked John Prescott 'whether he thinks either Burchill or, as it were, son or daughter of Burchill could offer a framework in which meaningful negotiations on both pay and modernisation could begin' (col 860). The reply for the moment was that the proposal 'has a number of cost implications. The existing costs are quite heavy ... Burchill accepts a negotiated wage framework, but has presented proposals which we and the employers consider effectively prevent any modernisation' (col 861). Since the FBU had been prepared to sign up to a modernisation agenda acceptable to the employers in November 2002, this appears to be a disingenuous statement from a Government now determined to humiliate the FBU in order to advance its broader anti-union agenda. Prescott went on:

> Hon. members will be aware that one of the cornerstones of the current terms and conditions of service is that there must be a constant level of crewing at fire stations around the clock, regardless of daily fluctuations in the number of fires that actually occur. That is neither right nor sensible, and it is certainly not right to assume that fire cover cannot be provided in another way. No other emergency service operates on this basis. Through the powers provided in the Bill, I will be able to change existing constant crewing requirements and allow Fire Authorities to match staffing to the real risks posed by fire (col 863).

Other Labour MPs joined in with pleas and arguments in favour of a negotiated settlement, with or without ACAS, and suggested that imposition and its threat posed a real danger to the wider trade union movement. For example Joan Walley, Kevin Barron and Alice Mahon all backed the Burchill proposals as the basis for a settlement without the need to attack the rights of firefighters to collectively bargain. In a long contribution Alice Mahon made the relevant points:

> On Professor Frank Burchill's proposals, like many of my colleagues, I attended an FBU briefing last night, which was useful. His proposals could settle the dispute to the satisfaction of the firefighters, their unions and the employers ... I do not like the Government's draft guidelines. They are all about cuts ... firefighters are members of a much-valued public sector work force and should be given the chance to have an honourable settlement ... the dispute is unnecessary. The Government must bear some of the responsibility for it and I am saddened that a Labour Government are trying to impose a settlement (col 884.5).

'THE HISTORY OF THE DISPUTE HAS BEEN REWRITTEN EVERY TIME A MINISTER HAS RISEN'

In a devastating attack on the Government's handling of the dispute from the start, John McDonnell spoke of the 'depth of anger about the Bill': 'many FBU members and firefighters across the country see this as a strike-breaking Bill – an attempt to break their strike'. He went on to widen the debate: 'the message that is going out to teachers, nurses and Local Government workers is that, if they enter into a dispute with this Government over wages and conditions, the Government will resort to the use of Parliament to impose a settlement ... Many in the public sector have already experienced reform, and it has meant privatisation, increased hours and worsening conditions, despite the investment that has gone in'. He then critically reviewed the Government's role in the dispute:

> We need to understand how we got into this mess – because it is a mess. In June last year an intervention occurred ... [and] that offer was blocked. That was the first disastrous Government intervention. Step two was industrial action. What was the Government's response? ... The Bain review. Then, in November, a clear deal was drafted. It was acceptable to employers and the unions, with the TUC present. Then came the second disastrous intervention. The third stage was the Government directing employers, straightforwardly, not to allow the November offer to go forward ... The Government's interventions destroyed trust, goodwill and any belief in the honesty of the discussions and negotiations that were taking place ... We now reach the fourth stage of the process. Mr Burchill comes forward. He is no running dog of Trotskyism, no lapdog of the militant trade union movement. He has proposals that the FBU leadership see as a basis for negotiation and for a settlement. What do the Government do? ... [they] say 'No, we will not fund it', and they invent

a figure of £100 million. There has been no negotiation with any Fire Authorities about the cost of Burchill. How do we know that? We know because the Fire Authorities have been asked, and they say they have not been involved in the calculations.

In a passionate conclusion he stated: 'this new Labour legislation marks an historic break between the party of Hardie, Attlee and John Smith, and New Labour. If it is passed, do not mention solidarity again; do not refer to "our movement"; do not expect the support of firefighters across the country and the many trade unionists who are behind them … this legislation is a disaster … it is a disgrace to our movement' (cols 894-898).

SUNSET CLAUSE – TIME-LIMITED LEGISLATION

The FBU's case for a settlement based on Burchill's bridge to Bain was restated many times by other MPs, including Alan Simpson – 'it seems somewhat perverse that we have gone through a process whereby we have plucked a settlement from the jaws of a national agreement and plunged it into the grip of a national dispute' (col 903); and David Winnick – 'if the Government said that the Bill was being introduced to facilitate a settlement of the present dispute, I might change my mind, but it contains no sunset clause. Regardless of what happens under the Bill the Government can impose a settlement whenever the Minister wants to do so' (col 909).

At 5.43pm, after over three hours of debate, Nick Raynsford, the relevant Minister, made the reply for the Government. He made four main points. First: 'I shall start with attempts to rewrite history … the reality of the Government's interventions in the dispute is that they were motivated solely by the requirement to make it clear that there are limits on what costs the Government will pick up' (col 918). He then dealt with the Burchill proposals:

> the employers made it clear that they had serious reservations about the way in which Frank Burchill had come forward with the proposals without ever consulting them, and without looking into the proposals' costs and implications. Given those reservations, I wrote to Professor Burchill on 10 April … 'I was surprised to learn that you had produced unilaterally a new package of pay and modernisation proposals, which goes beyond the employers' final offer to the FBU … as things stand it is difficult to see how these proposals could be funded from the employers' current budget'.

On 13 April Burchill e-mailed the Minister who read out the reply:

> 'the intentions behind "my" proposals were purely to keep open a line of communication and to gain time, if required – a potentially valuable commodity in light of surrounding circumstances'.

And Raynsford continued: 'that response is not a promising basis for a settlement' (cols 919.920).

As we have already noted above, Raynsford's reference to costings was entirely misleading and without basis in fact. Nothing in the proposals put forward by Burchill related directly to costings – he was simply facilitating an agreement based on implementing change by negotiations not managerial dictat or Government proclamation.

Raynsford ended with a comment to suggest that a secret ballot of FBU members would be timely, and that his main concern was with public safety and the end to the dispute. In this regard he repeated the Government's support for the employers' offer, that there was no additional transitional funding, and that he might concede a sunset clause during the committee stage (cols 920.921).

A SETTLEMENT IN THE MAKING

It took another two weeks for the employers to come back with a revised offer and for the FBU's EC to recommend it as the basis for consultation with a view to acceptance. First came indications that further industrial action was a real possibility:

> firefighters in East Yorkshire today warned a fresh wave of industrial action was now inevitable. It comes after they overwhelmingly rejected the Government's latest pay offer ... just 10 of the 1000 members of the FBU in Humberside backed the new offer ... A-division branch secretary Paul Applegarth, based at Hull's Calvert Lane Fire Station, warned ... 'the union is looking at holding two nine-hour strikes every week ... we hope our national executive will stick to this and not call off planned strikes while negotiations take place; we have made some tactical errors and lost momentum as a result' (*Hull Daily Mail* 14.5.03:17).

This was repeated elsewhere in the country: 'firefighters' leaders were today holding a crucial meeting which could lead to a call for fresh strikes' (*Coventry Evening Telegraph* 15.5.03: 5).

By the time the EC met on 15 May there were clear indications that the next meeting of the employers' side on Monday 19 May would be in a position to decide on a new offer. The EC decided to reconvene on 20 May to consider this offer, having 'agreed a strike strategy which is wholly dependent on the outcome of the employers' meeting'. So *The Guardian* could report: 'the executive of the FBU pulled back yesterday from naming walkout dates after disclosing that progress had been made during private discussions in recent weeks with local authority employers. The FBU meeting near Barnsley, South Yorkshire, agreed a timetable for stoppages, to be implemented if the talks stall and an employers' meeting on Monday fails to produce a settlement' (16.5.03:10).

The new offer, headed *Fire Service Pay and Conditions Agreement*

2003, was considered by the EC to be the basis for agreement to be recommended to the members for acceptance. In a circular of 22 May, the EC said, 'this proposed agreement differs significantly from previous offers made by the employers and meets many of the concerns expressed by members when rejecting those offers'.

On Duty Systems, the main stumbling block in previous negotiations, the EC had this to say:

> The proposed agreement on Duty Systems and working time arrangements is significantly different than any previous offer and maintains the existing Duty Systems in the *Grey Book*.
>
> If Fire Authorities wish to introduce other Duty Systems they need to be agreed with the Union and have to be justified to meet the Risk Management Plan. Change for change's sake and imposition by management is not provided for in the proposed agreement. If agreement is not reached then it can be referred to a Technical Advisory Panel, on which the Union will be represented.
>
> Alternative Duty Systems will need to meet certain safeguards on issues such as working time, safety and family friendly policies.
>
> Overtime will not be able to be used to support shortfalls in establishments and will only be on a voluntary basis.

The newspapers were full of the good news. Barrie Clement wrote in the *Independent* that: 'an end to the nine-month fire dispute was in sight last night as both sides unofficially endorsed a settlement' (20.5.03: 6). He explained:

> after several days of negotiation, FBU officials provisionally agreed a 16 per cent pay rise over three years [actually it was over two and a half years]. The blueprint is expected to be accepted today by the FBU's executive, which will recommend it to the 55,000 members. The prospective settlement will be put out to consultation over the next three weeks.

The next day the *Scotsman* joined in: 'the long-running fire dispute neared its final stages yesterday as union leaders agreed to accept the latest pay offer' (21.5.03: 2); and Roger Bagley wrote in the *Morning Star* that: 'FBU general secretary Andy Gilchrist said the new offer represented a "potential breakthrough" ... [and] Sir Jeremy Beecham said that he believed that there was now a "workable basis" for moving forward' (21.5.03: 4). The *Independent* still felt that there had been a 'fudge' over modernisation (21.5.03: 6), but the *Daily Telegraph* decided to continue its vendetta against the FBU leaders, with further pointless stories of largesse, and quotes from the head of the Retained Firefighters' Union, Derek Chadbon, who referred to the 'arrogance' of the FBU leadership (24.5.03: 5).

So the deal was done – following a simple endorsement from the parties the ink could dry in peace. Such an ending would have assumed some goodwill, and some clarity about the future of the Service on the part of the employers. It was now for the employers with a Labour majority to show their mettle. What resulted was a drawn out saga of retribution and revenge upon the FBU, its leaders and members. There seemed little concern for the future of the Service, public safety, political survival, and consensus. Instead we had another year of seeking to show the firefighters who was boss once and for all, and of course, by default, showing all other Local Government employees the same stick with which they could be beaten. All this was encouraged by Government Ministers, with Nick Raynsford and his senior civil servants particularly keen to block any final agreement which did not meet the Audit Commission's approval on costings.

JUNE 2003 – AN AGREEMENT IS ANNOUNCED

By early June the Fire Bill with its powers of imposition had passed through the House of Commons, despite a modest Labour rebellion and a concession allowing a sunset clause. It would soon be up to the Lords to further the debate and the legislation. For over four hours on 3 June, MPs debated a series of amendments to the Bill as it passed through the House in its third reading. Most of the comments had been made in the earlier debate, but those MPs friendly to the FBU kept up the pressure on Nick Raynsford, probing away at the Government's case and intentions. His response throughout was resplendent with the vocabulary of New Public Management: 'modernising the Fire Service … one of the keys to this is to set clear targets … and to insist on best value … flexibility is very much the objective … it is in all our interests that we have the most effective Fire Service possible'. Raynsford did not tell the House that in reality the agreement expressed the essence of the Burchill proposals by incorporating the requirement to implement change by negotiation. Neither did he concede that many academic labour lawyers and the TUC totally disagreed with his assessment of ILO convention 151, since it was clear that the Bill as drafted was designed to impose terms and conditions of employment.

He was more defensive when dealing with the apparent attack on collective bargaining, and spoke at length about the Government's strong preference for a negotiated settlement of the dispute. There were four points he made. First he conceded that: 'there is no wider application to any other industrial relations situation' (col 51). Secondly, he stated: 'all parties, including the local authority employers and the FBU, want a national agreement. They do not want regional bargaining or negotiation with individual Fire Authorities … the proposals that Professor Burchill made a couple of weeks ago are not on the table and do not form part of the current offer' (col 61). Thirdly, he denied that the Bill was against article 8 of the Labour relations (Public Services) convention, known as ILO convention 151: 'The article requires that settlement of disputes about conditions of employment of public employees should "be sought ... through negotiation ... or through independent and impartial machinery"' (col 62). Fourthly, he conceded a two year sunset clause: 'as a result of amendments made today, the powers in the Bill will have a limited life and will lapse two years after Royal Assent' (col 112). This was despite the advice from the Government's own lawyers that it breached their treaty obligations.

The other important aspect of the debate dealt with the uncertainty surrounding the proposed deal. As the Minister said in a reply to a question from Angela Atkinson: 'I agree that there are uncertainties. That is one reason why individual firefighters may have been nervous about accepting the generous 16 percentage offer on the table' (col 74). He tried to be reassuring about changes to the shift system, mixed crews, and overtime. So the bold modernisation plans upon which the Government had fought this encounter had apparently and suddenly become fairly marginal and largely voluntary changes in conditions of service. No wonder that many firefighters remained wary of an offer which required them to trust Ministers as well as their employers, a point forcefully made at the Recall Conference later in the month.

At 9.22pm Raynsford formally moved the third reading of the Bill, and on 19 June Lord Rooker formally moved its second reading in the House of Lords. Most of his contribution parroted that of Nick Raynsford in the Commons, but he spoke after the settlement, and therefore had to explain why the Bill was still needed even if only for two years. He did so by providing a timetable of what needed to be done:

> these issues include the agreement of a new pay structure by 31 October 2003; a new pay formula for 2005 and 2006 to be agreed by 31 July 2003; evaluation of the relative job weights of firefighters and control room staff to be completed by 31 July 2003; revisions to the so-called '*Grey Book*', the document setting out detailed conditions of service, to be agreed by 31 October 2003; a review of the current procedure for settling disputes to be completed by 31 October 2003; and proposals for the revision of the NJC's constitution to be made and ratified before the end of this year. The pay increases for stage two, which is November 2003, and stage three, which is July 2004, are subject to the completion of all negotiations and consultations (col 1016).

So the gun had to continue to be pointed at the collective heads of the employers and union. At 6.41pm Lord McCarthy rose to speak to an amendment. He had been a professor of industrial relations at Oxford University and architect of the original firefighters' pay formula in

1978. He went on to attack the Government and the Bill in savage mode.

THE GHOSTS AT THE BARGAINING TABLE

He started: 'some 25 years ago, I was responsible for the formula that settled the last Fire Service dispute; the Upper Quartile of the Manual Workers (Male) Index. Although it gave us peace for 25 years, it blew up at the end'. He then declared that in the interest of equity 'this Bill is not fair ... the Bill at this stage is an insane Bill. It is a botch-up ... It is halfway between a cock-up and a conspiracy' (col 1020). But most of his comments concentrated on the nature of arbitration, imposition and reserve powers. Invoking his fellow academics from the Donovan era, Flanders and Clegg, he restated the case for national collective bargaining and the use of textbook ACAS-style arbitration. He made it clear that: ' [the] Bill gives the Secretary of State as many bites of the cherry as he wants. He can interfere, as he has already, in the negotiation process ... he twice prevented a settlement. He was active among the employers, and then bobbed in and created a separate mediation theme. I say nothing against the Bain commission, but the chairman was not chosen by the parties and no terms of reference were agreed' (col 1021). That point made, he then discussed the real problems of the role of Government in public sector pay: the twin issues of the 'ghost at the bargaining table' and 'the Pooh-Bah dilemma of the three hat syndrome' – namely that the Government is pushed by the Treasury to keep the pay settlement down, but is pulled by the public who do not want industrial action, and pushed again in favour of fair pay for public sector workers such as nurses, teachers and firefighters. His solution is a system of 'independent arbitration' through pay review, *ex parte* arbitration, and mediation (col 1022).

RECALLED TO SETTLE

The week before, firefighters had been voting on the new recommended package, with very mixed feelings and results. In Devon, for example, a majority turned down the offer at Paignton, Exeter, Barnstaple, Bideford and Plymstock; but the other eleven stations voted to accept the deal. Andy Gould from Paignton was quoted as saying '"we voted 17-2 in favour of rejection because we feel there are too many grey areas in the package"'; and Mark Wileman from Torquay said his station had voted 25-20 in support of the deal because, he said of '"industrial action fatigue" and that "the stop-start nature of the dispute did not help things at all"' (*Herald Express*, Torquay 10.6.03: 2). The London regional leadership, as ever in favour of more action, urged rejection of the deal. They became increasingly concerned about the fate of long service pay, and were unsure about the details of a new pay formula due to start in July 2006. In a long interview with six of the leading activists from the London FBU their feelings were clear: the leadership had got the tactics wrong from February 2003; there should have been more and longer strikes; and, as a result of this failure of militant will, the union was now facing a very limited settlement, was damaged as a fighting force, and Andy Gilchrist in particular had let them all down. This line of argument was increasingly echoed by a small minority of activists at FBU meetings in 2004 and formed the basis for a challenge to the strike leaders early in 2005 (see chapter 6).

On the day of the Glasgow conference, the *Morning Star* reported Andy Gilchrist's mood when he explained why what was on offer was a basis for settlement:

> the employers have also accepted that retained firefighters should receive pay parity, with greatly enhanced hourly rates and attendance fees ... emergency control room operators, who are mainly women, will receive at least 16 per cent under the agreement, with the possibility of more, subject to the results of a job evaluation exercise ... the employers have also agreed to a new pay formula which will link firefighters' pay to associate professional and technical workers (12.6.03: 5).

The Recall Conference held on 12 June voted by a majority of 3 to 1 to accept the employers' offer. It recognised that 'this offer requires further detailed agreement within the NJC on a number of matters', and that the membership would be 'fully consulted prior to final agreement being reached on each of these issues'. The next day the press widely reported the reaction of firefighters up and down the land. Paul Matthewman, branch secretary of the south Yorkshire branch, told the *Star* in Sheffield that his branch opposed the offer by 2 to 1, and that the feeling was there were too many hoops to be jumped through to get the money (13.6.03). In South Wales, Neil MacPherson from Swansea told the *South Wales Evening Post* that: '"there was no great enthusiasm for the offer but it's gone on for such a long time and members wanted to bring it to a close ... it's not a bad deal but we are concerned about the changes in conditions linked to the offer"'(13.6.03: 2). Jeff Owen, chairman of the FBU branch at Scunthorpe Fire Station, said he was worried about job losses, but that his members had voted to accept what was on the table and then continue to negotiate (*Scunthorpe Evening Telegraph* 13.6.03: 7). North of the border a FBU member from Lothians and Borders remarked: '"they have led us into a dark tunnel. All we can do is wait and see what it's like at the end of it"'. And Tony Paterson, representing FBU headquarters staff in Scotland, was reported as saying '"I voted to accept this deal ... and it sticks in my craw"' (*Herald*, Glasgow, 13.6.03: 2). This mood of reluctant acceptance was taken up and used to attack the deal and the FBU leaders by the ultra-left groups. Despite the overwhelming vote by mandated delegates expressing the position of rank and file members, the agreement was portrayed as 'appalling' (*Socialist Worker* 10.5.03), and it was argued that 'pay rises come tied to cuts and attacks on conditions' (*Socialist Worker* 24.5.03).

Jeff Ord, President of CACFOA, was quick off the mark: 'getting the firefighters back to work is the first step in moving this essential Service forward ... the best people to deliver change must be the people who work in the Service. Consultation is specified in the deal now accepted, if this is to be meaningful, and not just sound good, then everyone in the Fire Service has a vested interest to take part' (CACFOA *Press Statement* 12.6.03).

So on 13 June 2003 the parties at the NJC agreed a collectively bargained national settlement. One that had been reached after strike action, the invasion of Iraq, new legislation threatening imposition, and with increasing rifts both within and between the two sides. The Government had directly intervened and thus had given the lie to its policy plank that employers and their employees could freely settle differences over pay and conditions of service.

The national press reported the FBU's decision with mixed accounts. The *Independent* was happy to point out that 'Andy Gilchrist ... was attacked by militant firefighters over his leadership of the organisation. But he believed the deal, tied to modernisation of the Service, was a good one'. The article went on to quote a leading dissident, Matt Wrack (FBU London regional organiser), thus, '"this is a very sad day for the union and for the Fire Service. Everyone is unhappy about this. The leadership has mishandled the dispute from the start and they should consider their position"' (13.6.03: 8). A more sympathetic *Guardian* reported the 'rancour' that 'marked the end of the 10-month fire dispute as leftwingers accused union chiefs of "selling out"'; but it also reported Andy Gilchrist's response: 'if anyone thinks we can overcome the state with a few periodic strikes then they are living on a different planet. If anyone thinks we can launch indefinite strike action and keep the members together they are coming from a different universe' (13.6.03:10).

How did the FBU negotiators view the June 2003 settlement? Mike Fordham was upbeat:

> I think, given where we were, it's certainly good enough. It comes back then to my only experience of the negotiations at that level and that's the 1977 strike. At the end of the 1977 dispute many of us, including me, thought it was a defeat. We had asked for a percentage pay rise of 30% and we got 10%, and we got a promise of a new pay formula without the detail of it. What is it we got? A forty-two hour week promise and we ended up negotiating stand-down time in the 1977 deal. They don't know about that. They've forgotten that we gave away stand-down time in the 1977 deal. I had this row the other night with some people who were actually in the strike. They've forgotten it. We agreed to a disputes

procedure in the 1977 dispute. We didn't have one before, and the employers insisted on conditions in the deal we didn't want. Many of the activists we recalled were prepared to reject a forty-two hour week and all the jobs that came with that because they didn't want a disputes procedure.

History is telling me that that was a great victory and one of the best the trade unions ever had. Now my feeling for this one is the same. It's a considerable step forward, it's a significant pay increase compared to anything else. Certainly what we've done with retained is groundbreaking, never mind just the pay, it's not just the pay for them. What is important is pay equality, and what changes that will bring about in the relationship between rural and urban areas, it's massively significant.

What we've done in control is significant, they've had a pay rise which other people would not dream of. Not everyone saw it was significant and not everyone would think they ought to get that, but the pay formula results will show how good or bad that is. It's a forerunner, giving us what we want, which is recognition of where we ought to be within certain staff categories.

No it's not £30k, but, interestingly, even this year, this financial year, once we've sorted this mess out many of our members will be on £30k now we've negotiated locally. So I think we are in that classic situation, we've built them up for something that we were not able to achieve. We've told them they are worth something that we weren't able to get. Then they are seeing changes throughout, and it's a Service that hasn't seen change for a long time. People don't like change and management are crap at doing it. They are incompetent, not just politically, they are actually incompetent at doing anything like that.

Of course the agreement was subject to close scrutiny by FBU activists and members. The overwhelming majority accepted what they had as the best available in the circumstances, but that was dependent upon the employers paying the increases and some muted optimism that the modernisation programme could be delayed and diluted at local level. The FBU's official strike bulletin (issue 70) put the questions and gave some of the answers rehearsed amongst brigade members throughout the UK Fire Service. First that the alternative to a settlement was more action; secondly, that the Labour Government was gearing up for more privatisation and public sector reform; thirdly that the Government still argued that we were at war in Iraq and therefore threatened drastic action against an emergency service on strike; and fourthly there was the threat of imposition contained in the Fire Bill. Andy Gilchrist's position was clear: 'we should not underestimate our achievements'. These included progress on equality issues for retained and control staff, the best pay rise anywhere in the public sector, and the saving of national negotiations for pay and conditions (*Firefighter*, July 2003: 2-3).

Most activists interviewed agreed: Jim Quinn from Northern Ireland said his members were not happy, especially with the proposed staging and the deal on long service increments; Linda Smith from London thought the deal was acceptable for retained members and control staff – a position supported by Val Salmon (EC for control staff), although she worried about job losses if regionalisation took off; an executive council member told me his members were split over the pay offer and had further worries about all aspects of the deal, but Helen Hill, representing retained members, said her members were happy with the move to parity pay. Brian Joyce (EC for Devon and Treasurer) thought the deal the best available but ruefully noted the damage done to the credibility of the leadership because – a point made by many others – the promise of £30k, although a negotiating position, had been seen as a genuine valuation of their worth and an achievable target.

THE WHITE PAPER FROM ODPM

Meanwhile the ODPM had issued its White Paper (*Our Fire and Rescue Service*) in late June. The *Independent* suggested that, while 'the White Paper falls substantially short of the radical changes suggested by Sir George Bain', yet 'the plans will enable fire chiefs to change the number of firefighters on duty at different times of the day'. The overall package was familiar to other public sector workers: in the name of efficiency and modernisation more power was to be located in the hands of senior managers on site, smaller units of activity would be closed or merged, and there would be fewer skilled staff available to deliver a service with a changing emphasis (1.7.03: 2). The FBU response was concerned with potential job losses, but otherwise adopted a wait and see stance to what might happen locally. As Mark Wileman, Torquay FBU, said: 'it is how they are going to be implemented that will be the real test' (*Herald Express*, Torquay, 1.7.03: 2). In Merseyside the mood was more defiant. FBU branch secretary, Les Skarratts, said: 'chief officers and Fire Authorities support the White Paper because it not only stops the FBU from opposing these moves [station closures] but also the communities that we serve ... our members have been very clear that we will oppose any reduction in jobs' (*Daily Post*, Liverpool, 2.7.03: 5). A more widespread view was expressed by a local FBU representative, Ray Grindod, as reported in *The East Grinstead Courier*: 'he was wary of the White Paper' (4.7.03: 7).

So the strike and subsequent negotiations had shifted the formal power relations within the Fire Service away from the employers and employees to a familiar combination of Central Government and senior managers. Thus both the employers and the FBU had lost some say over the running of the operational side of the Fire Service, and what now remained was how the two sides would redefine their own relationship up and down the country before setting about the longer term objective of chipping away at the new modernising agenda. Thus, after the settlement bargaining continued for another fourteen months, while the formal aspects of the agreement clashed with the informal aims of the parties.

JULY - OCTOBER 2003 – HARD BARGAINING AFTER THE EVENT

There then began four months of detailed talks to secure implementation of the agreement. On 9 July the EC circulated to members a provisional agreement for approval on a New Pay Formula which would link future pay rises for all FBU members to movements in the average pay for the Associate Professional and Technician classification in the New Earnings Survey carried out each year. This was overwhelmingly endorsed at Branch meetings and the agreement was finalised with the employers before the end of July. By 20 October substantive agreement had been reached on a position statement and on 21 October the General Secretary was able to circulate to members the following list for approval:

> Minimum of 7% from November 7 2003 on the basic pay of all members.
>
> Additional 3.2% for all Emergency Fire Control Staff from 7 November 2002.
>
> Pay parity for Retained members which equates to 13.74% from November 2003.
>
> A new National Pay Formula linking the pay of all Firefighters to the Associate Professional and Technical group of workers.
>
> A new non-discriminatory scheme to be negotiated based on Continued Professional Development will replace the Long Service payments (phased in over 2006-2007).
>
> Competence/Qualified pay reached after three years rather than four years.
>
> Opportunity to earn payments for additional responsibilities.
>
> Further 4.2% from 1 July 2004.
>
> Guaranteed minimum £25,000 for all 'competent' Firefighters at 1 July 2004 and for Control Members £23,750.

If accepted this will mean the ending of the union's overtime ban from November 7 2003. If accepted, with effect from 7 November 2003 as stated in the Fire Service Pay and Conditions whole time and part time employees on the shift, day crewing and day duty systems will be free to undertake retained duties where appropriate. There will be no barrier to any employee working on a combination of different whole time, part time and retained duty systems.

By early October much hard work had been done to clarify the agreement and to start work on its implementation up and down the country. At national level some repairs had apparently been made to industrial relations in the Service, especially between the FBU leadership and the LGA officers. As some employers broke ranks with their own association, on both regional and political grounds, so different versions of the agreement emerged. With that came renewed worries that with the new legislation about to be finalised and the White Paper as a policy directive, some employers would seek to alter the balance of power once and for all between themselves and the FBU. In Scotland, for example:

> the FBU accused the Scottish Executive of betrayal ... Kenny Ross [FBU Scottish secretary] claimed the Executive's document would remove the statutory minimum number of appliances attending incidents and scrap the maximum arrival time of five minutes. It would also scrap laws that required Ministerial approval before local fire chiefs could shut down stations (*The Times* 2.10.03: 13).

The internecine warfare that now broke out amongst the ranks of the Labour Party representatives was both political in nature – between those more and those less willing to hound the FBU – and constitutional – between those holding out for Local Government autonomy and those giving in to the demands of the ever more ruthless central state. Figures such as Val Shawcross were seen to be too close personally and politically to Ministers such as Nick Raynsford, who in turn was not trusted, partly because of his own close personal links with one of the more anti-union CFOs.

Such distractions fuelled the idea that the majority of employers had given in to Central Government, and that further attacks on the FBU and its members' conditions of service could be expected even after the settlement. There remained anxiety about the fifteen-year Long Service Increment (LSI), which, it was proposed, would be replaced by a new system of payments to reward Continual Professional Development. (This latter scheme will be introduced by 1 July 2006 to coincide with a phased reduction of LSI and will completely replace LSI by 1 July 2007. The new system will be funded by the money currently spent on LSI.)

Clarity on this and other questions was provided to all members in a circular dated 22 October. On Emergency Fire Control Room pay the employers agreed to a joint job evaluation exercise to assess the relative weights of the jobs. After a number of workplace visits and discussions, the job evaluation team agreed that the ECRO pay should be increased significantly, from 92% to 95% of the firefighters' rate. After consultation with the Control Staff National Committee, the EC agreed to accept the job evaluation report and the NJC subsequently ratified this backdating of payments from 7 November 2002.

While the principle of retained firefighters' pay parity was conceded by the employers early in the negotiations, the devil proved to be in the detail. After a number of meetings at officer level a new structure for the retained firefighters was agreed subject to consultation with the membership. This produced an overall annual increase of 13.74% at stage 2 to be paid from 7 November 2003. The new pay structure includes an annual retainer (10% of basic pay of a whole time fire-fighter), an hourly rate for work carried out, and a disturbance payment for every call out. These arrangements were approved by the Retained National Committee and therefore became part of the substantive agreement.

PHASING

It was expected that the position paper would be endorsed by the full employers' side of the NJC on 28 October and subject to membership approval by the FBU Executive on 3 November. But at their meeting on 28 October the employers' side agreed that the 7% Stage 2 payment due on November 7 2003 should be phased, with 3.5% payable (but backdated to 7 November) only when all the negotiations on Disputes and Disciplinary Procedures and the structure of the NJC had been completed, and the Audit Commission had confirmed that there was clear evidence of the implementation of new working practices at brigade level.

Although rumours had been circulating in early October that phas-ing or delay was being considered by the employers, this was never officially conveyed to the union side. On the strength of the rumours the General Secretary sought assurances from the Deputy Prime Minister and from the Audit Commission. The latter confirmed that it had no status in the implementation of the Pay Agreement, while Mr Prescott provided an 'avoid the question' answer to the General Secretary's letter – which had stressed the importance of full payment in November to the success of the Fire Service reforms and to improv-ing morale.

So there was widespread dismay when the employers' dropped their 'phasing' bombshell. The *Irish News* reported that: 'fears were grow-ing last night that the firefighters' dispute could flare up again in Northern Ireland' (28.10.03:19); and 'firefighters are considering renewed strikes after differences emerged with employers over the agreement … [they] want to introduce it in two stages, paying 3.5 per cent from next week and awaiting the result of an Audit Commission report into working practices before paying the second half in the new year' (*The Times* 1.11.03: 9). As we now know, FBU members had to wait until September 2004 for the final 3.5%.

NOVEMBER 2003 – UNOFFICIAL ACTION

Angry members in a number of brigades took unofficial action, including responding only to emergency calls. Some leading activists began turning their frustration inwards at their own leadership. Bob Pounder of the Greater Manchester FBU, and a leading activist in the Workers' Revolutionary Party, was quoted: 'the FBU pay claim has been a debacle with the national leadership handing over every gain that the previous generations of firefighters have won and defended' (*Manchester Evening News* 3.11.03: 4). In the run up to bonfire night there were various forms of unofficial action being pursued. About thirty-five of the fifty-nine Brigades reported some action:

> Dave Williams, of the FBU in Cheshire, said: 'most of the fire stations took a decision at 9 am to do emergency calls only' … Neil Day, secretary of the Norfolk FBU, said: '… our members are 100% taking part in this action. We are communicating in various ways – by telephone, fax, email, mobile phone and text message' … Matt Wrack, London regional organiser for the FBU, said: 'London firefighters are extremely angry at the employers' decision to stage the next phase of their pay increase' (*Guardian* 6.11.03: 6).

Despite this view no action was actually taken in London. Meanwhile, in Nuneaton: 'firefighters … have voted to withdraw their "goodwill" … Mark Rattray, the Nuneaton FBU branch secretary, said: "a motion was unanimously passed by the membership stating that all goodwill shall be withdrawn until further notice"' (*Coventry Evening Telegraph* 8.11.03: 1). Such views and actions were reported in the *Socialist Worker* with support both for the members' antipathy towards the Government-backed employers, and, especially, applause for attacks on the FBU leadership (8.11.03).

The EC decided to respond to the employers' provocation and the anger of the membership by going to a postal ballot of the whole membership to ask whether members were prepared to accept a phased payment of Stage 2. As the *Morning Star* reported: 'the FBU said yesterday that firefighters will vote over the next few weeks on whether to accept the staggered pay rise offered to them by the bosses' (11.11.03: 4). Such a move was aimed at legitimising the EC's position and thereby weakening ultra-left criticism of them, as well as heading off further unofficial action which might leave the union open to legal attacks from the employers and dissident firefighters. It worked for now. David Turner of the *Financial Times* was happy to report the planned revolt against the leadership and the intended vote of no confidence in them from the London regional committee (15.11.03: 3). By appealing over the heads of activists to the members, the EC had calculated that the ultra-leftists were the ones out of step with the membership. Again the *Financial Times* reported that: 'hardliners in the FBU were defeated when their general secretary won rank-and-file agreement on pay offer ... FBU members voted three to one in a postal ballot to accept the employers' offer' (29.11.03: 2).

North of the border in Scotland, Lynne Dickson – the employers' (Cosla) secretary – had stirred up more ill feeling with her comments on the nature of the deal. Ken Ross of the FBU had written a furious reply published in the *Glasgow Herald*: 'firefighters and control staff have complied with our side of the agreement. Rather than indulging in spinning untruths and misleading the public, Lynne Dickson, along with her colleagues at Cosla, should be ensuring that they comply with theirs. Otherwise, she and her colleagues will be responsible for more industrial unrest in the Fire Service' (12.11.03: 15). He later argued that the vote to accept the phasing 'has shown we are all reasonable people ... the actions of the employers, however, have shown we are dealing with unreasonable people' (*Glasgow Evening Times* 29.11.03: 2).

THE REASONABLE IN PURSUIT OF THE UNREASONABLE

The employers had by now shown that their intention was to keep the FBU dangling while they tried to whittle away at traditional conditions of service. This was their one big chance to roll back the FBU's frontier of control and to secure gains once and for all before the deal was bedded down and the new formula kicked in. The manner of the employers' enforcement of their temporary advantage was calculated to undermine the FBU leadership, hopefully split the union, and to sow the seeds of doubt amongst FBU members (and the wider audience of other Local Government workers) about whether industrial action and strong unions can actually defend long cherished working practices. The fact that such myopic employer strategies can lead to disillusion and demoralisation of the entire workforce, thereby putting the Service reforms and actions at risk, seemed to be unimportant. By sowing so much mistrust nationally it was unlikely that FBU branches would co-operate with any initiatives, making the Service less efficient not more. By summer 2004 the employers still had not paid in full the November pay rise, they had damaged the union and encouraged internal splits, and they had put in jeopardy the future of the Service. Some subsequently lost their seats at the June 2004 Council elections, partly due to the Iraq war, but also because of Labour voter abstentions over issues such as management of public services and treatment of well-respected public service workers, such as the firefighters.

Part of the employers' courage came from the Government's legislation which was about to become law. In the Commons on 12 November 2003 the final amendments were being debated and a fierce rearguard action was mounted by the Labour left to prevent the new Act from outlawing strikes by firefighters by the back door. In an important contribution John McDonnell MP made use of the arguments in the Lords by Professors Wedderburn and McCarthy. One example of the problem was given:

> Under clause 1(1)b, the Secretary of State may 'give ... directions to Fire Authorities about the use or disposal of property or facilities'. The fire authority has a statutory duty to comply with the direction contained in such an order. Wedderburn considers the example of a fire station closure and said that firefighters from the station under threat might persuade other firefighters to take industrial action against the closure and the removal of pumps, which threaten public safety, and indeed, jobs overall within the Service. It could be after a ballot and it could involve all the members of the FBU nationally. The union, Wedderburn states, would 'clearly be at risk' of liabilities 'for inducing a breach of the fire authority's statutory duty to comply with the direction'. Wedderburn further asserts: 'at present it is lawful for firefighters to strike against the closure of stations. Under the new law as the Bill stands it would not be lawful' (cols 320.321).

For the rest of the year talks continued on a new disputes procedure and a revised *Grey Book*. At the time most of those involved anticipated that these would be satisfactorily concluded well before the FBU Conference in May, so as to enable the early pay of the outstanding 3.5% (backdated to 7 November 2003) and prompt payment of the 4.2% (minimum) due on 1 July 2004 – provided that the employers showed good faith by honouring the agreements they had signed up to.

THE LONG GOODBYE: JANUARY TO AUGUST 2004

Four related issues now kept the pot boiling. In the early months of 2004 senior managers in the Fire Service started to implement the 'modernisation' agreement with special emphasis on re-organisation of control rooms and cutting the number of special appliances and associated jobs. This created tensions between the FBU in the relevant localities and the CFOs. This was not helped by some further pay increases to senior managers, seen as a reward for doing the Government's work for them, and these local spats in turn fed into the delayed and embittered national negotiations. These had virtually failed by late April.

In the east of England, for example, plans to merge centres from six counties were being drawn up as part of the Government's joint regional management boards. The worry for local people and the FBU was expressed by Sharon Peverett of the FBU: 'my main concern is the loss of the local service. In a merged control room we could have someone who knows the name of a village, but is not sure what county it is in' (*Luton Today* 6.1.04). A similar story was told by the *Bath Chronicle*: 'lives will be put at risk because of plans to amalgamate the south west's fire control rooms into one centre, according to the FBU.

The Government wants to get rid of local fire control rooms ... this means a call about a fire in Bath might no longer go to the control in Lansdown but to a centre as far away as Devon or Cornwall' (27.1.04: 5). And the *Coventry Evening Telegraph* reported: 'Moves to regionalise fire control rooms have been branded as "nothing more than a cost-cutting exercise" by the FBU Brigade Secretary for Warwickshire ... Norrie Henderson ... said ... "these moves would take the local aspect out of things"' (9.2.04).

Across the nation changes under the 'modernisation' plans began to cause concern, with cuts proposed in frontline staff. In Nottingham the local MP, Alan Simpson, said 'the whole thing is a cash-saving exercise, not a life-saving one. I'm very concerned about the moving of the aerial platform ladder. It seems madness'. This was endorsed by Notts FBU Secretary Alan McClean: 'to take a high rise appliance out of the city centre ... in my opinion is a suicidal gamble' (*Nottingham Evening Post* 14.1.04: 11). Elsewhere: 'More than thirty firefighter positions are to go in the West Midlands and up to a quarter of fire engines are to be redeployed for community use' (*Birmingham Post* 23.3.04: 3); and: 'the Fire Service in Greater Manchester is facing its biggest shake-up for more than fifty years ... Bob Pounder, FBU spokesman for Greater Manchester, said fifty jobs could be lost with the changes, in addition to sixty that are at risk if plans to replace the Service's control centre with a regional one go ahead' (*Manchester Evening News* 12.3.04: 17). Similar stories were reported in the north east, where FBU regional Chairman, Keith Walters, said, 'the public need to be aware that reducing the number of firefighters from nine to eight for every house fire means that firefighters will be taking short cuts' (*The Journal* 17.2.04: 15). In south Yorkshire the FBU accused fire chiefs of 'robbing Peter to pay Paul'; as Sheffield branch secretary, Gerry Pagan, said 'parts of this plan are cost-cutting, sometimes in areas where further cuts can hardly be made' (*The Star* 13.2.04). In south Wales there was a threat to the emergency crash tender in Llanelli – the FBU's branch chairman, Deiniol Lloyd, said, 'it could mean that there would be no crew available should the tender be required. The golden hour [the first hour following an accident] is crucial for the injured victim' (*Llanelli Star* 29.1.04: 3). In Scotland: 'firefighters are to be taken off front-line duty and ordered to "cold-call" every home in Lothian and Borders under plans to modernise the Service ... Union leaders have reacted furiously to the plan, which they say will compromise safety' (*Evening News* in Edinburgh 16.1.04: 5). In the south West: 'firefighters in Devon are threatening to strike after the county's fire authority yesterday voted to cut staff and effectively "mothball" an aerial platform used to fight serious fires' (*Western Morning News* 23.4.04: 5). Such stories tell the real tale of 'modernisation', namely that by cutting costs, providing more powers to senior managers, and redirecting resources away from core emergency work, the Service can become integrated within regions with other local authority activities, thereby reducing local account-ability and strengthening the central state and the market state.

To add fuel as well as evidence to this process: 'west Yorkshire fire chiefs have been awarded an inflation-busting pay rise in defiance of their national employers ... they are to receive 7.5%' – taking them up to between £112,000 and £120,000 salary (*Yorkshire Evening Post* 17.3.04); and down the road from there: 'CFO Paul Woods will now earn between £110,000 and £120,000 ... his deputy, assistant chiefs and head of human resources will also get significant increases' (*Nottingham Evening Post* 20.3.04: 5).

Such a combination of Government and employer betrayal, disillu-sionment with a campaign that did not deliver all that had been promised, and local aggravation, was a fertile breeding ground for the ultra-left to pursue their objectives of breaking away from the Labour Party, and winning FBU elections against the broad left incumbents. Thus *RedWatch* ('the voice of rank and file firefighters and control staff') claimed that: 'the vast majority of FBU members support this stance or support disaffiliating from New Labour ... the outcome of the pay dispute proved that New Labour is our enemy'. The argument continued with attacks on the leadership for calling a series of seminars to discuss the dispute with activists (27.1.04). We attended these semi-nars and found a wide range of argument about what had happened, but the majority of those that spoke, and with whom we spoke after-wards, supported the leadership's line that the strike had achieved a better deal than otherwise would have been offered, and that it was the Government that had caused the confusion and that deserved the great-est criticism. In February the ultra-left launched another propaganda sheet, *Grassroots FBU for a Democratic and Fighting Union*. Even its title tells the tale that it was part of a wider campaign under the umbrella electoral organisation, Respect, and behind that the SWP.

It was used to peddle the line, based on 'a new united rank and file grouping' aimed at trashing the FBU leadership, 'to support electoral challenges for union positions', and 'to build a network of activists' (Bulletin 1, February 2004). Bulletin 3 advised readers on the forth-coming conference, with support for motions to end Labour Party affiliation and to lambast the leadership again and again for the outcome of the strike. Bulletins 4 and 5 in March urged members to vote 'no' in the ballot to move ahead with implementation of the agree-ment. By June this had become a policy to stand against every incumbent associated with the broad left leadership and thus throw the union into a period of internal strife at a time of continuing external threat.

By early April these local disputes were overshadowed once more by a breakdown in the national talks on implementation of the June 2003 agreement. Again, as a deal appeared to be close, the union claimed that the Minister had put pressure on Labour councillors to attend the employers' side meeting and thereby 'scupper' the talks. As was widely reported, 'firefighters ... will be asked to vote for strike action after efforts to end the long-running pay dispute ended without agreement'; and, while the union blamed the Government, the LGA said that 'the sticking point had been over bank holiday pay and working conditions' (*Yorkshire Evening Post* 8.4.04). So once again the employers were to spring a late surprise.

STAND-DOWN

This time it concerned the issue of stand-down time. Under the old *Grey Book* arrangements, the hours of 12pm to 7am were designated as stand-down time, so that those covering the night shift (normally 6pm to 9am) would usually rest between midnight and breakfast except to cover emergency calls and other essential duties. What constituted other essential duties varied from brigade to brigade, and was often determined by custom and practice rather than written agreement. Brigades in inner city areas would occasionally use the early hours to carry out inspection work at night clubs and other places of late night entertainment, while others might intermittently check arrangements for commercial alarm systems during these hours.

For most brigades most of the time stand-down time was only interrupted by emergency call outs, with some nights busier than others, dealing with fires, road traffic accidents and many other incidents that required emergency and professional interventions. Bank Holidays were also treated as stand-down time, although the definition of essential activities usually extended to include fire station open days for the public, attendance at spring and summer fetes held on Bank Holidays, and other activities seen to be important as part of community fire safety work. The employers waited until early 2004 to raise this issue formally. They argued that they wanted stand-down removed from the revised *Grey Book*, giving local Fire Authorities total freedom to arrange shift patterns and working arrangements at all times of the day and year. The union argued that this issue was not part of the June 2003 agreement and therefore should not be part of the negotiations concerning the implementation of the agreement.

In reality, of course, there is precious little effective work that can be done between midnight and breakfast, except to deal with emergencies. Indeed there is considerable evidence to suggest that extra duties, which might include midnight lectures on some aspects of rescue work, are better done when the workforce is likely to be more attentive, and that extra duties could detract from the effectiveness of any emergency work carried out during the night. So it is very likely that ending stand-down could prejudice the health and safety of firefighters, and therefore the public safety in rescue situations. The fifteen-hour night shift requirement can only work in the public interest if firefighters are given adequate periods of rest between emergency calls. The union argued that, by keeping some central guidance on this issue in the revised *Grey Book*, the FBU membership and the public are protected against the temptation of local CFOs to end what they see as unproductive time.

This and the related issue of Bank Holiday stand-down arrangements appear to be minor matters. In real life there is very little worthwhile activity that can be carried out in the Fire Service during traditional stand-down times except the vital one of responding to emergency calls. It thus appears that, having wrung considerable concessions from the union in reaching the historic June 2003 agreement, some on the employers' side, egged on by Government Ministers and senior civil servants, were determined to prolong the dispute in order to both embarrass the union leadership and to extract every last advantage they could from what they saw as a favourable bargaining position. This is hardly the stuff of social partnership and dialogue. As we will see, the majority on the employers' side (an alliance of New Labour and Tory councillors) were to take this approach right to the brink of provoking a further national strike.

Parallel to the talks on all outstanding issues the Audit Commission was continuing its work monitoring progress on modernisation at brigade level, with a view to encouraging progress and clearing the way for the final 4.2% payment (the third stage), due to all firefighters on 1 July 2004 under the June 2003 agreement. By the end of the month the FBU leadership was confident that the employers could be pressed to pay the outstanding 3.5% due from November 2003 under stage 2 of the agreement, and that the verification process was on course to guarantee the final 4.2% by or soon after the agreed date of 1 July 2004. In order to test the membership views and to press the employers, the union leadership decided on a consultative ballot of the total membership on the basis of the progress made since the breakdown in October 2003 in all areas, except that of disciplinary procedures in the revised *Grey Book* and working conditions, revisions to the NJC constitution, IPDS, and the procedure for dealing with local disputes. The union material accompanying the consultative ballot form made it clear that on the issue of stand-down there was no agreement and that members were not being asked to agree with the employers' proposals at that time and to delete all reference to it. On 31 March the Audit Commission reported that the overwhelming majority of brigades (forty-eight of the fifty in England and Wales) had made progress towards modernisation.

CARRY ON NEGOTIATING

In early April the union announced a 62.8% 'yes' vote supporting the position reached and as outlined in the various summary documents. In the light of this and the recent report of the Audit Commission, the union pressed the employers for immediate payment of the 3.5% still owing from the previous November. The union leadership banked on some movement from the employers' side, particularly since it appeared to them that remaining differences were either slight or contrived and outside of the June 2003 agreement. Not for the first time in this long running dispute the union had misjudged the employers' position. The employers were in no hurry to reach agreement or to pay improved wages. Most of the employers saw no virtue in offering the union leadership a final settlement ahead of the FBU Annual Conference to be held in the second week of May 2004. So the employers, who individually or collectively were facing no financial loss, were delaying agreement, since they felt that they held all the negotiating cards as well as controlling the purse strings. They offered the FBU a further meeting on 5 May to resolve differences on the text of the revised *Grey Book* and the local consultation/negotiation procedure. The FBU EC was again put onto the back foot. In order to put pressure on the employers' side the FBU Executive decided that should the talks fail to agree immediate payment of the outstanding 3.5% backdated to November, then the union would pull out of the entire June 2003 agreement, thus placing in jeopardy the whole of the modernisation agenda. Some progress was made during April, with agreement achieved on a local disputes procedure, leaving only the issue of stand-down time still to be negotiated. On this the employers did make concessions, by accepting that some limitations be placed on the range of activities expected of firefighters in the small hours, and that, where possible, there should be adequate periods of rest between emergency calls.

Despite hours of negotiations, both informally at officer level before the 5 May meeting and at the NJC itself, the talks broke down without agreement on the stand-down issue. Indeed the employers turned the screw again by announcing that stand-down arrangements would no longer apply to Bank Holidays. The union leadership was anxious to be in a position to recommend to its Annual Conference, beginning on 14 May, the outline of a final settlement on all issues as the basis for a ballot of the membership. As we have seen the employers saw virtue in delay. So when the union, on the very eve of the conference, put a new form of words towards an agreement on stand-down arrangements, accepting in principle the right of Fire Authorities to organise the duties on night shifts in accordance with local risk assessment plans, the employers sent a non-committal reply, referring only to the need for further negotiations. According to the *Birmingham Post*: 'As a fresh firefighters' dispute is threatening to flare up after a sudden last-minute hitch to talks aimed at finalising the deal ... FBU sources accused some employers of wanting to introduce changes to the deal which were not part of the original agreement. One of the main sticking points involved "stand-down" time'; and 'the problem could lead to increasing calls for the FBU to disaffiliate from Labour' (8.5.04: 5).

Once again the FBU leadership was placed in a difficult position. The strike weapon was not available since it was perfectly clear that to call for industrial action would split the union. All sides knew this. In the past, industrial action short of strikes had been ineffective. In the event the EC decided to put the onus back on the employers by recommending to conference that the union pull out of the whole agreement and consult members about the best way of progressing the outstanding claim for pay justice. In effect the members were being asked to consider a campaign of non-compliance with management initiatives on training or new procedures not covered by the *Grey Book* or previous custom and practice.

The leadership could neither announce nor campaign for such a policy for fear of falling foul of the employment laws, thereby placing union funds at risk. To warn the Government off any move to impose a settlement, the conference was asked to support a resolution to call a ballot for industrial action should the Government use the draconian powers available to it under the Fire Services Act. Although this was a high risk strategy, the FBU Executive was reasonably confident that any Government imposition would unite the membership behind the leadership and could bring forward effective solidarity action from other sections of the trade union and labour movement. There was also the clear possibility that a few Fire Authorities and CFOs would react to a policy of non-compliance by disciplining FBU members, thus raising the stakes and creating new conditions for successful solidarity action.

ACTIONS SPEAK LOUDER THAN WORDS
Within a few days the situation changed dramatically. First: 'FBU delegates dramatically suspended their week-long conference on its opening day in Bridlington in North Yorkshire and voted to block implementation of a "modernisation" programme to prepare for a ballot on industrial action' (*Guardian* 12.5.04: 7). Of course this would happen only if the employers continued to refuse to pay the monies owing under the June 2003 settlement.

Secondly, Barry Dixon, the CFO of the Greater Manchester Brigade, suspended a group of FBU members for refusing to cover a new Incident Rescue Unit (IRU) unit based at Salford fire station. Following a short period of organised spontaneity, there began a period of widespread but limited unofficial action across the whole of the UK. Often this took the form of responding to 999 calls only, but the level of response varied from brigade to brigade. In some areas it was limited to a refusal to train on new programmes such as the New Dimension anti-terrorist operation. Within days the dispute had escalated, and:

> firefighters in Greater Manchester are on the brink of official strike action in the row over the suspension of thirty-two officers … last night

crews at fifteen stations across the county answered emergency calls only in a show of support for those suspended. Firefighters in five other brigades across the UK have taken the same action … nineteen firefighters from Salford plus thirteen from Ashton and Broughton were sent home without pay on Tuesday and Wednesday after refusing to sign an agreement to work with engines designed to deal with a terrorist attack (*Manchester Evening News* 20.5.04: 2).

And in *The Times*: 'The FBU said last night that it would immediately call for a national strike if any firefighters are dismissed over current wildcat action'. This was taking place in about a quarter of all areas such as the West Midlands, Gloucestershire, Wiltshire, Norfolk, Shropshire and Avon, Cornwall, Northamptonshire, Bedfordshire, Tayside, Derbyshire, South Yorkshire, Nottinghamshire, Leicestershire, Rutland and Merseyside; but not London (20.5.04: 2). Other reports put the number of brigades taking unofficial action as forty out of the fifty-eight in Britain (*Daily Telegraph* 20.5.04: 8).

By now: 'the number of firefighters suspended in Greater Manchester has risen to more than 120 and union officials are today facing calls for an immediate strike … it is understood that some of those suspended believe any plans for a ballot should be abandoned in favour of an immediate unofficial walkout' (*Manchester Evening* News 24.5.04: 2). On 28 May the GMC Fire Authority lifted the suspensions on the FBU members at Salford with no loss of earnings and accepted that the use of new IRU vehicles be delayed until there was agreement at national level on the implementation of the June 2003 agreement.

As so often during the dispute, industrial action by the FBU membership moved the position of the employers. Behind the scenes the national employers were actively putting pressure on the GMC Fire Authority to end the suspensions so that talks could proceed nationally to resolve the overall dispute. On 20 May, Phil White, the employers' side secretary, wrote to Andy Gilchrist proposing a new form of words to cover the stand-down issue. Indeed: 'the employers appear to be backing away from insisting chief officers should have wide flexibility to decide tasks … Christina Jebb … struck a distinctly more conciliatory tone after angering crews on Wednesday by accusing them of wanting to sleep on duty'. As she said, 'after a productive discussion we have come up with a proposed form of words we believe will at least give both parties the basis for more talks' (*Guardian* 21.5.04: 10). The next day *The Times* reported that: 'the FBU is expected to back a national strike ballot at its reconvened conference on 15 June, raising the prospect of another fire dispute' over the issue of stand-down time (22.5.04: 4). Within two days further talks over both stand-down time and the situation in Manchester were held in London (*Evening Standard* 24.5.04: 4), and by the Thursday of that week: 'an end to the firefighters' dispute looked likely last night after union leaders recommended members accept a new pay deal', which appeared to resolve the issue of stand-down time within the new *Grey Book* (*Independent* 27.5.04: 2). After talks at officer level and a bit of fine tuning, the FBU EC at its meeting on 26 May agreed to the employers' proposals on the wording, subject to their applying to Bank Holidays as well as night shifts. Further evidence of bitter splits amongst employers surfaced throughout local councils; for example: 'an acrimonious split saw members from Stirling and Clackmannanshire march out of the chamber with no decision reached' (*Falkirk Herald* 10.6.04).

A settlement now looked imminent. On 4 June Phil White wrote again to the FBU's General Secretary to reiterate that the employers were not prepared to maintain existing stand-down arrangements for public holidays. Once again the employers were making it clear that they were in no hurry to settle except on their own terms. At the same time the employers wanted to satisfy Government Ministers that the modernisation process was indeed well advanced at brigade level, and that this was verified by the Audit Commission, who were yet to produce a final report. Although vital time had been lost at the start of this process due to employer incompetence, the Fire Authorities were more determined to protect their backs against Government censure than they were to honour the pay agreement reached with the FBU.

Traditionally on Bank Holidays, including Christmas day, brigades were on an emergency calls only basis, although a number of brigades do carry out community fire safety work. Watches working Bank Holidays are paid double time and receive time off in lieu. Such agreements are not uncommon in unionised sectors where staff are asked to work on Public Holidays. The employers' side wanted to end this arrangement so that in future Fire Service staff would be expected to do a full range of duties on these days subject to the requirements of CFOs. Some employers were prepared to concede that the Christmas period could be excluded from their new proposals. The union wanted a negotiated agreement which would give clear guidelines to the sort of work to be carried out on Bank Holidays, rather than leaving the issue to be determined solely by the employers and CFOs.

Given the magnitude of the challenges faced and overcome over the previous two years, this issue may appear to be very small potatoes. To many firefighters it was yet another example of employer duplicity – since the question concerned was not covered in the June 2003 agreement – and yet another excuse to delay payments due under stages 2 and 3 of that agreement. To the employers it was another opportunity to exploit a favourable bargaining situation and to underline what they considered to be a new pro-employer balance of forces in the Service. Notions of social partnership and mutual trust had long been abandoned as the price for introducing modernisation. The lack of faith among ordinary members in the ability and willingness of their own bosses – let alone the Government – to safeguard themselves and their communities was expressed in a letter to a local newspaper:

Sir, – I feel that I have to respond to the article Safety Work by Fire Crews Spells Danger dated, May 14, 2004 and the Chief Fire Officer's comments that the Fire Brigades Union is mischief-making. Following The Fire Service Pay dispute of 2002/2003, the Government has abolished the National Standards of Fire Cover and produced a Fire Service Bill to modernise the Fire Service. This meant Staffordshire Fire and Rescue Service would have to produce a draft Integrated Risk Management Plan (IRMP) by the end of October 2003 and put the document out for consultation which closed on February 7, 2004. The IRMP focused among other things on community safety, operational response and attendance times; these were covered by national standards of fire cover, which laid down the number of appliances and the time it should take those appliances to arrive at the scene of an incident. The Government wants Fire Authorities to lay down their own operational responses and attendance times; these should not be worse than those the public and business communities of Staffordshire already have in place. Unions, as employee representatives, were formed into one of a number of focus groups and were consulted about some ideas that were contained in the draft IRMP, among these being the Fire Brigades Union thoughts on variable crewing – fire-fighters going out into the community in cars and vans fitting smoke detectors and doing home fire risk assessments (HFRAs) currently being carried out with firefighters crewing fire appliances and providing operational readiness. When Staffordshire Fire and Rescue Service did its consultation exercise the general public were asked for their concept of variable crewing. The answer was while the majority of people felt very positive about the concept of variable crewing when it was initially introduced, they were much less positive when it was explained that this might result in a slight delay in the arrival of a second fire engine at a fire (Source S-o-T & Staffs FA IRMP Consultation document).

With the introduction of variable crewing this will mean a 50 per cent reduction in whole time operational response at Hanley, Newcastle, Stafford and Burton, with back up of a second fire engine being provided by using retained crews, not necessarily from their own stations, thus increasing the time of arrival of a second fire engine at a fire. The Fire Brigades Union is totally opposed to these ideas, on the grounds of public and firefighter safety with the increased response times. Retained firefighters have to live within a five to eight minute travel distance at normal road speed to respond to a fire call. So firefighters who now arrive at an incident first are being put into a moral dilemma not only not knowing from which station the second fire engine is coming from but also how long will it take. Firefighters will now have to do a dynamic risk assessment as to whether or not to enter a building without suffi-

cient resources in attendance at the scene of a fire, even if there are
reports of people inside. Variable crewing forms only part of the draft
IRMP, we believe the Service also intends to reduce the responses to
automatic fire alarms of businesses, hospitals, care homes etc. With the
tragic fire at the Rose Park Nursing Home in Scotland resulting in 14
deaths, the Old Rectory Residential Care Home Pembrokeshire resulting in one death and a serious fire last week at the Edith Beddow Home,
Hanford, Stoke on Trent, can we afford to reduce responses to
Automatic Fire Alarms?

Regarding the Government's proposals, to regionalise fire control
rooms by September 2007, we believe these will have a detrimental effect
on the Service currently being provided to the community of
Staffordshire and could put members of the public and the lives of firefighters at risk, by cutting the number of control staff employed to crew
this new control thus increasing the workload and stress levels of our
members. The Fire Brigades Union is not mischief-making. We have
such grave concerns about the health, safety and welfare of both our
members and the public of Staffordshire we serve, that we formally
registered a dispute about the variable crewing proposals with the Chief
Fire Officer who dismissed it saying it was not disputable. The Fire
Brigades Union then tried to register the dispute with the Fire Authority
which also said it was not disputable and the proposals went live on
Monday. The public and business communities should be asking, why
the Government, fire authority and senior management are being
allowed to play God with people's lives?

Steve Hill, Brigade Chair, Fire Brigades Union,
Staffordshire (*Sentinel*, Stoke, 9.6.04: 12).

Once again the employers had raised fresh obstacles to the final deal
and so: 'the leadership of the FBU is to recommend a ballot for industrial action to its conference' (*Financial Times* 10.6.04: 4). Against this
background the FBU reconvened Annual Conference took place in
Southport during the week beginning 16 June. All were agreed that the
employers' position was unacceptable and that further initiatives were
required to progress a final implementation of the June 2003 agreement. While delegates were angry with the employers, they were also
uncertain about the response of FBU members, particularly since the
stand-down question only affected two-thirds of the membership. EC
members and regional officials were aware of a certain battle weariness,
of a desire to draw a line under the dispute and sort out any problems
arising at a local level. If push came to shove there was no longer a
certainty that the overwhelming majority of members would follow a
call for further industrial action. In a national emergency service, any
split of any size could represent disaster for the future of the union.
Both authors attended this conference and witnessed the deep sense of

betrayal by Government and employers alike, the feelings of bitter anguish at being messed about by senior managers, and a profound disillusion with any democratic process in this country. A fair case, fairly pursued, had led to vilification and victimisation of FBU members; and had allowed Government to mobilise the full force of the ruthless state with the intention of creating division and confusion in FBU ranks. Some of this was exploited by those who sought to advance their personal positions within the FBU hierarchy.

With this very much in mind, the EC decided to recommend to delegates that in the event of further employer prevarication and procrastination, the union should hold a consultative ballot of the whole membership. The questioned posed would be whether or not to pursue action in the face of the failure of the employers to honour the agreement. In the event conference voted by a significant majority for a more direct approach, which involved balloting for national strike action should the employers not pay in full stages 2 and 3 by 30 July. As reported: 'firefighters are preparing to push their pay demands to the brink once again, and will vote for strike action ... union leaders said they would ballot their members in five weeks as the row on wages rumbles on ... the move, which marks further escalation in the dispute, was decided by delegates yesterday at the annual conference of the FBU' (*Scotsman* 17.6.04: 13). Indeed emergency resolution 15 called on conference 'to recommend a ballot for discontinuous strike action' (FBU *Pay Campaign Update* no.1).

Despite the call for more action, the decision that grabbed the headlines was the one to quit the Labour Party. This issue is discussed in more general terms in the conclusions (chapter six), but the FBU, along with some other unions such as the RMT, had expressed concerns about the links with the Labour Party for some time. The dominant view of the EC was that links should be maintained, but that they should be increasingly targeted, so that explicit support was given to those MPs with views largely in line with FBU policy. Early in 2004 the EC considered cutting funds to the national party and redirecting them to regional campaigns, but by the time of the June conference activist opinion had swung behind the long time call from the ultra-left for disaffiliation. As the *Daily Mail* delightedly reported: 'the FBU yesterday voted to cut its historic links with Labour. It became the first union to leave the party, provoking fears that others might follow suit' (18.6.04: 8). This became: 'the left-right rift in Labour deepened yesterday as firefighters took their union out of the party' (*Independent* 18.6.04: 8); and *The Times* saw it as 'an overwhelming show of anger' against the Government (18.6.04: 11).

The official position of the EC at the Conference was:

> the Executive Council acknowledges and shares the FBU membership's anger at this Government's tactics used during our pay dispute.

However there is also a general disillusion with the direction of
Government policy, the abandoning of agreed Labour conference policy
without discussion and the dumping of manifesto commitments, like-
wise, before discussion.

Many within the Labour Party, not only other unions, are also deeply
unhappy with this Government. However, disillusion and anger at a
Labour Government is not the same as anger and disillusion with the
Labour Party and we should continue to work with others within the
Party who also wish to see meaningful change in policy direction and in
the conduct of Government (*EC statement on restructuring the political
work of the union*, June 2004).

John McGhee, writing in the July/August edition of the *FireFighter*,
commented: 'this year's Annual Conference was truly historic. An 86-
year chapter in the FBU's political history has ended. We rejected our
ties with the Labour Party in a resolution of less than 50 words'. He
went on to argue that the decision did not imply a move towards any
other party. In particular he rejected overtures from Respect (a newly
formed leftist group linked to Socialist Alliance), whose national chairman, Nick Wrack, is the brother of one of the leaders of the London
FBU, a long-time opponent of the FBU leadership. He then posed the
questions of how and where to spend the political fund since
Conference had only voted to split away from the Labour Party without further guidance on what to do next.

THE FINAL CURTAIN CALL
Throughout July negotiations continued, but under the shadow of a
strike threat from the FBU, as the union was pushed and pushed again
into considering such action as the employers dithered and dodged
their way through the talks. By this time the utter confusion in the
ranks of the employers was publicly evident, with contradictory statements, the sacking of their chairwoman, and several examples of local
Fire Authorities in confusion. Such disarray was hardly surprising
given the Government's own role in interfering with the settlement
even on matters of detail. This few weeks in the summer of 2004
showed clearly that Central Government had no trust whatsoever in
local authority employers, and that the whole intent of central state
intervention was to reduce the powers of locally elected councillors in
favour of greater central control, with senior managers directly
accountable to Central Government targets and audits. No choice here,
no local democracy, and no voice for those most involved.

By August, relations between the main parties had deteriorated
further, and only the united action of the FBU in threatening action
brought both Government Ministers and local fire authority leaders to
the bargaining table for a final 'good faith' agreement on implementation of the June 2003 settlement.

At this stage the TUC stepped in. Brendan Barber arranged informal talks with both sides and offered the TUC's expertise in facilitating a negotiated settlement of all outstanding issues. In a letter of 9 July to the FBU he identified the issues still to be settled and progressed, including the need to ensure that the Audit Commission's verification process did not hold back payment of the stage 3 award. The TUC was anxious to secure a commitment from the employers, subject to agreement on all outstanding issues, by the end of July, and in the 9 July letter, Barber proposed that negotiations be completed by 21 July.

Under the TUC's auspices the talks went well. The terms of appropriate grievance, disciplinary and capability procedures were agreed after hours of intensive negotiation. At long last a form of words was agreed on the stand-down and Bank Holiday working arrangements, which represented both the firefighters' needs to reasonable rest periods and the employers' requirement to use this time more productively for fire prevention tasks. The union gave ground on detail but secured the big prize of keeping such arrangements within the context of risk assessment plans, rather than being left to the whim of individual authorities and CFOs.

While huge efforts were being made by the negotiators to settle their final differences, the reality of the modernisation process began to create new tensions as those involved took it upon themselves to decide what it all meant. So the employers were split, and badly so. They were split at local level over the new power system in the Fire Service – the new relationships between Central Government agencies such as the Audit Commission, the senior fire managers, the much-weakened employers, and the FBU. For example, in Scotland: 'claims of a rift between firemasters and the Fire Authorities were dismissed'; but there was evidence that 'fire chiefs had threatened to go over the heads of local authority employers and ask Deputy Prime Minister John Prescott to impose a settlement' (*Aberdeen Press and Journal* 6.7.04: 11). There was further evidence that the President of CACFOA, Alan Doig, was urging Ministers to impose a national settlement over the heads of local authorities (*Morning Star* 6.7.04: 1), despite his comments to me in interview that he wanted a return to free national collective bargaining as the best chance of getting the modernisation plans implemented. Even the *Sun* reported splits between local authorities and Central Government on the issue of regionalised control rooms (9.7.04), with the former rightly concerned that the Government was minded to sell off local control rooms.

THE EMPLOYERS RENEGE

By the end of July pressure to complete the negotiations came not only from senior managers and the FBU, but from the real difficulties faced across the Service due to cuts and changes. The employers too wanted out by now, but the hand of Ministers was still firmly guiding the outcome of the negotiations, and it alone dragged out the dispute. Across the country reports of the impact of modernisation came in. In East Yorks: 'frontline firefighters are to be moved into community safety work ... it is also planning to send fewer fire engines to auto-mated alarm calls' (*Hull Daily Mail* 23.7.04: 4); and in Manchester, new targets mean that: 'the speed with which a fire engine is expected to be at the scene will be slower' (*Manchester Evening News* 24.7.04: 4). When the full NJC met, it was generally expected that the agreements reached under the TUC watch would be endorsed and the two-year dispute finally ended. What occurred that Monday morning almost matched the events of 21-22 November 2002 in their unconstitutional-ity as far as the NJC procedures were concerned.

After 113 hours of negotiations the TUC appeared to have brokered an agreement on all outstanding issues. So when the NJC met on 2 August under the chairmanship of Professor Burchill, for the first time in nearly two years, a settlement seemed to be a formality. Once again the employers' side were playing hide and seek. For reasons we shall examine later, the full employers' side of the NJC decided to repudiate the work of its own negotiators on the issue of stand-down time and thus put in jeopardy the whole of the June 2003 agreement.

At the NJC meeting Mike Fordham accused the LGA of wrecking tactics. A circular to all FBU members spelt out the union's view of what happened in terms of a political conspiracy, hatched in Whitehall, to delay settlement. It took the threat of further strike action, backed by evidence of overwhelming support from FBU members, to persuade Government Ministers and the employers that further prevarication carried far greater political risks than any temporary advantage that might be gained by attempts to embarrass the union leadership and thereby weaken the union.

The FBU circular of 3 August, sent out in Mike Fordham's name, pulled no punches. It reported that the employers had decided on the previous day by a vote of thirteen to ten not to reach an agreement with the union. It said:

> the vote was only able to be achieved by the flooding of the meeting by mainly Labour councillors from London on behalf of the LGA. Without this unconstitutional wrecking move, the vote would have been ten to six in favour of reaching an agreement ... it is clear that Nick Raynsford has once again intervened to wreck a deal, as he had on numerous occasions in the past. This is not just the view of the union, but of many on the employers' side.

Elsewhere the FBU publicity machine blew its horn: 'Government sends in wreckers. The TUC-sponsored talks have broken down after Government wreckers packed Monday's NJC meeting with stooges in order to block the release of the remaining Stage 2 and 3 payments' (FBU *Pay Campaign Update*, No.3).

So once again the union was claiming that political interference had broken a negotiated settlement, and once again it appears that Whitehall was not prepared to trust the LGA negotiators. In essence Whitehall wanted very tight control over every dot and comma of the final agreement, in order to maximise the freedom given to senior managers in organising duty systems; and it wanted further time to assess the Audit Commission report monitoring progress in implementing the Government's modernisation agenda. This interference had the effect of splitting the employers, resulting in the sacking of Staffordshire Liberal Democrat Councillor Christina Jebb. Their dirty linen was now being washed in full public view and they were being exposed as weak and divided creatures humiliated by Government in order to be permanently by-passed in the modernisation process. The London *Evening Standard* reported that: 'the conflict follows a claim by Christina Jebb, the employers' chief negotiator, that she was sacked for trying to agree a deal with the FBU ... Ms Jebb said she had been told to vote against the agreed deal and accused the LGA of packing the meeting with councillors she had never seen before' (6.8.04: 2). As the *Morning Star* reported:

> As the tide turned against new Labour wreckers and their Tory allies, employers' body the LGA was forced to convene a crisis meeting of its Fire Forum ... Thursday night's sacking of LGA negotiating team chairwoman Christina Jebb was clearly the last straw for local fire chiefs (7.8.04: 1).

In an unusually open spat Jebb went public. In a letter to *The Guardian* she said (9.8.04):

> Sadly the Local Government Association leaders (Letters, August 7) seem to be suffering more memory lapses. No 'binding agreement' was reached with the FBU. The provisional settlement, reached after many weeks of sensitive negotiations, facilitated by the TUC, was to be taken to the employers' side meeting on August 2 for consideration. A joint meeting with the union would follow when, hopefully, the agreement could be signed.
>
> The deal that was on the table would have given the LGA everything it wanted, as confirmed by fire chiefs throughout the UK. So I did not exceed the association's wishes – unless, of course, they wished it to fail. My role as chair of the national joint council negotiating body was to represent and act on behalf of Local Government in the whole country, rather than to be mandated to support a minority view from London.
>
> On the World at One programme, I answered a straight question – about the way I had voted – with a straight answer. Is that wrong?

An unnecessary confrontation with the FBU has now been provoked, and the only possible explanation is that senior figures at the LGA do not want a settlement.

TIME TO PAY UP

The majority on the employers' side were therefore happy to allow the negotiations to go on for another six weeks on this issue of arrangements for Bank Holiday working. At this stage the employers were confident of a 'no' vote in the FBU ballot, but such a position was not acceptable to either the FBU or TUC. Pressure was immediately put on John Prescott to intervene, and the FBU balloted its members on strike action in face of the employers' leisurely and unreliable approach to negotiated agreements and the pay owing to FBU members. For over a week the news was again full of broken promises, threats to strike, splits amongst the employers, and the shadowy role of Ministers. David Turner in the *Financial Times* got the ball rolling with suggestions that the Government had directly intervened by packing the employers' side with 'stooges', and that as a result the FBU would start the process of industrial action by 'notifying Fire Authorities of a planned ballot' (3.8.04: 3). Terms like 'wrecking' and 'scuppering' were widely used to describe Nick Raynsford's pressure on the employers, as Mike Fordham was quoted as saying: 'I am stunned and angry. A clear agreement was reached. A Government-inspired wrecking crew has been sent in to destroy the deal' (*Guardian* 3.8.04: 5). At the same time it was admitted that the Government could not provide proper safety cover if there was a strike in September – 'full national cover for a possible new wave of Fire Service strikes might not be in place in time' (*Financial Times* 5.8.04: 3).

By now the fiasco at the heart of New Labour's unsure handling of the dispute was on public view. Ken Livingstone, the London Mayor, began some behind the scenes bridge-building because it was felt he could put pressure on Val Shawcross – the chair of the London Fire authority, key anti-FBU hardliner and friend of the Minister Nick Raynsford – and skirt around the power clique linked with Central Government (*Evening Standard* 10.8.04: 2). On the same day the FBU launched its new ballot on strike action. Angry firefighters expressed their disbelief at Government antics as in this letter from Ray Dring in Derby:

> elements within the ODPM clearly do not want a settlement of this dispute at any cost! Their first attempt at wrecking the meeting involved pressurising the chair of the employers' side ... to cancel the meeting ... the second and successful attempt involved gerrymandering the vote by parachuting in a group of mostly London Labour councillors who had nothing to do with the NJC; nothing to do with the talks, and nothing to do with the Fire Service! (*Derby Evening Telegraph* 11.8.04: 4).

To show how that betrayal rebounded to stiffen the resolve of FBU members in the ballot, Frank Gendall of the Penzance fire station said: 'all of us are very unhappy with how the negotiations have gone and we are very disappointed with the way the employers have conducted themselves ... most ordinary people would be astonished if they knew what had taken place' (*The Cornishman* 12.8.04: 6). Further mixed messages came from fire chiefs and the employers: in Scotland the fire board chiefs wrote to every firefighter urging them to vote against the strike (*Scotland on Sunday* 15.8.04: 2); and, in contrast, the chairman of Avon fire authority called on the employers to re-open talks with union leaders (*Bath Chronicle* 16.8.04: 5). No wonder the FBU leadership was constantly surprised by the lack of strategy from employers, who were being pulled and pushed like rag dolls with no will of their own.

After a further five hours of talks on 12 August, Brendan Barber produced a form of words on public holiday working which proved acceptable to both sides. The union was satisfied that the agreement recognised that public holidays were not 'ordinary working days' as the employers had originally demanded, and that the arrangements would be subject to consultation with the union, while the employers took comfort in the requirement that staff would be expected to undertake a full range of duties subject to an understanding that 'distinctive circumstances apply throughout local communities on public holidays'. The critical moment now came, with the Audit Commission report providing evidence of 'excellent' progress on modernisation and therefore knocking away the last possible obstacle put in the way of the final settlement (*Morning Star* 20.8.04: 6). This, alongside stories of Government incompetence in preparing army cover for a possible strike (*Sunday Herald* 22.8.04: 4) completed the picture being painted in Whitehall – not the town halls – that the time had come for Central Government to take its foot off the windpipe of local authorities.

Just as Government action to help the FBU win a strike ballot seemed to have ended, unbelievably, there was another leak that told a still worse tale: 'private contractors could be used to requisition and operate modern red fire engines if crews strike next month ... officials in the ODPM have discussed paying commercial firms to support the hard-pressed military ... confidential talks are understood to have taken place with senior figures in Group 4 Securicor ... contractors could also be asked to cross picket lines' (*Guardian* 25.8.04: 2).

Once again the strength of membership feeling forced the employers back to the negotiating table sooner than they had planned. Rumours began to circulate that on a high turnout firefighters were again voting nearly nine to one for strike action. Apparently this impressed both Whitehall and the employers. When the FBU, as is its constitutional right, requested a full meeting of the NJC for 26 August, the employers agreed to further talks under the auspices of the TUC in preparation for the NJC meeting.

So 26 August was the day this dispute was finally settled. The end game was messy and showed how far Whitehall was prepared to go in policing the negotiations, and how far the Labour members of the LGA were prepared to accept interference from Central Government, even when such practices directly contravened the NJC constitution. In the end it was the tenacity of the FBU membership and its loyalty to the parallel strategy proposed by the leadership – of talk but prepare for strike – that won the day. This approach exposed the divisions and weaknesses on the employers' side, thus making possible a negotiated rather than an imposed settlement. In all of this the role of the TUC proved to be crucial.

CONCLUSION

The memory of the dispute will long be etched in the memories of the FBU membership. One feature, above all, will be in the forefront of their minds. This is the treatment they received from the Labour Government. The settlement achieved did not meet all their aspirations, but the more far-sighted knew that this was always likely to be the case, as the history of public sector disputes clearly shows. So whatever misgivings activists may have now, these are likely to fade as pay packets improve and new challenges, particularly on risk assessment plans, present themselves. What will not go away are the insults, the lack of understanding and empathy for the job FBU members do for society and the deliberately downplaying of what's involved in providing an emergency service, as if the time between call outs was for rest and recreation not recuperation. Some insults were political – accusing the FBU leadership of being Scargillite, meaning in Blair's thinking that the union never wanted a negotiated settlement but aimed to bring down the Government, or, as in Scotland, categorising the FBU as fascist; others attacked the job and the working conditions negotiated by the FBU – Spanish practices became an overworked term of abuse.

Writing in *Tribune* (13.2.04), *Guardian* political correspondent Kevin Maguire summed it up like this: 'What alienated firefighters was the Government's conduct of the dispute. Tony Blair's "Scargillite" smear and Downing St jibes about full time cabbies and part time firefighters, as the Prime Minister's strategy of painting crews as the enemy within, backfired so spectacularly'. He might have added to this Minister Raynsford's description of striking firefighters as being 'criminally irresponsible', or the many references in the Bain Report which downgrade the role and workload of the modern firefighter and emergency fire control room operator.

So with the end of the dispute comes the fallout for all the parties. Before trying to assess what that might be, we provide a brief analysis of the causes of the behaviour of Government Ministers and employers in their pursuit of 'modernisation' in a key public service.

PART 2: ANALYSIS AND AFTERMATH

Chapter 5

New Labour, Modernisation, and the Fire Service

INTRODUCTION

This chapter sets the 2002-4 dispute in the UK Fire Service within a wider context of developments in UK political economy. We discuss the influence of neo-liberalism on ideas and practices in British politics, and then show how this approach to civil society translates through Public Choice Theory to New Public Management of public services. This applies both to the management of those services in general and to labour management in particular. We then discuss how this becomes part of the actual reform of labour management practices throughout the public services, including greater management control over job regulation, a more limited role for trade unions and collective bargaining, and a greater level of flexibility at work. The chapter ends with a comment on the 'modernisation' of the Fire Service itself.

There has been much said about the differences between 'old' and 'new' Labour, and the particular role of Tony Blair in controlling policy direction. Too much of the debate is presented in terms of powerful personalities and contrasting leadership values; and it has become an example of the narcissism of small differences. For our limited purposes, the interest lies in the nature of European-wide social democracy in the aftermath of the Cold War, and the policy implications for public ownership and the management of public services.

The historical development of European-style social democracy was always a conflation of a competing set of values and practices (Miliband 1973, Aaronovitch 1981). So, for example, while most could embrace the general slogans of the French and Russian revolutions – equality, fraternity and liberty – for social democrats, these were best guaranteed within a capitalist political economy. This contrasted with the communist wing of the movement, which argued that only a socialist revolution could guarantee these social advances and that capitalism would always threaten the permanence of progressive reforms.

Hence for Social Democrats markets would exist and be encouraged; those controlling markets and benefiting from them would be allowed a large say over policy direction; and the role of politicians was, other than to be elected, to control and manage the social and political fallout of the inevitable inequalities and injustices that stemmed from market operations. A major aspect of social democratic policy and practice, therefore, was the development of popular, or at least acceptable, arguments for allowing private profit to dominate the economy and state functions, while mediating the failings and failures of market operations through social policies on health, education and social services.

In this task the rhetoric of equality was important to separate social democrats from conservatives, and thereby to win votes and enact reforms that prevented the worst aspects of poverty – now increasingly exported to Africa and Asia. Hand in hand with social amelioration went the need to support all parts of economic activity with state funds and state power (mainly through legislation) to improve its performance. Without a strong economy it was difficult to win elections, to convince voters to pay taxes to support social and security benefits, and to be portrayed as being in command. The state elite therefore invests in education and research, in training, in infrastructure improvements, in trade organisations, and in labour markets, to bolster economic performance. This happens because left alone no single capitalist would make that type and level of investment. But to convince those involved at every level of the benefits of such changes, the Government of the day needs to dress up limited reforms in the clothes of 'modernisation', while leaving the basic power and wealth structure of society alone. The political imperative of the day is to drag – and to be seen to drag – allegedly old-fashioned sections of society into the modern world.

'Modernisation' is not a neutral step forward but a highly coloured version of progress rooted in market-style efficiency. As part of that sought-after 'efficiency' gain, public sector managers are required to run their 'business units' within audited performance indicators. In labour intensive and highly unionised services, such as the Fire Service, this means changes to the traditional pattern of industrial relations. This in turn requires a new set of power equations – between local and national employers, local and national conditions of service, the FBU and employers, and employers and senior line managers. This tends to lead to changes to payment systems and levels, changes to other conditions, and changes to working practices. If the employers cannot impose these changes, Central Government will.

The modernising tendency of the British state had swept through most services by 2002. There was no hiding place for the Fire Service. Modernisation as defined by the Government was on its way. This was made clear to activists and members of the FBU through statements from the leadership, who constantly warned, certainly after 1999 when discussion was opened on a new White Paper on the future of the

Service, that the issue for the FBU would always be how to respond to modernisation rather than how to bury their collective head in the sand. Most members of the Cabinet made endless references to this process in the years before and during the dispute, and for those in any doubt here are a few tasters. Schools minister, David Miliband: 'we want head teachers in the lead, teachers focused on teaching and schools modernised to support high quality learning' (*Hansard* 16.8.02 col 379); Nick Raynsford, on elections, 'a multi-channelled approach has consistently been the long-term aim of the Government's electoral modernisation strategy' (*Hansard* 16.9.04 col 554WH); David Blunkett: 'we will invest in the modernisation of policing' (*Hansard* 19.7.04 col 24); and John Reid: 'if the Labour Government has one mandate it is to defend and modernise the national health service' (*Hansard* 8.7.03 col 1082).

The decision the FBU leadership and activists had to make with the support of their members was how and when to seek a national nego-tiated solution to the twin issues of falling relative pay and the modernisation of working practices. In this they had to take stock of their own history and situation, and to learn some of the lessons from the actions of other public sector unions fighting similar battles – such as, for example, the PCS, CWU and NATFHE (Beale 2000).

MODERNISING HEARTS AND MINDS: FROM NEO-LIBERAL-ISM TO NEW PUBLIC MANAGEMENT

The so-called and much-vaunted 'modernisation' of the Fire Service is best appreciated within a broader and deeper context of changes in British society and politics, and in particular as part of a global programme of market-style reforms of public services. These include from various forms of privatisation (selling off, leasing through PFI, and CCT); the creation of hybrid public interest companies such as Network Rail, Foundation Hospitals and City Academy schools; and marketisation, with more power being given to site managers within an ever tighter centrally-controlled corset of performance and financial targets. These messy halfway houses have been shown to be far less efficient than presumed, and far less popular than believed (Pollock *et al* 2002, Heritier 2002).

The intellectual basis for such changes is that private sector profit-making reality – or at least a mock form – is better than any form of public sector operation. Where aspects of social life remain in the public sector, as with the armed forces, the fire and police services and some elements of public health and education, they should be subject to artificially constructed market pressures, with financial audit, performance indicators and senior managers acting as if they were profit maximisers. In this regulatory system the Audit Commission plays a major role. Its reports on the Fire Service in 1986 and 1995 set the pace for modernisation, and its unusual task of policing the June

2003 settlement of the fire strike sets it aside from other such bodies. Their website tells us:

> We are an independent public body responsible for ensuring that public money is spent economically, efficiently, and effectively in the areas of Local Government, housing, health, criminal justice and fire and rescue services.
>
> Our mission is to be a driving force in the improvement of public services. We promote good practice and help those responsible for public services to achieve better outcomes for citizens, with a focus on those people who need public services most.
>
> Our formal governing board is made up of several Commissioners and includes a Chairman. Commissioners are appointed by the Office of the Deputy Prime Minister, following consultation with key stakeholders.

Hence it embraces the fundamental notions of modernisation contained within Government thinking and policy, and its leadership is answerable to and depends upon the ODPM, currently run by John Prescott, a key figure in the Government's handling of the fire dispute. Its independence, therefore, is limited and it operates within restricted boundaries of what constitutes good and bad management in a public service. It typifies the ways in which the central state functions through arms-length organisations, as part of the hegemony exerted by the neo-liberals.

This is part of a worldwide reversal of the gains made by the working-class movement after 1945 (Hobsbawm 1978), and has been given impetus by the collapse of the Soviet Union and the emergence of the USA as the predominant world power, with its insistence on the dominance of USA-style market controls. This climate allows the argument to gather pace and credibility – until it fails. So persistent is the dogma that even when it implodes, as with the railways in the UK, electricity supply in California, pollution in India, higher education in Spain, pensions in France, welfare in Germany, the entire Argentinean economy, and the media in Italy, few leading politicians or commentators allow the facts to get in the way of a good story. The case for public ownership and the delivery of public services by public sector workers goes by the board, and those proposing ideas that not long ago were widely accepted are painted either as extremists or as out-of-touch traditionalists pining for a bygone era. This matters, since much political debate within European countries, including the UK, concerns domestic policy on public services. We examine developments in the Fire Service within that context.

The key notion remains that of 'modernisation'. Whatever those involved and watching might think, it was a code for a reform package based on a mix of privatisation and private sector management practices, within a framework of Government audit, performance targets and greater central control over local delivery of services. As has been argued elsewhere (Ironside and Seifert 2003), public service managers have faced a gamut of centrally decided measures that require changes in service delivery methods.

Thus the central state, mainly through a coalition of Ministers, senior civil servants and a range of policy advisers taken from the business, media and academic worlds, enforces the political changes necessary to allow a dominant market-powered system to become centre stage (through legislation, policy, budgets). In other words we are living through a period in which the benefits of markets for the few are foisted on the rest of us by political leaders representing a powerful elite. In European democracies this also requires voters to be persuaded that their interests are best served through an expansion and deregulation of private markets – mainly through privatisation in all its various forms. It has meant the re-introduction of markets into those aspects of social and economic life from which they were partly excluded in the post-1945 period – areas such as health, transport, energy, education, Local and Central Government, and all forms of manufacture.

Markets are the central unifying theme, and they are introduced with the cloak of previously discredited economic theories promising a more efficient allocation of resources and a more efficient management of those resources. But in reality markets do not function in any sense 'freely' (Baran and Sweezy 1966). In practice, policies such as outright privatisation, compulsory competitive tendering, Best Value, PFI and PPP – aimed at promoting a least wasteful solution to public spending – rarely achieve this. Any marginal improvements in market efficiency trumpeted by Ministers have been largely offset by reductions in social efficiency.

In fact the re-creation of these new markets is intended not to raise efficiency, but to put into the private profit-making domain activities through which state funding can be channelled back into the pockets of the business community. For those sectors of the economy that for a variety of reasons remain public, such as health and fire, there are moves to replicate market discipline inside the systems. This is done by inventing business units (sometimes competitive ones, through league tables and performance indicators), which are controlled by Central Government directives and enforced through inspection and audit; in these, senior managers are persuaded (by exhortation and monetary incentives) to cease to act on behalf of the workforce and local community, and instead to act on behalf of Government through the mysterious interests of the public – the citizen-consumer (Hall and Jacques 1983).

NEO-LIBERALISM

Neo-liberalism has become dominant throughout the capitalist world and elsewhere, and all aspects of the lives of citizens – as electors, consumers, workers, owners, users of services, culture seekers, hobby-ists, members of families and individuals – are increasingly affected by the fallout (Chomsky 1999). This New Right political philosophy now criss-crosses traditional conservative and social democratic political groups, and its advocates passionately argue for the benefits of free markets as the best guarantor of efficiency throughout economic life. This is usually associated with an increasingly individualistic and liber-tarian approach to everyday life, social and health problems, and rights. Only when it goes wrong – when markets catastrophically fail, when there are riots, when the social disintegration of youth culture threat-ens both work and social discipline, when there are nationally and/or religiously based movements against the dominant world order – only then does the political class seek alternative solutions and admit to problems with the implementation of policy. But even then it rarely acknowledges problems with the policy itself (Cohen 1988).

In order to persuade voter-citizens that neo-liberalism in all its forms is the best way forward, its proponents suggest that it involves less central state involvement in civil society and greater choice for individuals. This is the opposite of the reality, but it is attractive to those who wish to believe that politicians and state bureaucrats get in the way of their lives and their businesses.

Most European social democratic parties, including the Labour Party in the UK, have abandoned much of what their supporters understood by social democracy – such as Keynesian welfare solutions, a thriving public sector, and ideals of social justice based on notions of equality (Sassoon 1997). In particular, in the attempt to break with the past, such party leaders scorn these old-fashioned remedies and embrace the new theories of the new right with abandon. As John Saville pointed out: 'the British Labour Party, since its early days, has always been a party of social reform whose ideas and policies have been largely articulated within a socialist rhetoric ... [and] whose aims and purposes are the introduction of social reform into the existing struc-ture of capitalist society; and whose objectives in no way challenge the fundamental property relationships of that society' (1980: 148). So the break with the past is in some ways more apparent than real, although the break-up of the rhetorical associations with socialism is more genuine and to the electoral point. But there remains within the labour movement fierce controversy on these issues, and today's leadership could well become tomorrow's outcasts.

PUBLIC CHOICE THEORY

One example of this is the inclusion of some variant of 'public choice theory' in the Labour Government's policy direction. Here, a popular and dangerous notion – that all politicians are similar and are not to be trusted – is turned into an argument that we cannot trust politicians to make rational decisions in the interests of citizens because they are too concerned to be re-elected in the immediate future. The argument also applies to bureaucrats, who cannot be trusted to make decisions in the interests of the population since they too have narrow vested interests to protect. Therefore both sets of key decision-makers will make poor decisions, leading to inefficient use of tax-payers money.

If current systems of decision-making lead, as is suggested, to grotesquely inefficient use of public funds to provide public services (Dunleavy 1991, Rowley 1993), then the only rational solution is to place the public service into 'a competitive environment'. That will result in optimal decisions about goods and services. Senior managers running these newly created business units should be given incentives to hit targets, manage all resources efficiently, and therefore manage staff more flexibly (Niskanen 1967, 1971). This also incorporates fashionable solutions around localism and mutualism. The argument here is that public services are to serve individual citizen-consumers, but, since they are paid for by taxpayers they need some accountability. This should now be local – not through elected councillors, but rather through newly elected members of school and hospital boards from a variety of constituencies, including patients, parents, staff and local residents. The fact that in both current practice and historical experience such experiments in 'handing back' to the people usually fail, either through complete lack of interest or through capture by extreme, often religious, groups, is ignored. Of course, by default, decisions are increasingly left to senior managers and thereby fulfil in part the requirements of public choice theory to eliminate democracy from the matter of business management.

THE THREE E'S

Competition in the pursuit of profit, according to the neo-classical model of the firm, is the motor that drives increases in efficiency, effectiveness, and economy (the Three Es) in private companies. Thus the absence of such a motor, for example in the public services, results in relatively poor performance with regard to the Three Es. The public choice position makes a neat link with the neo-classical model, justifying the involvement of private firms in public services by asserting that it results in the best allocation and delivery of services at any given cost. Politicians can avoid being trapped by the privatisation logic of this position by using the 'what works' argument – it is not necessary to assert that private enterprise is inherently better at delivering services than public enterprise, only that it should be involved where it is better, in terms of the Three Es.

A fundamental issue in this model, as well as for traditional public sector management, is the question of how Ministers and other senior decision-makers actually affect staff performance in the respective sectors. There can be policy initiatives, regulations, even legislation; but none in and of themselves guarantee that anything happens, and that what does happen is in line with intentions. In economics this is known as the principal-agent problem: the 'problem' in general is that owners (the principals) of companies have difficulties in ensuring that the managers (their agents) carry out the policies that are required.

Difficulties in defining the 'success' of any public service are also inherent in the complex political nature of the public sector. The Government, the citizens, the service users, the taxpayers, the local authorities, the service professionals – all may claim to be involved as principals in setting the objectives of services, and all may have different ideas about what constitutes success. Inevitably, there is always a bewildering array of objectives and sub-objectives, reflecting the different views within and between these groups, resulting in unresolved conflicts over how to define and test for success. Meanwhile, decisions about service planning and delivery are increasingly becoming management decisions, as the reforms reduce or remove democratic involvement at all levels – for example union bargaining at the workplace, political representation on employer boards, or parliamentary scrutiny of the executive. Those with the deepest pockets gain the greatest influence.

How does all of this help us to understand 'modernisation'? Well, the argument is that once political leaders adopt a neo-liberal approach to the running of society, they will seek to make all aspects of that society subject to some form of market system: either directly, through selling off public assets, or indirectly, by applying some market principles to remaining public services. This is done through public choice theories, which emphasise individual consumer choice over a basket of goods and services; and this becomes, in practice, New Public Management (Pollitt 1993). Dunsire summarises the position in his historical survey of public administration:

> It [NPM] covered a set of doctrines described as follows: a shift of concern from policy to management, emphasizing quantifiable performance measurement and investment appraisal; the break-up of traditional bureaucratic structures into quasi-autonomous units, dealing with one another on a user-pays basis; market-testing and competitive tendering instead of in-house provision; a strong emphasis on cost-cutting; output targets rather than input controls; limited term contracts instead of career tenure; monetized incentives instead of fixed salaries; 'freedom to manage' instead of central personnel control; more use of public relations and advertising; encouragement of self-regulation instead of legislation. These doctrines ... were a mix of 'public choice' and updated Taylorism (1999: 373).

Thus NPM contains two strands: Taylorism reborn as managerialism, which aims 'to gain more effective control of work practices' (Walsh 1995: xiii); and the establishment of new business units. These 'businesses' are supposed to be consumer-oriented and subject to Central Government controls through regulation, inspection and audit. In theory this should not be necessary, since the new type of senior manager will have incentives to achieve targets set by Ministers, and staff will obey because they too will now be motivated by the carrot of bonuses and the stick of job loss. In labour intensive sectors, such as most of the remaining public services, especially those with a history of strong collective bargaining backed by high levels of union membership, the implementation of these policies requires a major shift in labour management policies and practices.

NPM IN PRACTICE

We now present a few examples from the public services that show how changes to finances and structures aimed at setting up business units represent a 'modernisation' programme defined within the terms of NPM. We do so to show that the reforms of the Fire Service were not isolated from wider reforms, and that the 'modernisation' agenda was so dominant that no sector could remain aloof: the 'can of worms' was already being opened up by Government Ministers.

In the Civil Service, Ministers enacted the reforms directly, through the creation of Agencies with market testing and internal markets. Elsewhere the reforms were implemented primarily through a series of Parliamentary Acts, including, for England and Wales, the Local Government Acts 1988, 1992, and 1999; the Education Reform Act 1988; and the NHS and Community Care Act 1990. These initiated the creation of competing business units: in education through local management of schools and incorporation of further education colleges; in Higher Education through the abolition of the binary divide and the creation of the new universities in 1992; in health and social care through internal markets based on a purchaser-provider split (which remains largely intact despite Primary Care Trusts and Foundation Hospitals); and in Local Government and the NHS through CCT and Best Value.

Thus Central Government has created some of the conditions required by the public choice theorists of the New Right by setting up competition in the supply of services, alongside incentives for site managers and regulation of quality outcomes. As would be expected, these reforms focus on the supply side of the equation – making schools, hospitals and fire brigades more efficient – but have mainly failed to tackle the demand side of these brave new markets. Yet the demand for health care, education and fire prevention and rescue are not spontaneously generated by people's needs: they are constructed from people's lives and the role of work in them. Government Ministers have produced sets of performance indicators that are meant to indicate the extent to which service objectives are met. Regulatory bodies such as OFSTED (office for standards in education), NICE (national institute for clinical excellence), the Audit Commission, and the Social Services Inspectorate, have been established and strengthened, to enforce the Government's priorities through a process of inspection linked to sanctions and rewards.

The Government's drive for 'modernisation' in the public sector has gathered pace dramatically over recent years, becoming increasingly focused on human resource management (HRM) issues. In each service the message is the same: modernisation of services means modernisation of the workforce and of their terms and conditions of employment, as illustrated by the following examples.

The NHS Modernisation Agency was created in 2001, and within this there is a 'self-managed team' called 'New Ways of Working', which is involved with the implementation of 'Agenda for Change' and the 'Changing Workforce Programme'. Agenda for Change commits the signatories to work together:

> to meet the reasonable aspirations of all the parties to: ensure that the new pay and conditions system leads to more patients being treated, more quickly and being given higher quality care; assist new ways of working which best deliver the range and quality of services required, in as efficient and effective a way as possible, and organised to best meet the needs of patients; [and] assist the goal of achieving a quality workforce with the right numbers of staff, with the right skills and diversity, and organised in the right way.
>
> [...] pay modernisation is an integral part of the human resource strategies of the NHS (Department of Health 2003: 5).

In Local Government the employers and the Government have agreed a strategy that 'sets out a comprehensive approach to help ensure that Local Government has the right numbers of people in the right places with the right skills to deliver improved services, better productivity and greater customer focus in front line services'. Among the list of priorities, the following human resource management issues appear:

> Identifying successful approaches to managing productivity and performance and adopting them to help deliver continuous improvement of services throughout the sector. Creating a high performance people management culture across Local Government, with all authorities using quality people management as the foundation for improvement. Developing a successful partnership approach to employee relations. Creating a more flexible workforce, able to deliver high quality, customer focused services. This includes remodelling the workforce, achieving greater movement across professional and skills boundaries and taking advantage of new technology to develop 'win-win' outcomes from flexible working arrangements that achieve improvements in delivery and better work-life balance. Developing effective partnership

working and addressing the implications for the workforce and people management in the sector, including the tri-partite agreement on the 'two tier workforce' (Office of the Deputy Prime Minister and the Employers' Organisation 2003: 5).

The Local Government Employers' assessment of the case is simple: 'The drive to modernisation and improvement sponsored by Central Government demands high performance and greater capacity in Local Government. This requires considerable organisational change, including the introduction of a high performance working culture' (Employers' Organisation 2002b: 2).

Andrew Smith, Chief Secretary to the Treasury, set out the position for the Civil Service in his foreword to the Makinson Report: 'As part of its comprehensive plan for modernisation, the Government has recruited a team of top private sector managers to the PSPP [Public Services Productivity Panel] – with a remit to advise on improving efficiency and productivity' (Makinson 2000: 1).

Finally, the Bain Report on the Fire Service concludes that 'modernisation is long overdue. The challenge is great. Action is required to legislate for the changes; to negotiate alterations in terms and conditions of service; and to plan detailed local implementation plans and a new audit regime' (Bain 2002: vi).

NPM AND THE FIRE SERVICE

The programme of modernisation of the Fire Service is fraught with difficulties: definitional, political, managerial, and practical. What it means and what it might mean to various interested parties matters and is debatable. In light of our more general discussion we can see that there are essentially two opposing schools of thought, each with its own set of variations. On the one hand is the main thrust – although not always supported in detail and practice – from Government Ministers and their senior civil servants. Here is a familiar grouping of arguments around traditional welfare liberalism – that the free market is the best way of providing efficient services of any kind, that when some form of state ownership and/or control is required as with the emergency aspects of the Fire Service then it should be funded on a minimalist basis and with clear central direction, while allowing local employers and their senior managers to operate on a utilitarian consequentialist basis. In other words, pragmatic outcomes in terms of value for money should be the objective of the Service. This contrasts with a different tradition that also emerged with empire and industrialisation in the 1850s – of services free from market constraints, democratically accountable, planned, and managed with the full involvement of staff, the community and the Central Government. Such a tradition seeks governance based on social solidarity, shared risk and consensus, rooted in equality of power, not a false partnership of the unequal.

Such differences translate into wider debates on the nature of European social democracy (and hence New Labour), or the nature of socialist ideas in the UK today – and about the reality check that would be required to prevent market dogma from overwhelming us all. In the case of the Fire Service, its future structure, purpose, finance, staffing, control and management is unclear, and is subject to debate; it cannot be resolved through simplistic references to the workability or modernity of any given set of proposals.

So the meaning of modernisation of the Fire Service for Government Ministers and their advisers comes out as a set of pragmatic changes, wrapped in the rhetoric of community renewal but firmly rooted in the ideological soil of laissez-faire welfarism. This point is easily illustrated by reference to a recent set of documents: the report of the inspectorate in 2001, the Bain report in 2002 with the associated employers' evidence to Bain, and the Command Paper from the ODPM in 2003. All are linked together and sing from the same sheet, and all repeat the mantra of modernisation as part NPM (efficiency, effectiveness and economy), part PCT (more local decision making powers by senior managers), part neo-liberalism (markets and targets), and part liberal welfare utilitarianism (community benefits). The themes repeated so often are: best value incorporating value for money (through audit); reform to become more efficient and effective (through best practice and continuous improvement); more power to site managers (unilateral managerialism spiced with ever newer management techniques); reform of employment issues in terms of being more flexible and therefore reducing unit labour costs (deskilling); and restructuring into larger units (regionalism).

MODERNISING WORKING PRACTICES: LABOUR MANAGEMENT USA-STYLE

Brian Towers indicates that both union density and collective bargaining in the USA have been falling for over forty years. Alongside the lack of worker representation in unions goes 'the downward pressure on workers' living standards, employment conditions, and traditional rights' (1997:1). The convergence of UK policies with USA ones include: an increasingly deregulated labour market, partly achieved through privatisation; some 'institutional borrowing' around issues such as union recognition rights; shared anti-union ideologies, beginning with Thatcher and Reagan and continued, albeit with less rhetorical flourish, by Clinton and Blair; employers' attacks on collective bargaining, especially national wage setting; and the double-edged nature of some of the employment legislation (*ibid*: 2-8). This latter point was well illustrated by the operation of the National Labor Relations Act under the Clinton administration (Gould 2000). This thesis of Anglo-American convergence is supported by American academics such as Rogers (1995, and, with Dresser, 2003) and others (Logan 2002), suggesting that by 2003 the British Government was happy to move closer towards Bush and the new Reaganism, rather than to copy the limited attempts in the EU to establish greater power for information and consultation through works councils.

The basic nature of the employment relationship has remained unchanged for over a hundred years and varies relatively little from job to job and from country to country. In market economies most adult citizens have to sell their ability to work in a labour market in order to receive wages. For most people this is an economic and social necessity, and one for which they are prepared by years of schooling, family life, and endless and varied accounts of working, from cultural sources that include TV soap operas and religion. Unless one is very rich (by whatever means – inheritance, crime or the lottery), not working renders you very poor. Most of the time in most places being very poor is something to be avoided. Hence the need for paid employment.

As in most labour markets there are far more sellers of labour (workers) than buyers (employers), so wages will be generally held down. The more deregulated the market, the easier it is to hold wages down. There is nothing natural or fair in the operation of labour markets, but that is how many do function. Getting up in the morning and going to work is therefore an experience shared by about two billion people worldwide, and many more wish for paid work. This common activity is covered by the nature of the employment contract. Whatever the exact legal niceties of the contract, it is just an exchange – work for wages. Therefore industrial relations is about pay (the total remuneration package, that is, including pensions) and performance at work – the quantity and quality of labour (however measured, controlled and determined).

Once employed, how does this exchange alter if circumstances change? For example if the company expands and makes greater profits, if the public service requires new skills from the staff to deliver it, if competition becomes tougher, if the labour force develops, and if Government intervenes? Workers, individually and collectively, tend to have difficulty in improving their wages and conditions. If you adopt the Oliver Twist position and ask for more from the managers representing the employers, you might be sacked or victimised, you might be turned down, or you might get less than your demands. To overcome the weakness of the individual worker in relation to the employer, and to even up the problem of asking for an advance in wages, workers created unions, with union officials employed by the union and therefore untouchable by the employer.

Unions, therefore, first and last were formed to collectively bargain on behalf of their members, both individual and collective. The process of such bargaining is well known: it usually starts with a claim of sorts from the union negotiators put before the employers. The origins of the claim, its exact contents, the importance and urgency of various elements, the timing, and the support for it from members, are all part of the campaign, all part of the negotiations. Once tabled, assuming formal agreed bargaining systems are in place, then the claim is answered by the representatives of the employer(s). After a period of negotiation, which includes activities outwith the negotiating forum – such as rallies and demonstrations, political support, press statements and leaks – a variety of outcomes are possible. The most common is an agreed settlement, which represents a classic distributive compromise (Walton and Mckersie 1967).

If there is no agreed settlement, four things might happen: the parties agree to bring in a third party to conciliate, mediate, or arbitrate; the employer imposes a settlement; there is a strike; and there is a lock-out. All outcomes are well documented in the academic and other literature.

STRIKES

As the book is about the strike in the UK Fire Service in 2002-4 we need very briefly to discuss strikes and their main causes – pay and in particular pay comparability for the public services (see chapter 1).

To begin at the beginning: the contract of employment allows alterations in the terms of the contract and encapsulates the power relations between workers seeking more pay and more job controls, and managers representing employers wanting to pay the least possible in the prevailing market conditions and to have more control over performance. Therefore both the task itself (the skills applied to a range of work activities) and the circumstances under which the task is completed (fellow workers, work organisation, labour management, physical surroundings, equipment, support) are negotiable within a framework of job regulation and control. The issue is not whether we have control over all aspects of the job, but who controls what aspects – managers unilaterally (managers' right to manage), the workers (professional autonomy), or a mixed bag of joint regulation (pluralist and bargaining). Even if there are no trade unions involved these battles take place; and in the UK post-1945 it was part of public policy that, since conflict was endemic to the work situation, it was better to control work by sharing control (Flanders 1968). In other words, as the mafia say, keep your friends close but your enemies closer!

Therefore to defend and/or improve your lot at work is no easy business. One common solution has been for workers to set up trades unions and then to use them to bargain with employers. As part of that bargaining process both parties use threats, including the threat to strike. Strikes are no ordinary aspect of collective bargaining, however, because they raise wider and deeper issues of power and control in society. Hence there have been several studies of strikes (Knowles

1952; Edwards 1986; Lyddon 1998), including case studies (Lane and Roberts 1971; Hartley *et al* 1983; Winterton and Winterton 1989; Kerr and Sachdev 1991). Some left-wing activists and commentators provide sympathetic analysis rooted in various Marxist traditions of the strike as a weapon in the class struggle (Lenin 1902; Gramsci 1930; Kelly 1988; Hyman 1989), while other writers see them as a menace in and to civil society (Hayek 1944; MacFarlane 1981).

These contain debates on the morality and legality of strike action, on its effectiveness, its place in history, and, in the case of public services, on whether or not such action should take place at all. Most studies concentrate on causes, conduct, and consequences, both for those involved and for the 'public interest'. For our purposes strikes are defined as a temporary stoppage of work based on some rational calculation of success, and involve trade unions within a collective bargaining system (or the fight for such a system). But, as we know, such actions cannot be contained within the narrow confines of the combatants; as Engels makes clear, trade unions' involvement in wage regulation involves class struggle, which becomes a political struggle (1881: 510-516). Therefore there are underlying ideological debates, concerned with the role of the state itself, whether directly or indirectly involved; with the nature of union leadership at all levels of the movement from the TUC down to local activists (Undy *et al* 1981); and with the nature and usage of power through agencies such as the media.

PAY COMPARABILITY AND COLLECTIVE BARGAINING

Pay tends to be the main trigger and stated cause of most strikes. It is also a symbol of a wider protest against inequality embedded in the *status quo*. The vexed question of how you measure the worth and value of a worker's contribution and therefore how much they should be paid in a democratic society continues to puzzle most people. We tend to be stuck with a *status quo*, which is unfair, unequal and resented. Yet there seems little way out other than policy drift, market anarchy and to endure the frustrating injustice of the wage payment system. While in the private profit-making sector there is much talk of markets and wages being determined by market rates, yet this hardly ever represents the feelings of workers in terms of relative worth. In the public sector the pay hierarchy has been largely determined by skill/professional power, shortages, management priorities and a strange quirky mix of short-term Government policy and random allocation of priorities. Nobody pretends the system for wage setting in the public services is fair, or was ever intended to be fair, but most workers feel it ought to be fair. We exist within limited possibilities and strive for marginal and often short-term improvements in our pay and conditions of service. The ability to protect and/or improve our situation depends on many factors, including the nature of the employers' policies and budgets, the nature of the job, the job market, the union's power, and the attitudes and beliefs of those involved. Our recent history is littered with errors, Government opportunism, failures, strikes and struggles; there have been overall pay improvements in real historic terms, but a less impressive record in terms of relative/comparative pay.

In the public services, pay comparability is more important and more enduring as the main determination principle than elsewhere in the economy. This stems from the essential nature of the services provided, and from the specific historical circumstances under which successive British Governments have been pushed and pulled over public sector pay (Brown and Rowthorn 1990). The main mechanism for achieving pay 'fairness' has been collective bargaining.

Collective bargaining in all its forms remains the defining function and purpose of trade unionism. There is a strong case for a broad definition of collective bargaining to include both strike action and arbitration within its normal operations (Webbs 1897; Clay 1929; Phelps Brown 1959; Clegg 1976). The process itself, whatever particular form it takes, is concerned to achieve an acceptable set of *pro tem* outcomes in terms of improved and/or defended conditions of service, including pay, non-pay items, and union representation. The process usually starts with a claim from the union side, because it is the employees who tend to constantly lag behind the realities of the business situation. But asking for more is no simple task. Claims have regard to membership wishes and/or aspirations and/or expectations; union policies and rules; the situation of other workers; the employer's position; the impact on the sector and users of the sector; the attitude of the dominant section of the media; and of course the view of Ministers and other political leaders.

Public services are provided by staff employed largely by public sector employers. Their pay is determined through some kind of collective bargaining mechanism – either through traditional Whitley-style systems, as with those in Local Government, the civil service and parts of the NHS, or through review bodies, such as for nurses and teachers (White 1999, 2000). The original and dominant system was that of Whitley (Whitley 1919). It essentially created national joint councils/committees (NJCs or equivalent), within which the two parties' representatives could negotiate, in some cases under the eye of an independent chair. The outcome would be binding on all employers and was therefore an effective rate-setting device. It also allowed for local disputes procedures with national stages. But the *sine qua non* of the system was the recognition by the employer of the union's right to represent and bargain for its members.

In Local Government these Whitley mechanisms developed separately for most manual and white-collar staff, with additional systems for groups such as firefighters and schoolteachers. At national level the distinctive features include a multi-employer system, with employers themselves representatives of elected councils. The unions representing staff tended to include a range of general unions, and then special unions such as the FBU for firefighters. A feature of Whitleyism for most of the post-1945 period was that final national agreements were known by the colour of the cover of the book within which they were published – 'grey' for firefighters. This also meant that, since pay and most conditions were determined nationally, local industrial relations was often about the enforcement and interpretation of the conditions of service manual.

In Local Government generally, and for the Fire Service in particular this system began to be tested in the late 1960s. Several factors brought pressure to bear, including rising inflation, expansion of the services, mechanisation, more developed management systems, and a more active and in some cases left-leaning set of union leaders at all levels in the organisation. This new found 'militancy' lasted through to the mid-1980s and the historic miners' strike in 1984-5. Pay and conditions were clearly tied up with a range of other issues, such as rationalisation and privatisation, working practices and skill changes, management controls and worker labour process, and the increasingly powerful interventions by central state agencies. As part of this the debate about the impact of public sector pay on the economy as a whole came to the fore. The basic argument was that a large chunk of public spending was on pay; if such spending exceeded tax revenues then Government had to borrow (the PSBR); if that borrowing was too high, interest rates would rise and cause inflation. This would create a wage-price and price-wage spiral, destructive of economic stability and growth. As this conventional wisdom took hold throughout Europe, there began a long and painful process of Government tax cuts followed by cuts in welfare and relative cuts in public sector pay. This in turn led to workers fighting for better pay, and the question then became one of what the correct basis was upon which to base pay.

Labour markets matter in pay determination. Basic supply and demand models give us a starting point to understand wage levels and movements. If you have a skill in great demand, and if (and only if) everything else is equal, you should receive a high reward. You may of course have a scarce skill but not one in demand at present and therefore you cannot sell it at all! Public sector employers and ultimately the Government must be concerned with this, because some staff have direct equivalents in the private sector and can therefore be benchmarked across services. In order to recruit and retain such staff, the total employment package must be at least equivalent to that offered by the private sector, assuming some reasonable level of labour mobility (getting on your bike). Other groups may have no direct competitors: most nurses, teachers and firefighters effectively have to work in the public sector if they are to work at all. In these cases the state acts as a monopsonist (sole buyer), and is in a very strong position to hold wages down. But this causes other problems. There is the question of internal relativities: a teacher expects to earn more than a school secretary, yet the latter's pay may have a market value and be higher. In addition, the state needs to staff its services and therefore needs to persuade seventeen-year olds making career choices to enter this or that occupation.

A solution to both issues can be systems of pay comparison, or at least total employment package comparison, allowing trade-offs between pay levels and factors such as job security and satisfaction, pensions and holidays, rights and representation. While the force is with the Government in most cases, a counter-argument is quite popular, namely that some public sector workers have too much bargaining power. This is based on the elasticity of demand for the service – services such as education, health and the fire service are in such demand by the public that they cannot survive without them and they cannot be easily substituted. Therefore the threat of strikes by such groups could push up their wages above the going (market) rate, hence the phrase 'holding the country to ransom'. In the 1980s both Reagan in the USA and Thatcher in the UK sought to win the argument decisively, and to defeat the workers involved, by accepting the political and financial costs of defeating such groups.

THE UNION CASE

There are five main arguments used by unions to support pay and other claims. These are cost-of-living (prices have gone up by x% and therefore it is only fair that my wages go up by at least x%); comparability (me-too claims – others have seen their pay rise by y% so I want y%); labour market shortages (my skills have become more scarce and/or different and so pay me more or I will take them elsewhere); profitability/affordability (you have the money due to my activities so I want a share); productivity/workload (I am working harder and smarter so pay more – Wootton 1962). All of these are of course linked together in some way or other, and unions use them tactically to win member support and to persuade employers. We will focus on comparability for now, although the May 2002 FBU claim also focused on skill changes, with some reference to workload.

Comparisons are used in wage claims in three ways: against the Average Earnings Index (AEI) – a general measure of wage movements; with a specific other occupational group; and through internal relativities within the job hierarchy of an organisation, increasingly through job evaluation, as with recent agreements in Local Government, the NHS, and Universities. None are straightforward. Averages hide wide variation and do not take into account changes in other factors. Other groups are never the same and there can be a tendency to go around in circles – I am compared with you while you are compared with me! Job evaluation and subsequent job hierarchies are contested at every calcu-

lation, are unstable, and often reflect the dominant managerial definition of worth. What remains important, however, is union members'
sense of felt-fair comparisons, because when these are outraged it is
possible to mobilise (Kelly 1998) them to take action.

So it is through the mechanism of collective bargaining that unions
present their arguments for pay rises, and in the public sector this is
backed by membership support for action frequently fuelled by a
sense of unfairness caused by a comparable fall in pay. As Routh
argued forty years ago: 'unions protect individual workers against
arbitrary acts; they give collections of workers more control over their
own destiny than they would have as individuals and present the
possibility of pursuing social ends that might not otherwise be attain-
able. It is in pursuit of such ends that unions set about reducing
differentials' (1965: 153). Fifteen years later he was more convinced
than ever pay that patterns were maintained 'through the tensions of
perpetual disequilibrium, the system powered by moral energy: the
pursuit of what is right and fair' (Routh 1980: 205). There can be no
doubting the moral energy in pursuit of fairness that dominated the
FBU actions in 2002-4.

Part of the definition of this fairness is that it is equitable on 'historical, ethical or prestige grounds' (Wootton 1962:138). In other words:
what did we have that we have now lost – we need to catch up; it is fair
that our training, skills and bravery are properly rewarded; and if our
status falls so does that of the service and the confidence the public
have in us. This takes us back to the role of the central state; to the
policy conflict of staffing services and controlling the wage bill. Since
the late 1940s this has not been done well! Policy has emerged from a
series of Governmental botches, based on a combination of false
economies, reaction to disruption of services caused by shortages or
stoppages, and an unclear perspective on the direction of such services.
An increasingly familiar way out of difficulties, taken by successive
Governments, has been that of pay inquiries. These were popular in
resolving specific disputes, and their findings over many years, allied
with the normal bargaining process within Whitley, created a dominant
norm of comparability-based bargaining up until the early 1980s.

Much of the modernisation debate around the reform of the Fire
Service in 2002-4 has centred on changes in working practices of the
workforce. When workers deliver a service to the service users, when it
is labour intensive, and when it is locally delivered, improvements in
the management of the service and the management of labour of the
service must go hand in hand. But achieving this raises a range of familiar issues about the nature of paid employment, control over the job
(labour process) and the nature of change (through agreement and
bargaining, or through imposition). So reform of the labour-intensive
public services means reform of the jobs done by the employees who
deliver them, and therefore of the management of labour in terms of

work organisation and control over task. Managers therefore have to deal with a wide range of labour management and labour relations issues: 'the modernising Government programme encompasses a vast range of personnel issues and it sets a bewildering raft of performance targets and standards for public servants' (IRS 1999: 5).

Those workers still under direct public employment regimes have maintained their relative position in terms of pay and conditions of service in general, with the notable exception of those in the Fire Service (IDS 2002a). They have, however, been subject to significant changes in labour management practices (Boyne *et al* 1999), including weakening of union influence, loss of job autonomy, and a concomitant rise in management discretion over what constitutes good performance. In particular the workforce have experienced job loss, relative worsening of conditions of work, tougher performance targets resulting in speed-up and closer supervision, and deterioration of their rights, both as trade unionists and as individual employees (Pendleton 1999; Ironside and Seifert 2000).

Of course most of these practices are familiar to most groups of workers and are neither a unique feature of the current period or new in any sense of being modern. What is happening is a restatement of management power and authority in a period of dominant central state intervention in the provision of services' and the intervention is increasingly in the interests of owners of businesses and not of the voter-citizen. This re-marketisation simply reverses the push after 1945 towards a more socially responsive and economically just set of policies, and returns us to a more reactionary time. Then as now such changes are not without serious problems, not least the resistance of those affected (Carter and Poynter 1999). As Braverman points out such resistance is uncertain: 'it [the working class] protests and submits, rebels or is integrated into bourgeois society, sees itself as a class or loses sight of its own existence, in accordance with the forces that act upon it and the moods, conjunctures, and conflicts of social and political life' (1974: 378). Braverman's main focus was not on the nature of resistance, but on what it was that was being resisted: he uncovered the market-driven logic of labour management.

MANAGING COST CUTS

Exposing public service managers to the force of market-like competition over streams of income, through the twin pressures of tight budgets and competition for budget share, is intended to mimic the tendency for rates of profits to fall and the competition for market share confronting private sector managers. The latter have a range of possible responses open to them, including: closing the business or part of it; changing the product/service; changing the price of the product/service; seeking out new markets; or cutting wage rates/conditions of service. Even fraudulent reporting and accounting can become part of everyday management functions, as catastrophically illustrated amongst large US and UK corporations such as Enron and Shell.

Public service managers can exercise few of these options. Cutting unit costs is the only viable response to competition, and in labour-intensive industries this can only be achieved by cutting unit labour costs. As wage rates are still mainly determined through national collective bargaining and review bodies (White 1999), this means cutting unit labour costs by implementing one or more of the following: reducing staffing levels; increasing work rates; reducing the proportion of staff on higher grades; changing conditions of employment to reduce their cost; and introducing flexible work schedules, including the use of agency staff, to enable managers to deploy labour strictly in accordance with business needs in the right quantity, in the right place, at the right time, and at the right price. Measures to weaken the capacity and the resolve of trade union representatives to resist are implicit in such cost-reducing measures (Ironside *et al* 1997). No wonder the FBU and its members fought so hard to resist the application of such modern systems into their service!

This approach suggests the application of techniques to manage the performance of staff, based on 'scientific management' principles. where jobs are broken down into component parts and measured in order to facilitate deskilling (Taylor 1911). As in the private sector, the Taylorist logic applies to an increasingly wide spectrum of occupational groups, including professionals such as teachers, nurses, and social workers, a tendency identified by Braverman (1974). HRM techniques associated with the control of staff performance play a key role in the thinking of Government and employer decision-makers (see for example a range of Government and employer statements about the best ways to manage staff: DFEE 1998; NHS Executive 2000; DoH 2001; Employers' Organisation for Local Government 2001).

Reducing unit labour costs in this way does not automatically result in either efficiency or productivity gains. Efficiency is gained by increasing the ratio of outputs to inputs. Thus for the outputs to remain the same – students learn the same things, and patients recover as quickly, for example – an efficiency gain would require a reduction of the inputs. This could be achieved through technological advances that would transform the delivery of mass education and health care, reducing the quantity and changing the quality of labour needed to deliver the current level of output. However, while there are some rapid and far-reaching changes in surgical procedures, the main input into mass health care and education is still labour. Any reduction in the labour input would, if all else remained equal, produce a corresponding reduction in output. The question then becomes, can the labour input be maintained if the labour input cost is reduced? The answer is yes only if one or more of the following can be achieved without affecting the labour input: making the service delivery workforce smaller;

replacing higher paid employees with lower paid ones; reduce relative levels of pay and other conditions of service; using employment practices that allow for cost-free rapid adjustments of workforce size and composition.

Reducing unit labour costs does not reduce by an equal amount the amount of labour inputs necessary to maintain outputs, so it does not increase the efficiency or productivity of the service. It simply makes it cheaper, by achieving the same outputs from a cheaper workforce, with fewer employees working harder, mostly at lower rates of pay, with worse conditions of employment, with less job security, and with less trade union protection. This raises the very important question: can the objective of cheapening the workforce be achieved without worsening the quality of the service?

Service quality imperatives are built into both the market and regulatory mechanisms, imposing further constraints on managers. For example, parents of prospective pupils might have an eye on school league tables and OFSTED reports when selecting the school for their child. Competitive advantage can be gained by achieving better results than competitors, as measured by performance indicators and as certified by regulatory bodies. Where there is competition for service contracts, performance indicators are built in. Best Value is predicated on the use of performance benchmarks. National inspection regimes impose further discipline over managerial behaviour, setting national service norms and carrying with them the threat of sanctions in the event of 'failure'. Managers are locked into a system that requires them both to minimise the cost of the workforce, and to maximise the effort of the workforce devoted to hitting performance targets.

Public service employees face some very hard realities. Their managers are encouraged to attack their pay, conditions, and job security, make them work harder, make them pursue targets, supervise them more closely, and employ more lower paid and fewer higher paid staff. They must minimise trade union influence over such matters. They must break with the public service traditions that included a shared sense of priorities between service delivery workers and their managers. While this goes against the grain for many experienced managers, they have little alternative but to act in accordance with the market and regulatory pressures. Job evaluation-based single pay spines, which are being pushed into Local Government (Single Status), the NHS (Agenda for Change), and higher education (framework agreement for the modernisation of pay structures), provide the link between pay structures, pay levels, and the Taylorised division of public service labour. Trade unions, perhaps anxious to protect some semblance of national bargaining have, with only a few exceptions, agreed to the weakening of national agreements necessary to secure managerial flexibility at the level of the service delivery business unit. However, it is difficult to see how the weakened safeguards contained in these national agreements will be enforced at local level. Some trade unionists appear to have accepted the idea that elements of the Government's modernisation agenda do actually hold out real potential benefits for workers.

The key may well be the relative strength of local trade union organisation, and national unions will need to give greater support to their workplace representatives. The neo-liberalism that underpins modernisation leads directly towards Taylorism, with its assumptions that workers systematically under-perform when left to themselves; that managers can prevent underperformance through work study and related techniques such as job evaluation; that managers can establish the best way of organising work and workers; and that workers will co-operate with management decisions in return for praise and higher pay than they would get by not co-operating. In this environment the trade union movement faces big challenges if it is to retain influence and protect members.

MODERNISING THE FIRE SERVICE: THE POWER AND THE GLORY?

The radical reform of the Fire Service became a central issue from the start of the dispute. The FBU had long accepted the case for fundamental reform to create a risk-based service, with greater emphasis on fire prevention linked to the need to prioritise the saving of lives and injuries, rather than protecting buildings and property. To these ends the union had fully co-operated in the *Pathfinder* Trials; it had been centrally involved in negotiating the details of the new training and skills development programme known as IPDS, which would pave the way from a rank based Service to one based on roles; and had pioneered new approaches to Fire Safety legislation, Community Fire Safety and Equal Opportunities within the Service.

The employers had a different agenda. To them the essence of radical reform was to increase the ability of management at all levels to deploy resources without the need to secure union agreement. This is borne out by the employers' evidence to Bain and by Government statements during the dispute.

When the employers stated that any significant increase in salaries could only be conceded if the union agreed to sign up to a modernising agenda, the union's response was to argue that its members had always co-operated in service-improving measures and had made the major contribution to raising productivity and reducing fire deaths over the previous two decades. It was time, the union said, for these contributions involving greater skills level and more varied and challenging workloads, to be reflected in the pay packets of FBU members. Notwithstanding this, any changes the employers wanted could be brought to the NJC for discussion and possible agreement and, where agreement was not possible, subjected to arbitration.

It became clear during the dispute that the employers' objectives (backed by Bain) were to provide a reformed Fire Service within existing budgets. So the costs of putting extra resources into Fire Prevention were to be found by cutting costs in fire cover, and by replacing whole time firefighters – particularly the night shift – by pre-arranged overtime and rest day working. This was the employers' version of modernisation.

The union argued that to provide a better service brigades needed more not fewer firefighters, as evidenced by the *Pathfinder* trials, and that the extra resources needed for Fire Prevention should be provided by a reformed and more generous Standard Spending Assessment from Central Government. So instead of advocating the redistribution of scarce resources in a way which would almost certainly threaten public safety, the union's view was that the employers should join with the FBU to put a united case to Central Government for more investment in the Fire Service.

Until the 2001 General Election there was a widespread consensus about the range and contents of the reform necessary to deliver a better Fire Service. The draft White Paper, subsequently abandoned, was based on widespread consultation under the auspices of the then Minister, Mike O'Brien. Starting from a position of already high performance, particularly in intervention work, it was broadly accepted that there was a need to put more emphasis on Fire Prevention activities, as well as using resources, both of equipment and personnel, more flexibly. This latter requirement can best be described as a move from a Service based on prescriptive standards (a given number of appliances with a given number of firefighters should attend a particular incident in a given time varied only by the type of location involved) to one where local risk assessment plans determined the allocation of resources.

The Fire Service has a good recent record in reducing fire deaths and injuries. But it is recognised that the best way of substantially reducing fire loss, particularly fire-related deaths, is through fire prevention policies – prevention being better than cure. These involve a range of approaches, from community education – teaching kids about the danger of matches and persuading adults about the dangers of smoking and unattended chip pans – to building design, including the installation of alarm and sprinkler systems. It also means having a usable predictive model, which tells you where the greatest risks are. For example, most fire deaths occur in domestic premises at night and in socially deprived communities, with the old and the young being particularly vulnerable. So the argument has been how to get resources into fire prevention, and how to frame legislation to improve regulation of new building design and fire escape procedures in multi-occupied dwellings and industrial or commercial premises. In a sense the legislation is the easy part, although there is still argument about the cost-benefit outcomes of the wider use of sprinkler systems, and some hesitation about how far you can regulate private landlords without affecting levels of housing supply.

Getting extra resources into Community Fire Safety has been a bigger nut to crack. It is only in fairly recent years that this has become a priority, and it remains a greatly under-funded and under-researched area of activity. The assumption is that if you raise public awareness of fire hazards, particularly in communities identified as being particularly vulnerable, then you will reduce the level of fire incidents, allowing you at some stage to reduce or re-direct the level of resources currently put into fire intervention. Such a strategy involves advertising campaigns about fire dangers and simple fire protection strategies, visiting families at greatest risk and installing smoke alarms, installing fire doors, going into schools and old people's homes, producing and distributing leaflets, and setting up Fire Safety Centres usually at Fire Stations. For a number of reasons, the most cost-effective way of undertaking most of these activities is by using existing Fire Service staff and facilities. Experienced firefighters, with some training in presentational skills, are usually the best teachers of the Fire Safety message. For most – particularly the young, the old, and members of migrant communities – a small team of firefighters in uniform is a more credible source of information and knowledge than a teacher or an actor. And this is a two-way process. The firefighters get to learn much more about the communities they serve and some of the potential hazards they may have to face.

The major problems until now have been twofold. Firstly, some brigades are not totally convinced that the trade-off between investment in CFS and savings in fire intervention costs has been established. This is understandable given the dearth of research and monitoring material available. You can search the Bain Report from cover to cover and not find one research finding which firmly establishes the link. There are a few local reports which do back the intuitive reasoning behind the case for CFS, and there have been good successes with multi-agency work in arson prevention – but probably not enough at this stage to convince every hard bitten Station Officer that they should spend time mapping out a comprehensive list of school and home visits for front-line firefighters, particularly when these are not funded within existing budgets.

The second issue is that of the structure of existing shift duties and constant crewing requirements. It is argued by some that, since the greater number of call outs, and the better opportunities for carrying out CFS work, occur during the day shift (9am – 6pm), the Service needs more firefighters on days than nights if a better balance between intervention and prevention is to be achieved. Certainly this is the view of Bain, who spends three short paragraphs in his 159-page long report discussing these issues. For Bain, CFS work: 'needs to be scheduled during the normal operating hours of schools, businesses or community groups'. Clearly this is a difficult logistical problem. Bain's answer is to bring firefighters in on their rest days (on a voluntary basis, presumably at premium rates) to do CFS work. This seems to be rather an expensive and old-fashioned way of tackling the issue. It also relegates fire safety to an optional extra to be undertaken when there is nothing else to do. Our society is moving towards a 24-hour 7-day-a-week working culture. Many key groups from a fire safety perspective are most accessible in the early hours of the night shift (between say 8pm – 10pm). These include Youth Clubs and Tenant Associations, Entertainment Centres, hotels and residential homes; and many manufacturing plants are also open during these hours. If properly planned, much productive CFS work could be done on the night shift without the extra costs and pressures (on the firefighter) of regular overtime working. Similar arguments apply at weekends.

The FBU gives full support to CFS work. It argues, however, that at this stage, and without the necessary trialling experience or monitoring information, it would be reckless to scale down resources currently applied to intervention (particularly the night shift, on which most fire deaths and rescues occur) on the expectation that an expanded CFS effort now will automatically result in reduced fire incidents tomorrow. It may take a period of five years or so of consistent CFS work to make a real dent in fire loss statistics. What is needed now, the union argues, is a period of sustained expansion in CFS work, properly funded and monitored, which can then be assessed, with the results being built into future risk assessment plans. If this is allied to better building regulations and more safety inspections, plus a zero tolerance culture of fire deaths, then Fire Authorities might be in a position to safely scale down intervention activities and redeploy further resources in the direction of education and inspection. The two strategies, intervention and prevention, should be seen as complementary within an expanded Fire Service, and not as competitive within a modernising culture which is obsessed with cost considerations rather than those of service quality.

It does appear, then, that there was and remains a third way option between what existed (prescriptive national standards) and New Labour's version of modernisation (radical reform of working practices plus the freedom of managers to manage). Incremental change was on the agenda before the 2001 General Election. If the thinking of Mike O'Brien's draft White Paper had been carried forward, it would have meant a careful introduction of local risk assessment plans, with pilot schemes and detailed monitoring, and a change to the funding formula, giving more money for fire prevention activities.

BAIN: THE ARCHBISHOP OF MODERNISATION
On modernisation, Bain has been used to ditch the *Pathfinder* exercise.

Pathfinder was based on several years research and a number of pilot studies in selected brigades, to develop a new risk-based approach to fire cover which would take into account the contributions made by Community Fire Safety and Fire Protection activities, including Fire Safety legislation. This report, using both worst case scenario models and cost benefit analysis, found a number of shortcomings in existing levels of fire cover and recommended significant increases in investment levels, particularly in non-urban areas without whole time stations. It showed that for an investment of an extra £1 billion per year (50% of the current budget), lives and property could be saved, and NHS and other social costs reduced; and that overall society would make important savings as a result of additional investment in staffing and station facilities. The FBU were active participants in this process. It saw this as a logical extension of the draft White Paper produced before the 2001 Election, which looked forward to a new risk assessment basis for the work of the Fire Service. Following the 2001 General Election and after several delays *Pathfinder* was finally published, but it was immediately questioned by Government, who were able to identify some middle range problems with the report's methodology.

The union claims that with some further work these flaws in *Pathfinder* could have been ironed out without in anyway changing the main thrust of the report. *Pathfinder* made it clear that its proposals for radical reform could be introduced while maintaining the existing *Grey Book* conditions on duty systems. This was not only contrary to the Audit Commission's report *In the Line of Fire* (1995), but was also out of kilter with New Labour's approach, which insisted that new public sector investment could only be justified if it were accompanied by radical changes in the way a service was operated and managed.

Bain's overall approach to the firefighter's job is not that sympathetic, and he has precious little to say about the union, the FBU, which represents over 80% of all uniformed staff working in the Fire Service. Thus for Bain: 'the Fire Services workload has been growing slightly overall over recent years'; and he goes on to quote figures since 1996 of incidents attended. Many of the other figures quoted dealing with fires go back to 1990, and one suspects that the base for Bain's statistics is altered so as to put the best gloss on any particular argument. There is also a striking omission, and that is the extra workload undertaken on Community Fire Safety. If one uses a slightly larger time frame and bases output purely on the number of incidents attended, then it is clear that, over the last ten years, workload has increased by 55% with a workforce that has fallen in full time equivalents by 2.5%.

Bain also seeks to downplay the change factor, and forgets to mention altogether the trauma involved in rescue work, as if cutting a badly injured child out of a car is about as demanding as a welder's job. Industrial injuries happen every day and some industries are more acci-

dent prone than others. The fact is that danger is built into a firefighter's job and so is trauma. It is not an accident to be caught in a back
draft: it is the nature of fire. Firefighters consciously go into extremely
dangerous situations, while most industrial accidents are bolts from the
blue. On working hours and the shift pattern Bain says: 'The first day
starts off at 9am'; he omits to notice that this follows a night shift of
fifteen hours, nine of which were during the so-called day off. Similar
crass remarks are addressed to the issue of whole time firefighters
working on their rest days in the Fire Service, as retained or part time
firefighters. Bain says: 'FBU rules will not allow a full time firefighter
to work as retained on their four (sic) days off although invariably they
can do any other kind of work'. Here Bain shows absolutely no understanding of the Health and Safety reasons for keeping hours at a
maximum forty-two hours on variable shifts; nor that regular overtime
working threatens both jobs and overall pay levels in the Fire Service
because of the way that the previous pay formula operated. At various
times during the dispute John Prescott made great play of this alleged
great irony. The argument used by Bain and Prescott is that a number
of firefighters are known to have second jobs, and that this is made
more possible by the existing shift pattern. Therefore, why not allow
firefighters the freedom to work longer hours in a job for which they
are well trained, rather than doing a few hours minicabbing or window
cleaning. The union's position is clear. The FBU is against second jobs,
and is against pre-arranged overtime. The union has no control over
what members do in their spare time – and in a free society neither
should anyone else – but the union does have a say in what happens in
the Fire Service, and if members vote to ban pre-arranged overtime and
rest day working for entirely rational reasons, then the democratic will
of the majority should guide the Fire Service activity levels of all.

What did the FBU and others make of the Bain report so speedily
and uncritically accepted by Ministers? The FBU was deeply unimpressed with Bain's pay analysis and asked both a job evaluation
consultant and the LRD for a commentary on the report's findings.
Both submitted highly critical assessments of Bain's methodology and
findings, including the work done by Hay (2002).

The consultant wrote as follows:

> There are a number of questions to be raised over the Hay Group
> Comparability Study, as described in Appendix 8:
>
>> Whether the Hay system is a suitable job evaluation scheme for
>> measuring the job demands of Firefighter and/or Fire Control
>> Operator roles. The scheme was developed in the USA immediately
>> before and after World War II for use in large private sector organisa-
>> tions. It appears to work satisfactorily in banking and finance
>> companies, and for senior managerial roles in both private and public

sectors, but it may be less appropriate for direct service providing jobs in the public sector.

Whether the omission of any additional factors to reflect, for example, the physical effort, working conditions and hazards of the Firefighter role does not invalidate the salary comparisons made with supposedly equivalent jobs in Industry and Services generally and in the Public Sector.

Why the actual Hay evaluations have not been published in the report, so the evaluations have to be accepted on trust.

Over the selection of comparator roles. For instance, the Firefighter role was assessed as equivalent in size to 'the old "State Enrolled Nurse" role' (Appendix 8, para. 8). In fact, this job title has not existed since 1988, when clinical grading for nurses and midwives came into effect and most SENs were assimilated into clinical grade C, with those who were regularly in charge of a ward being placed in grade D. Since then the Enrolled Nurse qualification (also known as second level registration) has been abolished, with most of those who held it having undergone training to convert to first level registration, with the associated promotion to clinical grade D or E. Finally, the SEN roles have largely been replaced by what are known as Healthcare Assistants (HCAs), whose salaries vary from trust to trust. So, it would now be impossible to identify either an SEN role or the matching salary.

Whether the different mechanisms for paying for unsocial hours working have been taken into account by the Hay consultants. Ambulance technicians and prison officers, like firefighters, receive a total salary, which incorporates payment for unsocial hours working. Nurses and midwives, on the other hand, receive a basic salary, with an additional premium for working rotating shifts or other unsocial hours patterns.

Whether median pay is actually the most appropriate basis for the pay comparisons, when most Firefighters are at or near the top of the relevant incremental scales, while different pay systems and distributions may apply in the private sector comparator companies (cf Appendix 8, para. 28).

Why the author of Appendix 8 discounts the comparability evidence with other firefighting jobs, which indicates that 'firefighters and lead firefighters in the Fire Service are paid between 8 and 9 percent below' the closest equivalent public and private sector roles, on grounds that are not to do with pay comparability (Appendix 8, para. 31) and this evidence is not mentioned in the main body of the Report.

How the Job Profiles were drawn up and whether there was any consultation over their content, as some aspects appear outdated or inaccurate, for example, that Firefighters only administer 'first aid' at incident and the absence of the use of sophisticated cutting and other equipment; the absence of any reference in the FCO Job Profile of the impact on the work of, for example, mobile phones, dealing with callers for whom English is not their first language and the health risk of sitting for long periods at a VDU (Hastings 2002)

On the job evaluation exercises commissioned by Bain, the LRD (2002: 5-7) was also highly critical:

The suitability of the Hay system is not discussed, despite the fact that large parts of the public sector use alternatives, and the Hay system has been criticised by some unions.

Hay's 'standard' system seems to have been used without adaptation to reflect the importance attached by either the union or employers to factors specific to the Service.

The Hay data show that public sector workers at the job size assigned to fire fighters receive significantly lower basic pay than their industry and services counterparts. This underlines the importance of including the private sector in any pay comparisons.

The report says that there were 'in excess of 3,000 fire fighting jobs based outside the Fire Service, the majority with the Ministry of Defence and the armed forces'. These 'probably provided the closest matches in the entire working population with jobs in the Fire Service and should therefore be considered' (A8.30). The report found the median rate of £21,531 for a firefighter to be 8.5% below the market median, with bigger negative differentials for most of the higher Fire Service grades. In this case the 'caveats' are given in some detail, and revolve around the claim that other firefighters 'embrace change wherever and whenever it is required' and 'are paid to do the job that management needs to be carried out at the time'. This leads to the statement that: 'If Fire Service staff are to realise the pay of their private sector counterparts, it could be argued that a change in operational practice should accompany any uplift in pay' (A8.31).

The LRD report went on to argue that: evidence of higher pay for fire-fighters outside the Fire Service – the 'closest match' identified by the DLA MCG study – is dismissed on grounds that they 'embrace change whenever and wherever it is required'. No evidence is given for this. Enquiries by LRD showed that jobs and working practices for fire-fighters in the private sector vary, and confirm that earnings of £25,000 to £30,000 are available.

It would hardly be surprising if firefighters working as part of a much larger non-fire fighting workforce, in different circumstances to those under which the Fire Service works, do things differently. Informal comments from some of those we contacted suggest that not all have undergone radical 'change' and that this would, in any case, be subject to union consent even where 'flexibility agreements' have been entered into.

It is clear therefore that Bain's work on firefighters' pay was at best hurried, and by not setting out the various evaluations used the whole exercise was deeply compromised. Perhaps the biggest single example of prejudice and error is the approach to comparative pay for firefighters' pay in the private sector, where greatly superior wages are justified simply on the unsubstantiated grounds that such workers are amenable to change in working practices. The LRD research clearly shows this to be a nonsense. Whatever else Bain did, the Report does not satisfactorily address the issues and findings of the research commissioned by the FBU, which justifies a significant pay increase by showing changes in job content and a fall in comparative earnings, backed by evidence of substantial improvements in productivity.

The criticisms of Bain go beyond mere carelessness with the facts. Part of this goes back to the terms of reference Bain was prepared to accept. These included the breathtaking task of determining pay levels 'and their affordability across the economy'. Obviously the Government had great confidence in their man, but to suggest that an unelected professor should make recommendations with this scope in a three month review is astonishing. We know of course that in his younger days when a don at Nuffield College Oxford, Bain provided extra tuition in economics to a Ruskin student by the name of John Prescott. This was Bain's own initiation into the world of second jobs in order to pay the rent. But that he should make recommendations on affordability of pay rises across the economy is surely taking delegation too far. All that he says on firefighters' pay, and the way any modest increase is to be financed (essentially through job losses), is determined by these terms of reference.

To be at all useful in this situation, Bain needed to make some estimate of just pay for firefighters, taking into account the factors identified by the FBU-commissioned research. Then it would have been for the Government, the employers and the FBU to negotiate a way forward. Instead Bain closed the door on fruitful negotiations by meekly endorsing the Government's general strategy on pay and reform in the public sector.

Writing in the *New Statesman* Robert Taylor said this:

> It wasn't what the unions were expecting. Sir George Bain, head of the Government-appointed independent review of the Fire Service, has many admirers in the trade union movement and – although the Fire Brigades Union has refused to co-operate with him since the inquiry started in September – most observers thought he would at least offer emollient words and a pay offer in the realm of acceptability. Instead, his

interim report not only disputes the firefighters' claim for a 40 per cent rise but does so in the most dismissive terms (18.11.02: 15).

Another industrial relations academic made this comment:

> Overall the Bain report should be seen as essentially one ordered by the Government in response to the strike threat. In other words it could never be independent because it is unheard of in industrial relations modern history for such a review to be undertaken with the threat of a dispute when one party refuses to participate. Therefore Bain's position in disingenuous: it is not about the future of the Fire Service in terms of modernisation but about stopping the strike; and as a result his report and its timing have tied the hands of the employers (Seifert in *FBU Strike Bulletin*, November 2002).

This point was reinforced in a letter to the *Guardian* from Professor John Kelly of the LSE. He wrote: 'Bain has simply not engaged with the argument about fair pay and largely endorsed the employers' agenda by proposing that even a modest pay settlement would only be paid after agreement on far-reaching reforms to work practices' (14.11.02: 27).

An internal document produced at FBU Head Office came to the following conclusion on Bain:

> This is a deeply flawed paper designed to:

- Put a lid on public sector pay increases.
- Attack the FBU's position by undermining
  - (i) the right to joint regulation of duty systems and operational staffing levels
  - (ii) the NJC and national bargaining through:
    - (a) individual performance payments taking the lion's share of any available extra funding
    - (b) the recommendation to move towards local bargaining on a broader range of issues

- Introduce in the name of modernisation and equal opportunities
  - (a) attacks on the watch system and single entry recruitment and progression with all this could mean in the dilution of professional and operational standards particularly in Fire Incidents and Prevention work
  - (b) deeply old-fashioned notions like a longer working week in order to boost inadequate salaries

- Question the validity of a Pay Formula since this would obstruct further moves towards individual pay awards and local bargaining on a broader agenda.

The final word came from Lancashire Business School:

> As I prepare my lectures for a course on crisis management next semester, I will be obliged to comment on the proficiency and efficiency of the British service. As always, I expect to demonstrate that the fire service has a flexible approach to handling emergencies that is a model of excellence. I will go on to suggest that other businesses should follow the lead of the Fire Service in preparing for crisis situations. I will back this up with evidence.
>
> It is now clear that I will have to explain that the Bain report is clearly not independent. The analysis of the results of the army's role is premature and based upon faulty argument. The attempt at 'modernisation' is nothing more than a policy to reduce the effectiveness of the Fire Service in order to save money. All this will be necessary to maintain my proposition that the Fire Service is an effective and modern organisation. I will have to confront the substance with the Government spin.

Edwin Thwaites (*Guardian* 5.12.02: 25)

PARAMEDICS

The FBU document continued:

> In his interim report Bain strongly recommended that firefighters take on extra paramedic duties particularly when they are in a position to be first to the scene of an incident where such skills are necessary to save lives or reduce injuries. UNISON, which represents the majority of Ambulance Service staff, and the professional association representing paramedics, both wrote to Bain to protest at this recommendation pointing out that paramedics take 3.5 years to train and that their skills need constant updating. It was therefore impracticable, wasteful and a dangerous diversion to give extra responsibilities to the Fire Service – the urgent need is to invest more in the Ambulance Service and Paramedic training.

The FBU has similar policies to those of the bodies representing paramedics. When attending fire incidents crews provide necessary first aid and in extremis use resuscitation equipment and, in most brigades, defibrillators. The understanding is that it is very much a holding operation until the professional paramedics arrive. Training is given in all brigades to ensure that there are adequate first aid skills available on all watches. But in many brigades there are waiting lists for training, particularly the necessary updating and refresher courses, because of inadequate investment in such activities.

Much has been made by the LGA and other politicians about the use of defibrillators by fire crews. The argument is that if a fire engine can get to a non-fire incident before an ambulance, then firefighters should be used as a surrogate Ambulance Service in the interests of saving lives. In one or two rural areas there are co-responding agreements between the ambulance and Fire Service to use firefighters in this way. Generally speaking the FBU is against its members attending non-rescue incidents to carry out paramedic functions. It argues that extra investment is needed in the Ambulance and Paramedic Services to give the public a better service, and that, as a general rule, people with life threatening conditions are better attended by fully trained paramedics rather than firefighters with limited training in this field.

In the light of the above arguments Bain came to a more rounded position in his final report simply recommending that more co-responding schemes be negotiated between the two services. But this did not stop the Prime Minister arguing on 20 November that firefighters training as paramedics and the establishment of joint control rooms were 'not wildly unreasonable suggestions'. Based partly on the extraordinary circumstances of the military operations in providing an alternative Fire Service during strike days, Government Ministers made a deal of noise about the merits of moving towards joint control rooms for emergency services. This was also punted by Bain in his interim report.

Again UNISON wrote to protest on behalf of their Ambulance Service staff. In a letter to the Secretary of State for Health, dated 19 November, Karen Jennings, UNISON National Secretary (Health) wrote: 'the Control Staff function across the Emergency Services is not generic. Ambulance Control Staff have extensive skills which they deploy to assist 999 callers ... control staff save lives by giving telephone advice prior to the arrival of an ambulance'.

For the Fire Service, as Ministers and Bain must have known, the Mott MacDonald report published before the dispute in April 2000 specifically recommended against Joint Control rooms, arguing, after extensive research, that such arrangements would lengthen response times thereby threatening lives and would not be cost effective anyway. But this authoritative report did not prevent Bain from riding a Ministerial hobbyhorse. Subsequently Mott MacDonald has revisited the issue and confirmed its previous recommendations against Joint Control rooms (2003); and the FBU (2004a) has responded with its views on keeping control rooms separate.

CONCLUSIONS

Modernisation as expressed by the political leaders of the Labour Party is neither neutral nor necessarily progressive in terms of democratic accountability and rights, as in the quality of service provision for the public. As applied to the Fire Service, it has re-opened the door to a long-hours working culture, to multi-union bargaining and competition, and to much greater powers for unelected senior managers, particularly at CFO level. In structural terms it represents a move towards regionalisation and indirectly elected or appointed management boards rather than Local Authority based fire authorities accountable to directly elected councillors. Strategically, all key decisions will now be made by civil servants and CFOs, with no involvement of worker representatives and precious little by elected councillors.

New local risk assessment plans will shortly become operational. The signs are that the changes introduced are extensive; and, with the exception of new investment in the New Dimension programme to deal with the possible consequence of terrorist attacks, they present a general picture of cuts in service provision, including minor cuts to staffing levels. The real tests are yet to come, as regionalisation could result in a big cutback in Control Room numbers and contingent staffing levels. The pay question may have been settled in a way that guarantees industrial peace on this issue for a few years. But we can be certain that the struggle over resources, investment, cuts and working practices resulting from the introduction of the modernisation agenda will sharpen and intensify.

As with other public services, modernisation has meant the introduction of market forces. The form this takes is a combination of more authority to make decisions at the centre of Government, thereby by-passing locally elected councillors, and giving more powers to site-based senior managers, thereby by-passing the concerns of both the workforce and the local community. In order to achieve this in a labour intensive public service with a strong tradition of collective bargaining it is necessary to undermine national conditions of service, to reduce union influence, and to break up strong work groups. This has to be done covertly in the name of greater efficiency and greater local flexibility, as well in the name of the customer. This much is clear; the evidence from the NHS and now from the Fire Service is overwhelming. What remains a puzzle to many is the 'why' of it all.

If we have dedicated staff working in efficient sectors on behalf of an accountable employer, then what is the objective of this change of direction? Well, the best answer contains three elements: to control more tightly costs and performance for Central Government as the ruthless state takes greater powers to enforce greater inequality; to ease the path to privatisation through weakening opposition from unions, elected local councillors and professional experts; and to seize the ideologically dominant high ground associated with the delivery of efficient services and thereby undermine residual beliefs in welfarism and socialism.

Chapter 6

Closure and Aftermath:
The Balance Sheet

INTRODUCTION

> This has been an historic dispute, only the second of the Union's history
> and the first to challenge New Labour's overall approach to public sector
> pay, public service provision and management. It has achieved much but
> not everything we set out for. That is often the nature of campaigning.
> The Union has held together and the unity, dignity and determination of
> the membership has secured the best public sector deal this pay round,
> around £1500 per annum on average above what the old Pay Formula
> would have produced (*FBU Annual Report* 2004: 10).

In this chapter we revisit some of the main moments of the dispute in
order to provide a more analytical account of what happened and to
draw together some final comments.

AN ASSESSMENT OF THE ISSUES

At the end of any dispute it is natural for participants and commentators to make an assessment of the outcome. In the overwhelming
majority of cases there are no unambiguous winners, and this general
rule has been born out by the firefighters' dispute. The union made
significant progress on every aspect of its original claim but has had to
concede ground on its previous position of considerable strength in
jointly regulating conditions of service and working practices. Only
when the new locally based risk assessment plans have been fully rolled
out can a real assessment be made of their effects on jobs, working
conditions and workers' rights, including the right to an effective say
in the way the Service is managed. For the FBU the arena of struggle
has shifted. National framework agreements will remain extraordinar-
ily important, but local negotiations on everything other than basic pay
rates will become increasingly dominant. So when people ask how the
balance sheet of the dispute should be accurately drawn, we are

reminded of Chou-En-Lai, the Chinese Foreign Minister in 1949, who, when asked for his assessment of the French Revolution of 1789 replied that it was too early to judge.

In the meantime we can make some tentative appraisals. As we write it is clear that the union has emerged intact with membership levels, in density terms, among the highest in the British trade union movement. The national agreement will be less prescriptive and much will be devolved to brigade level. However, it remains in place, and its substantive and procedural arrangements will be of some significance for local bargainers, particularly on hours of work, health and safety, basic pay rates through the operation of the new Pay Formula, equal opportunities and family friendly working practices, and disputes and discipline procedures. Nationally the FBU will continue as the instrument of workers' rights in the Service, dwarfing both the RFU and the tiny Officers' (middle managers) organisations. The FBU will retain its majority position on all national bargaining bodies, except that for Chief and Assistant Chief Fire Officers. Similar arrangements will be replicated locally where, thanks to the unity and resilience of its membership, the FBU national leadership was able to force the employers to concede that change in working practices must be related to plans to improve fire safety, not simply cost-cutting measures; and should be agreed with the workforce, through the FBU, subject to arbitration wherever there is a failure to agree.

So cuts and redeployment cannot be made on cost grounds alone. If so inclined, CFOs will need to undertake the difficult task of persuading local communities that having fewer firefighters available somehow makes people safer in their beds at night. National standards of fire cover may have gone, but it is a measure of the union's achievement that all future change at any level must be preceded by consultation and agreement or arbitration, within the context of providing a better Fire Service for the people. After the breakdown of negotiation in November 2002, following the Government's intervention, the employers were encouraged to take a hard-line position which included the imposition of change at the behest of CFOs, linked to a 2% per annum for four years reduction in the whole time firefighters' establishment to fully fund a phased 16% increase. FBU negotiators were able to persuade the employers to drop the direct link with job losses and to move back to a position of change by agreement. These were, by any measure, significant victories. In these areas, jobs and working conditions, the union still has all to fight for at local level and, as in most of the public sector, these struggles are part of a constant war of position with the established powers.

While conducting our interviews with FBU local officials and officers, a view was expressed on a number of occasions that modernisation New-Labour-style could have been avoided if the union had been less aggressive with its pay claim. This reflects the union's thinking during the 1990s, or at least before the election of a Labour Government in 1997, when, despite the relatively poor performance of the Pay Formula, it was felt to be adventurist to consider challenging a Tory Government on pay. Better, it was argued, to protect conditions, jobs and services, and the Pay Formula itself, which in their view provided protection against cuts and moves towards regional pay and/or extensive outsourcing.

In our view these assessments are misguided. For the public sector, as a whole, 'modernisation' has been the Government's main domestic political objective since its re-election in 2001. Change is being driven through everywhere you look. The Fire Service may have been a back-water for years for local and national politicians, but it was a racing certainty that sometime this Parliament the Government would have acted. Looking back it is clear that *In the Line of Fire*, the Audit Commission's Report published in 1995, signalled a change of direction for state policy. This was the embryo of a radical 'modernisation' agenda. But after a successful propaganda campaign, the FBU was able to hold the line while the employers appeared to back off and decided not to attempt to force through such a programme in the late 1990s. Instead we had the Burchill Report (2000), which addressed one of the employers' main concerns, on the way the union was able to use the existing disputes procedure to block service changes; and then a Draft White Paper, drawn up after considerable consultation, in which the FBU was centrally involved, and finalised in early 2001 by the then Fire Minister Mike O'Brien (later a temporary victim of one of the early Mandelson scandals). Both the O'Brien paper, and to a lesser extent the more specialised Burchill Report, focused on modernisation and devolvement of some decision-making to local level. The FBU was fully involved in both processes and gave its enthusiastic support to Burchill and a general welcome to O'Brien's White Paper. So, as even Bain acknowledges, there was a broad consensus about the need to reform the Service, moving towards local risk assessment, with a far bigger role for Community Fire Safety and Fire Prevention. Indeed the lengthy discussions and negotiations around the IPDS process were intricately linked to an agreed radical reform of the Fire Service.

If introduced along the lines of O'Brien's White Paper (in a measured way over a number of years, with the careful monitoring of the impact and effectiveness of Fire Prevention measures and their rela-tionship to the level of Fire Cover required to protect the public), modernising reform could well have been introduced in a consensual manner. But since the 2001 General Election, the Government appears to have been seeking a programme of rapid change, overriding the views of the workforce and sidelining the influence of the union. This general approach is replicated throughout the public sector.

On the pay front the union secured what was one of the best public sector agreements in the pay round. Table 2 on pay indicates just how

Table 2: Fire Service Pay in 2005

Grade	FIRE SERVICE Qualified/ Competent fire fighter	LOCAL GOVERNMENT (E&W) Spine point 32 (min of old Senior Officer 2 scale)	NHS NURSES & MIDWIVES Minimum of scale G (Sister/Charge nurse)	POLICE Constable on completion of two years service	ARMED FORCES Sergeant level 1 lower band
2001	£21,531 (from November)	£21,702 (from April)	£21,605 (from April)	£21,015 (from September)	£22,926 (from April)
2002	4% from November, new salary £22,392	3% from April (more for lowest paid), new salary £22,353; and 1% from October, new salary £22,569	3.6% or £400 whichever greater from April, new salary £22,385	3% from September, new salary £21,645	3.7% from April (4.2% on lowest pay range), new salary £23,772
2003	7% from November, new salary £23,959	3.5% from April, (4.5% for lowest paid), new salary £23,358	3.225% from April, new salary £23,110	£402 (1.86%) from April (scale being shortened), new salary £22,047; and 3% from September, new salary £22,707	3.2% from April (3.7% on lowest pay range), new salary £24,532
2004	4.2% (4.34% Competent fire fighter) from July, new salary £25,000	2.75% from April, new salary £24,000	3.225% from April, new salary £23,860	3% from September, new salary £23,388	2.8% from April (3.2% on lowest pay range), new salary £25,218
Total 2002 to 2004	16% annual average 5.3%	10.6% annual average 3.5%	10.4% annual average 3.5%	11.3% annual average 3.8%	10% annual average 3.3%
	New formula for 2005 and 2006	2.95% from April 2005, new salary £24,708. April 2006 rise may be inflation-linked. 2002/3 deal followed industrial action and involvement of ACAS. 2004/6 deal commits local authorities to progress on grading and equal pay.	Salaries may rise on transfer to new Agenda for Change pay structure from 1 December 2004. 3.225% from April 2005. Pay review body recommendation or new Pay Negotiating Council from 2006	Future rises unknown but pay formula linked to private sector non-manual pay settlements	Future rises unknown but based on pay review body recommendation

Source: Labour Research Department

favourable the FBU settlement was compared to other public sector workers. The annual continual average for firefighters was about 6.5%, since in the end the deal was over two years and eight months, not over three years as stated. Of the four pillars in the original claim, two were achieved in full and one was substantially advanced. The shortfall was in the failure to achieve something like the central demand for £30,000 per annum for a qualified firefighter, on which the level of the other three demands was contingent. Here the final settlement at £25,000 by June 2004 fell some way short of the members' aspirations, and there remain some ticklish problems to resolve, such as the phasing out the service-based fifteen-year payment and the introduction of a new Professional Development payment.

The new pay formula will be introduced in 2005, and reviewed after the 2006 settlement. It is to be based on the movement in earnings of workers in the Associate Professional and Technical classification of the New Earnings Survey, which is conducted annually. This group includes many non-manual workers and also reflects movements in women's earnings. These are the groups that have experienced the fastest rate of earnings growth in recent years (with the exception of course of Company Directors and Chief Executive Officers in the private and public sectors). So, from a considerably improved starting point (up by a minimum of 16% for all and somewhat higher for those in the ECROs and Retained Firefighters), the potential of the new pay formula to produce better results than the old pay formula (see table 3) is extremely high provided that current trends continue.

The Emergency Control Room staffs have seen their pay arrangements up rated. Previously, grade for grade, they were paid 92% of the equivalent firefighter's rank. Now, after an extensive job evaluation

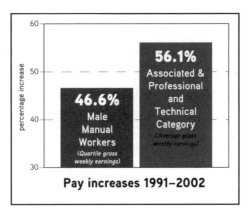

Table 3: 1991-2002 pay increases

exercise, this has been upped to 95%. So while pay parity has not actually been achieved, a big step forward has resulted from the industrial action. This group of workers, some 1700 strong and over 90% women, will however face considerable upheaval over the next few years, as the Government seeks to regionalise control centres, substantially reducing the number as local brigade-based centres are closed.

Nonetheless, even here some of the more outrageous and dangerous (for the public) Government proposals concerning joint control rooms with the police and ambulance services have been quietly dropped, at least for the foreseeable future. During the strike the Government made great play of the way in which what was a joint Army-Police control room operation led to greater efficiencies and better collaboration between services. What they forgot to mention was that less than 40% of the calls were responded to and that an authoritative report, the research for which was carried out when the Fire Service was operating at 100% response rates, showed that joint control rooms were a danger to the public (by increasing response time), and would not save the Fire Service a penny. Since the dispute has ended and there is no longer a pressing need for the Government to bad mouth the work of the Fire Service this research has been repeated, and it came to the same conclusions about the serious disadvantages of moving to joint control rooms for the emergency services (Mott MacDonald 2000, 2003).

It has been widely recognised that the Retained Section of the Fire Service has been seen as the poor relation for a number of years. Most retained firefighters rely on understandings from their main employers that, in the event of a call-out, they will be able to leave their job immediately. Others are self-employed, carers or unemployed. Their reward structure consists of a number of elements – a retaining fee, a turnout fee, an attendance fee, and a weekly payment for the required two hours training (drill night). So each retained firefighter has a different reward pattern, based on their level of actual activity over which they do not have total control (turnouts). The retained force operates mainly in rural areas and is around 18,000 strong. It is chronically understaffed. The FBU, which has campaigned long and hard for equality of status, under the slogan 'A firefighter is a firefighter is a firefighter', has sought pay, pension and training parity for the retained. So pay parity became one of the four pillars of the 2002 pay campaign.

For their own reasons the employers conceded the principle of parity early in the talks. No doubt they recognised a continuing recruitment problem, but they almost certainly also wanted to keep the retained on side should a dispute develop. While the FBU represents over half the retained workforce, the RFU has approaching 2000 working firefighters in membership (about 10% of the total), and over 30% belong to neither organisation. This non-union element (the RFU plus nons), together with a small number of non-FBU officer grade members, may have provided the core of a strike breaking workforce capable of attracting others if the dispute became protracted and difficult. In the event the FBU retained membership remained 100% solid for the strike and a few hundred RFU members joined the FBU. The Officer grade FBU membership was also 100% solid.

While the principle of parity pay, contrary to the preconceived ideas of Ministers and civil servants, was conceded as far back as July 2002, reflecting this in actual pay arrangements proved to be no easy task. After months of detailed negotiations the NJC agreed a model to reflect the 'typical' Retained Firefighter. This was based upon 200 calls per year producing 150 turnouts, thirty over one hour, and fifty attendances. Pre-settlement this typical firefighter would have received £5557 per annum, but from 7 November 2003 this figure would be £6406, which is a 15.3% increase. A further 4.2% would be added in June 2004. The position statement adopted also gave the Retained Firefighter parity in respect of training and skills development.

So on the pay front we have a mixed picture. The outcome on each of the four pillars has ranged from outstandingly good (the pay formula) to much better than most have achieved (the basic rate for firefighters). However you slice it, industrial action forced the employers, with some extra Government funding, to increase their original offer from 4% plus pie in the sky to 16% over two years and eight months. Assuming that without industrial action firefighters would have received average pay increases of around 3.5% a year (the going rate for the public sector), we can see that the average FBU member was £1500 a year better off by July 2004 as a result of their solidarity and unity in action and the final settlement negotiated by their leadership. That is £1500 every year until retirement, plus the value of a higher base rate from which future rises will be calculated. For example a 4% rise on £21,531 gives an increase of £861 while 4% on £25,000 gives an extra £1000. And every year these increases will be reflected in the final pension entitlements.

Despite some of the very positive features in the settlement and the campaign which made it possible, we found, at meetings of brigade level and Regional Officers and Officials of the FBU, levels of disappointment and anxiety about the future which surprised us. When we interviewed activists and elected officials, either individually or in small groups, we were struck by the force of their conviction that firefighters are worth £30,000 per annum and that the general public supported this position. It is as if the campaign itself was so successful in uniting the membership behind the £30,000 claim to produce such an outstanding and favourable vote (83% overall) for strike action if necessary, that any negotiated settlement less than £30,000 came as a disappointment. The union leadership, despite their public negotiating position indicating acceptance of a phased 16% increase linked to changes in working practices as far back as November 2002, never found a way of managing down the membership's expectations, or of combating the outrageous claims of Government Ministers, well into 2003, that the FBU's position remained 40% with no strings. This in our judgement has more to do with the strength of the FBU's democracy and the pressure exerted by leading activists on elected EC members than it does with any failure of leadership by the FBU negotiators.

Throughout the dispute the Government's use of the state machine and of a tame anti-union media was both effective and unprincipled. The list is long. It includes threats, deceptions, the effectively anti-strike legislation in the Fire Services Bill, the use of Professor Bain to underwrite Government policy, the promotion of anti-TUC pro-employer so called unions, the shock horror stories linking firefighters' pay to mortgage increases, the pretence that systematic overtime is compatible either with efficiency or family friendly working practices, and the disregard of international employment accords.

All of this has done harm to the labour movement. The beginnings of the decline in Labour's popularity can be traced back to the Government's handling of the firefighters' dispute. Certainly the concerns in the trade union movement about the direction of Government policies were considerably reinforced and this is reflected by a significant distancing from New Labour by important unions.

In his *Guardian* column, the long time SWP member Paul Foot described the outcome as an 'ignominious Government victory'. Other ultra-leftists, from the Workers Revolutionary Party to supporters of what used to be the Militant Tendency, just like the *Financial Times* and the *Daily Telegraph*, have cried defeat and blamed the elected leadership of the FBU. They provide us with the usual suspects for apparent defeat: if only the FBU had struck harder or later and harder, and if only the leadership had stuck to the letter of FBU Conference policy, then the Government would have been forced to concede considerably more than it did and existing conditions of service could have been protected by an unaltered national agreement.

We find all these criticisms to be wide of the mark. During our interviews we were impressed not only by the tenacity of the activists' belief in the justice of their pay claim but also by the unwillingness of the membership to engage in prolonged periods of strike action. The members are immensely proud of the service they provide for the public and deeply uneasy about taking strike action, particularly on pay issues. That is why, in our judgement, there have only been two national strikes in the history of the Fire Service. And it is why there is a pay formula, which, if kept up to date, obviates the need to take industrial action on pay issues. For the leadership to have ignored this history and experience by attempting to escalate strike action instead of taking every opportunity to create the best possible conditions in which to achieve a negotiated settlement would have been disastrous. All the reports are that following the very successful and totally solid eight-day strike at the end of November 2002 the membership had reached a point where a majority were no longer prepared to support further periods of lengthy strike action. The union would have been split down the middle and probably destroyed by such a strategy.

Our view is that the FBU achieved most of what it campaigned for but has paid a price in lost consultation rights and challenged representation positions at national level, and faces difficult challenges as the new local risk management plans are rolled out over the next year or so. But our overall judgement is that without the campaign backed by industrial action the advances on pay would not have been achieved, with the possible exception of a new pay formula (from a lower base of course) and some adjustment of retained pay and allowances to improve recruitment levels. All the changes to conditions and working practices which are on stream now or down the line would have come anyway, perhaps in a more draconian form, sooner or later, and with or without a pay campaign, as they have done in other sectors.

Given the lively debate within the FBU, especially amongst the activists, it might be helpful to end this account of the dispute with further analysis of key issues and turning points.

THE BIG ISSUES

THE CLAIM: BACK TO THE BEGINNING, WHY £30K?

To some commentators the size of the claim was the main reason why the firefighters were unable to obtain a negotiated settlement without recourse to industrial action. Senior LGA representatives Charles Nolda and Phil White certainly claim this, arguing that both a new pay formula and a decent annual pay rise could have been negotiated.

As we have seen the union justified the £30k claim for a fully trained firefighter after four years of service on a number of grounds. Since the introduction of the pay formula in 1978, firefighters' pay has slipped down the pay league such that IDS calculated that a 21% increase was required simply to restore their relative pay position to that enjoyed in the late 1970s. LRD research for the union (2002) showed how far firefighters' pay had slipped behind average earnings.

On the job content front, the union commissioned a report from Sue Hastings, an acknowledged expert in the field. That report showed that by using job evaluation techniques, the modern firefighters' job had grown by 16% since the late 1970s. A number of reports, including the employers' own figures, showed a remarkable increase in call-outs since the pay formula was introduced, while the numbers of firefighters had slightly reduced in the same period. So on a number of grounds, from the union perspective £30,000 was a reasonable negotiating position. The general public certainly supported the £30,000 figure, recognising the value people placed on the firefighters' courage and professionalism. A MORI poll showed

70% support in favour of the main pay claim (*Firefighter pay special*, September 2002: 3).

The politicians had mixed views. Nolda and White were in no doubt that this was a serious claim and that the union could organise effective strike action should this prove to be necessary. They also recognised that the case for a substantial improvement in earnings was justified and saw in this an opportunity to trade better pay for changes in working practices. As early as February 2002 notice was given by the union of the need to reformulate the pay formula and that the base for this should be a substantial pay increase in November 2002. By April the employers had advised civil servants that a big pay demand was in the pipeline and that in their view some sort of independent inquiry was needed to deal with the need to substantially increase wages and change working practices. This appears to have been put on the back burner during a period of departmental change for Fire Service affairs – in May 2002 the responsibility for the Service was transferred to the ODPM within the portfolio of minister of state Nick Raynsford. A Government sensitive to workers' demands and the strength of the firefighters' support for these claims could have intervened in a positive way by encouraging a negotiated settlement in July. Instead it delayed, making strike action inevitable in November. And by intervening again in late November it ensured a further period of intermittent strike activity at considerable public cost. In the end the 16% pay rise, first mooted by the employers in July, was still the basis for the final settlement, albeit phased over two and two-third rather than two years.

Once negotiations started in June 2002 the employers side immediately linked the pay issue to what it called 'modernisation' – in practice a long list of cost nothing changes to working practices which had been on their agenda for a decade or so. It is now clear that by early July the employers were prepared to offer a phased increase over two years, taking a qualified firefighter to a basic £25,000 per annum (a 16% increase on current salary) subject to union acceptance of changed working practices. But the Government intervened and prevented such an offer being tabled. At this stage in mid-July the employers again signalled that they saw no way forward within the traditional NJC process and that the best way to proceed was an independent inquiry linking pay to modernisation. The union's position was to seek a negotiated settlement based on the rate for the job, then as a united Fire Service to go to the Government to ask for extra funds to finance both the pay increase and any requisite modernising investment to improve the Service. Such an approach recognised that Fire Service funding arrangements were badly in need of reform, and that the Government had conceded this in its draft White Paper in 2001. Within the Fire Service itself there was a consensus that a step-change increase in pay was justified and that the Service had been underfunded for years, since the funding arrangements failed to take into account the high costs of providing specialist services (such as attending road traffic accidents) and fire prevention work, including Community Fire Safety.

The union also argued that changes in working practices should be negotiated at NJC level separately from pay. The FBU claimed that £30,000 per annum or thereabouts was what a firefighter was worth in 2002, and that firefighters had been modernising for years without proper financial reward by constantly undertaking new tasks and the training which went with this.

The union claim presented the Government with an opportunity to reform the Fire Service by agreement with all the social partners, if it was prepared to live with an exceptional pay rise in a small service within the public sector. Such an increase could have been justified as a special case and as a lever for big changes in the Service. This could have included new funding arrangements and locally assessed risk management plans, which, until they were actually framed, were difficult to cost, not least in staffing requirements. But the Government was not prepared to accept the risk that such an approach presented to its overall, if not clearly stated, pay policy for the public sector, with all that this could mean for its credibility with the financial markets, the CBI and the media. The Winter of Discontent still haunts the minds of many Labour politicians, who fear that their Government could be thrown off its neo-liberal course by the strength of trade union militancy. So rather than changing course and proceeding by agreement, the Labour leadership chose to tough it out, hoping that somewhere along the line the union leadership could be persuaded to accept the Government's line.

As far as finding a settlement was concerned, weeks were wasted while the Government prepared its defences. It tried to divert the union leadership by setting up the inquiry requested by the employers. The problem for the Government was that the union had made it very clear that it wanted nothing to do with such an exercise. In these circumstances it would be unusual to proceed with such an approach without the acceptance of all interested parties. Meanwhile necessary preparations were made to mobilise resources to deal with a possible strike – preparing the Green Goddesses, training thousands of military personnel in basic firefighting, and setting up a logistical chain of command to handle the emergency call centres.

While all this was going on the Government encouraged the employers to delay. The result of the strike ballot, with its massive support for strike action, concentrated minds. With great haste the Bain Inquiry was established without union support and with no meaningful consultations about the terms of reference. To hammer the point home the terms of reference specifically included Government pay policy and the effects of any recommendations on the overall economy. The strikes in mid-November again changed the balance of power and within a few weeks the employers, with Government approval, were back at the negotiating table. On that fateful night (November 21-22) the July 'offer' that was never made was back on the table, with some of the strings more fully spelled out. After several hours of negotiation an agreement was reached – the union had accepted that a significant phased pay rise (16% over two years) could be linked to progress in changing, by agreement, some working practices. Once again the Government intervened arguing that the final agreement was uncosted, and instructed the employers to withdraw their offer.

Despite the union's clear commitment to seeking a negotiated settlement, if necessary well below the £30,000 mark and including strings, the Government continued throughout the following months to argue that the FBU was demanding 40% without strings. This presentation was faithfully followed by most sections of the media and became part of the 'received wisdom'. It was a successful strategy which the FBU found difficult to combat, given the strength of feeling among the membership that £30,000 was a reasonable rate for the job they did for society.

Of course it is possible in theoretical terms for the union to have run a different kind of campaign. At the time long-term public sector agreements were in fashion. The problem for the FBU, however, is that there were few conditions of service which could be bargained away in exchange for pay rises based on cost savings, without compromising the safety of its members or the public. The biggest example of this is the shift system and constant crewing. For years the employers had been seeking to reduce numbers working the night shift, arguing that fewer incidents occurred in the night and much of the firefighters' time on this shift was spent resting. But the union could show that most life-threatening incidents and most rescues occurred during the night shift, and that any cuts to crewing levels would be dangerous for public safety and put members' lives at risk when carrying out rescue and fire-fighting duties. These arguments were thoroughly supported in official reports. Indeed any real attempt to modernise the Fire Service would cost, not save, public money in the short term, and would almost certainly involve higher levels of staffing. So, understandably, the union was not prepared to bargain increased pay for reduced staffing. The reality is that modernisation, properly understood, would result in increased costs to the Fire Service, with the resultant savings – in reduced fatalities, reduced insurance claims, and reduced fire loss – accruing to society as a whole.

In the end substantial progress was made by the firefighters on three of the four pillars of their ambitious claim. The evidence suggests that it would not have been possible to achieve the 16% phased rise without the threat and use of the strike weapon. The Government put the holding of the line on its pay policy much higher up its agenda than it did reforming the Fire Service or treating the firefighters as a deserving case for a catch-up increase in pay. Thus they blocked the July offer, and then dilly-dallied as far as a negotiated settlement was concerned until the strike vote came in. Then there was the rush to Bain, the blocking of a settlement until Bain was ready to report, and then the slight loosening of those purse strings to facilitate a settlement as the pressures of the Iraq invasion influenced Government thinking. Maybe the FBU negotiators could have secured a new pay formula for some time in the future without too much campaigning. But there was no way that a step-change improvement in earnings was going to be conceded without the strongest possible indication that members were prepared to take industrial action. To secure this expression of membership support required that the leadership present a bold claim followed up by intensive campaigning.

STRIKE STRATEGY

As we have seen there was a good deal of discussion on the strike strategy employed by the leadership. It has to be said that most of the discussion occurred after it became clear that the agreed strategy had failed to achieve a decisive breakthrough in the negotiations. Before the eight-day strike in late November 2002 the only voice heard criticising the flexible discontinuous strike strategy promoted by the leadership and overwhelmingly endorsed by the membership was that of the FBU's London Regional Committee.

During October a number of pre-arranged strikes were cancelled to give negotiators room to reach a settlement. In a sense, and in retrospect, it is clear that the employers were playing for time and waiting for Bain. No concessions were made to the union's position in exchange for cancelling strikes during this period. It was this the FBU London region criticised when meeting on 1 November 2002 to oppose any further cancellation of strikes. Despite London's position the full national EC agreed to cancel strikes selected for 6 November by sixteen to two.

The employers may have been waiting for Bain and for Prescott's 'fancy dancing', but by 22 November, before the Government's dramatic intervention, they had agreed the basis for a settlement which would have added a further 5% to the 11.3% recommended by Bain's interim report. It could be argued that by deploying flexible tactics and by constantly being seen to be ready to negotiate the FBU leadership almost carried the day. Any refusal to negotiate, with an inflexible adherence to previously announced strike dates, could well have handed the initiative to the employers and the Government in their attempts to isolate the FBU by branding them as irresponsible and unreasonable.

The point of writing history is to make sure that the actions and views of those involved are reported as they were at the time of the decisions and not re-invented afterwards. Pointless speculation – counter-factual history – about the what-ifs of life serve no purpose other than to undermine the decision capabilities of those involved. The question is did the FBU decision-makers at national level behave reasonably in the circumstances given their mandate to seek a negotiated settlement? The answer in our view is that they did.

BAIN AGAIN

We have already dealt in some detail with the so-called independent inquiry. In summary the union argued that the NJC, if necessary with Government involvement, should determine wages and conditions in the Fire Service – and not some hastily convened outside body without expertise in the Service, and with no responsibility for implementing or living with any settlement made or imposed. The union went on to criticise the terms of reference as too narrow on pay and far too wide on management issues – and ridiculed the time-scale given to Bain. The last such independent inquiry had taken three and a half years in 1970 (Holroyd), while Bain was given three and a half months.

Yet the decision by the FBU leadership was not taken hastily, particularly since there was some pressure from the TUC to co-operate. Leading officials did give this very serious consideration, but in the end stuck to the decision they had made in June when they were asked by the employers to jointly approach the Government requesting the setting up of an independent inquiry. The union leadership said no in June and no in September. At the time there were no voices in the union expressing support for involvement in the Bain Inquiry, although some members of the EC have expressed a view two years later that the union should have co-operated. This is clearly an important issue. Both Nolda for the employers and Barber for the TUC told us in interviews that they felt the FBU were wrong not to go along with the Bain inquiry, by formally submitting evidence and argument in support of their claim. Barber feels that Bain could have given the Government the opportunity to put more money into the Fire Service and cleared the way for an exceptional pay rise without provoking 'me-too' claims from other public sector unions. The TUC's public services committee had agreed not to jump onto any pay breakthrough.

While counterfactual hindsight is interesting, we can never know what might have happened. In September the FBU leadership were campaigning for a 'yes' vote for industrial action in support of their campaign for a favourable negotiated settlement. The membership, and in particular the activists, were convinced that this strategy would be successful. To have abandoned it in order to fully co-operate with Bain would have created a split in a then very united union. Of course it might have been possible to adopt a two-pronged strategy – pressing for a negotiated settlement backed by industrial action if necessary while giving evidence to Bain. But even this had high risks. It could well have compromised the campaign for a 'yes' vote for industrial action, with a substantial minority of members influenced by employers and press comment to take the easy route by relying on Bain rather than their industrial strength. On top of this, at that stage the union leadership was totally convinced that their strategy was much more likely than Bain to deliver the bacon. Until the early morning of 22 November they were almost certainly right in this assessment.

We have detailed various critiques of Bain earlier. In particular his hurried work on comparative pay is deeply flawed, proving that the FBU leadership were right to be concerned about the independence of such an exercise. Above all, as his work at the Low Pay Commission shows, he works within Government policy and its terms of reference. His report was always likely to recommend modest pay improvements, in exchange for job cuts and changes in management practices which reduced the firefighters' ability to control the job, and reduced union power, particularly at national level. All this is New Labour policy and Bain and the FBU leadership knew it. At one point during the November 21-22 negotiations the FBU had transcended Bain. Then, after the Government's intervention on that fateful morning, the FBU leadership, supported by a loyal membership, spent months trying to fend off many of the Bain reforms. This book has shown that the June 2003 agreement owes as much to this rearguard union campaign as it does to Bain's agenda, despite the Government's best efforts to present Bain as the only show in town.

THE KEY MOMENT: 21-22 NOVEMBER 2002

The events of the last two weeks in November can be seen as pivotal to the outcome of the dispute when, as a result of the Government's unprecedented and extra-constitutional intervention to block a negotiated framework agreement, the talks of 21-22 November failed to provide the basis for a settlement, triggering the first strike of eight days.

The events of the 21-22 November clearly marked a turning point in the dispute and were followed by a determined Government campaign, led by the Prime Minister's office, to change the balance of forces against the union, and for more Central Government control over both the negotiations and the future of the Fire Service.

The lead up to the NJC meeting on 21 November showed that the union side could deliver complete solidarity behind its strike calls, but that the effect of strikes was not necessarily as devastating as the employers and the Government had feared. Obviously luck played a part – if, for example, the big Edinburgh fire had occurred on a strike day with massive losses to a historic city as troops failed to deal with a complicated and major fire incident, the impact of the strikes would have strengthened the union's bargaining position. There were other factors: advertising of all kinds around fire safety messages had been stepped up since 2000 and was stepped up again during the strike periods, making the public more aware of fire hazards and safety procedures. Apart from the closure of underground railway systems, there were few secondary effects of the strikes – life went on as usual despite anticipation before the strike that big sporting events and other forms of live mass entertainment could well be halted for health and safety reasons.

In the event the armed forces coped quite well during the early strikes, aided as they were by firefighters leaving their own picket lines to deal with emergency situations and rescues, both fire related and road traffic accidents. The military was not providing a Fire Service but it was managing to paper over the cracks with some help from lady luck and from the humanitarian actions of professional firefighters. Whilst less than 40% of calls were actually attended and the person power employed was greater than that available to the Fire Service, the Government painted a glowing picture of the emergency operation, spuriously claiming that it had learned lessons for the future operation of the Fire Service in normal times.

That, on balance, the force was with the union in mid-November is illustrated by the events at the negotiating table on the 21-22 November. For the first time, on 21 November – nearly six months after the FBU claim had been submitted – the employers made what the union considered to be a reasonable offer, which involved substantial progress on three of the four pillars, and some concessions on the union's main demands for a step-change improvement in basic rates for whole time firefighters. The offer was substantially better than the Bain recommendations a month later.

So for the first time the union negotiators had something to get their teeth into, and they did so with some effect as far as changes to working practices and the management of the modernisation process. The employers' first offer on 21 November gave a substantial monitoring role to the Audit Commission in determining whether the agreement on new working practices was being implemented so that phased pay increases could be made. The three phases, spread over two years, were those contained in the Bain position paper published in early November. This was rejected by the union. The FBU indicated that it was prepared to recommend to members a phased 16% increase linked to modernisation, but that this should not be restricted to the Bain agenda and should include the union's own proposals for change. The union also suggested that the role assigned to the Audit Commission should be carried out by an independent panel consisting of a representative from the TUC and a representative from the Audit Commission plus an independent chair. This panel would adjudicate on any issues where negotiations failed to agree, and both the FBU and employers said they would guarantee to accept the results of this process. This then became a draft agreement which was accepted by the FBU but in the words of an employers' circular, issued the next day to CFOs and chairs of Fire Authorities, 'not by the employers following a last minute request from Government sources that the employers should not endorse the draft until Ministers had considered it. This is a new procedure of which we had been given no prior notice'.

It is clear from this that the draft agreement would have been signed by both sides if it were not for the direct Government intervention. It should be understood that there was no constitutional power for the Government to block the agreement and the employers were free to sign and then to join with the FBU in negotiating with the Government over the funding implications of such an agreement. But there were, of course, powerful political pressures, particularly on the New Labour councillors. In the event, an opportunity to reach a negotiated settlement was thwarted by Government. Some two months later the Minister at the centre of the dispute, John Prescott, was justifying to Parliament the need to take special imposition powers regarding the Fire Service pay and conditions, due to the inability of the NJC to reach a negotiated settlement some nine months after the union claim was lodged.

Prescott claims to have intervened (in a letter to MPs he denied blocking a settlement) because the offer was 'uncosted'. This appears disingenuous. The Government backed the employers' first offer which concluded:

the NJC recognises that the above package will impose significant additional costs on local fire authorities paybills over and above any efficiency savings that might be generated by modernisation, and existing budget allocations. We will explore with Government how this situation can be resolved. We urge the Government to respond to this as a matter of urgency (clause 6 of the draft agreement).

The negotiated draft agreement that Prescott blocked was unchanged on matters of pay. So on the face of it, if the first draft agreement was acceptable on costings to Government so should have been the second draft agreement. After all both were tied to a programme of modernisation which everyone, including Bain and the Government, knew would involve extra costs over and above wage costs in the early stages (Bain later found that it would be two years before his recommended cost savings based on job cuts paid for improved wages and modernisation). At issue for the Government was whether or not a modernisation package, which in Prescott's mind was mainly about cost savings, could be delivered by the NJC. In the first agreement the Audit Commission alone was given the role of monitoring and verifying the modernisation process, which was itself much constrained by the Bain proposals contained in his position paper. In other words a process approved by Central Government and imposed on the Fire Service negotiators was to be maintained by a Central Government agency – a real belt and braces job! The achievement of the FBU negotiators, greatly assisted by

John Monks and Brendan Barber, was to loosen these shackles and to take the modernisation process out of the straitjacket imposed by Bain and judged by the Audit Commission. The union negotiators in the second draft agreement had restored the right of the union to put forward its own modernisation agenda and for the process itself to remain within the NJC, subject to compulsory adjudication by an independent panel when there was a failure to agree. Since it was clear that the whole basis of the Fire Service was soon to change from prescriptive national standards shaping staffing levels to locally determined risk assessment plans, it was difficult if not impossible to put a short-term estimate on the likely costs of future modernisation. The employers could have said that 16% on the wage bill over two years represented about 4% per annum over and above the Local Government funding settlement, and would add some £56 million a year to Fire Service costs, all else being equal. But they stuck to the position outlined in paragraph 6 of both draft agreements, which called for talks with Government to find a way of resolving any funding deficit faced by local Fire Authorities as a result of the proposed agreement. In the circumstances, Prescott's talk of a 'blank cheque' was a cheap shot – the Government was being asked to take part in tripartite discussions about funding a modern Fire Service and, as virtual paymaster (it pays 80% of the bills), it would have retained a powerful position in such talks.

The key question is why the Government blocked the second agreement having approved the first. Certainly Brendan Barber was convinced that the early morning phone conversation between John Monks and John Prescott had cleared the way for an agreement and would have given the union the opportunity to call off the eight-day strike due to begin at 9am that same day. Indeed Monks and Barber went to see John Prescott in office hours that same morning to express their disappointment at the Government's intervention and further urged Prescott to, even at that late stage, accept the deal as the basis for a final agreement later that day so that the FBU leadership could consider calling off the strike. After a rather heated exchange, Prescott flatly refused to make any concessions. The likeliest explanation for the Government's actions is that they simply lacked trust in the ability of the Local Government employers to deliver their modernisation agenda so that the cuts demanded by such an agenda could pay for any pay increases agreed at the NJC. Once the Audit Commission and the Bain report had been relegated to secondary players the Government felt it would lose control of the modernisation and verification process. No doubt there were strong forces at the Treasury who would have frowned at a 16% settlement over two years, but these could be assuaged if cost cuts could be guaranteed under the stewardship of the Audit Commission. Once that guarantee was removed Prescott felt unable to stand up to the Treasury in the interests of the Fire Service and its democratic institutions, including the FBU.

The Government got a bad press following the breakdown of the negotiations. It now got Blair's support to attack the FBU, while Prescott poured scorn on the employers, presenting them as poor negotiators, implying that they were like putty in the FBU's hands. By the end of November the tide had turned again as the FBU leadership became increasingly aware that large sections of their members were unhappy with long strikes and were becoming weary of the dispute. By the end of the year the ACAS process had begun and early in the New Year the employers, encouraged by the Government, turned the screw.

BURCHILL'S SECOND INTERVENTION

Frank Burchill was throughout the dispute the chair of the NJC. As we have seen March 2003 saw a crucial breakthrough in the talks, brokered partly by Burchill's insistence that modernising reforms be negotiated and not imposed. When the FBU leadership failed to carry the union's delegate conference for this agreement, Burchill made his second and highly controversial intervention. To the informed outsider it looked as if Burchill was simply trying to replace the March agreement by taking on board some of the concerns about proposed new working practices expressed by union activists. Both the Government and to a lesser extent the employers wanted none of this. They calculated that, having got the FBU's EC to accept and recommend the March proposals, it was simply a matter of time before the rank and file fell into line or a damaging split would develop in the FBU. Either way the employers and the Government would be the winners.

In the background Prescott was seeking Parliamentary powers to impose a settlement. So to cloud the issue, particularly since a few Fire Authorities, including for example Staffordshire, had expressed support for the Burchill approach, first the employers and then, more extremely, the Government went into full attack mode. The employers made the obvious point (in suitable circumspect language) that it would be easier for them to impose change than introduce it by agreement. In their letter to Burchill they also revealed the essential point that Burchill was bringing forward proposals for negotiation and that his proposed wording was open to interpretation. In other words the doubts that employers expressed about constant crewing and shift hours could have been cleared up by talks and negotiations, particularly since Burchill made it absolutely clear that his proposals were within the context of local risk assessment plans. These would give local Fire Authorities much greater freedom to reform shift arrangements and crewing levels, provided that such changes could be justified on fire safety grounds and not on cost grounds alone. On the other hand the Government took a totally opportunist line, backed by extremely spurious arguments. Without providing a single piece of evidence, Raynsford claimed in Parliament that the Burchill proposals would add a further £70m to the costs of the settlement, and that with the already committed transitional funds (£30m to be repaid over three years by Fire Authorities), this would take the total extra costs to £100m.

Neither Raynsford nor anyone else knew what the final costs of Burchill would be. Unless the Government figures were simply picked out of the air, they could only have been based on some estimate of the cost implications of maintaining the existing shift, and crew remaining totally unreformed. Nobody believed this would be the outcome of negotiations around the Burchill proposals. The FBU leadership suspected that the Government had embarked upon a mischievous campaign to discredit Burchill, and since any valid estimate of costings could only come from individual Fire Authorities, the union cleverly turned the tables on the Government by asking Fire Authorities to provide evidence to support Raynsford's figures. None could and it is clear that Fire Authorities were not even consulted before Raynsford made his unfounded claims. Little more was heard from Government circles on this – their fox had been shot!

In the event the Burchill proposals gave the union time to regroup following the setbacks in March. This, together with the pressures on the Government following the invasion of Iraq, somewhat improved the union's bargaining position, and by early May both sides were ready to conclude an agreement finally reached in June. To no little extent this outcome was due to Burchill's insistence on all sides sticking with the central tenet of the NJC constitution – that progress should be by negotiation and agreement and not by dictat and imposition.

PUBLIC SECTOR PAY

In their commentary on the Wilberforce Inquiry into miners' pay which was the basis for settling the 1972 miners' strike, the Ruskin Research Unit had this to say: 'There is no doubt that we are here touching on a major unresolved problem. There have been several cases in recent years which, in various combinations, showed on the one hand high productivity and positive cooperation by the labour force, and on the other low levels of reward'.

The Wilberforce Report (1972) itself, in contrast to Bain, had this to say:

37. First there is what we may call the *periodic increase*, which is designed to take account of the cost of living and other considerations. We accept that for the present this is a fact of life and that negotiators on both sides expect that it will occur.

38. But, secondly, there is what we may call the *adjustment* factor. This means that a time may come in any industry when a distortion or trend has to be recognised as due for correction.

39. We are convinced, from the arguments we have stated, that the

present is a time when a definite and substantial adjustment in wage levels is called for in the coal industry.

42. We think it an essential part of the present settlement that the miners' basic claim for a general and exceptional increase should be recognised. We believe that in general this is accepted by public opinion and if it cannot be paid for out of the NCB's revenue account, in accordance with its statutory obligations, we think that the public, through the Government, should accept the charge.

43. We recognise that by accepting the arguments for a reassessment we are moving on to the difficult territory of placing a relative value upon different jobs. We are conscious of the difficulties of establishing any general principle, but we think that the need for a reassessment is clear and that it can be reasonably quantified in money terms.

As the events described in this book have shown, those issues and problems remain with us today. Over the intervening years various mechanisms have been introduced or discussed as possibilities for optimising outcomes and mediating the efforts of collective bargaining. We have had statutory and voluntary incomes policies on the Government side, and periodic attempts on the trade union side to co-ordinate pay claims amongst public sector unions. None of these efforts have been blessed with much success. Government intervention usually fails after initial successes, by its own lights, in the face of growing union opposition when real wages began to fall. On the trade union side it has not been possible to win acceptance for greater centralisation of multi-union bargaining under the auspices of the TUC because of inter-union rivalries and the suspicion held by some private sector unions that improvements in public sector pay will in some way crowd out the room for increases in the private sector. Attempts to argue for special case treatment for a particular union claim have either been rejected by Government, mainly because they doubt the TUC's ability to deliver, or because of opposition from some union leaders who fear criticisms from their own rank and file should other groups do substantially better in any given pay round. These are realities which cannot be gainsaid or wished away. Given this picture, public sector trade unionists have usually looked to their own bargaining power or a friendly Labour Government to advance their conditions at work. Sadly the overall experience with 'friendly' Labour Governments has not been a good one.

The firefighters' dispute was yet another example of a Labour Government being extremely hostile to a group of workers whose pay no longer reflected their contribution to society and had fallen some 21% in comparative terms since the pay formula was introduced in 1978. In 2002 the employers, the CFOs and previous Government Ministers all agreed that firefighters merited an exceptional pay rise and a new pay formula, and that the Service as a whole needed a new funding formula which took account of the much wider scope of activities undertaken by the modern Fire Service, and rewarded rather than punished success in reducing fire loss. Of course the employers wanted something in exchange for a step-change pay increase and their reform agenda was at the centre of the negotiations and the dispute.

All this occurred at a time when the events of 9/11 led to the Government putting yet more responsibilities on the Fire and Rescue Service, designating it as the lead agency in dealing with the immediate public safety consequences of any terrorist attack. At the same time a Government sponsored report, the *Pathfinder* exercises, had shown that increased investment in the Fire Service, particularly for increased staffing levels in non-metropolitan areas, would result in net savings for society as a whole as well as reducing fire deaths. What is more, the public finances were in good order and the real economic threat on the horizon was deflation rather than inflation.

THE ROLE OF THE GOVERNMENT

In general our analysis suggests that of the parties involved the Government must shoulder most of the blame for prolonging the dispute with all that meant in terms of costs to society and to Fire Service staff. Of course at one level Government Ministers argued that the dispute was a straightforward industrial affair to be sorted out by the employers and the union. This was part of the attempt to use a magical cloak of invisibility when dealing with such issues: the Government intervenes more while wishing to be seen to intervene less. In this situation only the Government could have provided the investment and short-term financing to facilitate a negotiated settlement. The employers knew this. As early as April 2002 they were flagging up to civil servants the possibility of conflict and the probability, from their perspective, that only a Government-backed inquiry could resolve the challenges posed by the union. For its part the union made it clear when submitting the claim that they were seeking a negotiated settlement which could only be paid for by extra Government support, and that the Fire Service as a whole, through the employers and the union together, should make the case for that extra support.

The Government refused to countenance the union's approach entirely, and eventually accepted the employers' position only on the eve of a strike and then in a highly restrictive way. The Government claims never to have intervened so as to block an offer from the employers, or the negotiating process. While this may be technically true, since the Government has no constitutional position within the NJC structures, in reality it is what happened. Technically the employers could have settled at any time, with or without Government, but this was always financially and politically impossible given that the Government effectively controls the purse strings.

In June the employers were working on a paper which indicated that they were preparing to offer a staged increase giving a qualified fire-fighter a basic salary of £25,000 by November 2003 (a 16% rise) in exchange for radical changes in working practices and the existing *Grey Book* including disputes and disciplinary procedures. This accepted the case for an increase way above the going rate. It is now clear that at the LGA conference in early July the employers had their cards marked by John Prescott himself. No extra money would be forthcoming to finance such an award and all public sector pay awards had to be self-financing through modernisation. So warned, the employers decided not to table an offer at the 9 July NJC, despite a previous commitment to do so. Instead they invited the union to join with them in calling for a Government inquiry into Fire Service pay and working practices.

By August 2002 the Government had realised that a strike was probable if Ministers maintained the position set out at the LGA conference. So contingency plans were laid for fire cover and the employers were encouraged to stall negotiations until the Government was ready to call an inquiry. While the employers tamely toed the Government's line, it was realised rather late in the day that some formal offer had to be made to create the conditions for FBU rejection and the consequent setting up of an independent inquiry. In this strategy the employers were entirely guided by Government Ministers and civil servants. It was no surprise therefore when the FBU's £30,000 claim was met with a formal offer of just over £22,000 at the 2 September NJC. So at every important stage from July onwards the Government had effectively determined the employers' strategy.

The events of late November have been described and analysed at length. Again the Government claims not to have blocked an offer – all Ministers did was to have it made it clear to the employers that not a penny piece would be available from central Government to fund the framework proposals negotiated in the early hours of 22 November. In the light of this information the employers' withdrew their support from the agreed proposals and therefore made no formal offer. As we indicated earlier the employers were less than pleased with the Government's approach but felt compelled to accept it.

Allied to these blatant interventions in the negotiations we have the rush to Bain, with its non-agreed and highly constricting terms of reference, and the constant hints that the Attorney General would activate his powers to injunct strike action on the grounds of threats to public safety. This was followed by two Acts of Parliament which impose bargaining structures on the NJC and limit its ability to bargain freely, by insisting that Government guidelines on pay and conditions parameters be accepted, while giving the relevant secretary of state powers to impose terms and conditions of employment as well as redeploying Fire Service assets by dictat.

Finally, we have the almost farcical situation which prevented final settlement in July 2004, when New Labour councillors without Fire Service responsibilities were used to pack a NJC meeting in order to overturn an agreement reached with the union by the Fire Service employers' negotiating team.

Thus at every stage the Government was actively involved in shaping negotiations and blocking settlements not to its taste. The result is a much more centralised Fire Service, with far greater direct civil service involvement in strategic decisions, and the prospect of greater regionalisation to replace or reduce the role of locally elected Fire Authorities.

In addition, the industrial relations arrangements have effectively destroyed single-table bargaining, by promoting the interests of tiny non-representative non-TUC organisations which on current membership numbers will continue to be far surpassed by the FBU. This could provide fertile ground for inter-union disputes. But for the state it provides alternative poles of attraction for both Officer grades and retained firefighters. Ministers were surprised by the support given to the FBU by its majority membership in these grades, who were seen by Government advisers as a potential strikebreaking force. So in order to weaken the FBU's bargaining power and to re-educate officer grades in new management techniques, the Government has created new structures which they hope will break the high levels of support currently given to the FBU by workers in these grades. No doubt the FBU will redouble its efforts to strengthen its links with both officer grade and retained firefighters, through recruitment efforts and special attention to the needs and aspirations of these workers. Only time will tell if the Government's anti-union strategy is to be successful.

THE ULTRA-LEFT'S CRITIQUE OF THE LEADERSHIP

In essence the small clique controlling the 30k website and Grassroots argue that the dispute was – in their words – 'lost', because leading national officials of the union 'sold out' the members in face of the pressures and blandishments of Labour politicians and TUC leaders. In other words they preferred to please their friends at the top of the labour movement rather than fight for firefighters' interests.

Leaving aside the fact that the settlement achieved was actually favourable to the members, and recognising that notwithstanding this there is disappointment in FBU ranks that the £30k was not achieved, what are we to make of the ultra-left criticism of the leadership? Let us begin by facing the facts. After the November 2002 eight-day strike, the majority of FBU members were not prepared to escalate strike action in pursuit of their pay claim. Everyone knew this to be the case, and for the union leadership to have ignored this would have been to gamble with the very future of the union, risking splits followed by loss of membership and a total loss of union authority in relationships with its rank and file. Similarly, the calling off of strikes earlier in the campaign in order to promote better possibilities for a negotiated settlement at the earliest possible time was a tactic widely understood and supported by the overwhelming majority of activists and members. They much preferred 'jaw-jaw to war-war', a position entirely consistent with the union's continuing commitment to have the best possible negotiated settlement. Of course it is always a judgement call as to how best to apply industrial pressure during a dispute. But in our view the leadership was right to err on the side of caution in order to give the employers and the Government no reasonable excuse to abandon the search for an early negotiated settlement or plausible pretext to present the union and its members as irresponsible militants. That the union was not entirely successful in preventing unprincipled attacks from Government Ministers and others does not gainsay the need to fight for the moral high ground in a dispute of this nature and to carry public goodwill with you.

The members expected nothing less from their leadership and accordingly public support for the union's objectives remained high throughout the dispute. Mistakes were made as the pressure grew. With the benefit of hindsight it is clear that the EC overreacted to the pressure exerted by Ministers and employers in the run up to the March 2003 Recall Conference. But apart from this their judgement had been sound precisely because they listened carefully to what the members were saying in words and actions. And throughout the dispute all members of the elected leadership acted with total integrity by putting the FBU members' interests first.

In the light of these events and developments it is a total travesty of the facts to present the leadership's actions as a betrayal of the rank and file. And it is absurd to explain the alleged betrayal of the rank and file as being due to the leadership caving in to the pressures exerted by senior labour movement figures. It is a central part of the ultra-leftist theory to present all trade union officials as being eminently susceptible to the pressures of the people they negotiate with, be they employers or politicians. This arises, they argue, because officials, even those who come from the job and are elected by the members, become divorced from the rank and file.

Of course such pressures exist. But it is generally the case that the more democratic a union's structure is, the less likely it is that such pressure will be effective, let alone a decisive influence on developments. The FBU is a very democratic union in which all major decisions are taken by elected representatives and administered and implemented by elected officials, all of whom have considerable experience as working firefighters or control room operators. Far from sucking up to Labour politicians, the FBU leadership, usually through Andy Gilchrist, criticised Ministers in press articles, media interviews, letters to MPs and statements to members. No fair-minded observer could accuse the FBU leadership of having anything but a robust independent approach to politicians in the search for a negotiated settlement, which, as all trade union agreements do, involved elements of give and take.

CONCLUSIONS

Like most serious industrial disputes in the public sector, the strikes and subsequent considerable costs to the public purse could have been avoided, given Government action empathetic to strongly held workers' feelings of injustice. This was not forthcoming. Indeed it often appeared that the Government's main objective was to discredit the FBU leadership and to tough it out whatever the wider costs to the labour movement and society.

While the FBU leadership was fully aware that their membership could not advance their relative positions in the pay league without struggle, it probably overestimated the union's industrial strength and underestimated the sheer pig-headedness of the Government's determination to see off what it saw as a challenge to the core policies of New Labour.

The FBU is a fine union with an outstanding record of work on behalf of its membership and a broadly progressive policy platform on social and international questions. But because of the way the old pay formula operated its leadership was relatively inexperienced in the cut and thrust of pay bargaining, as were the elected employers' representatives. This explains why the employers too quickly cut and ran to look for a Government inquiry, rather than pursuing their initial July 2002 position of 16% over two years with strings, a position which was not developed into an offer until the fateful events of 21-22 November. It also explains why the union never took up the employers' offer, again expressed very early on, to open up negotiations on payments for special services outside of firefighting duties. It should be said, however, that such bargaining could not have made headway given the Government's insistence that improved salaries could only be financed by savings made in other costs such as cuts in staffing levels.

Recent history, both under the leadership of Ken Cameron and Andy Gilchrist, had also been kind to the FBU membership. When it came to serious industrial disputes at brigade level, the union had come out on top time and time again throughout the last decade. A certain hubris developed which gave many activists a feeling of invincibility. This was allied to the isolation from the rest of Local Government and the unions involved, which often comes with a single service industrial union. This probably shielded many FBU members, especially those in London, from the realities of painful change which both the Thatcher and Major Governments had foisted on other workers in Local Government.

Above all what comes through from this dramatic conflict is the solidarity and determination of the FBU membership, their ability to campaign for what they saw as pay justice. Not unlike the miners in 1984-5, they fought together rather than retreated in disarray. They may have fallen short of their ambitions but they did secure important progress towards what they see as pay justice.

Not surprisingly, an industrial struggle of this intensity conducted over two years has left some bitterness in its wake. As we have seen, however, the FBU has maintained its membership and its predominant unchallenged position as workers' representative in the Fire Service. In our view the national leadership acted with total integrity throughout the dispute and was always receptive to membership views. It took the best decisions it could in the circumstances after intensive democratic debate and consultation. In our view the union took few wrong turns, but by keeping the membership united made important gains. The pain that it took to reach where we are now is down to a mixture of Government policy, Government and employers' malice, and Government and employers' incompetence. Scarcely could a more favourable set of circumstances have been available to a Labour Government wanting to justify an exceptional pay rise for a vitally important and small group of public servants. Instead of taking this opportunity, the Government chose confrontation, backed by intervention to prevent any negotiated settlement that increased Government financial support for the Service by any more than 1.5%, a figure significantly lower than that provided to secure the recent pay deal in the Police Service (of about 4.5%). Only when the strike threat became real did the Government attempt to head it off with the appointment of the Bain inquiry, which was given perversely wide terms of reference on management reform and extremely narrow restraints when it came to pay determination.

As we have seen, the dispute has left the FBU in reasonably good shape. Clearly there is a degree of disillusionment among activists concerning the failure to secure total victory. This was expressed in organised opposition to national and regional officials standing for re-election in 2004, including some important and fairly spectacular defeats for incumbents. This was by no means universal, and many existing officials at regional level continued to be re-elected unopposed. The decision at the reconvened Annual Conference in June 2004 to disaffiliate from the Labour Party united various small ultra-left political forces within the FBU with the majority of purely industrial activists who felt short-term anger with what most saw as New Labour's treachery. But membership numbers have held up and throughout the two-year dispute the FBU has been able to present a united front backed by an ability to organise effective industrial pressure when this was required.

What of the other parties to the dispute? The employers not only proved to be ineffective; they lost the respect of Government and the trust of their workforce. They also effectively surrendered the future of the Fire Service to unelected bodies led by an expanded civil service secretariat. The strategic role of CFOs has also been greatly enhanced. In the guise of devolving responsibility to the local professionals the Service has been centralised, with much greater influence being given to the Audit Commission and senior civil servants within the ODPM. In the short term it is elected local politicians and the democratic institutions representing the workforce who appear to lose out. This is an unstable political settlement, which recent experience suggests will not serve the public well. For most public services, including the Fire Service, are labour intensive and are best developed or modernised by responding to the needs and expectations of local communities. Without the involvement of the workforce change will not be effectively introduced, and without the direction of locally elected and accountable politicians, change will not reflect the interests of those relying on the Fire Service to provide an efficient, professional and public-spirited service. The involvement of the workforce, through the union, in helping to plan and implement strategic change is more likely to succeed in reducing fire deaths and providing excellent rescue services, than an agenda driven by managerialism and cost reduction.

From October 2002 and to mid-December 2002 the fire dispute was barely out of the news. Despite all the attempts of the Government spin machine, firefighters retained majority public support for the broad outlines of their case for pay justice. Despite the setbacks of November 2002 and March 2003, the union was able to recover enough initiative to secure a negotiated settlement in June 2003. It was a settlement a great deal better than that recommended by Bain in December 2002, and in important respects somewhat better than that of March 2003. However, due mainly to the employers' duplicity encouraged by some Ministers, it took a further fourteen months of union campaigning to force the LGA to honour the terms of the settlement.

Given the strength of the forces ranged against it, the union's achievements were considerable. These achievements owe most to the remarkable resilience, unity and determination of firefighters and control room workers. They also pay testimony to the strength of the union's democracy, the depth of its democratic culture, and the integrity and judgement of the elected leadership at national level. Of course in the heat of battle mistakes were made, but never, in our judgement, for the wrong reasons. At all stages, the membership was fully consulted and their views painstakingly assessed by the national leadership. We hope that our account makes a contribution to the understanding of what was by any standards an extraordinary dispute, involving over 50,000 public servants striving for better pay and more say under a Labour Government.

References

Aaronovitch, S. (1981) *The Road from Thatcherism*, London: Lawrence & Wishart

ACAS (1977) *Industrial Relations in the London Fire Service*, Report 8, London: ACAS

Ashworth, W. (1986) *The History of the Coal Industry. Volume 5: 1946-1982, the Nationalized Industry,* Oxford: Clarendon Press

Audit Commission (1986) *Good Management in Local Government*, London: HMSO

Audit Commission (1995) *In the Line of Fire*, London: HMSO

Bain, G. (1983, ed.) *Industrial Relations in Britain*, London: Basil Blackwell

Bain, G. (2002) *The Future of the Fire Service: Reducing Risk, Saving Lives*, London: Office of the Deputy Prime Minister

Bailey, V. (1992a, ed.) *Forged in Fire: the History of the FBU*, London: Lawrence & Wishart

Bailey, V. (1992b) 'The early history of the FBU' in Bailey, V. (1992a), 3-100

Bailey, V. (1992c) 'The "spit and polish" demonstrations' in Bailey, V. (1992a), 158-175

Bailey, V. (1992d) 'The first national strike' in Bailey, V. (1992a), 229-269

Baran, P. and Sweezy, P. (1966) *Monopoly Capital*, Harmondsworth: Penguin

Beale, D. (2000) *New management initiatives and trade union responses in the public sector*, Ph.D. thesis, UMIST

Beaumont, P. (1992) *Public Sector Industrial Relations*, London: Routledge

Boyne, G., Jenkins, G., and Poole, M. (1999) 'Human Resource Management in the Public and Private Sectors: an empirical comparison' in *Public Administration*, 77(2), 407-420

Braverman, H. (1974) *Labor and Monopoly Capital*, New York: Monthly Review Press

Brown, W. and Rowthorn, R. (1990) *A Public Services Pay Policy*, London: Fabian Society

Burchill, F. (2000) *Inquiry into the machinery for determining fire-fighters' conditions of service*, Cm 4699, London: The Stationery Office

Burchill, F. (2004) 'The UK Fire Service dispute 2002-2003' in *Employee Relations* 26(4), 404-421

CACFOA (2002) *Final Submission to the Independent Review of the Fire Service*, London: CACFOA

Cameron, K. (1997) 'Foreword' to FBU (1997a)

Cap Gemini Ernst & Young (2002) *The true challenge: the cost of fire, flood and road traffic accidents to the UK economy*, London: FBU

Carter, B. and Poynter, G. (1999) ' Unions in a changing climate: MSF and Unison experiences in the new public sector' in *Industrial Relations Journal* 30(5), 499-513

Chomsky, N. (1999) *Profit over People: Neoliberalism and the Global Order*, New York: Seven Stories Press.

Clay, H. (1929) *The Problem of Industrial Relations,* London: Macmillan

Clegg, H. (1972) *The System of Industrial Relations in Great Britain*, Oxford: Basil Blackwell

Clegg, H. (1976) *The Changing System of Industrial Relations in Great Britain*, Oxford: Blackwell

Coates, K. and Topham, T. (1982) *Trade Unions in Britain*, Nottingham: Spokesman

Cohen, G. (1988) *History, Labour and Freedom,* Oxford: Clarendon Press.

Corby, S. and White, G. (1999 eds.) *Employee Relations in the Public Services*, London: Routledge

Couch, S. (2002) *The relevance of traditional leadership paradigms for the Essex Fire and Rescue Service in the 21st century*, D.Ed. Anglia P

Cully, M., Woodland, S., O'Reilly, A. and Dix, G. (1999) *Britain at Work*, London: Routledge

Cunningham, C. (1971) *Report of the Committee of Inquiry into the work of the Fire Service*, Cmnd 4807, London: HMSO

Darlington, R. (1997) 'Workplace union resilience in the Merseyside Fire Brigade' in *Industrial Relations Journal*, 29(1), 58-73

Davies, M. (1980) *A consideration of management development in the British Fire Service, with particular reference to the role of the Operational Station Officer*, M.Phil thesis, CNAA

DFEE (1998) *Teachers Meeting the Challenge of Change*: Technical

Consultation Document on Pay and Performance Management, London: DFEE.

DoH (2001) *The 10th Annual Report of the Chief Inspector of Social Services*, DoH, Crown Copyright

DoH (2003) *Agenda for Change: Proposed Agreement*, London: DoH

Donovan (1968) *Royal Commission on Trade Unions and Employers' Association*, Cmnd 3623, London: HMSO

Doyle, J. (1996) *The management of improved performance in the fire service*, M.Phil. thesis Bradford University

Dresser, L. and Rogers, J. (2003) *Part of the solution: emerging workforce intermediaries in the United States*, Oxford: Oxford University Press

Dunleavy, P. (1991) *Democracy, Bureaucracy and Public Choice: Economic Explanations in Political Science*, New York: Harvester Wheatsheaf

Dunsire, A. (1999) 'Then and Now: Public Administration 1953-1999' in *Political Studies*, 47(2), 360-378

Edwards, P. (1986) *Conflict at Work*, Oxford: Blackwell

Edwards, P. (1992) 'Industrial Conflict' in *British Journal of Industrial Relations* 30(3), 361-404

Edwards, P. (2003) *Industrial Relations: theory and practice*, Oxford: Blackwell

Employers' Organisation for Local Government (2001) *Putting People at the Heart of Improvement: A National HR Framework for Local Government*, London: Employers' Organisation for Local Government

Employers' First Submission to the Bain Review, October 2002a

Employers' Organisation for Local Government (2002b) 'Pay, performance, and modernisation', *Pay Advisory Bulletin*, no. 3

Engels, F. (1881) 'Trade Unions' in *Marx and Engels on Britain*, Moscow: Foreign Languages Publishing House 1962 edition

Ewen, S. (2003) 'Central government and the modernization of the British Fire Service, 1900-1938' in *Twentieth Century British History*, 14(4), 317-338

FBU (1997a) *Twenty years ago we realised things would never be the same … reflections of the 1977 strike*, London: FBU

FBU (1997b) *Members' Handbook*, London: FBU

FBU (2001) *Report of Proceedings and Record of Decisions*, 78th Annual Conference, London: FBU

FBU (2004) *Integrated Risk Management Planning: The National Document*, London: FBU

FBU (2004a) *Out of Control*, London: FBU

FBU (2005) *You and Your Pay*, London: FBU

Fitzgerald, I. and Stirling, J. (1999) 'A slow burning flame? Organisational change and industrial relations in the Fire Service' in *Industrial Relations Journal*, 30(1), 46-60

Flanders, A. (1968) *Management and Unions*, London: Faber & Faber

Flockart, J. (1992) 'The Glasgow strike' in Bailey, V. (1992a), 386-401

Fryer, R. (1989) 'Public service trade unionism in the twentieth century' in Mailly et al, 17-67

Gould, W. (2000) *Labored Relations: Law, Politics, and the NLRB*, Cambridge Massachussets: MIT Press

Gramsci, A. (1930) *Selections from the Prison Notebooks*, London: Lawrence & Wishart 1971 edition

Hain, P. (1986) *Political Strikes: the State and Trade Unionism in Britain*, Harmondsworth: Penguin

Halcrow, M. (1989) *Keith Joseph: a single mind*, London: MacMillan

Hall, S. and Jacques, M. (1983) *The Politics of Thatcherism*, London: Lawrence & Wishart

Hartley, J., Kelly, J. and Nicholson, N. (1983) *Steel Strike: a case study in industrial relations*, London: Batsford

Hastings, S. (2002) *The changing role of the firefighter*, London: FBU

Hay Group (2002) *Reward in Support of Strategic Change in the Fire Service*, Paper for the Independent Review of the Fire Service

Hayek, F. (1944) *The Road to Serfdom*, London: Routledge

HM Fire Service Inspectorate (May 2001) *Managing a Modernised Fire Service: Bridging the Gap*, London: Home Office

Heritier, A. (2002) 'Public-interest services revisited' in *Journal of European Public Policy*, vol 9(6), 995-1019

Heseltine, M. (1987) *Where's There A Will*, London: Hutchinson.

Hobsbawm, E. (1978) 'The forward march of labour halted?' in *Marxism Today*, September

Holroyd, R. (1970) *Departmental Committee on the Fire Service*

Horner, J. (1992) 'Recollections of a General Secretary' in Bailey, V. (1992a), 279-358

Hughes, J. and Moore, R. (1972) *A Special case? Social Justice and the Miners*, Harmondsworth: Penguin

Hyman, R. (1989) *Strikes*, London: Macmillan

Incomes Data Service (1991) *Pay in the Public Sector*, London: IDS

IDS (1994) *Pay in the Public Services 1993/4*, London: IDS

IDS (1995) *Pay in the Public Services 1994/5*, London: IDS

IDS (1996) *Pay in the Public Services 1995/6*, London: IDS

IDS (1997) *Pay in the Public Services 1996/7*, London: IDS

IDS (1998) *Pay in the Public Services 1997/8*, London: IDS

IDS (1999) *Pay in the Public Services 1998/9*, London: IDS

IDS (2002a) *Pay in the Public Services 2002/3*, London: IDS.

IDS (2002b) *Report 867*, October

Ironside, M., Seifert R., and Sinclair, J. (1997) 'Teacher union responses to education reforms: job regulation and the enforced growth of informality' in *Industrial Relations Journal*, 28(2), 120-135

Ironside, M. and Seifert, R. (2000) *Facing up to Thatcherism: the History of NALGO 197993*, Oxford: Oxford University Press

Ironside, M. and Seifert, R (2003) 'The significance of comparability in national pay bargaining in the public services: case studies of the 1980 and 1989 local government white-collar strikes' in *Historical Studies in Industrial Relations* no. 16, 81-116

Ironside, M. and Seifert, R. (2004) 'The impact of privatisation and the marketisation on employment conditions in the public services' in *Radical Statistics* 86, 57-71

Industrial Relations Services (1999) *Managing high performance in the public sector*, No. 690, October

IRS (2000) *Single status: the story so far*, No. 710, August

JCACR (1998) *Out of the Line of Fire*, Home Office

Jones, C. (1993) *A new management, a new industrial relations? A case study of the Merseyside Fire Brigade*, MA dissertation , Liverpool University

Kelly, J. (1988) *Trade Unions and Socialist Politics*, London: Verso

Kelly, J. (1998) *Rethinking Industrial Relations*, London: Routledge

Kerr, A. and Sachdev, S. (1991), 'Third Among Equals: An analysis of the 1989 Ambulance Dispute' in *British Journal of Industrial Relations*, 29(1), 127-143

Knowles, K. (1952) *Strikes – a study into industrial conflict*, Oxford: Blackwell

Labour Research Department (1996) *The Fire Service Pay Formula 1979-1995: A Report for the FBU*, London: LRD

LRD (2002) *Bringing the formula into the 21st Century*, Report for FBU

Lane, T. and Roberts, K. (1971) *The Strike at Pilkington*, London: Fontana

Lenin, V. (1902) *What is to be done?* Oxford: Oxford University Press 1963 edition

Linn, I. (1992) *New management Initiatives in the Fire Service*, Barnsley: Northern College

Logan, J. (2002) 'Consultants, lawyers, and the "union free" movement in the USA since the 1970s' in *Industrial Relations Journal* 33(3), 197-214

Lumley, R. (1973) *White-Collar Unions in Britain*, London: Methuen

Lyddon, D. (1998) 'Rediscovering the Past: Recent British Strike Tactics in Historical Perspective' in *Historical Studies in Industrial Relations*, 5, 107-152

Lusa, S., Hakkanen, M., Luukkonen, R. and Viikari-Juntura, E. (2002) 'Perceived physical work capacity, stress, sleep disturbance and occupation accidents among firefighters working during a strike' in *Work and Stress*, 16(3), 264-274

Mailly, R., Dimmock, S. and Sethi, A. (1989, eds.) *Industrial Relations in the Public Services*, London: Routledge

Makinson, J. 2000. *Incentives for change: rewarding performance in national government networks*, London: HM Treasury.

Mathieson, H. and Corby, S. (1999) 'Trade Unions' in Corby and White (1999 eds), 199-221

MacFarlane, L. (1981) *The Right to Strike*, Harmondsworth: Penguin

Miliband, R. 1973. *The State in Capitalist Society*, London: Quartet Books

Millward, N., Bryson, A. and Forth, J. (2000) *All Change at Work?*, London: Routledge

Moran, C. (2001) 'Personal predictions of stress and stress reactions in firefighter recruits' in *Disaster prevention and management journal*, 10(5), 356-365

Morris, G. (1986) *Strikes in Essential Services*, London: Mansell

Mott MacDonald (2000, 2003) *The Future of the Fire and Rescue Service Control Rooms in England and Wales*, Original report and update, London: ODPM

NBPI (1967) *Fire Service Pay*, Cmnd 3287, report 32, London: HMSO

National Board for Prices and Incomes (1967), *Pay and Conditions of Service of Manual Workers in Local Authorities, the National Health Service, Gas and Water Supply*, Cmnd 3230 Report 29, London: HMSO

NHS Executive (2000) *Human Resources Performance Framework*, London: Department of Health

Niskanen, W. (1967) 'Nonmarket Decision Making: The Peculiar Economics of Bureaucracy' in *The American Economic Review*, LVII(2), 293-305

Niskanen, W. (1971) *Bureaucracy and Representative Government*, New York: Aldine-Atherton

Nolda, C. (2004) 'Industrial conflict in local government since 1997' in *Employee Relations* 26(4), 377-391

Office of the Deputy Prime Minister and the Employers' Organisation (2003) *Pay and Workforce Strategy for Local Government*, London:

Office of the Deputy Prime Minister and the Employers' Organisation

Office of the Deputy Prime Minister (June 2003) *Our Fire and Rescue Service*, Cm 5808, London: HMSO

Office of the Deputy Prime Minister (2004) *The Fire Service*, London: the Stationery Office

Peak, S. (1984) *Troops in Strikes*, Cobden Trust

Pendleton, A. (1999) 'Ownership or competition? An evaluation of the effects of privatization on industrial relations institutions, processes and outcomes' in *Public Administration*, 77(4), 769-791.

Phelps Brown, H. (1959) *The Growth of British Industrial Relations*, London: McMillan

Pollock, A., Shaoul, J. and Vickers, N. (2002) 'Private finance and "value for money" in NHS hospitals: a policy in search of a rationale' in *British Medical Journal* 324, 1205-1209

Pollitt, C. (1993) *Managerialism and the Public Services: Cuts or Cultural Change in the 1990s?*, Oxford: Blackwell.

Pyper, R. (2003) 'Firefighters' dispute: playing with fire' in *Parliamentary Affairs*, 56(3), 490-505

Roberts, Z. (2002) 'What's going on with the firefighters' strike' in *People Management* 8(25), 11

Rogers, J. (1995) 'A strategy for labor' in *Industrial Relations* 34(3), 367-81

Rose, E. (2004) *Employment Relations*, Harlow: Pearson

Routh, G. (1965) *Occupation and Pay in Great Britain 1906-60*, Cambridge: Cambridge University Press

Routh, G. (1980) *Occupation and Pay in Great Britain 1906-1979*, London: Macmillan: 1980

Rowley, C. (1993 ed.) *Social Choice Theory*, Aldershot: Elgar.

Roxburgh, B (1992) 'Unofficial action on Merseyside' in Bailey, V. (1992a), 402-4

Sassoon, D. (1997) *One Hundred Years of Socialism*, London: Fontana

Saville, J. (1980) 'Hugh Gaitskell: an assessment' in *Socialist Register*, 148-169

Saville, J. (1992) 'The CP and the FBU' in Bailey, V. (1992a), 225-228

Segars, T. (1989) *The Fire Service: The social history of a uniformed working class occupation*, PhD thesis, Essex University

Segars, T. (1990) 'Industrial relations' developments in the fire service' *The Industrial Tutor*, 5(1), 77-82

Seifert, R. (1992) *Industrial Relations in the NHS*, London: Chapman & Hall

Seifert, R. (2000) 'Some comments on the economics of the public sector with regard to the provision of public and private goods by some agency of the state, and the role of public choice theory in government decision-makers' policies on privatisation', *Communist Review*, no 37,10-16.

Shepherd, D. (1984) *Fire Service Pay and Government Pay Policies*, Diploma in Labour Studies, Polytechnic of Central London

Smith, M (1992) *Management strategies and labour relations in the UK fire service: a trade union perspective*, MA dissertation University of Warwick

Stern, S. (2002) 'Don't quack like your silly old dad. Modernise!' in *New Statesman*, 131(4616), 13

Stiglitz, J. (1986) *Economics of the Public Sector*, New York: Norton and company.

Swabe, A. and Price, P. (1983) 'Multi-unionism in the fire service' *Industrial Relations Journal*, 14(4), 56-59

Taylor, F. (1911) *Scientific Management*, New York: Harper and Brothers

Thatcher, M. (1993) *The Downing Street Years*, London: Harper Collins

Towers, B. (1997) *The Representation Gap: Change and Reform in the British and American Workplace*, Oxford: Oxford University Press

Turner, H. (1964) 'Trade union structure: a new approach' in *British Journal of Industrial Relations*, II(2)

Trades Union Congress (2002) *Report of Congress*, London: TUC

Undy, R., Ellis, V., McCarthy, W., and Halmos A. (1981) *Change in Trade Unions: The Development of UK Unions since the 1960s*, London: Hutchinson

Vincent-Jones, P. (1999) 'Competition and contracting in the transition from CCT to Best Value: towards a more reflexive regulation?' in *Public Administration*, 77(2), 273-291

Walsh, K. (1995) *Public Services and Market Mechanism: Competition, Contracting and the New Public Management*, London: Macmillan

Walton, R. and McKersie, R. (1967) *A Behavorial Theory of Labor Negotiations*, New York: McGraw Hill

Webb, S. and Webb, B. (1897) *Industrial Democracy*, London: Longmans, Green and Co.

Whelan, C. (1979) 'Military intervention in industrial disputes' in *Industrial Law Journal*, 8, 222-231

White, G. (1999) 'The remuneration of public servants: fair pay or New pay?' in Corby, S. and White, G. (eds)

White, G. (2000) 'The pay review body system: its development and impact' in *Historical Studies in Industrial Relations*, No 9, 71-100

Whitley, J. (1919) *Interim Report on Joint Standing Industrial Councils*, CD 8606

Wilberforce (1972) *Report of a Court of Inquiry into a Dispute between the National Coal Board and the National Union of Mineworkers*, Cmnd 4903

Winterton, J. and Winterton, R. (1989) *Coal, Crisis and Conflict: the 1984-5 Miners' Strike in Yorkshire,* Manchester: Manchester University Press

Wootton, B. (1962) *The Social Foundations of Wage Policy*, London: Unwin University Books

Index